AMERICAN SUICIDE

HOWARD I. KUSHNER

American Suicide

A PSYCHOCULTURAL EXPLORATION

July 1991

Fr Bob -
whose ideas + questions
led me in the direction
that made this
possible.
Howard

RUTGERS UNIVERSITY PRESS
NEW BRUNSWICK AND LONDON

First paperback printing, 1991
Originally published in 1989 as *Self-Destruction in the Promised Land: A Psychocultural Biology of American Suicide* (cloth: ISBN 0-8135-1377-4)

Library of Congress Cataloging-in-Publication Data

Kushner, Howard I.
    American suicide: a psychocultural exploration
        p. cm.
    Bibliography: p.
    Includes index.
    ISBN 0-8135-1610-2 (pbk.)
    1. Suicide—United States—History. 2. Suicide—United States
—Psychological aspects. 3. Suicide—Physiological aspects.
I. Title.
HV6548.U5K87 1989
362.2—dc19   88-18351
                                                              CIP

British Cataloging-in-Publication information available

To My Colleagues and Graduate Students
at SDSU

CONTENTS

LIST OF FIGURES AND MAPS

LIST OF TABLES

ACKNOWLEDGMENTS

MY introduction to suicide came one spring day thirty-two years ago in a message whispered from desk to desk in my seventh-grade music class. A classmate, Harry Trapp,* had jumped in front of a freight train and killed himself. His sister, also a seventh-grader, had identified his remains, contained in plastic bags—at least that was what we heard or told each other. Trapp, who had been left back twice, seemed so much older than the additional two years of life that he had attained over the rest of us. Having passed through the puberty that the rest of us were only then experiencing, Trapp had stood, the tallest of the tall boys, in the back row of our junior high choir. With pegged pants and a "duck-tail" haircut, Trapp was to my mind (given my comfortable middle-class existence) from the wrong side of the tracks on which he met his end. With the sort of bravado that hid our deeper ambivalences, our band of boys renamed that section of railroad track "Trapp's Crossing." Perhaps, as nihilistic as it was, Trapp's suicide served as the first subversive challenge to the unquestioned optimism of the 1950s that we, the children of upwardly mobile classes, shared. Not that we reflected on it or even discussed it much, but our black humor testified that it had touched us deeply. Although I doubt that I ever exchanged two sentences with him, Harry Trapp's suicide has remained fixed in my memory as one of those formative childhood experiences that contained some hidden truth that I supposed would be revealed to me one day. I no longer expect that I or anyone else can ever fully comprehend or explain the causes of

*a pseudonym

suicide, but I have become convinced that any such transcendent act—Dostoevsky once held suicide up as the ultimate test of free will—must involve psychology, biology, and society.

The intellectual roots that inform this study are conventional, although only the self-deceiving would deny a connection between scholarly pursuits and early ambivalences. My interest in the history of psychiatry and particularly in the application of psychoanalysis to history was aroused over two decades ago when I was invited to participate in the monthly Group for Applied Psychoanalysis, led by Howard M. Feinstein at Cornell. In the mid-1970s, my participation in two seminars led by Joseph Afterman at the San Francisco Psychoanalytic Institute rekindled my curiosity about the causes of suicide and I considered turning my attention to a history of suicide. I began collecting data at the San Diego County Coroner's Office in 1981 for a study of suicide in the nineteenth century and there, one hot August morning, I met a pathologist, Howard Robin, who suggested a wider project involving recent findings claiming a link between the neurotransmitter serotonin and suicide. Given my psychoanalytic sympathies, I was skeptical about these biochemical explanations, but I joined with Robin and others, including Floyd E. Bloom, then at the Salk Institute in La Jolla, to formulate a grant proposal. As a result, I was introduced to Bloom's exciting research in behavioral neuropathology. Robin, Bloom, and John H. Morrison, also at Salk, opened new vistas in my thinking about the links between psychoanalysis and neurobiology. The results of this rethinking are evident in the pages that follow.

Over the past seven years I have sought and received valuable critical advice and useful suggestions from colleagues in the academic and medical communities. All those I called upon have given me generously of their time, and the advice that I received was uniformly thoughtful and stimulating. Of this large group, I owe my greatest debts to Howard M. Feinstein, Joel Kovel, Richard Steele, and Francis Stites, all of whom have read my manuscript with great critical care. Over the last several years I have received particularly valuable suggestions from the late Andrew B. Appleby, Michael Bulmash, William Goodman, William Issel, Kathleen Jones, Donald Kripke, Roger Lane, James K. Martin, Michael McGiffert, Stephen Roeder, Peter N. Stearns, and Christine Tomlinson. I owe a special debt (among many) to Carol R. Kushner, who balanced her expertise as a professional editor with the tact and forbearance required of one whose dual roles are critic and spouse.

The research that informs this work would not have been possible without the assistance of the staffs of many libraries and archives. The San Diego County Coroner David Stark and his staff provided me with access to the county coroner's records. The staff of the San Diego Historical Society was always helpful in my quest for nineteenth-century materials. Roberta Zonghi of the Department of Rare Books and Manuscripts at the Boston Public Library helped me uncover hitherto unknown eighteenth-century coroners' reports in the Adlow Collection. Katherine S. Menand, director of the Archives and Records Preservation Project of the Massachusetts Supreme Judicial Court, not only located sixteenth-century suicide documents, but also gave generously of her time, directing me through Boston's myriad holdings and opening many doors for me. The staffs at the Suffolk County Court and the Social Law Library at Boston's New Court House also were extremely helpful. I owe a special thanks to San Diego State University's Love Library Interlibrary Loan Department for their efficiency and good humor. I am particularly grateful to my colleague in sociology, Aubrey Wendling, who generously shared his raw data on San Diego suicides in the 1960s and 1970s with me. My two graduate research assistants, Thomas Walsh and Edward Gorham, have my everlasting thanks for work that exceeded the meager pay my grants provided.

I owe a continuing debt to my literary agent Sandra Dijkstra for her persistence and encouragement. I was fortunate that both Marlie Wasserman and Kenneth Arnold were not only persuasive advocates for Rutgers University Press, but also first-rate professionals. Although the process of publishing a manuscript often drives the neurotic to insanity, my experience with Rutgers University Press from acquisition to production has been wonderfully pleasant and pleasantly supportive. Finally, I am grateful to my copyeditor Cynthia Perwin Halpern for her insight and useful suggestions.

Much of the research for this project was made possible by support from the Graduate Division of San Diego State

University, through a series of grants-in-aid and research travel grants. The College of Arts and Letters also generously provided several grants and much-needed released time from my teaching duties. I wish to thank Barbara Aguado and Lorissa Boxer of the Geo-Graphics Place of the Department of Geography of San Diego State University for preparing the maps that appear in this volume and Rhian Arvidson of Chula Vista, California, for preparing the illustrations and graphs.

Over the past decade I have tested my preliminary views about suicide in a series of scholarly presentations and in several published articles. Parts of these articles appear in revised form in this book. A reader of these essays will discover that I have substantially altered many of my earlier arguments and conclusions. Much of chapter 2 appeared in "American Psychiatry and the Cause of Suicide, 1844–1917," in *The Bulletin of the History of Medicine* 60 (Spring 1986): 36–57. Small sections of chapters 2 and 7 originally were taken from "Biochemistry, Suicide, and History: Possibilities and Problems," *Journal of Interdisciplinary History* 16 (Summer 1985): 69–85 (© 1985 by The Massachusetts Institute of Technology and the editors of the *Journal of Interdisciplinary History*). Much of the information (but with a somewhat revised argument) in the sections on gender in chapter 4 appeared as "Women and Suicide in Historical Perspective," in *Signs: Journal of Women and Culture* 10 (Spring 1985): 537–52. The section on Meriwether Lewis in chapter 5 first was published in a slightly different form in "Suicide and the Death of Meriwether Lewis: A Psychoanalytic Inquiry," in *The William and Mary Quarterly* 3d ser. 38 (July 1981): 464–81. Finally, parts of chapter 6 were taken from my article "Immigrant Suicide in the United States: Toward a Psycho-Social History," which appeared in *The Journal of Social History* 18 (Fall 1984): 3–24.

In the process of delivering scholarly presentations and preparing drafts for publication I often received constructive criticisms and suggestions, many of which were in the form of anonymous critiques by journal referees. Most valuable, however, were the comments and suggestions that I received from my colleagues and graduate students here at San Diego State University, who for almost a decade have endured my earlier drafts and incomplete formulations. More often than not, these women and men have lived up to the expectations that lured me to the academy in the first place. And with my heartfelt thanks I dedicate this book to them.

Howard I. Kushner
San Diego, California
July 1988

SELF-DESTRUCTION
IN THE PROMISED LAND

INTRODUCTION

Late one November afternoon in 1893, while hunting in a canyon in the outskirts of San Diego, Edward Grenville discovered the body of a neatly dressed young man. The dead man's outstretched right hand held a revolver. When the coroner later examined the corpse, he "found that one cartridge had been exploded, and a hole in the right temple showed where the bullet had gone." The victim's pockets contained "a silver watch, twenty cents in change, a tin-type picture of the young man, and a pocket-book containing visiting cards bearing the name 'M. E. White.'" White's pockets also yielded a library card and a slip of paper with the names of several local firms. Alongside each name White had written notations such as "come again," and "favorable." Mr. W. E. Howard, whose name appeared on the list, identified White's body as that of a man who had applied unsuccessfully for work at two o'clock on the day of the suicide. Howard "remembered that the applicant was slightly cross-eyed." The coroner concluded that "from the condition of his hands and the fact that shorthand writing was in his papers, he [White] was unused to hard work."[1]

Max White was only one of many suicides reported by American newspapers in 1893. Often the press and other experts tied what they perceived as an increase in the incidence of suicide to the Depression of 1893, the most severe economic downturn in America's experience until that time. Several months before White's death, the editors of *The San Diego Union*, fearing a suicide epidemic, published a long editorial warning that "suicide has become so frequent as to attract little attention. Day after day the rehearsal of these crimes goes on in the daily press, and," *The Union* feared, "the horror, which such acts should produce, is giving way to indifference, or a morbid condition of the public mind which accepts self-murder as excusable and the natural outgrowth of modern conditions of life."[2]

The suicide of nineteen-year-old Max White seemed to confirm this assessment. During the previous three years, White, a native of Hungary, had lived periodically at his uncle Samuel Fox's ranch in rural San Diego County. At other times, he rented a room in San Diego while he searched for permanent employment. For a brief period White appears to have been employed as a baker. Despondent over his inability to find work, White purchased a pistol with which he intended to kill himself if he did not secure a position by 7 November. White recorded his final thoughts in a diary found in his possession:

> An indescribable feeling agitates me as regarding the position I am in hopes of receiving. The suspense is painful to me. If I should unfortunately be refused I should feel it to be my death warrant. I pray to God Almighty that I be given the place, as hunger and death stare me in the face. As for me, I feel so wretched and despair at the slightest ill-fortune.
>
> My God, how willingly would I that I should not be. The misfortune of being brought into this world! I must think of Sam [Samuel I. Fox] for all he has done for me. I can really never really repay for what he has done for me. Ah, I would rather have remained in the dominion of an emperor and become his minion than be in this land of the free and suffer.
>
> Ah, you false friends, who with your mouth claimed your friendship and with your hands withheld it! My curse upon you. May you ever feel misfortune blighting your whole career. My hatred is indescribable against you.[3]

During the period when Max White took his life, a French moral statistician named Émile Durkheim (1858–1917) began writing a volume that purported to explain why people like White were particularly vulnerable to suicide, Durkheim's 1897 study, *Suicide: A Study in Sociology*, lent scientific credence to the analysis offered by the editorial writers of *The San Diego Union*: modern life was the killer. Although Durkheim outlined four major types of suicide— egoistic, altruistic, anomic, and fatalistic—his study was concerned mainly with what he asserted to be the statistically verifiable increase in egoistic and anomic suicides, which seemed to mirror Max White's experience.

Anomie, Durkheim explained, "throws open the door to disillusionment and consequently to disappointment." Durkheim's description of the notes left by anomic suicides matched White's proclamation: "very many expressed primarily irritation and exasperated weariness. Sometimes they contain blasphemies, violent recriminations against life in general, sometimes threats and accusations against a particular person whom the responsibility for the suicide's unhappiness is imputed." The typical anomic, Durkheim found, was "a man abruptly cast down below his accustomed status [who] cannot avoid exasperation at feeling a situation escape him of which he thought himself the master, and his exasperation naturally revolts against the cause, whether real or imaginary, to which he attributes his ruin." Such a man has two options. "If he recognizes himself as to blame for the catastrophe, he takes it out on himself; otherwise, on someone else. In the former case there will be only suicide; in the latter suicide may be preceded by homicide or by some other violent outburst." [4]

Like the editorial writers of *The San Diego Union*, and unlike Max White, Durkheim denied that factors such as unemployment were themselves responsible for individual suicides: "If . . . industrial or financial crises increase suicides, this is not because they cause poverty, since crises of prosperity have the same result; it is because they are crises, that is, disturbances of the collective order." The breakdown of moral order, not its particular manifestation, was the culprit. Modern urban society tended to free people from traditional restraints, and this social disintegration formed the basis for egoistic suicide. "When a society is disturbed by some painful crisis or by beneficent but abrupt transitions, it is momentarily incapable of exercising this [moral] influence; thence come the sudden rises in the curve of suicides." For Durkheim, "egoism" and "anomy" were "regular and specific factor[s] in suicide in our modern societies; one of the springs from which the annual contingent feeds." [5]

When Durkheim's book appeared, a Viennese neurologist was on the verge of developing a new hypothesis for the etiology of hysteria that soon would become the foundation for modern psychoanalytic psychiatry. If Durkheim's *Suicide* is the starting point for most modern sociological investigations, Sigmund Freud's writings, particularly *Mourning and Melancholia* (1917), have become the classic texts for psychoanalytic discussions of suicide. [6]

In contrast to Durkheim, Freud (1856–1939) would have located the etiology of Max White's suicide in intrapsychic conflicts. According to the logic of Freud's analysis, the complaints of the nineteen-year-old White, even if grounded in some verifiable external problem such as unemployment, would seem too exaggerated to take at face value. For Freud, suicide was an extension of melancholic (depressive) behavior. Like melancholics, the suicidal exhibited "profoundly painful dejection, cessation of interest in the outside world, loss of the capacity to love, inhibition of all activity, and a lowering of the self-regarding feelings to a degree that finds utterance in self-reproaches and self-revilings, and culminates in a delusional expectation of punishment."

Drawing an analogy to mourning, Freud found that both melancholics and mourners experienced the loss of a loved one. Unlike the mourner, for whom "it is the world which has become poor and empty," Freud suggested that the melancholic appears to have lost "the ego itself." A melancholic displays "an extraordinary diminution in his self-regard" and "he reproaches himself, vilifies himself and expects to be cast out and punished." The melancholic, like the suicide, gives up "the instinct which compels every living thing to cling to life." These feelings of self-hatred, which often take the form of public display, resulted, Freud explained, from repressed anger at a deserting love object that melancholics have displaced onto themselves. Thus Freud suggested that suicide always contains an earlier repressed desire to kill someone else: "no neurotic harbours thoughts of suicide which he has not turned back upon himself from murderous impulses against others."[7]

Max White seemed to fit into Freud's characterization. On the one hand, White confided in his diary that he "despair[ed] at the slightest ill-fortune." He articulated a simultaneous wish to kill and be killed. He condemned his imagined enemies with vehement bitterness: "May you ever feel misfortune blighting your whole career;" and he announced his own self-destructive response to rejections that had yet to take place: "If I should unfortunately be refused I should feel it to be my death warrant." On the other hand, White's admission of despair was coupled with his expressed desire for "domination," with admissions of low self-esteem and laments that he had ever been born. And, as Freud might have predicted, White had experienced traumatic losses. His mother had died when he was twelve or thirteen years old and, almost immediately, White's father had sent the youth to live with his maternal uncle in a strange new land.[8]

Although Durkheim's contentions seem to contradict Freud's proposition that suicide results from intrapsychic conflict, there were broad areas of possible agreement. Both Durkheim and Freud portrayed the etiology of suicide in terms of "moral crisis." For Durkheim, social disintegration led to suicide only when individuals like Max White could no longer locate a connection between their personal condition and their social and cultural values. It was not a particular social crisis such as unemployment, poverty, or war, which led to suicide, but rather the way that crisis affected a person's relationship to the moral order. Durkheim found that more education led to an increase in the incidence of suicide among Protestants and Catholics, while similar experience did not have the same impact upon Jews because "the Jew . . . seeks to learn, not in order to replace his collective prejudices by reflective thought, but merely to be better armed for the struggle. For him it is a means of offsetting the unfavorable position imposed upon him by opinion and sometimes by law." Because a Jew's motivation for obtaining an education was different from a Protestant's or Catholic's, he had "all the intelligence of modern man without sharing his despair." Thus, for Durkheim social crises had psychological and cultural content because their impact depended upon the meaning any group or member of a group attached to them.[9]

On the other hand, Freud's analogy between melancholics and mourners provides a link to sociological factors. As melancholics, suicides like White were mourners, but with a difference. Most mourners are encouraged to participate in ceremonies such as funerals that function therapeutically as an organized social mechanism to deal with the anger, remorse, and guilt that loss brings. Like mourning, melancholia as Freud described it is also an attempt to master the ambivalent feelings that loss generates; it is a symptom as well as an illness. Like the mourner's, the melancholic's response and actions have a therapeutic goal. Although societies and cultures generally provide a structural mechanism for mourners, they rarely provide rituals for those who suffer other severe losses such as desertion or unemployment. The Freudian dynamic suggests that many, if not all, suicides are "mourners" who have been denied adequate cultural mechanisms for coping with loss.

Implicit in Freud's theory, then, is the notion that it is not an actual loss itself that drives individuals to suicide, but the extent to which

loss can be effectively ritualized that determines whether an individual turns to self-destruction. From this perspective, the way that
mourning is experienced depends upon both cultural and intrapsychic factors. Viewed in this way, Durkheimian and Freudian theories, though often presented and pursued in opposition, could have
been brought together to provide a productive starting point for a
psychocultural analysis of the etiology of suicide.* That this did not
occur, especially in the United States, was as much an outcome of
historical circumstance as of the apparent theoretical contradiction.[10]

Simultaneous with Durkheim's and Freud's elaborations, a German professor of psychiatry, Emil Kraepelin (1856–1926), offered
an alternative explanation for suicide that relied on neither cultural
nor psychological factors. The most influential spokesman for what
would evolve as the somatic school of psychiatry, Kraepelin believed
that organic disturbances underlay depressive disorders. He dismissed Durkheim's assumption that the incidence of suicide could
be reduced simply by alleviating external pressures, and because he
was certain of the organic etiology of depression, Kraepelin also totally rejected Freud's psychoanalysis.[11]

Had Kraepelin read Max White's diary, unlike Durkheim or
Freud, he would have disregarded its specific contents. What White
wrote or said would have been less significant for Kraepelin than the
manner in which White expressed his thoughts. Kraepelin would
have been concerned with an entirely different set of issues from
either Durkheim or Freud. He would have wanted to know how
White had presented himself to others; whether he had experienced earlier episodes of depression and mania; and if there were a
history of depressive disorders in White's family.

Contrary to Freud, who sought to elicit the etiology of a disorder
from the interpretation of a patient's thoughts and dreams, Kraepelin insisted that the form of a patient's thought process was more
significant than its particular content. Instead of examining in great
detail idiosyncratic personal factors like dreams, Kraepelin urged
psychiatrists to concentrate their energies on uncovering the similar-

---

*Freud, moreover, shared with Durkheim a belief in the cultural origins of unhappiness.
For instance, in *Civilization and Its Discontents* (1930) Freud argued that "what we call our civilization is largely responsible for our misery, and that we should be much happier if we gave it
up and returned to primitive conditions." Sigmund Freud, *Civilization and Its Discontents*, trans.
and ed. James Strachey (New York: W. W. Norton & Co., 1961), esp. pp. 33–45.

ities or differences in the course or outcomes of a disorder in groups of patients. Employing this model, Kraepelin drew a distinction between single-episode depressions such as melancholia, and recurrent depressive disorders, which he labeled "maniacal-depression." Kraepelin acknowledged that melancholia often was brought on (but not ultimately caused) by "external influences," such as "emotional shocks and especially the death of near relations." Although melancholia sometimes resulted in suicide, the manic-depressive was in greater danger of committing suicide because maniacal-depression was a recurrent disorder, which because of its organic nature erupted "without any very tangible cause." "Maniacal-depressive insanity," Kraepelin wrote, was "rooted in the intrinsic disposition of certain individuals" and their families. By mistaking manic-depression for melancholia, psychoanalysts, argued Kraepelin, were making a grave diagnostic error. Even though psychiatric science had not yet located the specific disease entities that led to manic-depression, its practitioners should not, warned Kraepelin, be led astray from their search by misleading constructs like those offered by Freud.[12]

Max White, Kraepelin would have assumed, suffered from maniacal depression rather than from cultural disintegration or intrapsychic conflict. And, Kraepelin would have found evidence to sustain his assumptions in the fact that testimony at the coroner's inquest indicated that White had experienced frequent fainting spells and had confessed to recurrent bouts of despondency both to friends and acquaintances.[13]

No doubt, were he alive today, Kraepelin would believe that his views have been vindicated by recent discoveries in neuroscience. The apparent success of psychotropic drugs in treating a variety of psychiatric disorders has led to an array of speculations about the link between depressive behavior and malfunctions or abnormalities in those chemical messengers in the brain called neurotransmitters. Specifically, these studies have associated low levels of the neurotransmitter serotonin with suicide.[14] Moreover, neurobiology seems to have provided Kraepelin's followers with additional ammunition in their war against psychoanalytic psychiatry. Studies in what has been labeled "brain plasticity" have demonstrated that the connections between neurons are not fully developed at birth and increase dramatically during the first two years of life, continuing to develop until approximately the twelfth year. Because memory transmission and storage appear to depend upon these connections, early childhood experiences, according to some neurobiologists, cannot be remembered. As a result several neuroscientists have argued that early object loss, rather than having been repressed as psychoanalytic theory assumes, more likely is not even recorded in memory.[15]

Like neuropsychiatric critiques of psychoanalysis, the rise of specialization, at least when it comes to suicide, has served more as a mechanism for uncovering the flaws in competing theories than it has as a vehicle for resolving the fundamental question about suicide: That is, *why, when faced with a similar set of circumstances— whether cultural, psychological, or biological—does one person commit suicide while another does not?* Any theory that attempts to explain the etiology of suicide ultimately must address this issue. Yet, after almost a century, the followers of Durkheim, Freud, and Kraepelin seem no closer to finding a satisfactory answer to this question than the masters themselves. I am convinced that the major impediment to resolving this dilemma has been the very professionalization and specialization that grew from the theories first offered by Durkheim, Freud, and Kraepelin.

The predecessors of Durkheim, Freud, and Kraepelin, distrusting explanations based on specific causation, had assumed that suicide like other diseases was a consequence of the interaction of emotional, constitutional, and habitual imbalances. The way a person lived, ate, and felt was viewed as inseparable from the course and outcome of any disorder. For the nineteenth-century physician, the moral issues that suicide raised could not be isolated from its constitutional components. Thus those who exhibited suicidal tendencies were subjected to an amalgamation of pharmacological, social, and psychological interventions, which practitioners labeled the "moral treatment."

By the 1890s, however, the consensus about the causes of suicide became unglued as bacteriological medicine and the rise of the social sciences jointly served to call into question eclectic diagnoses. The renewed doctrine of specific causation of disease quickly spilled over into a constellation of explanations for social behavior. The rise of specialization, which followed the bacteriological revolution of the 1880s, made the moral treatment appear scientifically suspect. Ridiculed and devalued, the moral treatment was abandoned by medical practitioners. The psychiatry—both somatic and psychoanalytic—that evolved in the early twentieth century increasingly confined diagnosis and treatment to a disease model that attempted to explain suicide, like other disorders, as resulting from specific causation.

Although American sociologists emphasized social disintegration rather than intrapsychic conflict or somatic disorder as the cause of suicide, they too adopted a disease metaphor. Urbanization and social disintegration became the specific hosts for a variety of social infections that if left unchecked led ultimately to suicide.*

Ironically, the belief in specific causation had served to separate medical, psychological, and cultural explanations for behavior into competing and mutually contradictory models. The rise and institutionalization of medical and academic specializations, born with these theories, ensured that any attempt at synthetic approaches to human behavior would be resisted as unscientific and amateur.

No example better illustrates the impact of this separation on our understanding of human behavior than the competing explanations offered by specialists for the causes of suicide. Because careers, even entire disciplines, rested upon these contradictory theories, resistance to integrated and cross-disciplinary approaches was informed by more than the usual baggage of professional conservatism.

Nowhere was the separation of culture, mind, and body more fully articulated and adopted than in the United States. The competing theories offered by Durkheim, Freud, and Kraepelin provided additional ammunition and confirmation for American theorists already split into competing professional groups. The rise of sociology, psychoanalysis, and neuropsychiatry exploded the nineteenth-century American synthesis on suicide. The subsequent growth of specialization in the United States, with boundaries more well-defined and protected than in Europe, exaggerated these cleavages. If Durkheim, Freud, and Kraepelin wrote the epitaph to the nineteenth-century consensus that had assumed that emotional disorders like suicide resulted from a interaction of environmental, psychological, and organic factors, their American followers, in a

---

*It is not surprising that Durkheim's followers adopted disease metaphors. As LaCapra pointed out, Durkheim had a "fascination with medical metaphors." Durkheim envisioned the sociologist as "the doctor who lucidly diagnosed the ills of society and prescribed rational remedies." LaCapra, *Emile Durkheim*, p. 7.

relentless pursuit of specialized professionalism, have jealously guarded and secured their borders against those who would attempt to transcend professionally sanctioned expertise.

It is my thesis that adherence to the twin doctrines of specific etiology and specialization has made it impossible to answer the fundamental questions about the causes of suicide because these doctrines have erected a barrier to an interdisciplinary approach. The goal of *American Suicide* is to demonstrate how the apparent contradictions among sociological, psychoanalytic, and neurobiological explanations of the etiology of suicide may be resolved. Only through a reintegration of culture, psychology, and biology can we begin to construct a satisfactory answer to the questions first raised by Durkheim, Freud, and Kraepelin.

American Suicide is divided into two parts. The first half traces American attitudes toward suicide from the seventeenth century to the present. It shows how the atomization of American experts' views on suicide was influenced more profoundly by the requirements of professionalization and specialization than it was by the logic of scientific discovery. In the second half, in four connected topical essays, I propose a model for the reintegration of sociological, psychoanalytic, and neurobiological contradictions into a psychocultural biology of suicide. This psychocultural biology offers the most promising path toward answers to the fundamental question: Why, when faced with similar circumstances, do only some, but not all, people commit suicide?

I have focused this investigation on North American suicide, although, when it is appropriate, I have offered comparisons to other western cultures. The etiology of suicide in the United States, or even in the West, is not unique, but, as I have suggested, there are conditions in the American experience that justify a national study. Of course, I hope that those interested in other cultures will find useful connections and contrasts for their own investigations.

I begin with the Puritans because they were the first Americans to offer a systematic integrated explanation of the causes of suicide. Moreover, like later psychiatrists and sociologists, Puritans participated in a public debate over the nature of the causes of melancholia and suicide. Though their vocabulary differed from ours, the Puritans were concerned with issues that inform modern views: individual responsibility, mental illness, and social disintegration.

PART ONE

From Satan
to Serotonin

1

FROM CRIME TO DISEASE: THE TRANSFORMATION OF ATTITUDES TOWARD SUICIDE IN AMERICA, 1630–1843

On Saturday morning the first of February, 1724, John Valentine, seventy-year-old former provincial attorney general,* left his Boston house to speak with Robert Auchmuty, a fellow attorney. Not finding Auchmuty home, Valentine had waited for some time before departing. No one had seen him since. Later that afternoon when Valentine had not returned, his wife sent servants around town to look for him. Apparently, Valentine had been depressed and he had been acting so strange that his family feared for his safety. They searched every room and closet in the house and at 7:00 P.M. Valentine's dead body was discovered in the attic hanging from a rafter. He appeared to be "resting upon his knees," as if in prayer.[1]

The coroner, Captain Jonathan Pollard, who was notified immediately, instructed a constable to summon a jury of eighteen men that evening. The jury, including justices and attorneys, all of whom were acquainted with Valentine, agreed with his widow that her husband had been "afflicted by a deep Melancholly which brought on

---

*Valentine had served as advocate general for Massachusetts, Connecticut, and Rhode Island from 1718 to 1720.

the Loss of his Reason" and returned a verdict of *non compos mentis*.[2] Valentine's family quickly arranged for a funeral to be held on the following Tuesday.

Because the coroner's jury decided that Valentine had been insane when he took his life, his death was not officially considered a suicide. Under Massachusetts law, suicide as *felo de se* was a felony and, like murder, both intention and motive had to be demonstrated. Without intention there could be no felony. If there were no felony, there was no suicide. On the other hand, had Valentine been found of sound mind at the time of his death, the law required that he be denied a Christian burial; that his body be buried near a highway or a crossroads; and that "a Cart-load of Stones" be laid upon his grave "as a Brand of Infamy, and a warning to others to beware of the like Damnable practices."[3]

When Chief Justice Samuel Sewall learned the results of the coroner's inquest, he was outraged. Sewall believed that news of the suicide had been kept from him purposely because Valentine's family knew that he would have opposed a *non compos mentis* verdict. His suspicions were increased by the hastiness of the inquest. On Sunday evening when the coroner showed Sewall the jury's verdict, the chief justice objected that the jury had failed to take written affidavits from the witnesses as the law required. Moreover, Sewall was astonished to learn that Valentine's family had made arrangements for a funeral without first making application to the lieutenant governor or to anyone else.[4]

Samuel Sewall (1652–1730) is perhaps best remembered for his role as a judge in the special court that tried and executed Salem's witches in 1692, a role that he later deeply regretted. Scholars of Puritan life are familiar with his massive *Diary*, which has served as a valuable source for our knowledge of the late seventeenth and early eighteenth century.[5] Chief Justice Sewall was opposed unconditionally to suicide and throughout his career as a jurist he advocated full legal sanctions against those who attempted or succeeded in killing themselves.

Sewall used his considerable influence to attempt to reverse the coroner's jury verdict and to deny Valentine a Christian burial. He accused the widow Mary Lynde Valentine of having defied "the Terrible Providence of God" by having arranged a Christian funeral service for her late husband. On Tuesday, 4 February, church bells called the mourners to the funeral service. When the mourners arrived they learned that the minister, Reverend Samuel Myles, persuaded by Sewall's outburst, had changed his mind and had decided that he could not in good conscience read the Office of Burial. Promptly, two of the pallbearers, Judge Addington Davenport and Colonel Thomas Fitch, announced that they too wished to be excused from their obligations and left. Interrupted, the funeral and burial of John Valentine nevertheless proceeded.[6]

Sewall openly rebuked the coroner and jury for their part in finding Valentine insane: "What good is it to know countless things and to unravel cases," he asked in Latin in *The Boston News-Letter*, "If you run away from what has to be done; if you do what should be run away from?"[7]

Mary Valentine, understandably, resented Sewall's intrusions. Against the advice of friends, she published a likeness of her late husband along with eulogies in *The Boston News-Letter*, *The Boston Gazette*, and *The New England Courant*. Proclaiming that her husband was "a Gentleman for his Knowledge & Integrity most Eminent in his Profession, Clear in his Conceptions, and Distinguishable happy in his Expressions," she explained that his life came to an end because "It pleased God, some short time before his Death to deprive him of these Excellent Endowments by afflicting him with a deep Melancholly which brought on the Loss of his Reason."[8]

The eulogies brought an angry response from Sewall. From Cotton Mather, the chief justice obtained a copy of the Reverend Increase Mather's 1682 sermon, *A Call to the Tempted. A Sermon on the horrid Crime of Self-Murder*.[9] On 19 March, Sewall published the elder Mather's sermon and apparently sent a copy to Valentine's widow. "Self-murder," Increase Mather had argued, "is the worst kind of Murder." A man "cannot disgrace himself more than by commiting such a sin." Melancholy, rather than a defense, was merely additional evidence of criminal culpability because Satan tempted the afflicted to commit suicide. The section of the sermon that may have upset the widow most was Mather's proof for Satan's participation in all suicides:

Yea, Satan has a most peculiar Hand in the perpetration of the crime: As is evident from the strange manner, how sometimes it is accomplished—by Drowning, in a small Puddle of Water;—Hanging, upon a small Twig not

enough to bear the weight of a man—*or with Knees resting on the Ground.** Satan
must needs have a great hand—the Invisible World is most sensibly at work, in
such things as these![10]

To a modern reader Sewall's behavior may seem odd. One early-
twentieth-century writer described Sewall's action as "contemptible
and malicious" and "almost inhuman in its malevolence." Whatever
animosity Sewall felt for Valentine was certainly increased by Valentine's having been both an attorney and an Anglican. Because Puritan doctrine opposed the idea that anyone should profit from dis-
putes that arose among them, Puritans distrusted lawyers. Men like
Sewall made no secret of their dislike of appointed officials whose
announced first loyalty was to the crown and the Anglican Church.
Moreover, Valentine had made many enemies over the course of his
life. In particular, he had aroused popular enmity when, during a
Boston town meeting in June 1720, he had insisted that Bostonians
be required to swear an oath of allegiance to the Crown. Sewall attributed Valentine's behavior then and at other times to an attraction for hard drink.[11]

Nevertheless, whatever his personal animosity toward John Valentine may have been, the objections Sewall raised in 1724 had historical significance that transcended the particular circumstances
surrounding Valentine's suicide. Sewall, in his seventy-second year,
saw himself as an embattled defender of Puritan values that had all
but disappeared by the 1720s. His Puritan forebears, both in the
Old World and the New World, had resisted seventeenth-century
evolutions in English thought that portrayed melancholy—what
modern clinicians would characterize as depressive behavior—as a
disease.† Although it was not synonymous with the devil's temptation, melancholy, especially among Massachusetts' Puritans, was

---

*The position in which the body of a suicide was discovered was regularly offered as evi-
dence of Satan's participation and thus for a determination of *felo de se.* For instance, the Reverend William Adams reported in 1672 that the body of a suicide, Mrs. Thomas Whitteridge
of Wenham, was found "with her face thrust into a little puddle of water not sufficient to
cover all her face." "Memoir of the Rev. William Adams, of Dedham, Mass.," *MHS, Collections,*
4th ser. (Boston, 1852), 1: 17–18.

†As Stanley Jackson has shown, since the late seventeenth century when "melancholia" began to be restricted to a disease, "*melancholy* remained both a synonym for melancholia and a
popular term used with a breadth and diffuseness not unlike our use of the term *depression* today. And remarkably similar trends occurred in many of the other vernacular languages of
Western Europe." Stanley W. Jackson, *Melancholia and Depression: From Hippocratic Times to
Modern Times* (New Haven, Conn.: Yale University Press, 1986), pp. 5–7.

portrayed as a condition that made one vulnerable to the devil's temptation to suicide. Thus Puritans viewed suicide by the melancholic as evidence of individual submission to Satan and therefore of a conscious and purposeful rejection of salvation. New England's Puritan founders wanted to establish a "Government of God," and it made no sense to them and to their successors to condone a legal pleading—*non compos mentis* due to melancholy—that seemed to allow submission to diabolical temptation to be used as a defense against criminal punishment.[12]

The attempt of old guard leaders like Sewall and the Mathers to retain the criminal sanctions against suicide replicated earlier battles in England. Indeed, Samuel Sewall manned ramparts that already had been overrun, not only in England and other American colonial jurisdictions like Providence Plantations and Pennsylvania but also by coroner's juries in Massachusetts and Virginia. By the end of the eighteenth century, melancholy behavior followed by suicide was almost uniformly connected with mental illness in England and in the new United States. As we shall see, the American Puritans' success in linking melancholy with suicide ironically undercut their insistence that suicide be treated as a criminal act.

What follows then is significant not for its uniqueness but rather for the window it provides for seeing the *mentalité* that informed traditional views on the causes of self-destructive behavior. Moreover, it offers a glimpse of how opinion in the Old World and the New moved from a medieval conception toward a "modern" consciousness about suicide. The descendants of America's Puritan experiment were among the most reluctant to accept these changes. Their reasons help us comprehend why the traditional world saw suicide as a criminal act and how adherence to that belief led dialectically to the acceptance of the contrary belief that suicide resulted from mental illness.

SUICIDE IN EARLY MODERN ENGLAND

To understand Sewall's attitude toward suicide, we must review briefly the historical context of the legal definition of suicide in early modern England. Building on seventh-century canon law, King Edgar decreed in 967 that the goods of a person who committed suicide must be forfeit. In the mid–thirteenth century the English jurist Henry de Bracton explained that, like murder, suicide was a crime: "Just as a man commit felony by slaying another, so he may do so by slaying himself, the felony is said to be done to himself."[13] After Sir James Hales took his own life in 1562, the court held that Hales had committed murder, which it defined as "killing a man with malice prepense. And here the killing of himself was pre-pensed and resolved in his mind before the act was done."[14] An early seventeenth-century handbook for local justices proclaimed that suicide was "a greater offence than to kill another man." Justices were instructed that suicides' "goods are confiscated, and their dead bodies (from the terror of others) are drawn out of the house, etc., with ropes by a horse to a place of punishment or shame, where the dead body is hanged upon a gibbet."[15] Another handbook ex-plained that "he is *Felo de se* that doth destroy himself out of a pre-meditated hatred against his own life, or out of a humour to destroy himself, forfeits all his Goods and Chattels to the King, and also his debts real and personal, with specialty and without, and all simple Contracts."[16] William Blackstone's eighteenth-century *Commentaries* affirmed the classification of suicide as *felo de se*. Because "the sui-cide," Blackstone wrote, was "guilty of a double offense; one spiri-tual," and "the other temporal" it is "among the highest crimes, making it a peculiar species of felony, a felony committed on one's self."[17]

Attempted but unsuccessful suicides could be tried as felons and if found guilty they were punished.[18] Those who succeeded in kill-ing themselves were denied a Christian burial and their bodies, with wooden stakes driven through their hearts, were buried at cross-roads under a pile of stones.* In September 1590 a coroner's jury determined that Amye Stokes, the wife of a London sawyer, "Fall-inge from god hanged or murthered her selfe." Her body was or-dered to "be carried from her sayd house to some cross way" and a "stake dreven throrowgh her brest and so buried with the stake to

---

*The practice of burying suicides under crossroads under a pile of stones or with stakes through their hearts comes from ancient fears, no doubt based on the unarticulated under-standing that suicide is often an act of anger aimed at those left behind. These burial practices were therefore aimed at ensuring that the suicides would not return from the dead to wreak vengeance on those at whom the suicide was aimed in the first place.

be seene for a memoryall that others goinge by seeinge the same myght take heede for commitinge the Iyke faite."[19]

Suicide was a crime that not only punished the victim but also the victim's heirs. Because the movable property of suicides was forfeit, there were good reasons for families to disguise a self-murder and for the same reasons, juries were careful in returning a verdict of *felo de se*.[20] The law stipulated that to prove suicide a jury had to be satisfied that both intention and motive existed. To persuade a jury of intent, there had to be evidence presented that a suicide had "resolved of [in his mind] to be done, before it be done." Coroners were instructed that "If a man kills himself (either with [pre] meditate[d] hatred against his own life, or out of distraction, or other humour) he is called *felo de se*.[21] As historian Michael MacDonald has explained, motives acceptable to juries tended to be universal rather than unique. So, shame, loss, and pain served as convincing motives for suicide when supported by evidence. Specifically, disgrace (unwed motherhood or an accusation of dishonesty), economic troubles, the death of a loved one, or physical illness (pain) were the most commonly accepted motives.[22]

There were however exceptions in Tudor and Stuart England. Physical illness could serve as an excuse if the severity of pain caused by the illness could be demonstrated. A person also could not be found guilty of the crime of suicide if he or she were too young or too mad to know the consequences of the act: "If one that wanteth discretion, killeth himselfe (as an infant, or a man *non compos mentis*), explained Michael Dalton's 1619 *Countrey Justice*, "he shall not forfeit his goods, &c." But, Dalton explained, "If a lunatike person killeth himselfe" while lucid, "he shall forfeit his goods."[23] Yet what exactly constituted *non compos mentis* was open to interpretation. It was troubling whether or not melancholy fit the category. This issue was complicated by the arguments of early seventeenth-century physicians like Robert Burton, who asserted that the melancholy that often preceded a suicide was a sign of somatic disease that manifested itself in the form of a mental illness. English juries, influenced by physicians and lawyers, increasingly accepted melancholy as evidence of *non compos mentis* in suicide cases.[24] When in July 1624 a servant, John Blackman, killed himself, the coroner's inquest determined that he was not guilty of the crime of suicide because at the time of his death he suffered from a severe physical "sickness" that had caused him to be "distraught and light headed."[25]

Puritans vigorously opposed decisions like the one that obtained in the Blackman case in which irrational behavior was used as a defense against punishment for suicide. Although Puritan ministers like John Sym accepted the argument that juries should not condemn those "destitute of understanding, or of the use of reason . . . as a child without discretion, a naturall foole, a mad man in his mad fits," suicides connected to melancholy were another matter altogether.[26] Richard Capel warned in a 1633 essay, *Tentations*, that to resist the constant temptation to self-murder one must "fight it out against Satan, by setting the Word and Christ against him."[27] In 1637, John Sym published *Lifes Preservatives against Self-Killing*, which attributed suicide to the desire to escape "trouble of the minde," or what we would call depression.* But, Sym warned, those who took their own lives assured themselves eternal damnation in "a second death farre exceeding the first in misery." "There is," he wrote, "a death of dissolution, and a death of torment; the former brings the subject to an end, the latter brings the subject of it to all miseries."[28]

These warnings seem to have gone unheeded. In 1653 Sir William Denny reported that "Mine Eares do tingle, to hear so many sad Relations, . . . concerning Severall Persons of diverse Rank, and Quality, inhabiting within and about . . . London, that have made away, and Murder'd Themselves." This outbreak of suicides moved Denny to publish a poem in twelve cantos entitled *Pelecanicidium: Or the Christian Adviser against Self-Murder*. Denny warned his readers not to confuse the self- sacrifice of the pelican for its young with the baser desire to escape life's troubles through self-murder:

> Stay, Desperate Souls! Let's have a word or two!
> Examine Well, what you by Once can do!
> Can any Fiend allure with such a Call,
> That you must post, and run into the Fall!
> Or is your Conscience cozen'd with false hope,
> That Heaven is t'ane by Water, Knives, or Rope?
> For no man sure seeks Hell; Nor sets his Will

*Like other Puritan writers, Sym saw suicide as a "command of the Devill, who himselfe a murderer, and also moves man to practice it; both upon others, and upon himselfe; thereby to dishonour God." (pp. 246–250, 269–270.)

On Purpose to bring forth the Fruits of Ill.
Man was, and is betray'd with specious Show;
And meets with Losse in seeking More to know.[29]

SUICIDE IN MASSACHUSETTS BAY COLONY

Not surprisingly, when the Puritans assumed power in England in the late 1640s, they opposed sanctioning automatic verdicts of *non compos mentis* for those who were allegedly suffering from melancholy when they killed themselves. This resistance proved short-lived, for with the Restoration came an increasing acceptance of melancholy as a legitimate excuse.[30] However, this was not the case in the Massachusetts Bay Colony, which initially was dominated by Puritans who were unalterably opposed to the social, economic, and legal transformations taking place in England. For them a suicide was both a criminal and a sinner. So melancholy continued to serve as evidence for suicidal intention. Because they insisted that suicide resulted from individual free choice, Massachusetts Puritans aimed punishment at those who attempted and completed suicide, but not at their families. Thus, suicides were denied Christian burials, but, contrary to English custom, their goods were not confiscated.[31]

The insistence that suicide was an act of free will seems, at first glance, to be at odds with orthodox Calvinist views of predestination. Yet, the doctrine of "preparation," which was widespread (if sometimes controversial) among New England's Puritans, sustained a belief that individuals could and should prepare themselves to receive God's grace. For instance, the Reverend Samuel Willard (1640–1707) emphasized that the "Covenant of Grace" did not erase an equal obligation to a "Covenant of Works." This latter contract included a duty to choose God's ways over the temptations offered by Satan. Thus, preparationist doctrine provided a rationale for human beings to accept or reject divine grace. Within this framework Puritan ministers denied that suicide could be preordained by God; rather, it was an act freely chosen.[32]

In 1640 when a servant named William Richards was found hanging in his master's outhouse, Governor John Winthrop convened a jury who determined that Richards, "seduced by malice and

instigation of the devill . . . murdered himself and was guilty of his
owne deathe." Denied a Christian burial, Richards was buried along
a highway under a cart-load of stones.[33]

Those who attempted but failed to kill themselves also were punished. In 1672, William Citterne was found guilty having tried to
take his life with poison. The Suffolk County Court sentenced "him
to bee whip't with twenty stripes & to pay fees of Court & to stand
committed to prison till the next Court of this County."[34]

In addition to official records, colonial diaries suggest the extent
of suicide in seventeenth-century Massachusetts.[35] Samuel Sewall's
Diary, for instance, records suicides as if they were commonplace.
During the smallpox epidemic of 1677, Lawrence Hammond, a
deputy of the Massachusetts General Court, recorded five suicides
in the span of three months.[36] This incidence seems unusually
high, given Boston's population of approximately four thousand,
but the numerous sermons warning against the temptation to suicide suggest that suicide was frequent in late seventeenth century.[37]

Historian Emory Elliott claims that theological developments in
New England in the 1640s and 1650s bred inner tensions that resulted in numerous "nervous breakdowns and suicides."[38] For
example, a suicide note left by a Hartford, Connecticut, youth,
Abraham Warner, who drowned himself in 1660, lends some credence to this suggestion:

> O Father, I have kept my soul as long as ever I could; My ruine was, the pride
> and stubborness of my tender years, which should have been fetcht out with
> sharp correction, and evill counsel and company hath been my undoing. I
> have a young brother that follows my steps, he is going the wide way to de-
> struction, I beseech you take pains with him & correct him as well as counsel
> him, that he may not be undone soul and body as well as I.[39]

Developments in provincial law indicate that Puritan leaders
viewed suicide as a serious social and religious problem. In October
1660 the General Court outlawed suicide: "This Court considering
how far Satan doth prevail upon several persons within this jurisdiction, to make away themselves, judgeth that God calls them to bear
testimony against such wicked and unnatural practices, that others
may be deterred therefrom." In framing this statute, the General
Court allowed no exception for those suicides connected with melancholy. In fact, its opening paragraph explicitly rejected such a

defense.[40] In contrast, a 1647 statute in neighboring Providence Plantations decreed that "an infant, a lunatic, mad or distracted man" could not be punished for self-murder.[41] Although by the 1680s English and most colonial coroners' juries accepted pleas of melancholy as evidence for *non compos mentis*, Massachusetts Bay Colony continued to impose its more traditional interpretation.

Like English common law, Massachusetts statutes allowed the defense of madness if an individual could be shown to have been insane for a substantial period prior to suicide. So, when in April 1688 Samuel Marion's wife hanged herself from a rafter in her bedchamber, the jury allowed her a Christian burial because witnesses swore that "she was distracted, and had been for some time."[42]

Melancholy or periodic delusions followed by suicide were another matter—for these betrayed diabolical agency and thus could not serve as an acceptable defense for either suicide or homicide in Massachusetts. For instance, in 1638 the Court of Assistants condemned Dorothy Talbie to be hanged for the murder of her young daughter even though they concluded that Talbie suffered from "melancholy and spiritual delusions." John Winthrop wrote in his *Diary* that assistants had heard testimony that indicated that Talbie had previously attempted to kill her husband, her children, and herself. These earlier events supplied evidence for Winthrop and the court that the defendant "was so possessed with Satan, that he persuaded her (by his delusions, which she listened to as revelations from God) to break the neck of her own child, that she might free it from future misery."[43] Although Winthrop was convinced that Talbie was insane, she was not pardoned. In England Talbie would have more likely received a royal pardon than a public execution.[44]

The case of a sixteen-year-old girl, Elizabeth Knapp, was comparable. In the fall of 1671 she suffered a series of seizures that included several suicide threats. Knapp's threats were connected to her melancholic behavior, which the Reverend Samuel Willard, a contemporary observer, and Knapp herself attributed to Satan's temptations. Willard also tied her destructive impulses to diabolical temptation. Satan, according to Willard, often had attempted to persuade Knapp "to make away with herself." On one occasion, he reported, "she was going to drown herself in a well, for looking into it, she saw such sights as allured her, and was gotten within the curb, and was by God's providence prevented." In 1672, Willard wrote an account of the Knapp affair, which he entitled "A Brief Account of a Strange and Unusual Providence of God Befallen to Elizabeth Knapp of Groton," and he sent a copy to Increase Mather in Boston.[45]

Increase Mather was receptive to Willard's interpretation of the causes of suicide. Mather feared that acceptance of a plea of mental incompetence would signal the erosion of one of the moral and legal cornerstones of the Puritan experiment in Massachusetts—individual choice in the face of Satan's worldly temptations.* Many of the issues that had concerned Willard in the Knapp case were addressed in Increase Mather's 1682 *A Call to the Tempted. A Sermon on the Horrid Crime of Self-Murder*, which he delivered originally as a sermon in response to the suicide of a prominent Bostonian, William Taylor. The merchant, who was reported to have been "very melancholy for some months before," hanged himself "with his own bridle" in July 1682. Mather, who had made several unsuccessful attempts to dissuade Taylor from killing himself, was moved to deliver a sermon on the relation between melancholy and suicide.[46]

Satan, Mather argued, took advantage of the afflicted, tempting them to reject the Lord's salvation. "Distress of Conscience," Mather proclaimed, "is that which the Devil does many times, takes occasion to Tempt Men unto the Sin of Self-Murder." When a melancholy person committed suicide, it was synonymous with intention because by choosing to end their lives, individuals simultaneously were abandoning faith in God's eternal grace:

> The Burden of a Guilty & Wounded Confidence, it is Intolerable. It is said, Prov. XVIII 14. Who can bear it? Poor Creatures having Such a Wounded Spirit, & being under the strong Delusions of Satan, often think to obtain some ease by ruining of themselves. Especially when inward and outward Troubles meet together (as oftentimes they do). Miserable Creatures are in Danger of becoming Guilty of this Crime. Satan Takes Advantage to Tempt them unto it. . . . Such Temptations are not from the Holy & Blessed GOD. Let no man say when he is thus Tempted, I am tempted of God!

For Mather, as for other orthodox Calvinists, melancholy could never serve as a defense against the legal punishments for suicide

---

*Indian servants and black slaves also were subject to the statutes on suicide: When "Thomas, an Indian and very usefull Servant of Mr. Oliver, hang'd himself in the Brewhouse" on 5 October 1688, the Coroner's Jury "ordered his burial by the highway with a stake through his Grave." Sewall, *Diary*, 1: 179; Sewall, *Diary*, 1: 47, 56; 2: 695.

because melancholy, when followed by suicide, was *prima facie* evidence of intention and thus of felony.[47]

The charter revisions, which were imposed on Massachusetts after the Glorious Revolution (1691), created an obligation on the colony to incorporate post-Restoration evolutions in the common law, including those relating to suicide.[48] Partly in response to what such changes might bring, Increase's son, Cotton Mather, reminded his fellow Bostonians in 1692 of the diabolical causes of suicide. It was, Mather warned his congregation, an "ordinary impulse of the Devil" that led to "Wounds on Peoples *Consciences*." Satan creates "such a *Consternation* . . . that they can't pitch upon any other Project for their *own* Repose than that of *Hanging, Drowning, Stabbing, Poysoning*, or some such Foaming piece of *Madness*." But, Mather argued, madness was no excuse; and an individual must overcome such temptations: "in God's name, *think again*, before you do so vile a thing! Think, by whose *Impulse* 'tis that you are dragg'd into this curs'd Action." Mather offered the skeptical a case study of how Satan tempted people to suicide:

> One that came to me with a *wounded Soul*, after all that I could plead with him, left me with these Words, *Well, the Devil will have me after all!* And some Company just then *hindering* me from going after him, as I *intended*, e're I could get at him, he was found sitting in his Chamber, choak'd unto death with a *Rope*, which *Rope* nevertheless was found, not about his Neck, but in his *Hand* and on his *Knee*.[49]

Although Cotton Mather's stricture served as a powerful reminder to the regenerate, this group represented a declining minority in an increasingly heterogeneous population. The revision of province laws completed in 1701 reflected the broadening of the common law excuses for suicide. Coroners were instructed that if an incident "appears to be selfe-murder, the inquisition must [first] conclude" that the perpetrator knew the consequences of the act and had "*voluntarily and feloniously*, as a felon, of himselfe did kill and murder himselfe, against the peace of our Sovereign lord the King, his crown and dignity."[50] These changes made it more difficult for Massachusetts coroners' juries routinely to deny Christian burial to those whom an inquest might find incompetent at the time of their suicide.[51]

Nevertheless, Massachusetts courts and juries remained much

more reluctant than English or other colonial jurisdictions to accept *non compos mentis* pleadings. No one followed the letter of the law more closely than Judge Samuel Sewall. In April 1707, Sewall, then a justice of the Superior Court, issued a warrant declaring that Abraham Harris, a Boston "white-washer," who "felloniously and willfully Murthered himself, by Hanging himself with a Neckcloth . . . is denied Christian burial—being Felo de se." Sewall ordered the constables "to Cause the Body of the said Abraham Harris to be buried upon Boston Neck near the High-way, leading to Roxbury over-against the Gallows, and to Cause a Cart-Load of Stones to be laid upon the Grave of the said Harris as a Brand of Infamy."[52]

And in April 1724, two months after John Valentine's suicide, the coroner's jury declared that Hopestill Foster, who "hanged himself on ye stairs of his cockloft, with a bag round his neck under ye rope," was *felo de se*. In fact, Foster's suicide occasioned a sermon by Benjamin Wadsworth, pastor of the First Church of Boston and later president of Harvard College. Sewall reported in his *Diary* that "Mr. Wadsworth made an excellent Discourse from 2 Cor. 2 II. against Self Murder." Although provincial law now provided that melancholy served to excuse a suicide from criminal penalties, Wadsworth reiterated the arguments of earlier Puritan ministers and jurists that suicide must be resisted "Lest Satan get an advantage."[53]

Of course, Satan did not always win. Increase Mather claimed that his 1682 sermon, *A Call to the Tempted*, saved at least one listener from the "Temptations to *Self-Murder* [which] were impelling" him "with a *Horrible Violence . . . at that very Time*."[54] Mather himself had sustained these temptations to self-destruction. Admitting that even he had been subjected to "Hypocondriacal affection," Mather acknowledged nightmares in which Satan attempted to take advantage of his depressive state. He admitted considering what modern clinicians would describe as a common suicidal fantasy of revenge. Angry at his congregation for its lack of appreciation, Mather fantasized about the reaction to his death: "When I am gone, my poor people will believe that the grief which I sustained by their neglect and mine, was unprofitable for them." Faith, of course, came to the rescue.[55]

Some Massachusetts Protestants continued to connect suicidal thoughts with diabolical temptation far into the eighteenth century, as the following examples from confessions made during the Great Awakening illustrate. Hannah Heaton reported in 1751 that "in years back I use[d] to be worryed to make away with my self when sudden trouble come on me and when my little daughter dyed Satans tone was go hang your self, go hang your self, and when I saw a convenient place I could hardly keep from it sometimes." Heaton recalled "lamenting, roaring, and crying" at those times. Another woman, Susan Anthony, confessed that the devil tempted her with melancholy in the 1740s. Believing that she "was an outcast, rejected of God," Anthony decided to "put an end to my life." Fortunately she came upon a copy of *Advice to Sinners Under Conviction, &c. with some Scruples of the Tempted Resolved.* This volume prevented her from "that soul shuddering sin, self-murder" because "Satan felt the force of these commissioned lines, and fled the field."[56] Nathan Cole reported that in 1745 he was tormented by Satan into doubting the authenticity of his conversion experience: "Satan comes upon me and says there is one way to know quick; destroy your self says he and you will soon know; for if you be converted you will certainly be saved; and if not you never will be converted, therefore destroy your self and you will know at once." Cole resisted "this horrible temptation."[57] Such examples demonstrate a persistent belief as late as the mid-eighteenth century, at least among the regenerate of Massachusetts, that suicide during an attack of melancholy remained a sin and thus a crime. But, by the mid-eighteenth century, these examples increasingly were the exceptions.

Emergence of a Disease

Ironically, the strongest endorsement of Sewall's views came from the English jurist William Blackstone. By the mid-eighteenth century, coroners' juries in England and the colonies increasingly returned verdicts of insanity in suicide cases. This situation caused Blackstone to complain that juries tended to find "that the very act of suicide is evidence of insanity; as if every man who acted contrary to reason, had no reason at all." Blackstone worried that such reasoning could set a precedent, "for the same argument would prove every other criminal *non compos*, as well as the self-murderer." The law, Blackstone insisted, "very rationally judges, that every melancholy or hypochondriac fit does not deprive a man of the capacity of discerning right from wrong."[58]

Blackstone's warnings served to indicate how commonplace

insanity pleadings had become in suicide cases. For instance, a recent study of suicide verdicts in early modern England concluded
that beginning in the 1640s, *non compos mentis* verdicts began to su-
persede *felo de se* and by the end of the eighteenth century "*non
compos mentis* [was] the usual verdict in all cases of suicide."[59] By the
mid-eighteenth century the number of self-deaths determined to
be "lunatic" had increased so substantially that one writer com-
plained that juries seemed to have decided that whenever someone
committed suicide they "must of course be Lunatick."[60]

At this time, a debate was taking place in Europe over the right to
suicide. Enlightenment thinkers like Montesquieu, Madame de
Staël, Voltaire, and especially David Hume, insisted that suicide was
a rational and therefore legitimate personal option. Others, including Jean Dumas, Charles Moore, John Adams, and Jean-Jacques
Rousseau, condemned suicide as an immoral and cowardly act.[61]
Both sides, however, agreed that suicide was a decision made by the
free rational will of the individual. Although educated Americans
were familiar with these writers, there is no evidence that this debate
had much impact in North America. Instead, Americans continued
to focus on the issue that had concerned the Puritans: Was suicide a
sin and thus a crime, or was it a disease over which an individual had
no control?

The vehement resistance of Sewall and others in Massachusetts to
non compos mentis determinations reflected the extent to which they
perceived that traditional values were endangered by these determinations. These anxieties were not misplaced. Attitudes toward
suicide were indeed transformed in the decades following John
Valentine's death. By the mid–eighteenth century, evidence of melancholy increasingly formed the basis for a successful pleading of
non compos mentis.

Why had these changes taken place? Part of the answer lay in the
Puritans' success in linking suicide with Satan and melancholy. Ironically, this served only to erode the claim that suicide was an act freely
chosen. For, by the mid–eighteenth century, most coroners' jurors
in Massachusetts had come to believe what many English physicians
had argued since the seventeenth century, that melancholy was a
disease. And, as a disease, melancholy could not be used as evidence
of criminal intent.[62]

Even some Massachusetts's ministers, swept up in the rationalism of the age, began to hedge on the connection between diabolical temptations and suicide. For instance, in a 1740 sermon delivered on the occasion of the suicide of a seventeen-year-old undergraduate, the Reverend Solomon Williams issued the usual exhortations about the dangers of pursuing gratification while neglecting God's rules. Nevertheless, Williams attributed the youth's "distraction" and subsequent suicide to a lifelong sickness that was exacerbated by "too hard study and the measles which he had in the beginning of the past winter."[63]

A quarter century later Samuel Phillips, a minister at Andover, still rehearsed the Mathers' arguments that "the horrible crime of suicide" was "the most dangerous of Satan's devices." Satan is greatly pleased, Phillips explained, "when he can prevail with any Person to destroy his own life." But Phillips's advice on how to avoid succumbing to these temptations reflected the rationality of the late eighteenth century. Because the Devil exploited physical as well as emotional weakness, Phillips urges the tempted "to seek . . . relief, as soon as possible" from a physician. "Don't say, as many do, that no Physician can relieve us, because our Trouble is altogether a Trouble of Mind, and Body is not at all affected." This, Phillips insisted, was "a very great Mistake; for very often, this Trouble of Mind takes its Rise from bodily Maladies; and unless the body be relieved, and the Dark Cloud which hangs over the Brain be scattered, it will be to little purpose, to offer them the best Instructions, because they are, at Present, *uncapable* of weighing matters according to their true value."[64]

What had occurred in Massachusetts represented the last attempts in the English colonies to retain medieval practices and attitudes toward suicide. Even these attempts, like Puritanism itself, were fraught with ambiguities and contradictions that ultimately led to the unraveling of older values and practices. Suicide remained a crime in Massachusetts until the late nineteenth century, but its penalties decreasingly were invoked:[65] For instance, from 1731 to 1800 Suffolk County (Boston) Coroners' Juries returned one *non compos mentis* determination for every 2.5 felonious determinations; but from 1801 to 1828, there were two insanity determinations for each felony suicide. After 1810 the word "suicide" only rarely can be found in a Suffolk County coroner's inquest.[66]

In other colonies where theoretical divisions were less well drawn, the enforcement of criminal penalties for suicide had been far less consistent. As in Massachusetts, coroners' juries increasingly resisted findings of felony suicide in favor of *non compos mentis*. For instance, in colonial Virginia the law required that a suicide's property be forfeit, but by the mid–eighteenth century this practice rarely was enforced.[67] When, during the American Revolution, Thomas Jefferson revised the statutes of Virginia, he insisted that the law ought to be practical and reflect the public sentiment against criminal sanctions in suicide cases: "That men in general too disapprove of this severity is apparent from the constant practice of juries finding the suicide in a state of insanity; because they have no other way of saving the forfeiture. Let it then," Jefferson argues, "be done away." Rejecting the allegation that "the quasi-punishment of confiscation" would prevent suicides, Jefferson reasoned that a man "who can determine to renounce life, who is so weary of his existence here as rather to make experiment of what is beyond the grave, can we suppose him, in such a state of mind, susceptible of influence from the losses of his family by confiscation?"[68] Thus the revised laws of Virginia institutionalized Jefferson's belief that "Suicide is not to incur Forfeiture, but considered as a Disease."[69]

As in Virginia, the American Revolution became the occasion, though not the reason, for other jurisdictions to do away with forfeiture of a suicide's property. In 1776 this was done in the new constitutions of New Jersey and Maryland and after the revolution, in North Carolina. In 1790 Pennsylvania's revised constitution reaffirmed that state's colonial commitment to consider suicide the same as a "natural death."[70] Thus, by the later eighteenth century, jurisdictions from Massachusetts to Virginia, whether by statute or practice, had come to accept the notion that suicide was an act whose commission was itself sufficient punishment.

Historian Louis Masur argues persuasively that a belief in the "perfectability of mankind," which pervaded the values of many leaders of the Revolutionary War, influenced several state legislatures to revise their criminal statutes to reduce "the number of crimes for which a convict might be hanged."[71] Because many of these revisions simultaneously included the abolition of the criminal penalities associated with suicide, a parallel argument could be constructed. Nevertheless, as we have seen, the trend toward the elimination of sanctions against suicide had a long history. At most, the revolution created the conditions that allowed legislatures to enact into law what had been for some time everyday practice.

By the end of the century, religious faith, once seen as a defense against the temptation to suicide, was increasingly being portrayed as a cause of illness and self-murder. Many agreed with Jefferson's friend, the novelist Charles Brockden Brown, who insisted that religious enthusiasm led to melancholy and insanity. Brown's 1798 romance, *Wieland or The Transformation*, connected Theodore Wieland's madness and suicide to his Puritan-like obedience to what he interpreted to be God's will. Like his Puritan forebears, Theodore also heard voices tempting him to murder and suicide. Rejecting man's reason and law as fallible, Wieland submitted only to the voice of God. Unlike Increase Mather or Samuel Sewall, Brown insisted that religious fanaticism, not Satan, was responsible for Wieland's madness. Religion diseased Wieland's mind and led to his suicide.[72]

Not surprisingly, religious leaders like the Presbyterian Minister Samuel Miller of New York rejected such views. In *The Guilt, Folly, and Sources of Suicide*, two sermons that he delivered and published in 1805, Miller insisted that suicide was "a crime of the deepest dye —a crime which has become alarmingly frequent in our land, and in our city." Denying that "the victim of depression and melancholy" has lost all "capacity" to overcome "his infirmities," Miller insisted "that there is not an individual breathing who can, with propriety, plead in defense of despair and suicide" that he might not choose to live. Suicide, Miller argued, was not the result of "mental disease," but "is generally prompted by the most sordid and unworthy *selfishness*. It is a crime which sacrifices every thing on the altar of *individual feeling*." Finally, Miller upbraided magistrates and jurors for their tendency to ascribe insanity as the cause of all suicides:

> Can you reconcile, either with your obligations as men, or with the official oath which binds you as public functionaries, the manner in which you are accustomed to treat suicide when called to consider cases of this melancholy crime? Believe me, when you attempt to cover, by a verdict of *lunacy*, the odium which ought ever to rest upon the memory of the deliberate self-murderer, or when you give countenance to such verdicts, you not only wrong your own souls, but also you inflict an injury on society.[73]

Although Miller had condemned suicide with the same vigor as Sewall and the Mathers, unlike his Puritan forebears, Miller did not

assert that Satan stood as the tempter behind suicidal urges. By ignoring the devil's agency, Miller opened the door to the very argument he sought to condemn, that those who killed themselves were
by and large irrational, if not mentally ill.

This issue arose even more clearly in two sermons against suicide
published that same year by the Reverend Joseph Lathrop, pastor
of the First Church in West Springfield, Massachusetts. Unlike
Miller, Lathrop admitted that "In most cases . . . this violence [sui-
cide] is the unhappy, but guiltless effect of insanity." Lathrop's concern was with those "cases, in which it cannot be imputed to this
cause."[74] The fact that even a Presbyterian minister, who condemned all suicide as an "atrocity," was willing to accept insanity as
the cause of most suicides, indicates how far attitudes had evolved by
1805. By the beginning of the nineteenth century one can no longer
identify distinct regional variations in American attitudes toward suicide. Coroners' juries in Massachusetts acted in much the same way
toward suicide as those in Virginia and Pennsylvania. A postrevolu-
tionary national consensus had emerged that suicide was an action
that resulted from forces beyond an individual's will or control.

By the second decade of the nineteenth century, suicides increasingly were viewed as resulting from mental illness and rarely were
denounced. In Massachusetts, where an official determination of
suicide continued to constitute a crime, coroners' inquisitions routinely determined that those who killed themselves did so either
through "accident," "misadventure," or "mental derangement"—
none of which fit the criminal definition of suicide. In fact, from
1810 to 1834 the word "suicide" did not appear on any coroner's
inquest in Suffolk County (Boston). When the designation of "suicide" reappeared in 1835, it invariably was qualified as "suicide while
laboring under aberration" or suicide due to "derangement of
mind." The result of these qualifications, of course, was that these
self-murderers were excused from criminal and ecclesiastical sanctions because they were not legally suicides under Massachusetts
statute.[75]

As the following examples illustrate, by the 1820s deaths that
unambiguously would have been considered suicides in colonial
Massachusetts regularly were excused from the stigma of a criminal
designation. For instance, when a Boston machinist hanged himself
on 3 August 1827, the coroner's jury refused to rule the death a sui-

cide. Accepting testimony that indicated Michael Boling, Jr., had been "much distracted" because of unspecified "family troubles," the inquest concluded that Boling was deranged when he came "to his death by hanging himself."[76] When nineteen-year-old Hannah Winslow, after a fight with her husband, threw "herself into the Mill Creek" and drowned in October 1827, the coroner's inquisition determined that she had done so by accident, even though her husband and other witnesses reported that they saw Winslow "go directly toward the water—and jump right into the Mill Creek."[77] William Bond, a thirty-one-year-old unemployed master mariner, "came to his Death by discharging the contents of a large pistol into his head" on 27 March 1828. Nevertheless, the jury did not find suicide because it accepted testimony that Bond had been "quite down-hearted" prior to his death.[78] A sailor, Jacob Wilson, who hanged himself in 1828 with "his suspenders round his neck," was determined to have done so "in a fit of insanity."[79]

When the word "suicide" reappeared in Suffolk County coroners' inquests in the mid-1830s, it routinely was qualified to differentiate it from felony suicide. For example, on the strength of the testimony of his wife, a coroner's jury determined that George Duffett, "unemployed due to illness," had "cut his throat" in April 1843 as a result of "partial insanity . . . thereby committing suicide."[80] In other jurisdictions, where suicide was not a crime, deaths were listed as suicides,* but the causes as in Massachusetts were increasingly attributed to insanity.[81]

A decade earlier Alexis de Tocqueville observed that "in the midst of American society you meet with men full of a fanatical and almost wild spiritualism, which hardly exists in Europe. From time to time strange sects arise which endeavor to strike out extraordinary paths to eternal happiness. Religious insanity," concluded Tocqueville, "is very common in the United States."[82] Tocqueville also remarked on a "strange melancholy which often haunts the inhabitants of democratic countries in the midst of their abundance." Sometimes this melancholy "seizes upon them in the midst of calm and easy circumstances." Although he claimed that "in America suicide is rare,"

---

*By the 1840s the qualified use of the designation of suicide became standard practice. Thus Winthrop Smart, who drowned himself in July 1843, was determined to have come to his "death by suicide" due to his "derangement of mind." "Coroner's Inquest," Winthrop Smart, 28 July 1843, Adl. 631.

Tocqueville discovered that insanity is "more common there than anywhere else."[83] Tocqueville underestimated the extent of suicide in America, as he may have exaggerated democracy's tendency toward melancholy. But if he confused a growing concern in some quarters about madness with popular behavior, his comments are more easily understood. For Tocqueville had uncovered without realizing it an important change in attitudes and perceptions. By the 1830s melancholy and suicide, no longer religious or legal issues, had become almost exclusively the concern of medical men. And if melancholy were a disease, a melancholic individual was no more responsible for committing suicide than for contracting smallpox. This transformation of consciousness signaled the medicalization of suicide that had emerged unchallenged by the 1840s.

2

RISE AND DECLINE OF
MORAL TREATMENT, 1844–1917

I<small>N</small> 1844 the officers of the New York State Lunatic Asylum in Utica established the *American Journal of Insanity.*[1] In its first volume, the editors published several articles that connected melancholy to suicide and both to disease. One of these, which reproduced six typical suicide cases, intended to illustrate "the importance of early treatment in preventing suicide." In "most of the cases," the editor explained, "the individual was known to be melancholy, and partially insane." So frequently did melancholic individuals attempt to take their lives that the editors urged intervention at the earliest appearance of symptoms to "secure these unfortunate individuals from the too often fatal consequences of this disease." The early signs of suicide followed a predictable pattern: "Whenever the occurrence of illness or circumstances in a man's social, domestic, or other affairs, is followed by a striking change in his character or conduct, there is reason for apprehension of dangerous results." Specifically, "if he becomes reserved and melancholy; loses his affection for his family and his business; prefers to be alone; is undecided in his purposes, and restless and sleepless at night; there is indication, that immediate action in his behalf may be necessary to his safety." Society must recognize that these individuals are sick and that "the only security that such persons have, is the constant care of a judicious friend, or what is still better for their recovery, a residence in a well-directed Lunatic Asylum—for usually such persons need medical treatment."[2]

The six cases were chosen to illustrate the thesis that melancholy, if left untreated, led inevitably to suicide. Three of the six victims allegedly had been driven to despair by their religious enthusiasm. One, a woman of twenty-seven, "became insane from continued religious excitement, in connection with the doctrine of Miller, who prophesied the speedy destruction of the world." The woman, who "thought she committed the unpardonable sin, became very melancholy, restless, and sleepless, and manifested a tendency to suicide, and endeavored to cut her throat." At the asylum she was given extract of conium [white hemlock] and carbonate of iron, together with sulphate of morphine, the latter in sufficient doses to procure sleep." The morphine "appeared to cure her," because when she was taken off it, "she became worse." Another, a forty-year-old farmer, "became much distracted in mind while attending a protracted religious meeting." The man "soon became melancholy, and despaired of his salvation. He continued in this state for four or five months before he came to the Asylum, much of the time melancholy, with no disposition to attend to business, or to labor, and says that all feeling and affection for his family and friends have left him." Diagnosed as "dyspeptic" and suffering from "some biliary derangement," he was given "a slight mercurial course for a short time, with laxatives and warm bathing. This was followed by extract of conium and iron, with elixir proprietatis [patent medicine], and he soon began to recover." The third, a twenty-year-old woman, allegedly became suicidal as a result of too "much attention to religion during a revival." She experienced disturbing dreams that left her "nervous and sleepless," and caused her to lose "interest in her domestic duties." With "her melancholy increasing, her friends became apprehensive of her committing suicide, as she said she had no wish to live." When bleeding, blistering, and cathartic medicines provided no relief, she was "brought to the Asylum." There, treated with "warm bath, laxatives, and extract of conium and iron, together with morphine . . . she regained her health and spirits."[3]

Charles Brockden Brown's earlier insistence that religious enthusiasm caused rather than cured melancholy and suicide had become medical dicta by the 1840s. For instance, in 1845 the *American Journal of Insanity* warned the American public of the danger of "protracted religious meetings, especially of those held in the evening and night." Such events led to numerous "delusions," resulting in "suicides, insanity, and every species of folly," because they created "an excitement bordering on disease." Pointing particularly to Millerism, a religious movement popular in the early 1840s that predicted the imminent destruction of the world, the editors reported that asylums throughout the nation were overflowing with "individuals who became deranged from attending upon the preaching of this doctrine," many of whom remained institutionalized in an "incurable" condition. "Thousands," of others, "who have not yet become deranged, have had their health impaired to such a degree as to unfit them for the duties of life forever; and especially is this the case with females." Thus, the editors concluded, "We have no hesitation in saying that . . . the prevalence of yellow fever or of the cholera has never proved so great a calamity to this country."[4]

The transformation of suicide from a crime to a disease coincided with the growth of institutional psychiatry in antebellum America. By the 1840s, much of the discussion of suicide in the United States had moved from the pulpit and the courtroom to medical journals. Increasingly, expert opinion concerning the etiology of suicide became the province of that small group of physicians charged with administering asylums for the insane. In 1844 they organized themselves into the Association of Medical Superintendents of American Institutions for the Insane (AMSAII).[5] Although alienists were not psychiatrists in the contemporary sense of the term, that is, they had no specialized or uniform training outside of general medicine, asylum superintendents self-consciously portrayed themselves as experts on insanity and the organization that they founded (AMSAII) evolved into The American Psychiatric Association in the early twentieth century.*

Alienists' views of insanity and suicide were influenced, as were medical therapeutics, by wider cultural, economic, and political developments. As urbanization and factories began to make their first serious inroads into American life in the 1840s, a growing national consensus emerged (outside the slave South) that emphasized self-discipline as an alternative to external authority. Fed by a belief that

---

*I follow the practice of those medical historians who refer to these early practitioners as "alienists" rather than as "psychiatrists."

like the environment individuals were malleable, suppressive modes of control were deemphasized in favor of more repressive behaviors. What was desired in the emerging factory society, especially in the Northeast (as it had been desired several decades earlier in industrializing England), was that factory workers, public school pupils, as well as criminals, identify with and internalize the moral standards of the emerging bourgeois culture. Whether these changes in consciousness preceded or resulted from developments in the growing market economy is debatable, but by the 1840s ideology and economy seemed to be having a reciprocal influence.[6]

These values were evident in both the attitudes toward and the treatments of madness, including suicide. Earlier methods of beating and punishing patients had reflected the idea that the insane were beasts who must be controlled. Like nature and Satan, madness was considered unchangeable. Simultaneously with the decline in the belief that diabolical forces underlay self-murders, the more general notion emerged that like the environment, the insane could be reshaped. Not only could artisans, farm girls, and immigrants be molded into good factory workers, but also, insisted asylum superintendents, many madmen and madwomen could be transformed into useful and productive citizens. Thus, a conviction emerged that the insane could be reformed and that the suicidal could be cured.[7]

While asylum superintendents were as much captives of bourgeois ideology as were other social reformers, they were influenced on a daily basis by more parochial concerns. Not least of all, these men sought stable employment in the medical profession at a time when, buffeted by competing medical sects, medicine promised neither prestige nor a regular income. A career as an asylum superintendent offered a solution to the contradictions between humanitarian desires to help others and a quest for economic security. First, however, the asylum had to be made safe for professionalism and that requirement provided the impetus for the founding of the AMSAII in 1844. In retrospect it seems that the asylum served the needs of the superintendents as much as, if not more than, the needs of their patients. Like most professionals then and now, these asylum physicians saw no conflict between an increase in their professional power and the improvement of the condition of the patients they served. Indeed, they viewed the former as essential for the latter.

Medical explanations for the causes of suicide were influenced profoundly not only by cultural values and clinical experience, but also by the rivalries that surrounded the establishment of the psychiatric profession as it grew from a collection of asylum superintendents in the 1840s into the competing specialties of neurology and psychological psychiatry at the beginning of the twentieth century.

A PROTEAN DISORDER

American asylum superintendents shared with other mid-nineteenth-century physicians and with much of the public an environmental or protean view of the etiology of both physical and mental disorders. As Charles Rosenberg explains, "health and disease" were assumed to result "from a cumulative interaction between constitutional endowment and environmental circumstance." Thus, health depended upon the combination of diet, atmosphere, climate, work, and lifestyle. "Each of these factors," according to Rosenberg, "implied a necessary and continuing physiological adjustment. The body was always in a state of becoming—and thus always in jeopardy."[8] This construct was useful especially for explaining the etiology of nonspecific psychiatric disorders.* Alienists like Edward Jarvis attributed insanity to "a part of the price we pay for civilization. The causes of the one increase with the developments and results of the other."[9] Suicidal behavior in particular fitted easily into protean environmental formulations and lent itself to what medical superintendents called "moral treatment."

Nineteenth-century alienists had believed that any imbalance or irregularity (such as fever, constipation, or diarrhea) in a person's physical system could have a debilitating effect on the nervous system or on the blood. If left untreated, an imbalance could develop progressively from melancholy to general insanity, culminating in suicide. Therefore treatment concentrated on symptomatic inter-

---

*Medical literature in the 1840s divided mental illness into four general categories: mania, melancholia, monomania, and dementia. Mania was similar to what later would be called manic disorders; melancholia mirrored modern depressive behaviors; monomania (or partial insanity) was a form of melancholia in which the afflicted focused on one thought or belief; while dementia served as a nonspecific diagnosis for ideational (for instance, schizophrenia) as opposed to affective forms of madness. In making diagnoses, alienists often blurred the distinctions among these categories.

ventions whose aim was to keep the body in balance or equilibrium. The suicidal were treated (or subjected to) a wide variety of emetics, cathartics, diuretics, and bleeding. Most of these heroic interventions appeared to work, because in combination they served to calm the violent and to turn the morose to concerns of more immediate bodily functions. Those inadvertently poisoned or otherwise killed in the course of therapy were believed to have been so progressively diseased that no interventions would have been able to alter the course of their disease.[10]

By the 1830s, asylum treatment of the suicidal began to downplay more extreme heroic interventions, especially bloodletting, in favor of newer pharmacological treatments. Clinical experience and new theoretical constructs served to undercut Benjamin Rush's earlier assessment* that bloodletting was an effective treatment for the suicidal because the procedure calmed even the most violent patients.[11] Experience had convinced many practitioners that stimulants and sedatives were often more effective in treating the manic and melancholic symptoms of suicide than purgative and depleting interventions.[12]

In addition, the popularity of phrenology, the belief that protuberances on the skull represented specific localized centers of mind functions such as intelligence and moral character, served to undercut another assumption of heroic therapy toward madness in general and suicide in particular. Rush had argued that insanity was essentially organic in etiology because it was accompanied by other somatic disturbances.[13] Madness could not be a mental disorder, because it was assumed that, although the brain could be diseased, the mind (which was equated with the soul) was immortal. Phrenological theory helped to change that view. Arguing that environment and behavior could affect specific locations in the brain, which themselves could be identified as disease centers, phrenological psychiatrists established a bridge between psychological treatment and the organic approach that had dominated medical psychiatry. This

---

*Rush insisted that "what is commonly called madness [was] a disease of the blood-vessels of the brain. All the other and inferior forms of derangement, whether of the memory, the will, the principle of faith, the passions, and the moral faculties, I believe to be connected more or less with morbid action in the blood-vessels of the brain, or heart, according to the seats of those faculties of the mind." Benjamin Rush, *Medical Inquiries and Observations Upon the Diseases of the Mind*, 1812, Reprint (New York: Hafner Publishing, 1962), 26–27.

bridge gave scientific credence to what was labeled the "moral treatment," which emerged first in England and then in the United States.[14] And bringing things full circle, the moral treatment meshed with bourgeois ideology as it informed the assumptions of antebellum alienists.

Beginning in the 1840s, the *American Journal of Insanity*, the sole journal of American psychiatry, published specific case histories as examples of the way that organic, social, and psychological factors combined in suicide and how the moral treatment provided the most efficacious form of intervention. For instance, in January 1845 the editors reported a case of a thirty-eight-year-old man who had been in "poor health for some time from dyspepsia." The man "gradually became melancholy, lost interest in his business" and "passed much of his time in useless regrets about his unhappy condition." He "twice attempted to commit suicide, and had frequently secreted knives with this object in view." Unsuccessful at killing himself, the man decided to "procure his death by killing another, but on being told that he would be acquitted on the ground of insanity, he relinquished this expedient." Because the causes of suicide had three components, the moral treatment logically combined organic, psychological, and social interventions. Committed to the New York State Lunatic Asylum in Utica, the man was given "a combination of laxatives and tonics, and of remedies to restore the tone of the digestive organs—the use of warm baths, and the change of circumstances and associates attending his removal from home and residence here" improved his health. After two months of treatment, his physical health was restored and the patient was sent home. Subsequently he wrote to the asylum superintendent thanking him "for the care that prevented him from consummating his former suicidal intentions."[15]

Sometimes, however, therapy reverted to more powerful interventions. For instance, one case of attempted suicide that the editors believed would be "of great practical utility" to American psychiatrists concerned an English merchant who, "having met with pecuniary losses, became depressed, and had a strong desire to kill himself." Unable to sleep, he experienced "extreme agitations. No language can describe his sensations. Self destruction appeared his only resource." A surgeon was called in and, upon seeing him, the patient "cried, Bleed me or I shall cut my throat." Hardly had the blood begun to flow when the merchant proclaimed, "Thank God, I am saved from self-destruction!" Since that time, the *Journal* reported, "he has not had a return of the symptoms mentioned."[16]

Like other nineteenth-century medical doctors, alienists turned to nosology, or the classification of diseases based upon external symptoms. They hoped that statistical analyses of categorized groups of symptoms would lead to a deeper understanding of their causes.[17] Because of its finality, suicide especially lent itself to nosological methodology and statistical analysis. Like their European counterparts, early nineteenth-century American alienists saw suicide as a key to understanding other forms of mental illness. American practitioners expected that an examination of suicide statistics would confirm a widely shared assumption that insanity in general and suicide in particular resulted from a combination of organic and emotional predispositions, exacerbated by the pressures of "modern" civilization.

Beginning with its first volume, the *American Journal of Insanity* reported annual suicide rates for New York State and occasionally for other jurisdictions.[18] The *Journal*'s editors relied upon suicide statistics in much the same manner that Durkheim later would, as a primary source for understanding the etiology of suicide.

Suicide statistics seemed to confirm the environmental assumptions of American therapeutics. In particular, the statistics appeared to demonstrate that urban life was a prime contributing factor in the etiology of suicide. In an 1845 analysis of suicide statistics, the superintendent of the New York State Lunatic Asylum in Utica and editor of the *American Journal of Insanity*, Dr. Amariah Brigham, found that although suicides were "alarmingly frequent" in the United States as a whole, in cities suicide had reached epidemic proportions. For instance, he pointed out that "as many [suicides] have been committed some years in the city of New York alone, as are assigned to the whole State." Relying on the "Reports of the City Inspectors of New York," Brigham found that rates for New York City, which had averaged 12.7 suicides per 100,000 since 1805 (see Table 2.1), far exceeded the 1840 rates of France (8.1) and England and Wales (6.3). Compared to the principal capital cities of Europe, New York City fell just below Vienna, which was reported to have a rate of 15.6 suicides per 100,000 people (see Table 2.2).[19]

In 1847 the *Journal* reported that the disparity between the urban

Table 2.1.
SUICIDES IN NEW YORK CITY, 1805–1839

Years	Rate per 100,000
1805–1809	15.1
1810–1814	7.9
1815–1819	15.9
1820–1824	11.2
1825–1829	13.3
1830–1834	12.3
1835–1839	13.1

SOURCE: "Reports of the City Inspectors of New York," 1805–1843, in the *American Journal of Insanity* 1 (January 1845): 232–233.

and rural rates of suicide continued to grow. The editors cited the 1845 New York State Census, which showed that the suicide rate for New York City was almost three times greater than that for the state as a whole.[20] The following year the editors found that the gap between urban and rural suicide rates had widened significantly. These results, they noted, mirrored "like observations made in France and other countries." Given the fact that "the occurrence of suicide has been more than four times as frequent in the city of New York, as in all other parts of the State," the editors suggested a mathematical formulation for the calculation of urban suicide:

> ... *in great cities* when compared with the country, all human passions are exercised with more than fourfold constancy and intensity, and that reverse of

Table 2.2.
SUICIDES IN CHIEF CAPITALS OF EUROPE, 1813–1834

City	Years	Rate per 100,000
Palermo	1831	0.6
Naples	1826	0.6
London	1834	3.7
St. Petersburg	1831	4.8
Prague	1820	6.3
Vienna	1829	15.6
Milan	1827	31.3
Paris	1836	37.5
Hamburg	1822	55.6
Copenhagen	1804–1806	100.0
Berlin	1813–1822	133.0

SOURCE: *American Journal of Insanity* 1 (January 1845): 234.

fortune and disappointments of desire, are more frequent by fourfold, and
are accompanied by a shock of the intellect or affections, more than four times
as severe, and by more than four times the liability to that temporary or continued overthrow of reason, which induces self-destruction.

These "reflections," the writer concluded, "should teach the coun-
tryman longing for the town, contentment, and should warn the
dwellers in cities, of the vast importance of the most rigid discipline
both of body and mind."[21]

These views were affirmed in the popular press. For instance, in
August 1859 the *New York Times* reviewed twenty-six suicides that
had appeared in its pages over a two-week period and warned of
"A New Epidemic" of suicides. In a companion editorial entitled
"The Alarming Increase of Suicides," the *Times* attributed these suicides to the conditions fostered by urban life. In rural America, the
newspaper explained, men and women were so wrapped up in their
daily chores that they had no "time for any mischievous thoughts of
ropes, razors and morphine." Transfer these same people to cities,
warned the editorial writer, and a combination of rising aspirations,
leisure time, and temptations to vice would form "the train of causes
that lead to self-destruction." Urban centers encouraged "the use of
intoxicating beverages, the inordinate consumption of tobacco, the
use of opium," and "nocturnal dissipation and the infamous solitary
vices that blazon themselves publicly in the shrunken, pale and
prematurely-aged faces of so many young men." These conditions
"are sowing for us a horrid harvest of suicides at an early day."
Moreover, "the wicked devotion to business, scarcely intermitted for
a day through the year," combined with "selfish employers who
grudge their employees a week's relaxation in the year from inces-
sant toil" were responsible for "many of the suicides that the daily
press will hereafter chronicle." Only "temperate habits," which included "respect unto the laws of our physical nature, early hours,
moderation even in healthy sports, . . . and the tenderest nurture
of domestic virtues, will nip in the bud all thoughts of self-
destruction."[22]

Publicity and imitation were additional environmental factors in
the etiology of suicide. "No other fact is better established by science," Dr. Brigham insisted, "than that suicide is often committed
from imitation." Newspaper reports of suicide, he asserted, led
readers to self-murder: "A single paragraph may suggest suicide to

twenty persons. Some particulars of the act, or expressions, seize the imagination, and the disposition to repeat it, in a moment of morbid excitement, proves irresistible."[23] Those who inherit "a propensity to suicide," warned an 1849 *Journal* article, are particularly vulnerable to imitation if "a relative or friend" commits suicide. "There is good reason to believe," the editors commented, "that the list of victims to this crime is greatly increased by the publicity which is given . . . by the newspaper press throughout the country."[24]

In the 1840s a few physicians argued that although suicide generally was connected to insanity, sane suicides also were possible. "That many insane persons commit Suicide is doubtless true; nay, the propensity to it may be said to constitute the prominent symptom of some lunacies," wrote an anonymous "Southern Physician" in *The American Whig Review* in 1847. "But those err," he explained, "who make it the essential element of a separate order of insanity." An expert who asserts "that the suicide is always insane . . . falls into the most obvious inconsistencies . . . for there is no act of human life that can be proved more rationally and consistently planned, than the act of leaving it in an infinite number of instances."[25] Nevertheless, even those physicians who agreed that some of the suicidal were sane concentrated their analyses on the links between environment and suicide.

Given the eclectic nature of therapeutic environmentalism, medical students were offered general rather than specific formulations for building diagnoses. For instance, at Columbia Medical College in New York City in the 1860s, students learned from Dr. John Ordronaux that "the higher development and the increased susceptibility of the emotions, in an advanced state of civilization" created those "disorders upon the mind" that culminated in suicide. "The causes which tend to develop the suicidal tendency," Ordronaux explained, "while they are, doubtless, remotely physical in character (as in the delirium of fever), are for the most part to be traced to disorders of our mental or moral nature."[26]

Due to the nonspecific nature of the causes of suicide, the primary concern of most alienists centered on the treatment rather than the etiology of suicide. If the causes of suicide were environmental, moral treatment offered both a prevention and a cure: incarceration and care in a rural asylum. Many insane persons, the *Journal of Insanity* noted, had a "disposition to suicide," but never "commit the act." The reason was "that the awful deed of self-murder is rarely committed in well regulated Christian communities by persons of sane mind—that is *suicide is generally one of the accidents of insanity.*" Thus the treatment that provides the "best security for persons known to be melancholy or partially deranged, is the constant care of a judicious friend, or what is still better for their recovery, a residence in a Lunatic Asylum."[27] In October 1847, the *Journal* published several case studies of homicides and suicides by the insane, which the editors hoped "may serve in the first place, to awaken attention to the importance of carefully watching and guarding the insane who are at large, as in several instances, it will be noticed that the insanity was known to exist before the commission of the act. This," the editors warned, "is particularly true as regards the numerous suicides."[28]

Because the leaders of American psychiatry were most concerned with those aspects of suicide that demonstrated to the rest of American society the urgent need for increased public support for the building and maintenance of insane asylums, they emphasized that suicide was preventable. In a long analysis of Louis Bertrand's 1857 *Traité du suicide,* a prominent asylum superintendent wrote that Bertrand had "not given sufficient attention" to the prevention of suicides. "Early treatment in an asylum of the suicidally disposed insane," the reviewer insisted, would be of "more real benefit" than any "legal measures to outlaw suicide."[29]

Similarly, an 1856 review of Alexandre Brierre de Boismont's *Du Suicide et de la Folie Suicide* in the *American Journal of Insanity* admitted that "there are occasionally circumstances in life in which suicide, without ceasing to be reprehensible and culpable in a moral sense, can, however, be readily accounted for by a state of mind far removed from insanity." Indeed, medical superintendents were willing to accept de Boismont's contention that decreasing the number of suicides could be accomplished by solving the "great social questions of the day—pauperism, labor, and wages." However, the reviewer was most interested in the book's main concern "that an intimate knowledge of the causes of insanity should be able to furnish numerous lessons for those to whom is intrusted the government of society." In this regard, the reviewer found that de Boismont's work was a "highly valuable one, particularly in reference to suicidal insanity—the principal object, in a word, of the studies of the author." Readers of the *Journal,* of course, had particular sympathy with de Boismont's suggestion that in the case of the suicidally insane, "frequently it is necessary to resort to seclusion, to coercive measures, and to therapeutical agents—such as long continued baths; shower-baths [to calm the patient] also are found serviceable in the acute stage of the malady." Like American asylum superintendents, de Boismont endorsed a combination of somatic interventions and moral treatment for the suicidal:

> Cold affusions and anti-spasmodic preparations and tonic may be employed with great success; also external irritation, such as friction of the skin, and likewise depletion and blistering, may prove beneficial. It is sometimes necessary, in cases of prolonged refusal of food, to introduce nourishment into the stomach by means of the oesophagus tube. The administration of morphine appears at times to be useful in the treatment of suicidal insanity. When the acute period of disease has passed, the pleasures of the family circle are of great service. During convalescence, country air, traveling, gymnastic exercises, amusements, and intellectual as well as manual labor assist materially in the cure. The recovery may be attributable to a physical or moral crisis.[30]

Taken to its logical extreme, the environmentalist explanation of suicide could be used as an argument for the radical reform of modern urban society. In an 1875 article entitled "Suicide in Large Cities," which rehearsed many of the arguments that would later appear in Durkheim's *Suicide,* a prominent psychiatrist and neurologist, Dr. Allan McLane Hamilton, claimed that statistical investigations of suicide had absolutely connected the "moral and physical" symptoms of suicide with the conditions of urban life. "The motive, behavior, and characteristics of the individual who takes his own life," Hamilton explained, were exacerbated by "certain sanitary conditions" as well as "the habits, tastes, and moral culture of the people," including their "national characteristics." Both the rich and poor increased their risk of suicide by living in cities. "The busy life men lead in the metropolis, and the necessity for brain-stimulus, accelerate the *facilis descensus.* The disgrace of men in high position, impending ruin and other facts," Hamilton asserted, "will often prompt suicide as a mode of relief." The poor, on the other hand, were moved to sin and self-destruction by the "tenement house system," which colonized "many thousand people in a limited space, much too small for them." In such an environment, "every vice becomes, to a great degree, contagious" and "moral contact of the vicious with the pure is certain to occur." The growth of prostitution and the destruction of health that result "are powerful inducers of suicide."[31]

Modern urban life, according to Hamilton, had produced a suicide epidemic. In New York City alone, he found that the suicide rate had increased 300 percent in seven years. To defeat the "moral and physical causes" of suicide, therefore, would be a "stupendous undertaking." To reduce its incidence, Hamilton wrote, "would require an attack upon our whole social system." Hamilton's program included "a diminution of working hours, the necessity for regular meals and habits, and means to prevent large cities from being overstocked by the agricultural classes, who imagine themselves in these days particularly fitted for business and professional pursuits." The number of suicides could be diminished if "immoral entertainments, advertising quacks, so-called anatomical museums, and obscene and sensational literature" were abolished. Along with the regulation of the sale of poisonous drugs, Hamilton suggested that "careful watch should be kept on all persons who go up into high public buildings, church spires, and other eminences." Finally, in line with Durkheim's similar suggestion in *The Division of Labor* (1893), Hamilton urged that agencies be established "for procuring work for immigrants, [because] freeing cities from the surplus of these people, would prevent much desperation, misery, and self-destruction."[32] Hamilton's views served as a summary of the environmentalist position rather than as a model for those psychiatrists who soon would follow.*

Because moral treatment rested on vague notions of the environmental causes of suicide, it generally avoided confronting the issues of determinism versus free will that had informed seventeenth- and eighteenth-century debates. Yet, the role of free choice (and thus of moral responsibility) in suicide was never completely submerged in alienists' discussions about suicide. Indeed, this issue formed the subtext of an almost forty-year-long public debate between two of the most prominent asylum superintendents, Isaac Ray and John P. Gray. Although their disagreements also were informed by an equally long professional rivalry, there is no doubt that each man

*Hamilton subsequently rejected many of his environmentalist views in favor of organic explanations.

was committed fully to his position. As important, this debate about
free will and medical predestination exposed both the therapeutic
and theoretical limitations of the moral treatment and contributed
to its ultimate decline.

Dr. Isaac Ray, director of the Butler Hospital in Providence,
Rhode Island, and one of the founders of the AMSAII, alleged the
existence of "moral mania," a somatic disease caused by social conditions that deranged moral behavior without any effect on "intellectual faculties." The stress caused by external factors, such as grief,
jealousy, religion, politics, and urbanization could create, according
to Ray, organic pathological conditions that altered normal moral
behavior. Because immoral (suicide) and criminal (homicide) behavior, like other forms of insanity, resulted from somatic alterations in
healthy brains, the implication was that neither the suicide nor the
murderer was responsible for his or her actions.[33]

In his five editions of *Treatise on the Medical Jurisprudence of Insanity*,
which spanned the years 1838 to 1871, Ray claimed that almost all
suicides were committed by "those who have been affected with
some pathological condition of the brain." Evidence for this conclusion rested upon his assertion that the "propensity to suicide [is] connected with an obviously melancholy disposition [which] is now
universally recognized as a form of monomania, for its symptoms
are plainly indicative of cerebral derangement." Ray explained "that
suicide is often committed under the impulse of mental derangement . . . has been confirmed beyond a shadow of a doubt, by the re-
searches of recent inquirers." Along with the French psychiatrist,
Jean-Pierre Falret, whom he cited, Ray believed that the "propensity
to suicide" had a "hereditary disposition." While insisting that in the
autopsies of most suicides "the brain or abdominal viscera are found
to have suffered organic lesions," he admitted that often "the most
careful dissection will sometimes fail of revealing the slightest devia-
tion from the healthy structure." This, Ray explained, was because
"sometimes the pathological change may not have gone beyond its
primary stage, that of simple irritation, which is not appreciable to
the senses, but the existence of which we are bound to believe on the
strength of the symptoms." Suicidal mania, Ray believed, was best
treated by confinement.[34]

The chief critic of Ray's "moral insanity" was Dr. John Gray, the
medical superintendent of the New York Lunatic Asylum in Utica

and editor of the *American Journal of Insanity* from 1854 to 1886.[35]
Although Gray agreed with Ray that insanity could always be traced
to an organic cause, Gray denied that suicide necessarily resulted
from insanity. He questioned the existence of "moral mania," claiming that "moral influences alone . . . are insufficient to induce insanity." Gray was adamant in his belief that immoral actions always
resulted from individual free choice. Insisting that no organic evidence had been uncovered that linked immoral behavior to mental
illness, Gray also rejected any connection between heredity and suicide. "It is not clear," he asserted, "how the doctrine of heredity can
possibly apply to suicide of sane people, any more than to homicide,
or theft, or gambling or burglary." Gray admitted that patterns of
imitation might take place, but he was "unable to see how the parent
could impress upon the organization of the offspring a mental bias
favoring self-destruction."[36]

Believing that "suicide is always an unnatural [and immoral] act,"
Gray argued that "in the large proportion of cases, if not the majority, it is committed by sane people." Gray did allow that some people
who killed themselves could be classified as insane. "The dread of
poverty and want," he explained, "are frequent causes of suicide
both among the sane and insane." Likewise, "remorse is also a frequent cause of suicide." What distinguished the sane from the insane suicide was not its social cause—poverty or remorse—but
whether or not an individual's evaluation of his or her situation was
reasonable: "Delusion" served as "the test and touch-stone in the
diagnosis of insanity." Thus, poverty led to suicide among the
sane "who have seen better days and have gradually sank [sic] into
helpless and hopeless poverty." But, "among the insane who commit suicide from dread of poverty, the great majority," Gray found,
"are well to do or rich, but are laboring under the delusion that they
have lost everything and are about to be put in a poor-house or
prison."[37] Although Gray admitted that some suicides were connected with delusion and insanity, he insisted that these were
exceptions.[38]

The debate between Gray and Ray exposed the limitations of the
moral treatment to provide a comprehensive explanation for the
causes of suicide and it supplied ammunition for those opponents of
asylum psychiatry who questioned its efficacy in the first place. Practitioners of the moral treatment agreed that physiological distur-

bances underlay the etiology of mental illnesses. If, as Isaac Ray and others assumed, suicide were an illness, a pathological condition had to be uncovered. If none could be located, suicide could not be classified as a disease. Because there were almost no pathological data or other anatomical evidence supporting claims that all suicides suffered brain lesions, the validity of Ray's underlying assumption, that suicide was a disease, was called into question. On the other hand, Gray's insistence that most suicides resulted from immoral behavior seemed to fly in the face of both clinical observations and current wisdom. Ironically, nineteenth-century alienists, who had sought to replace the Puritan discourse on suicide with medical explanations, found themselves bogged down in a debate about whether suicide was an act of free will or somatic predestination.

In the final analysis, the failure of nineteenth-century alienists to escape the moral concerns of their Puritan forebears created an opening for a more "scientific" psychiatry, which rose to challenge the power of the asylum superintendents in the 1880s and 1890s. The neurological psychiatry that emerged at the end of the century accepted the call for a more precise and scientific investigation of the organic causes of mental illness, while it ridiculed and rejected both Ray's construct of moral insanity and Gray's moralistic assumptions as superficial.

The Transformation of Psychiatry

The last two decades of the nineteenth century witnessed a transformation in American psychiatric practice. Bacteriological discoveries called into question the eclectic assumptions of moral treatment and, ultimately, undermined the authority of asylum physicians. By the end of the nineteenth century, increasing numbers of practitioners believed that like other diseases, mental disorders resulted from specific pathological conditions. "The result," according to medical historian Gerald N. Grob, "was a vague perception that psychiatric theory was dated, and that psychiatrists were growing apart from their medical colleagues." Neurology promised them a much more systematic investigation of brain pathology.[39]

What was also important was that neurology offered many non-asylum psychiatrists and neurologists a vehicle for breaking the monopoly that medical superintendents had held over both psychiatric practices and career advancement. In 1875 the American Neurological Association was formed and in apparent retribution for years of discrimination by the AMSAII, the society voted to exclude asylum superintendents from its membership. The *Journal of Nervous and Mental Diseases* soon was established to compete with the *American Journal of Insanity*. Led by men like Edward C. Spitzka and William A. Hammond, the association began a relentless attack on the competence of asylum superintendents, an attack that in 1879 spilled over into the editorial pages of the *New York Times*. A year later Spitzka and John P. Gray clashed as expert witnesses on opposing sides at the insanity trial of President Garfield's assassin, Charles J. Guiteau.[40]

Neurologists' assaults on asylum psychiatry were exacerbated by demands by state and governing boards that asylums admit more patients. Faced with growing patient populations and shrinking budgets, the asylums' functions moved increasingly from care to custody.[41] In an attempt to widen its base of support, the AMSAII changed its name in 1892 to the American Medico-Psychological Association and widened its membership to include assistant asylum physicians. (In 1921, the organization adopted its present name, the American Psychiatric Association.) To defuse further criticism from neurological circles, the Medico-Psychological Association invited one of its leading neurologist critics, S. Weir Mitchell, to address its 1894 annual meeting. Mitchell's message, however, was unrelenting. He informed his hosts that recent medical advances demonstrated the complete failure of asylum treatment. Noting that the annual reports of medical superintendents contained no "reports of scientific study, of the psychology or pathology" of their patients, Mitchell concluded that the "want of original work" was "the worst symptom of torpor the asylums now present."[42]

Nevertheless, as Mitchell's invitation to address the American Medico-Psychological Association suggests, American psychiatry had begun to abandon the assumptions that underlay moral treatment. While maintaining their separate identity, like their neurologist rivals, American psychiatrists launched themselves on a search for the specific organic and psychological causes for mental disorders. In relation to suicide, that meant that the consideration of those cultural and social factors that had earlier been connected with the incidence of suicide was abdicated to the emerging social sciences.

Although neurologists on the whole would not attempt a systematic analysis of the causes of suicide until the second half of the twentieth century, they viewed environmental explanations of the etiology of suicide as unscientific and as unworthy of serious consideration. In the same year that Durkheim published *Suicide, A Study in Sociology*, Edward Cowles, one of the leaders of the new American psychiatry, wrote, "How marvelous have been the changes that have brought us the conceptions we hold to-day of the scientific principles that underlie our medical art." Cowles believed that new methods of medical practice would clear "away much of the mystery and obscurity which have surrounded mental disorder." He extolled "the great progress of modern medical science," which had demonstrated "the close relationship of mental to general diseases." Mental disorders, he predicted, would soon be diagnosed and treated in a manner similar to other organic diseases.[43]

The professionalization and medical specialization that emerged at the turn of the century rejected eclectic approaches to behaviors like suicide. For all their limitations, nineteenth-century psychiatrists armed with the moral treatment had assumed that suicide resulted from a complex interaction of organic, psychological, and social forces. Their twentieth-century successors, split as they were into the disciplines of psychological psychiatry, neuropsychiatry, and sociology, tended to view the etiology of suicide in ways that excluded the insights that their professional rivals might provide. Of course, psychiatrists continued to pay lip service to the importance of social factors, as sociologists gave superficial attention to the organic and psychological components of suicide. Nevertheless, the rise of professional specialization, whatever its benefits, created conditions unfriendly to an integrated approach to suicide.

These developments did not take place in a vacuum. The growth of the "progressive" movement at the end of the century bolstered attacks on eclectic constructs like the moral treatment and provided an intellectual context for what historian David J. Rothman has labeled "civic medicine." Rothman is correct in noting that these "new orientations were so much a part of Progressivism that psychiatrists themselves . . . are best understood within the context of the movement." Psychiatrists shared with other social reformers an unflagging commitment to a "scientifically" ordered society brought about under expert guidance.[44] Nevertheless, important tactical differences surfaced between psychiatrists and social science experts' therapeutic solutions to mental illness. To a large extent, the way that psychiatrists attempted to obtain social order reflected the nature and structure of psychiatric practice. If progressive ideology paradoxically promised both unlimited individual self-transformation and social efficiency, its psychiatric offspring accepted the causes of mental illness as resulting from an inefficient social order, while insisting simultaneously that treatment must concern itself exclusively with altering individual behavior.[45] Although what emerged as American psychiatry shared common progressive roots with sociology—in particular, a commitment to "scientific" solutions to social problems—the fact that psychiatric practice was patient-centered contributed to a climate that proved to be hostile to sociological approaches to the causes of mental illness.

PSYCHOPATHOLOGY AND SUICIDE

The growing biological orientation of medical practice gave increasing relevance to the somaticist tendencies exhibited earlier in the arguments between Isaac Ray and John Gray. As long as American psychiatry was centered in asylums, most psychiatrists seemed willing to integrate cultural and organic explanations for the etiology of suicide because the treatment, no matter what the cause, included institutional incarceration. But as moral treatment was replaced by individual psychiatric practice, older, more eclectic explanations for suicide were replaced with new theories that insisted upon the individual rather than social or moral etiology of suicidal behavior. Nevertheless, American neurologists, for all their somatic tendencies, proved much more open to nonorganic, psychological explanations for suicide. As hopes for neurological breakthroughs diminished, private practitioners were attracted to a variety of psychological theories and to treatments that emphasized individual ual psychotherapy.[46]

American psychiatric journals had exposed their readers to the writings of European psychological psychiatrists like Jean Charcot and Pierre Janet. The fact that these European psychiatrists were also neurologists served to legitimize their psychological explanations of psychopathological behavior. In the early twentieth century, influenced by both immigrant and native neurologists like Adolf Meyer and William Alanson White, many American psychiatrists turned toward psychological psychiatry and the practice of various forms of psychotherapy.[47] A consensus soon developed among practitioners according to which emotional (affective) disorders, such as melancholia and suicide, were characterized as psychological, while ideational disturbances like schizophrenia generally were viewed as organic in nature. Thus organic and psychological explanations of mental disorder were seen as complementary, rather than as mutually exclusive.

At the 1905 meeting of the American Medico-Psychological Association held at San Antonio, Texas, the medical superintendent of The Glenwood of Dansville, New York, J. W. Wherry, presented a psychological explanation for the causes of melancholia, a form of behavior that since Puritan times had been linked to suicide. Melancholia, according to Wherry, was not the result of organic brain disorder but rather of unreasonable fears, because "Disease of the brain will find its expression, if it finds it at all, in disorders of the intellect, not in any intensification of the emotions." Wherry argued that melancholia was "unquestionably an emotional condition," which could have no origin in the brain, because, "there is no source of emotion" in the brain. Evidence for this view was strengthened by the fact that "melancholia . . . has been almost the *only* curable form of insanity." And, Wherry explained, "no curable disease of the brain ever produced insanity." Nevertheless, he accepted the views of his neurologist colleagues that melancholia resulted from conditions unique to the individual and that cures could be effected only by individual treatment.[48]

The connection of these views to suicide was made explicit at the 1906 Boston meeting in a paper entitled "Insanity and Suicide" delivered by Dr. Charles Pilgrim, the president of the New York State Commission on Lunacy. Pilgrim warned that "insanity and suicide are increasing out of proportion to the increase of population." He accepted the statistical data that indicated that only a minority of suicides were insane. Pilgrim, like Wherry, drew the distinction between the insane, whose disorders were organic, and other mentally ill people, like depressives, whose disorders were psychological in nature. Those whose suicidal tendencies proved to be caused by organic insanity should be placed in psychiatric hospitals under "general medical treatment indicated by the physical condition" and should be subjected to "constant supervision . . . for the prevention of suicide." Unlike Gray, Pilgrim accepted hereditarian explanations of suicidal behavior. There "is nothing more firmly established," he argued, "than the fact of the transmission of the suicidal tendency." Pilgrim suggested that "considerable good" can be accomplished "by the efforts of our own profession to prevent marriage where any hereditary trait exists."[49]

It was the second group of mentally ill patients, those with affective disorders, who although they were not clinically insane were in need of psychotherapy. Pilgrim seemed to accept that environmental factors played a role in depressive suicides. For instance, he admitted that many of these suicides appeared to have valid social reasons for their self-destruction—all of which he fit into the general category of the pressures caused by the conditions of modern life. Yet, unlike Hamilton or Durkheim, Pilgrim argued that it was the patient and not the society that must be changed. Psychotherapy, rather than social reform, provided the best hope for those who seemed driven to suicide by modern conditions. Melancholia, which displayed this irrational tendency more than any other form of mental illness, should become the main focus for clinical psychiatrists who wished to control the increase of suicides. Because "pessimism and depression more often follow ease than struggle," Pilgrim prescribed "occupation for body and mind" as "one of the best remedies in the early stages of the disease." Once "the interests of the would-be suicide can be directed into channels where his attention will be fully absorbed, he may, in a little while, be induced again to face life with interest."[50]

At the 1914 meeting of the American Medico-Psychological Society Association, Tom A. Williams, president of the Washington, D.C., Society of Nervous and Mental Diseases, rejected the idea that suicide had any neurological or physiological origin. Suicide, "is not," he insisted, "a matter of physical defect of the brain or body at all." Rather, "the act of suicide," he explained, "is psychological, a perversion of the instinctive will to life and power, by means of a conditioning of that reflex into its opposite by stimuli we may call pathogenic." Because "suicide generally denotes disturbance of an individual's power of social adjustment," its psychotherapeutic treatment must include a careful examination of the prior events of the patient's life.[51]

The transformation of psychiatric explanations for the etiology of suicide had a profound impact upon the diagnosis and treatment of the suicidal. The following case illustrates how much medical attitudes toward the causes of suicide had changed since the 1840s: A twenty-year-old youth was referred to Dr. Williams. The youth had first tried to drown himself and then, after having been rescued by his younger brother, he attempted suicide by swallowing landanum. Williams conducted the youth's treatment in hospital, insisting that "the maximum of freedom was allowed the patient from the first, the greatest tact being urged upon those who nursed him." The doctor uncovered "no physical disorder," but "discovered that there existed a serious psychological situation, which no one had even suspected." The patient's father had died four years earlier, when the youth was sixteen and his brother was fifteen. The duties of managing the family farm devolved on the older sibling, but the younger son soon proved successful in undermining the patient's authority and, along with neighbors, he convinced their mother that the patient was unfit to remain in charge of the farm. Curiously, the patient did not resist his brother's supplanting him. Interviews in the hospital suggested that this response mirrored the way he had dealt with other, earlier challenges. However, the patient became depressed after these events and finally attempted to kill himself, telling Williams that he had decided he "should be better off dead." After lengthy discussions with the patient, Williams decided that the youth's failure to assert himself after his father's death and his subsequent suicide attempts resulted from extreme guilt feelings over the practice of masturbation, which he had engaged in steadily "until he was 18, and had then ceased to do so, and other boys teased him about it, and said that he would be impotent, as he had ruined himself; hence he was very much ashamed."[52]

As late as the 1880s, such a youth would have been routinely diagnosed as suffering from insanity brought on by masturbation. In fact, "masturbation madness" was a designated disease, serving as a common explanation for lethargy and melancholy among youths. Many nineteenth-century alienists had insisted that when masturbatory practices went unchecked, they led to insanity and often to suicide.[53] But by the second decade of the twentieth century, Williams and his colleagues had rejected such constructs totally. Instead,

Williams's treatment consisted of attempting to relieve the patient's
overwhelming feelings of guilt by assuring him "that he was quite
mistaken about the effects of onanising (masturbation)." In a short
time the youth was, Williams claimed, "perfectly cured, and has
been at work and in good spirits" for nine months.[54]

Like Sewall and the Mathers, Wherry, Pilgrim, and Williams favored the view that the causes of suicide were located in melancholic
behavior that could be treated only in the context of individual case
histories. On the other hand, these twentieth-century psychiatrists
substituted the idea of "mental illness" for what Puritan ministers
had identified as immoral behavior. By the early twentieth century,
American psychiatrists had identified two categories of mental disorder: organic insanity, which required institutional interventions, and
emotional disorders such as melancholia, which could be treated by
psychotherapy. That these two areas of mental illness paralleled in
many respects Sigmund Freud's distinction between psychosis and
neurosis made his explanations of these conditions more palatable
to American psychiatrists. American psychiatry insisted that psycho-
pathology could be understood only in the context of individual case
histories, and this created an atmosphere that would prove friendly
to psychoanalytic psychotherapy. Thus, even before Freud traveled
to Clark University in 1909 and before publicists such as A. A. Brill,
James Jackson Putnam, and G. Stanley Hall set out to champion
Freud's theories, American psychiatry had evolved into a specialty
that would prove particularly receptive to psychoanalysis.[55]

When Sigmund Freud published his classic essay *Mourning and
Melancholia* in 1917, American psychiatrists already were inclined
to accept Freud's thesis.[56] Like Pilgrim and Williams, Freud located
the etiology of suicide in internal psychopathologic conflicts. Freud
too connected suicide with melancholic behavior.[57] Although Freud
also had opened the door to sociological factors with his analogy between melancholics and mourners, American psychiatrists proved
unwilling to enter.

Conclusion

Émile Durkheim's *Suicide: A Study in Sociology*, published in 1897,
with its emphasis on statistical analysis and moral arguments,

seemed methodologically primitive and scientifically quaint to the new leaders of American psychiatry. They ignored Durkheim's *Suicide* because it appeared to reflect a discredited version of nineteenth-century therapeutics, one uninformed by scientific advances in bacteriology and neurology.[58] The reluctance of twentieth-century American psychiatry to integrate Durkheim's sociological theory into its explanations for the etiology of suicide resulted as much from the developments within the American psychiatric profession as it did from the theoretical divisions between sociological and psychiatric theory. On the other hand, mid-nineteenth-century American alienists would have been much more receptive to Durkheim's sociology of suicide than their twentieth-century successors, primarily because little of what Durkheim wrote in 1897 would have seemed either new or startling to them. Indeed, early nineteenth-century constructs like the moral treatment informed much of Durkheim's assumptions about the etiology of suicide. Like Durkheim, medical superintendents had relied upon official statistics to identify and explain the causes of suicide. They too had concluded that the breakdown of the traditional moral order led to an increase in the incidence of suicide. The dominant psychiatric treatment for suicidal individuals, removal to a rural asylum, spoke to Durkheim's connection of suicide rates to the distributions caused by urbanization.

As a result of the transformation of American psychiatric practice, support for Durkheimian views appeared in the popular press and in fictionalized portrayals of suicide rather than in medical literature. For instance, simultaneous with the publication of Durkheim's *Suicide,* Robert N. Reeves wrote in the *Popular Science Monthly* that "suicide and education increase at an equal rate." Like Durkheim, Reeves rejected insanity as the sole cause for growing incidences of suicide: "Insanity, heredity, financial reverses, and domestic complications may be direct incentives to suicide, but back of them all is the real cause—the growth of a nervous, disordered temperament in the American people. The steady habits of our colonial ancestors," Reeves lamented, "no longer satisfy us, and, as a consequence, those amusements, those ventures and schemes which excite the mind and the nervous system to the highest degree are becoming more and more prominent." These effects of modern life were "the fundamental cause of all suicide." Although "drink and crime are responsible for a large proportion of the daily self-murders," urban society was the real criminal: "Poverty and disease," Reeves found, were "strong incentives to self-destruction. Suicide," he argued, "is often regulated by the price of bread." Urban life had brought about poverty, and poverty, suicide. "Where the population is dense and the law of health neglected, where dirt is common and vice flourishes, where the poor are concentrated, and where fortunes are made and lost in a day," Reeves wrote, "will always be found the highest rate of suicide." If suicide is to be reduced, the condition of the poor must be made "more enjoyable by giving them ampler provisions for pleasure and recreation, making their surroundings more cleanly and agreeable, and by faithfully executing thorough and most effective sanitation."[59]

Reeves's views were reinforced by portrayals of suicide in turn-of-the-century American fiction. Theodore Dreiser's depiction of the causes of George Hurstwood's suicide in *Sister Carrie* (1900) paralleled the complaints recorded in Max White's suicide note. Like White, Hurstwood found himself without work and friends in a society that excluded all those without capital. Dreiser used the saloon as the symbol of a community whose access was limited to those who could pay. Hurstwood, the impoverished former saloon keeper, could no longer participate in modern urban life. He became nothing and no one, rejected by Carrie and isolated from society. Hurstwood's self-destruction was laid on the doorstep of the culture created by American capitalism.[60] Similarly, Edith Wharton's *House of Mirth* (1905) tied Lily Bart's suicide to a social world in which she was forced to choose between economic security and emotional attachment. Lily Bart's ambivalence signaled that she would attain neither security nor love. Left without even the skill to obtain employment, Bart had no alternative but suicide.[61] Finally, in Jack London's *Martin Eden* (1909), the protagonist's life is shattered by his compulsion for material success. Eden chose a career as a novelist, not out of a commitment to literature, but because it provided him with a vehicle for wealth, fame, and social acceptance. Like William Dean Howell's *The Rise of Silas Lapham* (1885), Eden's social ascent is contrasted with his moral decline. The suicide of his best friend and the loss of the woman he loved demonstrated the emptiness of a world where success was measured by material rather than individual worth; where people became objects. The American dream of bourgeois self-transformation was translated into Martin Eden's nightmare of self-destruction.[62]

American social reformers and novelists concluded that the tensions in the social structure were the root causes of suicide at the very moment when American psychiatrists were moving toward a consensus that suicide could be understood only as a symptom of individual rather than social dysfunction. The demise of moral treatment meant that Durkheim's explanation of suicide would be ignored by mainstream American psychiatrists. European psychiatry, which continued to influence practice in the United States in the early twentieth century, did not ignore Durkheim, but it too proved hostile to his sociological analysis. In 1924 Maurice de Fleury attacked Durkheim and his followers in *L'Angoisse Humaine*. Maintaining that suicide was always the product of some psychopathological or biological condition, de Fleury claimed that sociology could make no contribution to an analysis of suicide.[63] Extending this argument, François Achille-Delmas concluded that because suicide represented such a small proportion of the population, social factors could not possibly play a significant role in its etiology.[64] Given this context, it is not surprising that Karl Menninger's classic 1938 psychoanalytic study, *Man Against Himself,* did not even refer to Durkheim's *Suicide.* On the other hand, Freud's psychoanalytic explanation of the cause of suicide was more easily integrated into American psychiatry because Freud's writings seemed to reinforce views already accepted by mainstream American psychiatrists.[65] The wider social implications of Freud's theory, which did not fit as easily into American psychiatric practice, were ignored.

By the twentieth century, two contradictory explanations for the causes of suicide had emerged in the United States. Social and popular theorists attributed suicide to the conditions brought about by modern urban civilization, while psychiatrists insisted that suicide's etiology was rooted in individual disorder—whether organic or psychological. This contradiction led to contrary prescriptions for the prevention of suicide: Sociologists urged social reform, while psychiatrists insisted that individual behavior, not social structure, must be altered.

3

SPECIALIZATION AND
ITS CASUALTIES, 1917–1988

Since 1917, sociologists, psychoanalytic psychiatrists, and neuropsychiatrists have pursued the causes of suicide in mutually contradictory directions. Over the years the gaps have tended to widen rather than narrow, as each specialty has increasingly restricted itself to methodological considerations. The result has been that sociologists, psychoanalysts, and neuropsychiatrists* each explain the etiology of suicide by denying explicitly the validity of the others' assumptions. Sociologists and psychoanalysts have tended to ignore those aspects of Durkheim and Freud that could connect sociology with psychoanalysis in favor of literal interpretations of Durkheimian and Freudian texts. The followers of Kraepelin, on the other hand, rejecting both Durkheim and Freud as unscientific, have pursued a mixed bag of physiological interventions ranging from bizarre applications of focal theories of infection to questionable neurosurgical procedures.

The discovery of psychotropic drugs in the late 1950s offered the first solid evidence that a century of neuropsychiatric hunches had

---

*In what follows I use "neuropsychiatrist" to identify those nonpsychoanalytic psychiatrists who are persuaded that organic dysfunctions underlie most psychiatric disorders. I use the label "psychopharmacologist" to denote those neuropsychiatrists who rely on pharmacological interventions as their main course of treatment.

some foundation. The result was a revolution in psychiatric practice that continues today. As this new psychopharmacology began to make significant inroads into psychiatric practice, psychoanalysts adopted a defensive posture, while sociologists simply included biological factors as another variable to be placed alongside other quantifiable statistical data. Psychopharmacologists, on the other hand, believing that they had at last found both the cause and proper treatment for those depressions that resulted in suicide, dismissed both psychoanalytic and sociological explanations as cultural lags from a prescientific era.

In what follows, I review the major methodological and theoretical developments in sociology, psychoanalysis, and neuropsychiatry in the United States since 1917 as they relate to suicide. My purpose is to offer an overview rather than an exhaustive institutional history.

SOCIOLOGY

Durkheim's sociology was less concerned with the lives of the suicidal than with the more widespread social phenomena that suicide exposed. The incidence of suicide served as an index for Durkheim to measure the general health or pathology of a society. When he attempted to explain individual suicides, Durkheim abandoned statistics in favor of social meaning. "Each victim of suicide," Durkheim wrote, "gives his act a personal stamp which expresses his temperament, the special conditions in which he is involved, and which, consequently, cannot be explained by the social and general causes of the phenomenon."[1]

Unlike Durkheim, American sociologists have believed that statistical analysis could provide a basis for coming to terms with both social and individual causes of suicide. Influenced as much by their native antecedents as by Durkheim, modern sociologists have been less concerned with social pathology than with suicidal etiology. Adopting Durkheim's statistical methods while ignoring his wider ideological concerns, most American sociologists have attempted to connect variations in the incidence of suicide with particular social traumata, such as unemployment, war, or social dislocation, in a search for the "proximate" causes of suicide.[2]

Epidemiologists* and sociologists increasingly employ sophisticated quantitative techniques to interpret official suicide data.[3] Unfortunately, almost all of this data has been and continues to be notoriously unreliable.[4] Suicide statistics are deficient because they lack uniform definition and because those responsible for their collection are often influenced by unspoken assumptions about what constitutes a suicide. Whether a particular act ultimately is classified as a suicide is determined by the official definition of suicide.† Thus, the rate of suicide in any society reflects what the society believes constitutes a suicide.

Although most sociological studies of suicide begin with a caveat about the unreliability of official statistics, most proceed, ignoring their own warnings.[5] In great part this is due to the methodological assumptions that have informed sociology since the 1920s, when statistical analysis became the foundation for American academic sociologists' claims to scientific objectivity.[6]

In the 1920s sociology in the United States was dominated by a group of urban sociologists who taught or were trained at the University of Chicago. Led by William I. Thomas, the "Chicago School" employed the local survey method to explore a constellation of urban social disorders.[7] Like their nineteenth-century predecessors, these experts found that urbanization was a crucial factor in the inci-

---

*Epidemiology provides one of the few bridges between medical and sociological approaches to suicide. Growing out of the public health movement at the turn of the century, epidemiology originally focused on epidemics of infectious disease, combining the medical model of disease with the tools of Durkheimian sociology. Trained in statistical methods at graduate schools of public health, epidemiologists investigate the frequency and distribution of a disease or a condition and the factors influencing its distribution. Epidemiologists analyze the frequency of suicide among different groups over time in order to determine which variables or combination of them—such as age, gender, marital status, religion, employment—are most characteristic of suicides. Once the populations "at highest risk" are identified, the epidemiological data are supplied to officials in the hope that they will be used to formulate programs for prevention and control.

†There is no single official definition of suicide in the United States. Moreover, within most states no uniform system exists for collecting data on what constitutes a suicide. In California, for instance, each county has its own method for determining if a particular action was a suicide and each uses a different instrument for collecting data. A review of the certification of suicide as practiced by 191 coroners in eleven western states found "extensive variation in the backgrounds, professional resources, operating procedures, and governing statutes of coroners and coroners' offices in policies concerning" the determination of suicide. The report concluded that "the extent of variation found here calls into question the validity and comparability of reported suicide rates." Franklyn L. Nelson, Norman L. Farberow, and Douglas R. MacKinnon, "The Certification of Suicide in Eleven Western States: An Inquiry into the Validity of Reported Suicide Rates," *Suicide and Life Threatening Behavior* 8 (Summer 1978): 75, 82.

dence of suicide. One of the school's chief exponents, Ernest Burgess, wrote that urban growth "is accompanied by excessive increases in disease, crime, vice, insanity, and suicide."[8] Since the twenties the urban thesis has gone virtually unchallenged.* Instead, sociologists of suicide have refined their statistical skills in an attempt to determine *which* urban factors play the greatest role in causing suicide.†

Ruth Cavan's 1928 study *Suicide* was the most comprehensive study of suicide to emerge from Chicago School sociology. Cavan wrote her masters and doctoral dissertations under the direction of Ellsworth Faris, chairman of Chicago's Sociology Department and editor of the *American Journal of Sociology*. Relying on data from earlier monographs and published federal mortality statistics, Cavan concluded that suicide rates did not simply increase with the population of a city. Rather, rates were highest in those cities, like San Francisco, Spokane, Oakland, Los Angeles, and Seattle, where

*One exception is Olive Anderson's study of suicide in nineteenth-century England and Wales. Anderson found that young men and women living in rural towns and villages were more likely to kill themselves than their cohorts in industrial cities. This, Anderson argues, "casts doubt both on the traditional sociological theory that the spread of modern industrial society was accompanied by high general levels of anomie and egoism, and upon the rather newer school of sociology which associates it with local social disorganization and ecological problems." Olive Anderson, "Did Suicide Increase with Industrialization in Victorian England?" *Past & Present* 86 (February 1980): 149–173; esp. 165–166. Also see Anderson, *Suicide in Victorian and Edwardian England*, pp. 54, 83–91, 101–103. The assumption that if the incidence of suicide can be shown to be greater in rural than in urban areas, then the connections between anomie, egoism, and suicide will be exploded, may be somewhat unwarranted. As many recent studies have demonstrated, industrialization has a direct impact on everyday life, even (if not especially) in rural areas. Because the growth of urban centers depends largely upon their ability to exploit the labor and resources of less-developed sectors, rural life proves to be even more vulnerable to the disruptions of industrialization than urban society is. This is confirmed in Michael Lesy's *Wisconsin Death Trip* (New York: Pantheon Books, 1973), which linked the economic depression of the 1890s with increased violent and suicidal behavior in rural areas of Wisconsin.

†In *Violence in the City* (1979) Roger Lane challenged the Chicago sociologists' assumption that increased suicide rates supplied an index for social disintegration. Lane found that as nineteenth-century Philadelphia was urbanized, its suicide rate grew proportionally greater than its homicide rate. Murderers, Lane reasoned, defy civil order, while suicides, by turning violent urges inward, internalize social regulation. Lane concluded that the increasing incidence of suicide in late nineteenth-century cities served as a barometer of social integration because suicide, unlike homicide, indicated the internalization of social anger. Lane rejected the connection between urban suicide and social disintegration, but nevertheless he affirmed the Chicago School's conclusion that urbanization was the underlying cause for a rise in suicide rates. Roger Lane, *Violent Death in the City: Suicide, Accident, and Murder in Nineteenth-Century Philadelphia* (Cambridge, Mass.: Harvard University Press, 1979), pp. 33–34, 115–134. A similar argument is made by Louis Chevalier in *Labouring Classes and Dangerous Classes in Paris During the First Half of the Nineteenth Century*, trans. Frank Jellinek (London: Routledge & Kegan Paul, 1973), pp. 280–292.

traditional social institutions were the most fragmented. To the extent that social fragmentation intruded on rural areas, their incidence of suicide also increased. Suicide rates were highest in those sections of the city with the weakest social organizations. Where institutions "such as the family, church, school, commercial and industrial organizations, recreational facilities" were the most pervasive, the incidence of suicide was the lowest.[9]

Cavan attempted to use her statistical data to build a model for explaining the causes of individual suicides. When family, church, schools, and other social support organizations were weak, personal crises—unemployment, alcoholism, illness, and social dislocation—were more likely to result in suicide because there were fewer impediments to an individual's acting on the belief that suicide was a legitimate solution to personal problems. "With apparently few exceptions, suicide in contemporary America," Cavan wrote, "is a symptom of complete loss of morale, a result of personal disorganization." Cavan supplied numerous descriptive case studies as examples for her argument, but she could not demonstrate that those who committed suicide lived in less stable social settings than others who did not kill themselves. For instance, although Cavan showed that the unemployed had a higher incidence of suicide than the employed, she was unable to prove that those unemployed who committed suicide came from a more disorganized segment of society than those unemployed who did not kill themselves.[10]

Cavan had attempted to integrate sociological and individual psychological factors and failed because she was unable to link her statistical data to her descriptive examples. This problem has plagued American sociologists whenever they have attempted to employ social statistics to uncover social meaning. Rather than return to Durkheim's insights that suicide statistics were inadequate to explain individual choice or personal motivation, later sociologists have ascribed Cavan's failure to lack of methodological rigor.[11]

Statistical methodology, although questioned from time to time, has underpinned subsequent American sociological studies of suicide. This has been reinforced in the education of American sociologists, which increasingly has emphasized the demonstration of sophisticated skills in statistical methodology as a prerequisite for certification. Indeed, the claim of contemporary sociologists that they are engaged in "scientific" investigations rests almost entirely on their ability to perform sophisticated manipulations of statistical data.[12] Whenever a colleague's studies were ambiguous or otherwise unsatisfying, sociologists tended to attribute that result to a lack of precision in the selection and analysis of data.

Representative of a more rigorous statistical approach were Louis Dublin's *To Be or Not to Be* (1933) and its 1963 revision, *Suicide: A Sociological and Statistical Study*. Dublin, chief statistician for the Metropolitan Life Insurance Company, was concerned with both the prediction and prevention of suicide. Like Cavan, Dublin relied on federal mortality statistics, which he supplemented with Metropolitan Life's own vast mortality data. A sophisticated statistician, Dublin crosstabulated age, sex, marital status, race, ethnicity, and religion with more general social, economic, and geographic variables in order to construct an epidemiology of American suicide.[13]

Ironically he found that "environmental factors—economic conditions, city life, religious affiliation, social customs, and laws and traditions—" were only precipitating events, because "countless persons, faced with what appear to be the same provocations, do not commit suicide." "The suicidal drive," Dublin wrote, "in the last analysis, is from within the individual rather than from without." It resulted from "a complicated psychic drama, the final response of a person to his own needs, desires, and circumstances."[14]

If Cavan proved unable to connect her data with personal motivations, Dublin proved unwilling to follow up the logic of his having done so. Demonstrating that official statistics were inadequate for explaining the etiology of suicide, Dublin ignored his evidence. Instead, being tied to quantitative methodology, he erected an elaborate rationale for its utility. Statistical methodology, Dublin asserted, offered the only sensible approach for the development of a model for discovering the etiology of suicide. The uniqueness of individual psychologies, he explained, meant that cultural rather than psychological causes were more significant in determining the incidence of suicide. If suicide resulted from a combination of individual predispositions exacerbated by social and cultural conditions, it was far easier to control the latter than the former.[15]

Unwilling to confront the issue he had raised, Dublin confirmed in his investigation what social reformers had assumed since the mid-nineteenth century, that the "uncertainties and insecurities" of modern life "have helped to drive thousands to despair and ultimately to self-destruction." Like Cavan, Dublin was convinced that "the prevailing social order" was the "basically important element," because "suicides are precipitated by [the] economic and social maladjustments under which we all live." Social conditions such as unemployment and slums "cause suicide to multiply," and the only way to "make any real headway in solving the problem of suicide," Dublin argued, was to "make changes in our social order which would avoid conditions that have driven people to self-destruction in the past." Eradicate an array of urban ills like poor housing, inadequate recreational facilities, unemployment, illness, and inequitable distribution of income, and Dublin insisted the suicide rate would decline.[16] Whatever else it had done, Dublin's more sophisticated use of quantitative methods had moved no closer to the specificity he had sought.

Other attempts to use statistical methods to bridge the gap between sociological and psychological variables have been no more successful. For instance, in *Suicide and Homicide* (1954) Andrew F. Henry and James F. Short compared suicide and homicide rates with fluctuations in the business cycle. Employing a series of sophisticated quantitative procedures, they asserted that increases in frustration (brought about by downward cycles in the economy) led to increases in aggressive behavior, such as homicide or suicide. A decrease in frustration, they argued, led to diminished violence. Whether frustration resulted in suicide rather than in homicide depended upon the "preference" of one's reference group.[17] Given their methodology and their reliance on official suicide and homicide statistics, Henry and Short could not demonstrate that the additional suicides or homicides reported during troubled economic times actually were committed by individuals who themselves were directly affected by these business cycles. Moreover, the frustration/aggression model rested upon the undemonstrated and mechanistic psychological assumption that frustration automatically transformed itself into aggressive behavior.[18]

Sociologists have been reluctant to admit that suicide statistics are inaccurate tools for measuring individual responses to social crises. But, like those studies I have highlighted, subsequent attempts to link personal motivation with social dynamics have met with similar frustrations. Those who have emphasized economic fluctuations, such as the Great Depression, as having been responsible for increases in the incidence of suicide have failed to explain why some people, who suffered more severe economic losses than others, did not commit suicide. The same issue arises for other proximate causes, such as severe illness. Why, for instance, do so few of the terminally ill kill themselves? The constancy of this problem has led Jack D. Douglas to urge his colleagues to take seriously Durkheim's earlier insight that the impact of social events on individual behavior is determined always by the meaning that individuals give to those events. Sociologists who depend on official statistics, Douglas argued in the *Social Meanings of Suicide* (1967), whether they intend to or not, become locked into the assumption that social meaning is the same for everyone; "that aspirations, failure, etc., are everywhere defined in basically the same manner in the United States, so that there are no cultural differences in these matters, or in suicidal matters, between classes."[19]

Given their scholarly investment in statistical methodology, it is not surprising that few American sociologists have followed Douglas's lead. As the British sociologist Steve Taylor has written, "Despite the general critical acclaim that [Douglas's] *The Social Meanings of Suicide* quite rightly received, it has had very little influence on the ways in which sociologists actually study suicide. In the first place many subsequent studies of suicide rates make no reference to Douglas and second, those who do mention him tend to side-step, rather than confront his arguments."[20]

By the late 1960s many American suicidologists had concluded that federal compilations of suicide data (vital statistics) were inaccurate measures of the incidence of suicide. But, they resisted Douglas's wider argument that statistical methodology itself was an inappropriate tool for understanding the cause of suicide. Instead, like Ronald Maris, American sociologists portrayed Douglas's criticisms as if they were merely "a plea for different sources of data," rather than a rejection of statistical approaches to suicide.[21]

Even before Douglas published *Social Meanings,* some suicidologists had grown suspicious of vital statistics as accurate indicators of the extent of suicide. In the mid-1950s, Edwin S. Shneidman and his UCLA psychologist colleague, Norman Farberow, suggested that researchers ought to look at actual coroners' reports rather than the official data compiled from them. Along with psychiatrist Robert E. Litman, Shneidman and Farberow developed an instrument to reconstruct what Shneidman later called a "psychological autopsy" from coroners' reports. Shneidman and his colleagues, however, were more interested in suicide prevention than in wider social theory. They established the nation's first suicide prevention center in Los Angeles and later they organized the American Association of Suicidology, whose main function was the dissemination of information on suicide prevention to health professionals.[22]

Following Shneidman's lead, several sociologists were persuaded that coroners' reports offered data that could link the social causes of suicide with its psychological components and ultimately satisfy the type of criticism that Douglas had raised about statistical methodology. Maris's *Pathways to Suicide: A Survey of Self-Destructive Behaviors* (1981) represents the most ambitious of these attempts. The writings of Maris, former president of the American Association of Suicidology and editor of its official journal, *Suicide and Life-Threatening Behavior*, are viewed as authoritative by the vast majority of American suicidologists. His methodological approach and conclusions in *Pathways* serve as a paradigm of current American sociological approaches to suicide.

In terms of statistical methodology and overall scope, *Pathways* is one of the most comprehensive and sophisticated sociological studies ever published on American suicide. Building on data compiled from his 1969 *Social Forces in Urban Suicide*, Maris employed a sample survey of 1,349 Cook County, Illinois, coroner's reports for the period from 1966 to 1968. Of these, 517 white suicides' relatives were selected for interviews. Two hundred sixty-six completed interviews resulted. These data were contrasted with a group of natural deaths and a sample of nonfatal suicide attempters from Baltimore County, Maryland, for the years 1969–1970.[23]

Following the American sociological tradition, Maris's objective was "to determine if there are any unique predictors of suicidal behaviors." Examining "the relative strengths of the traits or predictors related to suicide," Maris subjected a wide range of economic, social, and psychological variables to multivariant analysis. Suicide, according to Maris's analysis of his data, resulted when an individual was "either *unable* or *unwilling* to accept life as it presents itself to them." Maris labeled this pattern of response "a suicidal career." The more one experiences "suffering, disease, failure, lack of individual and social supports, pain, hopelessness, etc., . . . the more likely one is to end experience itself." But, Maris argued, a suicidal career was "more than simply a function of an exceedingly trying existence." It included "something extra." Suicide resulted when these "trying experiences" collided with any or all of a constellation of factors, including the lack of nonsuicidal alternatives; the availability and acceptability of suicide as a resolution to real or perceived conditions; individual unfitness—whether biological, psychological, or social—for life's struggles; weak tolerance for adaptation to problems; alcoholism or drug addiction; aging; and negative interpersonal relationships.[24]

The comprehensiveness of Maris's construct of "suicidal careers" betrays both its strength and its weakness. On the one hand, Maris considered a large number of variables and by the use of crosstabulation, he subjected many assertions made by other experts to careful scrutiny. On the other hand, given the wide range of variables he identified as contributing to suicide, Maris seemed to suggest that random life experience itself was the major variable determining a suicidal career. This appears to undercut his major conclusion that *"real types of suicide tend to have dominant traits and relatively predictable life and death courses."*[25]

On its own terms Maris's study suffers from some of the same methodological limitations that he criticized in earlier works. For instance, Maris decided to eliminate black suicides, because as he explained, "given our budgetary limitations, we could afford only about 500 interviews with the coroner's informants for suicides. Thus, we reluctantly decided to eliminate all black respondents and to focus on white respondents. *It is well known that suicide rates tend to be highest among whites, especially among older white males."*[26] The exclusion of blacks is unfortunate for several reasons. First, recent studies have demonstrated that black suicide rates have steadily increased since the late 1960s.[27] Second, Maris earlier questioned the validity of studies that relied on vital statistics. Yet, it is from the conclusions of these studies that Maris drew his assertion that "suicide rates tend to be highest among whites." By eliminating blacks from his study, Maris invited the charge of endorsing the very data he had rejected. Finally, it is important to discover why, if it is true, that blacks commit suicide less frequently than whites.

Equally troubling was Maris's use of comparative data. He selected the suicides for his study from one region, Cook County, Illinois, while his controls came from another county, Baltimore, Maryland. Moreover, the suicides, nonsuicidal deaths, and suicide

attempts were separated by several years. Maris justified these decisions, explaining: "After convincing ourselves that there were probably no significant differences between suicides, nonfatal suicide
attempters, and natural deaths in Cook County and Baltimore
County, and already being convinced that some comparison groups
were better than none at all, we elected to draw the non-fatal suicide
attempter and natural death samples from Baltimore. . . . In any
event to do otherwise was financially impossible."[28] Because so
many other studies have found that both region and year are crucial
variants in suicide incidence, it seems unusual to eliminate these
beforehand.

The above criticisms are not fatal, if one accepts the assumptions
implicit in a statistical approach. Given more funds and a greater
number of research assistants, Maris or another researcher could include every conceivable type of data in his statistical study. However,
more substantive problems suggest that the defects in statistical
sociological studies cannot be corrected merely by subjecting additional variables to quantitative manipulation. For the real issue ex-
tends to assumptions about the efficacy of the statistical paradigm
itself. Neither *Pathways* nor any other statistical study of suicide has
dealt successfully with the conundrum first raised by Douglas two
decades ago. That is, statistical studies of suicide continue to assume
that each unit of datum (the individual suicide) acts just like every
other unit in response to external forces. Their authors are therefore locked into the fiction that social, economic, and political events
have the same meaning for all persons in their sample.

Nevertheless, whatever the limits of current sociological methodology, sociology has made two important contributions that we must
not abandon. First, sociologists have been more open than other suicide specialists in including the findings of other specialists in their
overall approach to suicide.[29] Second, only sociology, especially in
its alternative classical incarnation, is committed to uncovering the
links between individual actions and wider social processes.

PSYCHOANALYSIS

Alongside Freud's analytic writings stand a parallel set of works that
generally have been described as his metapsychological explorations.

In *Totem and Taboo* (1913), *Beyond the Pleasure Principle* (1920), *Civilization and Its Discontents* (1930), and *Moses and Monotheism* (1939), Freud acknowledged in a Durkheimian fashion the role of culture in the genesis of neurotic disorders. For instance, in *Beyond the Pleasure Principle*, Freud speculated on the relation between culture and suicide that he had first described in *Mourning and Melancholia*. When a powerful external event elicited a repressed memory of a childhood fantasy, anxiety resulted. In an attempt to master anxiety, individuals reacted with a "compulsion to repeat . . . what has been forgotten or repressed" through dreams and/or by other forms of behavior. Freud found that this process often was accompanied by melancholia. And, he argued, it was well known that depressive disorders "are temporarily brought to an end by intercurrent organic illness." Physical illness itself could serve as a mechanism for dealing with these anxieties. The goal of all these strategies was to restore organic equilibrium. When all attempts at mastery failed, self-destruction offered to "*restore* [the individual to] *an earlier state of things* which the living entity has been obliged to abandon under the pressure of external disturbing forces." In short, Freud's speculations suggested that childhood fantasies acquired their full psychological meaning only when later mediated by cultural forces.[30]

Although practicing psychoanalysts claim to consider social and cultural elements in their diagnoses and treatments, few take Freud's metapsychology seriously. Indeed, the demands of everyday practice make difficult, if not impossible, the treatment of the underlying social conditions that may contribute to a patient's disorder. As a result, psychoanalytic studies have emphasized individual maladjustment and intrapsychic conflict at the expense of wider cultural dynamics. Drawing on the methodology of clinical practice, psychoanalytic investigations of the etiology of suicide concentrate on the suicidal event itself, which typically is read back into the suicide's life history, reframing previous incidents as foreshadowings of an inevitable tragic end.

Freud warned his followers about confusing practice with theory. The aim of psychoanalytic treatment, he wrote in 1904, "will never be anything but the *practical* recovery of the patient, the restoration of his ability to lead an active life and of his capacity for enjoyment." The "recognition of our therapeutic limitations," Freud wrote in 1909, "reinforces our determination to change other social factors so that men and women shall no longer be forced into hopeless situations."[31] Psychoanalytic theory, as historian Russell Jacoby has pointed out, stands in dialectical opposition to the goals of psychoanalytic practice.[32]

Until the 1930s, American psychoanalysts seemed content to rely on the clinical insights into suicide presented in *Mourning and Melancholia* (1917). Beginning in 1933 in a series of separate professional lectures and journal articles, Gregory Zilboorg and Karl Menninger defended and elaborated the psychoanalytic position on suicide against what they viewed as encroachments by sociologists. Although their arguments have been made more explicit by psychoanalysts since the 1930s, along with *Mourning and Melancholia*, Zilboorg's and Menninger's studies continue to provide the foundation for psychoanalytic thinking about the etiology of suicide.

Born in Russia, Gregory Zilboorg (1890–1951) emigrated to the United States with his parents when he was only a year old. Trained in psychiatry, Zilboorg traveled to Berlin in the 1920s to be analyzed by Hans Sachs, a member of Freud's inner circle. One of the founders of the *Psychoanalytic Quarterly*, Zilboorg became a leader of the New York analytic community in the 1930s.[33]

In the thirties Zilboorg wrote a series of papers on suicide that established him as a leading critic of both sociological methods and conclusions. Citing Dublin's 1933 *To Be or Not To Be* as his example, Zilboorg dismissed "statistical studies of suicide" as "well-nigh useless" because the "data, dis-individualizing the person as such, concentrate on statistics with the result that we are more than ever removed from the psychology of suicide." In addition, Zilboorg asserted that "statistical data on suicide are compiled from vital statistics and are therefore never complete since they represent only those cases which lay judgment, i.e., the coroner's, accepts as suicide." Although he claimed that sociological and psychological orientations were "not mutually exclusive but rather complementary," by denying the validity of statistical methodology, Zilboorg effectively had rejected American sociologists' studies of suicide. "It seems fair to say," Zilboorg wrote, "that statistics, wholly or partially divorced from the study of the pathogenesis and etiology of suicide, are more liable to lead to a misconception than an understanding of the problem."[34]

Zilboorg dismissed as well Freud's metapsychology, singling out

Beyond the Pleasure Principle, because "when applied to the problem of suicide, [it] seems to be rather tautological and either adds to, or at least does not subtract from, our confusion." Clinical practice, Zilboorg concluded, provided the only "empirical psychological data." Drawing on his clinical cases, Zilboorg claimed that "only those individuals who appear to have identified themselves with a *dead* person and in whom the process of identification took place during childhood or adolescence, at a time when the incorporated person was actually dead, are most probably the truly suicidal individual." A child who "loses a father, brother, mother or sister at a time when he or she is at the height of their oedipus complex or transition to puberty," faces "a true danger of suicide" if they experience psychological ("neurotic") disturbances later in life.[35]

The controlling factor in suicide for Zilboorg was not the loss per se, but a later psychological trauma, like depression. Ironically, this put Zilboorg much closer than he realized to endorsing the sociological paradigm that he had criticized. The difference was that whereas Zilboorg located secondary psychological traumata as the triggers to suicide, sociologists would have substituted social traumata, such as unemployment. Moreover, because not all depressives who have experienced earlier childhood losses kill themselves, Zilboorg's construct seems self-fulfilling. If a person who had experienced such an early loss did not commit suicide, Zilboorg would have been forced to conclude that s/he did not suffer severe enough neurotic distress later in life. Even though he insisted that psychoanalysis was compatible with a social analysis, Zilboorg's model was no more successful in providing social meaning than the sociologists he criticized.

Like Zilboorg, Karl Menninger also was analyzed by an important disciple of Freud, in his case by Ruth Mack Brunswick in Vienna. The son of Charles F. Menninger, founder of the famous Menninger Clinic in Topeka, Kansas, Karl (b. 1893) attended Harvard Medical School. After graduation, he returned to Topeka to practice at his father's clinic and to take up a post as professor of clinical psychiatry at the University of Kansas Medical School. In 1942, Menninger was elected president of the American Psychoanalytic Association.[36]

Menninger collected and expanded his earlier papers on suicide in his 1938 classic *Man Against Himself.* Like Zilboorg, he dismissed

sociological studies of suicide because "sociologists . . . are committed
to principles of mass reorganization and cannot become interested
in the psychological study of the individual. And," he argued, "because they ignore this more penetrating psychological examination
of the individual they fail to understand certain aspects of mass action."[37] Menninger too began with Freud's *Mourning and Melancholia,* which he supplemented with selected examples from his own
practice. Focusing on a "psychopathological" fixation at the infantile
oral stage, Menninger argued that "no suicide is consummated unless" there is "the wish to kill," the wish "to be killed," and the wish
"to die." Menninger admitted that the causes of suicide were "un-
doubtedly complicated by extraneous factors" such as "social attitudes, familial patterns, [and] community customs," but he insisted
that these influences only exacerbated "those distortions of reality
incident to an incomplete personality development." Rather than resulting from any particular social event, the origin of all suicides
according to Menninger lies in "the steady progression of self-
destructive tendencies first appearing long before the consumma-
tion of the critical act."[38]

Although Menninger agreed with the sociologists that socially isolated individuals are more likely to kill themselves than those who
are socially integrated, he disagreed over why this was so. For sociologists, like Cavan, Dublin, and Maris, social isolation causes suicide,
but for Menninger individuals tend to isolate themselves for the
same reasons that they tend to kill themselves, because they are
mentally ill. Both sides seem to neglect what, according to Anthony
Giddens, is the crucial issue: "under what conditions does social isolation become psychologically 'translated' into a phenomenal situation which the individual defines as 'suicidal'?"[39]

In *Mourning and Melancholia* Freud had argued that melancholics
experienced mental reproaches between the self and an internalized
"other." Freud called this other person-brought-inside an inner "object."[40] Building on this idea, Melanie Klein and her followers, especially Donald Winnicott and John Bowlby, developed what has come
to be known as object relations theory. Migrating from British analytic circles in the 1960s, object relations theory soon dominated
American psychoanalytic practice.[41] Because they had emphasized
the role of the fantasized other ("the object") in the etiology of suicide, Zilboorg's and Menninger's studies of suicide proved especially

compatible with object relations theory. Object relations theorists refined but did not substantially alter these earlier arguments.

Unlike Maris's *Pathways,* there is no single contemporary psychoanalytic work that stands out as an illustration of an object relations overview on suicide. It is possible, however, to construct an overview from the writings of object relations theorists who have been concerned with the etiology of suicide, including Bowlby (1960), Kurt R. Eissler (1955), Robert Jay Lifton (1979), Margaret Mahler (1974), George H. Pollock (1962, 1978), and Martha Wolfenstein (1966, 1976).[42]

Classical Freudian theory holds that people harbor ambivalent feelings about those with whom they have the closest emotional ties. Freud argued that when a parent, sibling, or spouse dies, the survivor not only experiences great loss, but also feels anger and responsibility because at times they have wished, if only unconsciously, for their loved one's departure or death. The process of mourning allows survivors to affirm loss, excise anger, and admit complicity in the death of those closest to them.

Like Freud, object relations theorists find that many depressives seem to act like mourners. Generally someone who is depressed has experienced a recent object loss, perhaps rejection by a lover or loss of employment. Often, the depressive's acts—refusal to eat, threats of suicide—have the effect of forcing the deserting lover to return, if only temporarily, to view the damage that has been done. In bringing the deserter back by such maneuvers, the depressive may succeed in externalizing his or her hostility toward the returned lover that heretofore could only be directed inward. In short, like mourners, depressives adopt complex strategies to work through feelings of loss and abandonment.[43]

Extending this reasoning, Pollock suggested that those who tended toward suicide were more vulnerable because they had experienced an earlier, severe loss that had been incompletely mourned. Any perceived loss, such as a divorce, desertion, or the loss of a limb can be seen as an object loss, but, Pollock argued, the death of a loved one during childhood served as the most graphic illustration of this process.[44]

Loss of a parent or a sibling during childhood, according to both Wolfenstein and Bowlby, increased the risk of incomplete mourning, because children often are removed from the mourning process by those who wish to protect them from the horrors of death. Yet, children as much as adults are ambivalent toward those to whom they are closest. In fact, children are less likely than adults to repress totally these ambivalent feelings and often wish consciously for the removal of a rival sibling or otherwise loved parent. It is not uncommon for children to proclaim to those they love, "I hate you and wish you were dead!" Since children tend to believe in the power of wishes, when one of their suppressed desires comes true as the result of a death, a desertion, or a divorce, they feel responsible for its occurrence. Because of both their weaker position and, paradoxically, their belief in the magic of wishes, children often feel more responsible for loss than adults do. If they also are shielded from rituals of mourning, this feeling of guilt intensifies. While their immediate reaction may be the repression of the unhappy event in their childhood, they remain particularly vulnerable to object loss later in life.[45]

In some cases, in an attempt to deal with their earlier repressed loss, incomplete mourners may repeatedly place themselves in a position that ensures continued object losses. But they face a difficult task. Because the objects they desire to bring back are not the immediate ones who have deserted them, but loved ones who are both dead and insufficiently mourned, guilt and hostility cannot be displaced and may in fact intensify and lead finally to suicide.[46]

Suicide, according to Lifton, also may be viewed as a desperate attempt to continue to live, if only in the memory of the survivors. It may be the final acting out of the child's threat to run away so that "they'll miss me when I'm gone."[47] In terms of incomplete mourning, this wish reveals the suicide's attempt to be transformed into the lost love object. Suicides fantasize that after death they will become an object loss for others. Thus, identification with the loved/hated deserter comes full circle.[48]

Because not all who experience incomplete mourning kill themselves or even attempt suicide in later life, most of these psychoanalysts have concluded that to a greater or lesser extent all those who have come into contact with death or desertion experience some incomplete mourning. However, to the degree that mourning fails to satisfy the need to admit and resolve ambivalence toward the departed, the risk of later self-punishment increases. In many cases incomplete mourning manifests itself through a life history of risk-taking. Like depressives, incomplete mourners often take actions that have the effect of placing them in actual physical danger. Excessive risk-taking—even attempting suicide—can be viewed as testing one's self-destructive urges in order to purge oneself of guilt—a sort of ritual attempt to avoid suicide.[49]

The theory of incomplete mourning emphasizes—some might say overemphasizes—individual meaning, but, all protestations aside, it dispenses with social meaning. The construct of incomplete mourning always turns out to be idiosyncratic. That is, what constitutes incomplete mourning depends on the meaning that any individual gives to a loss. But, whatever its intrapsychic content, mourning historically has been structured also by social and cultural elements. An object relations approach seems defective to the extent that it has provided no social theory to come to terms with cultural or historical variations in the meaning of mourning.

What is required is an integrated approach. In *Suicide and Scandinavia* (1964) Herbert Hendin, one of the few psychoanalytic critics of the current object relations model of suicide, suggested that differences in suicide rates among Danes, Swedes, and Norwegians could be understood in relation to the "different fantasies and attitudes toward death" found in each of those societies.[50] More than two decades later, these suggestions appear to have been largely ignored. What is needed still, Hendin recently argued, is a "psychosocial perspective" that "aims at understanding how psychic, social and cultural factors are interwoven to produce suicidal behavior in Americans from very different backgrounds. The organizing issue of a psychosocial frame of reference," according to Hendin, "must be the connection between psychic and social conditions." Any theory of suicide must deal with the fact that motives "are dependent on cultural expectations, on the degree to which an individual does or does not incorporate them, as well as on personal capacity to fulfill them."[51]

Beyond Hendin's concerns, an object relations approach is open to the criticism that it is unscientific, because like most psychoanalytic theories, it is not falsifiable. In other words, there is no way in which it can be tested. Its categories are so broad that any event in early childhood can be used as evidence for incomplete mourning. Conversely, many people experience severe early loss and do not commit suicide. Any theory that wishes to tie loss to suicide is obligated to explain these exceptions.[52]

Beyond these reservations, a substantial challenge to the psychoanalytic paradigm of suicide has arisen from recent neurobiological investigations. Studies on brain plasticity have shown that neural pathways develop rapidly during the first two years of life. In fact, the dendrites and axons that form these pathways continue to increase in length and branching until puberty. Memory systems, therefore, appear to be underdeveloped in young children. This suggests that those portions of children's brains are not sufficiently developed for recording memories during early childhood. Rather than being repressed, early loss may not be remembered in the first place.[53]

Informed by neurobiology and biochemistry of the 1970s and 1980s, psychiatric practice increasingly has turned from psychoanalysis to psychopharmacology. This change in psychiatric practice has led to a third paradigm of suicide, which stands as an alternative explanation to both psychoanalytic and sociological paradigms for suicide.

PSYCHOPHARMACOLOGY

Assumptions of an organic basis for insanity have their roots in the earliest medical theories about the etiology of melancholia. As we have seen, nineteenth-century psychiatrists like Isaac Ray and John Gray believed in the somatic etiology of at least some suicides.

The most influential spokesman for the somatic school in the late nineteenth and early twentieth centuries was the German psychiatrist Emil Kraepelin, whose views on suicide were presented in the introductory chapter. In the late 1890s Kraepelin's theories received a great deal of attention in the United States thanks to the influential American neurologist Adolf Meyer, who had visited Kraepelin's Heidelberg clinic in 1896. By the end of the first decade of the twentieth century, American psychiatrists, again led by Meyer, began to question the usefulness of Kraepelin's clinical construct and many of the most prominent abandoned somaticism in favor of Freud's psychoanalysis.[54]

Although no conclusive evidence emerged linking depressive disorders to organic causes until the 1960s, a significant number of neurologists and psychiatrists remained wedded to Kraepelin's belief that suicide has both organic and inherited causes. Recently,

Kraepelin has been rediscovered by American neuropsychiatrists and has been hailed by one of its leading publicists for having laid "the foundation for . . . the modern biological revolution in psychiatry."[55]

As Elliot Valenstein demonstrated in his impressive volume *Great and Desperate Cures* (1986) that "even though the neurologists had no treatment to offer seriously ill mental patients, they were . . . extremely reluctant to accept any ideas that might tarnish their image as scientists studying physical realities." Given their unquestioned allegiance to somatacism, neuropsychiatrists from the 1920s to 1960s developed what seems in retrospect to have been a series of bizarre theories and interventions. Nowhere, Valenstein shows, was the reception of these "great and desperate cures" more enthusiastic than in the United States.[56]

One of the most radical of these therapies was the "focal infection theory" promulgated by Henry Cotton, the medical director of the New Jersey State Hospital in Trenton, who had studied under Kraepelin in Munich. "Toxins produced by bacteria at infection sites in different parts of the body," Cotton argued, were "transported to the brain where they often produce mental disturbances." Valenstein describes how Cotton, beginning in 1919, performed a variety of surgical procedures ranging from the removal of previously filled teeth, tonsils, and sinuses to major interventions like colon resections and hysterectomies. Although Cotton's theories were criticized by some psychoanalysts, on the whole Cotton's approach won widespread endorsement by nonpsychoanalytic psychiatrists.* Throughout the 1920s Cotton's methods were adopted by many practitioners.[57]

In the 1930s, new therapies to treat depressives were developed based upon the theories of the Viennese physician Manfred Joshua Sakel. Sakel had mistakenly administered an overdose of insulin to a mental patient, who lapsed into convulsions and then into an insulin coma. When he had recovered from the coma, the patient's schizophrenic condition seemed to ameliorate. This convinced Sakel that convulsions had the effect of inducing epilepsy, which, Sakel reasoned (incorrectly), was the opposite condition to schizophrenia. Induced epilepsy, Sakel concluded, could reverse schizophrenia. Thus

*As late as 1933 the *American Mercury* magazine described him as "one of the leading psychiatrists in the United States."

convulsive therapy was born. Sakel's work was translated into English and in the 1930s and 1940s his procedure was adopted widely by American institutional psychiatrists.[58]

Simultaneously, a Hungarian neurologist, Joseph Ladislas von Meduna, introduced a camphor-like drug, metrazol, which he claimed was more effective in inducing convulsions. It became apparent, however, that induced convulsions were more successful in treating depressions than schizophrenia. In the United States, electroshock, developed in 1938 by two Italian neuropsychiatrists, Ugo Cerletti and Lucio Bini, quickly became the convulsive treatment of choice.[59] By the 1940s, electro-convulsive therapy had become the most widely used (and abused) intervention for depressive patients.* Even though it continues to be highly controversial, electro-convulsive therapy has experienced renewed support from a growing number of practitioners.[60]

Valenstein's analysis of psychosurgery covering the period from the 1930s to the 1960s goes beyond the bounds of this discussion, but it bears citation because it provides another example of how neuropsychiatrists, wedded to the assumption that mental illness had an organic cause, were willing to pursue interventions that in retrospect seem ludicrous and dangerous. But at the time and given what was known about the brain and disease, these procedures seemed to be on the cutting edge of science. We must remind ourselves how very little we know today about the chemistry of the brain in contrast to what there is to understand. Indeed, the recent discoveries in neurobiology seem like great advances because they stand in stark contrast to the earlier explanations of men such as Cotton, Sakel, and the psychosurgeons of the 1940s and 1950s. In terms of the major concern of this book, suicide, many of the same assumptions that informed Cotton's and Sakel's theories continue to inform neuropsychiatric research—in particular, the notion that depression and resultant suicidal behavior have an *exclusively* organic etiology.

Beginning in the early 1950s, neuropathological discoveries indicated a connection between certain behaviors, especially violence and depression, and malfunctions or abnormalities in those chemical messengers in the brain called neurotransmitters.[61] One of

*When in a 1939 interview Sakel was asked to explain how convulsive therapy worked, he " 'frankly declared he does not know how and why his cure works,' but that it 'indubitably works.' "

those neurotransmitters, serotonin, has been linked to suicidal behavior.

When serotonin was first identified, researchers theorized that it
was related to psychotic disorders like schizophrenia.[62] For the next
two decades, aided by refined chemical assays and increased data,
investigators rejected the schizophrenia thesis in favor of a relationship between serotonin and affective (depressive) disorders. They
found that by elevating the amount of serotonin and of another
neurotransmitter, norepinephrine, depressions seemed to be alleviated in a significant number of patients. This discovery occurred
serendipitously in the early 1950s. Patients who were being treated
for tubercular pneumonia with the drug isoniazid reported experiencing mood elevations. It seemed logical to assume that isoniazid
could be administered to alleviate depressive episodes. Thus experi-
ments were conducted with iproniazid, a drug similar to but with
fewer side effects than isoniazid.[63]

Iproniazid, it was later discovered, operated as a monoamine oxidase (MAO) inhibiter. When a neuron in the brain is stimulated, a
chemical is normally released from its axon into the synaptic gap or
cleft, the space separating two neurons (see Figures 3.1, 3.2). This
chemical is taken up by the receptor of the second neuron, which se-
quentially repeats the process, sending messages along neural paths.
A certain amount of the neurochemical is left in the synaptic gap
and either is broken down into inactive components or taken back
into its releasing neuron and broken down by an enzyme called
monoamine oxidase. Monoamine oxidase renders the excessive
serotonin into 5–hydroxyindoleacetic acid (5–HIAA), which eventually ends up in the cerebrospinal fluid (CSF). A monoamine inhibiter like iproniazid inhibits the enzyme monoamine oxidase from
breaking down excessive serotonin into 5–HIAA. This in turn serves
to raise levels of brain serotonin because it ensures that the serotonin
retaken into the releasing neuron will be available for later transmission instead of being broken down by an enzyme. In the late 1950s
a second class of antidepressants called tricyclics was developed.
With fewer severe side effects than MAO inhibiters, these drugs increased the levels of serotonin and norepinephrine by blocking
re-uptake.[64]

In 1976 Marie Åsberg and her associates at the Karolinska Institute in Stockholm announced that they had found a demonstrable

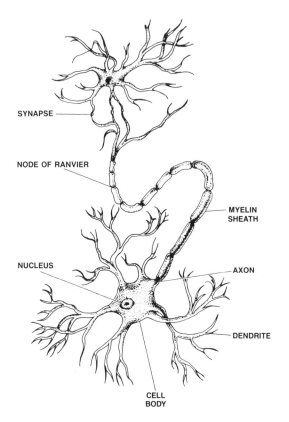

SYNAPSE

NODE OF RANVIER

MYELIN
SHEATH

NUCLEUS

AXON

DENDRITE

CELL
BODY

Figure 3.1 Two Neurons in Synaptic Contact

association between low concentrations of brain serotonin and clinical depression.[65] Almost simultaneously Herman van Praag and his colleagues at the State University of Utrecht in the Netherlands announced similar results. Indeed, van Praag had suggested this connection fifteen years earlier in his doctoral dissertation.[66] Subsequent studies, however, contradicted one another concerning the precise relationship between serotonin and depressive disorders.[67]

The effects of antidepressants on serotonin and norepinephrine concentrations have been used by most psychopharmacologists as evidence for the conclusion that depression has a chemical rather than a psychosocial etiology.[68] Thus, clinical treatment centers on pharmacological interventions because depressive episodes often may be alleviated or controlled by raising the available levels of these

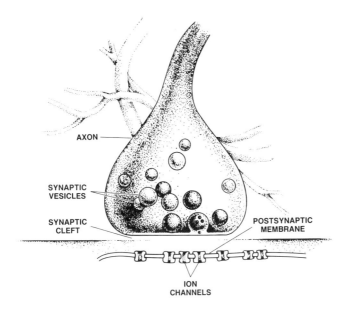

Figure 3.2 The Synaptic Cleft (Gap)

neurotransmitters in the brain.[69] While brain levels of both seroto-nin and norepinephrine have been associated with depressive dis-orders, serotonin has been particularly identified with suicidal behavior.

In July 1981, a joint team from the National Institute of Mental Health in Bethesda, Maryland, and one from the Karolinska Insti-tute announced that they had isolated a " 'suicide factor' in human spinal fluid that can be measured by a simple laboratory test."* The study was conducted by a joint team of American and Swedish re-searchers led by Lil Träskman (who had worked on the earlier Åsberg studies), and it appeared in the AMA's *Archives of General Psychiatry*. These researchers had measured for levels of serotonin and found that it "was especially low in those who choose violent methods and/or were successful in suicide."[70]

The contribution of the Träskman study was that in specifying a "strong association between violent suicide attempts" and low

*On its front page (11 July 1981) the *Los Angeles Times* proclaimed that the "new test can separate the truly suicidal from the depressed or otherwise disturbed patient. . . . It can help doctors decide which patients need longer hospital stays, as well as which patients should re-ceive new drugs that appear to alter levels of the 'suicide factor.' "

concentrations of serotonin, it appeared to resolve some of the contradictions of earlier studies.[71] Träskman's findings seemed to offer
additional clinical evidence for chemical interventions in those depressive patients who had been diagnosed as showing a high risk
for committing suicide. Subsequent investigations appear to have
confirmed these findings. At a meeting of the New York Academy
of Sciences in September 1985, a research team from Albert Einstein College of Medicine reported that they had found that "a low
level of serotonin seems to be a biochemical marker for those depressed people who are most prone to suicide."[72]

Although the technical sophistication of these studies is impressive, the connection between depression, suicide, and serotonin
remains tentative.[73] For instance, the conclusion that low concentrations of serotonin exist in a causal relationship with depression and
suicide has yet to be demonstrated. Moreover, the more scientifically
complex investigative procedures become, the more they tend to ignore the cultural and psychological context in which the behavior
they seek to explain takes place. This would matter less if taking
these into consideration had no impact on scientific results, but that
is not the case. From an epidemiological point of view, biochemical
studies of suicidal behavior display several limitations. I will focus on
the Träskman study.

The first of these limitations or defects is the relatively small
sample involved in most studies. Compared to others, the Träskman
population of eighty-five people was large. However, it is not at all
unusual to read studies in the *Archives of General Psychiatry* in which
the number of authors almost equals the number of subjects studied. Often the sweeping conclusions suggested seem inappropriate
given their limited population.

Because those who employ firearms are the most "successful" in
their suicide attempts, biochemical studies of suicide attempters generally include very few, if any, subjects who resorted to firearms. For
instance, no one in the Träskman study's population employed firearms, even though this is generally considered to be both the most
violent and the most lethal method of suicide. Moreover, data indicate that in the United States almost one-half of all successful suicides resort to firearms.[74]

These investigations, as a matter of course, further exclude alcoholics, because alcohol directly affects neurotransmitter systems.
From an epidemiological standpoint, however, an alcoholic has ten

times the greater likelihood of dying by suicide than a nonalco-
holic.[75] No subjects taking drugs that had antidepressant characteristics were included either, even though toxicological results of
postmortem examinations indicate that substantial numbers of suicide completers took or were taking tranquilizers and/or antidepressants immediately prior to their suicides.[76] Although the reasons
for excluding such persons from studies seeking to determine concentrations of particular neurotransmitter levels is experimentally
desirable, it is epidemiologically unsound.

Approximately 30 percent of all completed suicides are committed by women.[77] In the Träskman study, however, women made
up a disproportionate 63.3 percent of the sample.[78] Since women
attempt suicide at a rate 2.3 times greater than men, they are more
available to psychiatric researchers than men are. Although others
have discussed the limitations of concentrating on completed suicides in order to develop a clear understanding of the etiology of
suicide, the goal of the Träskman study was to determine which sec-
tor of the population was most likely to *complete* suicide.[79] Its sample
ought to have been controlled to reflect the epidemiological gender
distribution of suicide completers. This problem is not mitigated by
the study's conclusion that there are no gender-specific differences
in the etiology of suicide "since there was also a difference in CSF
5−HIAA level between violent and nonviolent *female* suicide attempters."[80]

Moreover, such investigations ignore the larger problem: can we
generalize about the nature of suicide by examining those who attempt suicide rather than those who actually kill themselves? Recent
sociological studies have argued that researchers should not form
conclusions about suicide from observations made about attempters.
"It must be emphasized," Ronald Maris points out, "that those individuals who *complete* suicide are very different from those who
'merely' attempt suicide."* Maris found that 75 percent of all "successful" suicides had made no previous attempts to kill themselves.[81]

Although we may be sympathetic with the fact that particular patient populations may limit the ability of any one study to establish

---

*Maris argues that the contents of suicide notes of completers, when distinguished from
those of attempters, demonstrate that one should not generalize from the actions of attempters in order to understand motives of successful suicides (pp. 275−279).

an epidemiologically valid sample, researchers must take these limitations into consideration when formulating their conclusions. Even a cursory epidemiological examination shows that studies of the relationship between neurotransmitter concentrations and suicide are misleading insofar as the populations they examine are atypical of suicide completion.[82]

A second category of limitations of biochemical approaches to suicide is their lack of cultural perspective. Most important, biochemical researchers seem to be unaware of both the changing incidence of suicide among populations and of the specific correlations between cultural experience and suicidal behavior.

Most sociological studies have demonstrated that suicide is not distributed randomly over time. For instance, most investigations report that the incidence of suicide completion by women has increased over the past century.[83] According to the logic of biochemical studies, changes in female suicide patterns must be due to alterations in the neurochemistry of women's brains over the past one hundred years. If that is so, no such biologic evidence has been introduced.

Also, suicide rates are ethnic-specific; that is, some cultures and ethnic groups consistently have had a greater incidence of suicide than others. Beginning in the mid–nineteenth century, Germans and Danes have had the greatest recorded incidence of suicide, while Irish and Italians have among the lowest. Moreover, suicide is connected with migration and immigration. European immigrants to the United States have had a higher incidence of suicide than those of their nationality who have remained in their native countries. Thus, Germans, Danes, and Austrians have had the highest rates in both the old and new worlds, while the rates of Irish and Italians have been consistently lower.[84] Can serotonin levels be higher among Irish and Italians than among Germans and Danes? Does immigration lower concentrations of specific neurotransmitters in Germans and Danes?

CONCLUSION

The sophisticated methodology that underlies much of recent psychopharmacology has reinforced psychiatric attitudes toward sociological studies. The promise of biochemical research has presented psychiatrists who are unsympathetic to psychoanalysis with additional ammunition in their war with psychoanalysts. It has produced a response toward psychoanalytic psychiatry that bears a striking similarity to the impact that bacteriology had upon moral treatment a century ago. As a result American psychiatric practice in general has turned increasingly away from psychological therapeutics in favor of pharmacological interventions.

The reaction of many orthodox psychoanalysts and sociologists to the psychopharmacological paradigm has been predictable. Arguing that their existing theories already provide sufficient explanations for the issues raised here, they contend that biochemical studies merely report what is obvious—that the conditions that drive some people to take their lives also have a physiological impact. To mistake neurotransmitter abnormalities for the causes of suicidal behavior, they insist, is to confuse a symptom with a disorder.[85] Although these responses no doubt contain some truth, they too often mask an unarticulated fear that to the extent that biochemical claims are accepted as valid, sociological and psychoanalytic analyses are invalidated. As has been the case historically, the resistance to alternative explanations for the etiology of suicide seems to arise as much from professional fears and jealousies as it does from methodological contradictions. Nevertheless, it is doubtful that any one side can make much headway by continuing to ignore the findings of the other side.

The rise of specialization has become both an impediment to and a necessary step toward the development of a comprehensive theory of suicide. On the one hand, explanations of the causes of suicide seem to tell us as much about the values of the explainers as they do about the etiology of suicide. Our understanding of the causes of suicide has been further obscured by the fact that studies of suicide often have been used as vehicles to justify wider concerns. Durkheim's *Suicide*, for instance, was aimed as much at legitimating the discipline of academic sociology as it was at providing an explanation for suicide. Like sociology's, psychiatry's search for the cause of suicide has been circumscribed in large measure by wider professional concerns. On the other hand, by singlemindedly pursuing one paradigm at the expense of the others, specialists have provided us with the insights essential for the construction of a synthesis.

Since the late nineteenth century, sociologists, psychoanalysts, and neuropsychiatrists have applied a disease metaphor to suicide. However, they differ fundamentally about the cause of behavioral "diseases" like suicide. Sociologists have claimed that suicide is a social disease; psychoanalysts have assumed it results from intrapsychic conflict; while neuropsychiatrists have insisted that suicide is an organic disorder. Although protestations have appeared regularly from members of each profession asserting that they have considered the insights of the other, the demands of professional orthodoxy have made it difficult for a true synthesis to emerge from the ranks of any of the three specialties. Yet, without such a synthesis, we will have moved no closer to the answers we seek than Durkheim, Freud, and Kraepelin had almost a century ago.

PART TWO

Toward a Psychocultural Biology of Suicide

4

OFFICIAL STATISTICS
AND CULTURAL MEANING

T HE goal of all theories of suicide is to explain why some people kill themselves and others do not. Although sociologists, psychoanalysts, and neuropsychiatrists have posited answers to this question, none have done so to the others' satisfaction. Moreover, each disciplinary theory has contradicted the underlying assumptions and methodological approaches of the others. This professional competition presents the most formidable barrier to our understanding of the causes of suicide. This is not because Durkheim, Freud, and Kraepelin were necessarily wrong, but rather because they (and their followers) have pursued their insights in a singleminded manner. Nevertheless, there is nothing inherently contradictory in sociological, psychoanalytic, and neurobiological explanations. Indeed, only an integrated psychocultural biology offers us the opportunity to answer the most fundamental questions about the etiology of suicide.

The first half of *Self-Destruction in the Promised Land* presented the history of the schism that gave rise to competing paradigms for the causes of suicide; this half suggests, in four connected topical essays, how these apparent contradictions might be resolved. Because this is a complicated process, I will concentrate first on the issues that separate sociological and psychoanalytic approaches, with the aim of providing a psychocultural theory of suicide. Then, I will suggest how this psychocultural approach can be integrated into what we know about the biochemistry and neurobiology of suicide.

A basic methodological issue separating the followers of Durkheim and Freud involves the viability of statistics as a tool for illuminating the causes of suicide. Sociological studies generally have assumed that official suicide statistics provide accurate data, which when subjected to rigorous analysis, yield clues to the etiology of suicide. Psychoanalysts, beginning with Zilboorg and Menninger, have been contemptuous of statistical studies, claiming that they fail to consider the intrapsychic conflicts that inform all suicides.

At least when it comes to the incidence of suicide, the sociological model seems to have triumphed. Almost every generalization about the incidence of suicide in America ultimately relies on official statistics. These data, whether issued by local, state, or federal agencies, are compilations of coroners' reports of completed or "successful" suicides. For the past decade Americans have been bombarded with media reports claiming that the United States currently is experiencing an epidemic of teenage suicide.[1] The evidence for a contemporary teenage (epidemiologically defined as people between the ages of fifteen to twenty-four) suicide epidemic rests almost entirely on official statistics that indicate that both the percentage and the rate of teenage suicides have increased substantially in the past two decades.[2]

Accepting these statistics as valid, experts have sought to uncover the underlying causes for the teenage suicide epidemic. A consensus has emerged that American teenagers are experiencing a greater sense of emotional dislocation than did previous generations. "Increasing numbers of children and young adults find it difficult to cope with today's independent lifestyles, tumble into fits of depression and commit suicide," claims Atlanta child psychiatrist Quentin Smith. Marianne Felice, chief of adolescent medicine at the University of California Hospital in San Diego, concurs: the "world is harder to live in," especially for teenagers, "a jungle of sorts with pressures so intense that no generation before has ever known anything quite like them."[3] Dr. Eva Deykin of Harvard's Graduate School of Public Health explains that "the increase in adolescent suicides has coincided with a dramatic increase in divorces and geographic mobility." Like Deykin, other experts find that America's teenagers are confused as they attempt to seek their identities in the complicated and contradictory society and economy of late twentieth century America.[4]

How accurate are the data that inform these explantions? Is it reasonable to develop a theory of the etiology of suicide based on manipulations of statistics that report the incidence of completed suicides? An intensive evaluation of one of the most persistent conclusions of statistical studies—that men are more suicidal than women—reveals both the strengths and limitations of such an approach and provides insight into claims that the United States is currently experiencing a teenage suicide epidemic. As important, such an investigation points the way toward rethinking the assumption that the motives for suicide may be gleaned from the histories only of those who succeed in killing themselves.

GENDER AND SUICIDE

Since the early nineteenth century, investigators have reported that approximately three out of every four successful suicides in both Western European countries and the United States were men.[5] In the United States, national mortality figures were first collected in the 1850 federal census, which was released in 1855.[6] However, before any substantial national statistics on the incidence of suicide were compiled or made public, experts already had convincing data from both local and state compilations as well as from various European authorities demonstrating that men were much more likely than women to commit suicide.[7] Although contemporary data continue to report that male suicides substantially outnumber female suicides, the data also indicate that the gender gap has been narrowing for the past hundred years.[8]

In San Diego County the ratio of male suicides had been even greater during the past century than that reported in federal census returns (see Table 4.1, Figure 4.1).[9] In 1880 women accounted for 12.8 percent of all completed suicides in San Diego County, even though they made up about one-half of the population. Reflecting the national trend, the percentage of female suicides grew by approximately 10 percent of its base per decade. Thus, by 1970

Table 4.1.

SUICIDE PERCENTAGES BY GENDER, SAN DIEGO COUNTY, 1880–1972

Years	Males	Females	Number
1880–1900	87.2%	12.8%	148
1911–1925	85.0%	15.0%	484
1938–1942	75.4%	24.6%	207
1948–1952	74.4%	25.6%	262
1967–1972	62.4%	37.6%	1,294

SOURCES: San Diego County, Coroner's Reports, 1870–1980, San Diego County Coroner's Office; Anita M. Muhl, "America's Greatest Suicide Problem: A Study of Over 500 Cases in San Diego," *Psychoanalytic Review* 14 (1927): 320; Aubrey Wendling, "Suicides in the City of San Diego, 1938–1942, 1948–1952," unpublished ms.

women accounted for 37.6 percent of all suicides in San Diego County (see Table 4.1).*

Roger Lane's Philadelphia study notes a similar trend (see Figure 4.2). In the 1870s the suicide rate for white women in Philadelphia was two per 100,000. A century later, the rate had reached 10.8 per

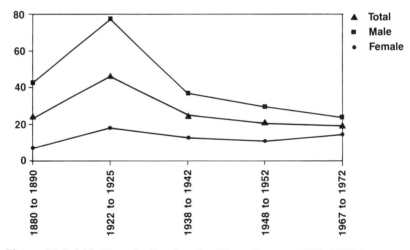

Figure 4.1 Suicide Rates by Gender, San Diego County, 1880–1972 (rates per 100,000)
SOURCES: Same as Table 4.1

*Rates per 100,000 of the living population provide a more accurate indication of the extent of suicide in a given population than percentages. As Figure 4.1 shows, in a century the rate had more than doubled for women, from 6.7 per 100,000 to 14.4 per 100,000.

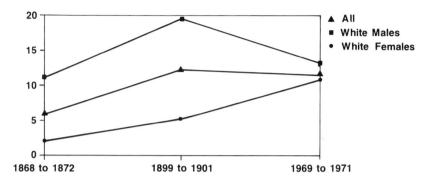

Figure 4.2 Suicide Rates by Gender, Philadelphia, 1868–1971 (rates per 100,000)
SOURCE: Roger Lane, *Violent Death in the City: Suicide, Accident, and Murder in Philadelphia* (Cambridge, Mass.: Harvard University Press, 1979), p. 29.

100,000—an increase of 540 percent.[10] Researchers studying suicides in Alberta, Canada, have arrived at similar conclusions.[11]

But, while the differential between the numbers of men and women committing suicide has diminished, official statistics continue to report a much higher rate for men. In fact, no study has uncovered a greater incidence of suicide completion for women than for men in any jurisdiction in the United States or Europe.

Explanations

Beginning in the mid-nineteenth century commentators have sought to tie the disparity between male and female suicide rates to what they believed to be different motivations. In 1846 *The Whig Review* explained that "in men, real or fancied impotence is very apt to induce self-destruction;—and among women, we cannot help always suspecting the dread of the consequences of secret loss of honor."[12] This essay was widely circulated and reprinted in several journals, including the *Democratic Review* in 1854 and *Harper's New Monthly Magazine* in 1859.[13]

"In regard to sex," reported the *New York Times* in 1861, "only about one-fourth of the whole number [of suicides] were women . . . [even] though by the last census there is an excess of females over males . . . in New York." That American women seemed to commit suicide even less frequently than their European counterparts was due according to this account to "the greater facility of divorce" in the United States, since "a large proportion of female suicides attribute their act to domestic unhappiness." "Besides," explained the *Times*, "it is a well known fact that women possess greater courage and patience under misfortune than men, and less readily give way to despair and the vices consequent upon it."[14]

By the middle of the nineteenth century, popular characterizations of women's suicides meshed with the ideology described by Barbara Welter as that "of True Womanhood, by which a woman judged herself and was judged by her husband, her neighbors, and society." Adherence to the virtues of "piety, purity, submissiveness and domesticity" translated into the belief that "a 'fallen woman' was a 'fallen angel,' " unworthy of the celestial company of her sex." Loss of purity, according to the periodical press, "brought madness or death." And these dominant values, Welter argued, portrayed "Death Preferable to Loss of Innocence."[15]

American fiction reinforced this ideology. Illustrative is Nathaniel Hawthorne's *The Blithedale Romance* (1852), in which Silas Foster finally realizes that Zenobia has been spurned by her lover Hollingsworth:

> "And so you think she's drowned herself?" he cried. "What on earth should the young women do that for?" exclaimed Silas, his eyes half out of his head with mere surprise. "Why, she has more means than she can use or waste, and lacks nothing to make her comfortable, but a husband. . . ."[16]

Nineteenth-century fiction is littered with the corpses of such women. Whether it was Zenobia; Emma in Flaubert's *Madame Bovary* (1857); Anna in Tolstoi's *Anna Karenina* (1875); or Lili Bart in Wharton's *The House of Mirth* (1905), the cause was always the same: rejection after an illicit love affair that led a despairing female to the only honorable (and predictable) resolution—suicide.*

This was, of course, a literary convention, but one that gained credence from its similarity to nineteenth-century American newspaper articles about women's suicide. During the last century the American press reported the details and backgrounds of most sui-

---

*Suicide by women often was presented as frivolous. One author suggested that "had Zenobia paused to think how unseemly and repulsive her form would look in this condition she never would have committed the rash deed." L. J. Bigelow, "The Aesthetics of Suicide," *The Galaxy* 2 (November 1866): 472.

cides in a manner that is uncommon today except in tabloids. A typical portrayal of the suicide of a woman appeared on the front
pages of newspapers from coast to coast in early January 1890: "A
Depressive Girl's Suicide," headlined the story in a San Francisco
newspaper:

> New York, January 1st. Gabrielle Oberbauer, a talented young crayon artist,
> shot herself, dead to-day in her apartment at 210 East Eighty-first street where
> her brother also lived. These two had become alienated from the other mem-
> bers of the family. Gabrielle had recently learned that William Brill, a wealthy
> glove manufacturer, who had been paying her marked attention, was about to
> marry another woman. This made her despondent and led to her suicide. Brill
> could not be seen today.[17]

These portrayals translated into the dictum that suicide rates
among women reflected individual emotional acts, while male suicide rates were taken as a barometer of national economic and social
well-being. Self-proclaimed nineteenth-century suicide experts,
citing federal census returns, tied suicide by a woman to her social
role as wife and mother. Albert Rhodes explained the suicide differential this way: "The woman's mode of death is usually less violent.
Copious weeping relieves the woman, and often saves her, while this
relief is denied to man. Besides, when the hour for the act comes,
her courage is apt to fail." When women commit suicide, Rhodes asserted, they do so for very different motives from men: "Women
appear to be more subject to moral influences, such as disappointed
love, betrayal, desertion, jealousy, domestic trouble, and sentimental
exaltation of every description."* Men, on the other hand, "are
rather affected by trials of a material order, such as misery, business
embarrassments, losses, ungratified ambition, the abuse of alcohol,
the desire to escape from justice, and so on."[18]
    In 1881, in a widely republished article entitled "Suicidal Ma-
nia," William Knighton suggested that a combination of "religious
restraints" and the possession of "a larger measure of that hope
which springs eternal in the human breast," accounted for the fact
that women "were less prone to commit suicide . . . than men."

---

*Contrary to this view, Olive Anderson found that women who committed suicide in
nineteenth-century England did so because of "sheer primary poverty," rather than because
of "disappointed expectations or reduced circumstances." Olive Anderson, *Suicide in Victorian
and Edwardian England* (New York: Oxford University Press, 1987), p. 144.

"Women," wrote Knighton, "cling to life much more strongly than men."[19]

Whenever an increase in suicide among women was reported, it was attributed to their adopting roles that nature and society had assigned to men. "It has been observed," wrote Robert N. Reeves in 1897, "that as woman approaches man in her mode of life she also becomes more familiar with those abnormal conditions which have previously been peculiar to man." This leads to an increase in suicide among women because "the comparative immunity of women from self-destruction in the past has depended greatly upon the relatively less harassing part she has taken in the struggle for life." As women move "deeper into . . . vocations," such as "art, literature, finance, and even politics," they "must expect to suffer the consequences. Already," Reeves warned, "it is noticeable that feminine suicide is not entirely due to the sentimental causes of disappointed love, desertion, and jealousy, but to those trials of a more material order such as have led men to the act of self-destruction."[20]

Twentieth-century experts who have attempted to explain the reasons for the alleged gender-specific disparity in the suicide rate have not moved far from the characterizations implicit in nineteenth-century novels and newspaper reports. Louis Dublin, author of the authoritative *Suicide: A Sociological and Statistical Study* (1963), concluded that "suicide . . . may be called a masculine type of behavior." Dublin suggested that suicide by women resulted from "maladjustment." Those women who committed suicide, Dublin asserted, must have experienced a "marked increase in . . . schooling and employment. . . . Greater economic and social independence . . . played a role." The therapeutic implications of his study were that to ensure mental health, women should avoid such masculine activities as schooling and paid employment. Dublin concluded that "it is fortunate for mankind that the people who are least likely to lose the will to live are producing and rearing the oncoming generation."[21]

A leading British suicidologist, Peter Sainsbury, explained the gender differential this way: "When the biological and social roles of the two sexes are compared, the female role appears more precisely, and her biological and social functions more harmonized." Males, on the other hand, are "less restricted by social conformity" and are "encouraged" to be individualistic and "aggressive." A man is responsible "for [the] support and welfare of his family" and as a result "he is more subject to the stresses of mobility and change."

Thus, the "male's more arduous social role" explains "the marked liability of the male" for suicide as opposed to females.[22] Such analysis restates the belief that women are happier and more adjusted in their domestic roles than are men who bear the heavier social burden; indeed, when a woman kills herself, it is because she has attempted to act like a man!

The prestigious American Public Health Association's *Mental Disorders/Suicide* (1972) quotes the Sainsbury analysis at length and endorses it, although its authors wonder, almost as an aside, why the rates differ so greatly between the genders, "since women are exposed to some of the same factors" as men, for instance, social isolation, lack of employment, and loss of status.[23] Richard Davis's "Female Labor Force Participation and Suicide" (1981) affirms the conclusions of its predecessors, concluding that "the greater the female labor force participation . . . the greater the rate of suicide."[24]

Thus the dominant explanation for and interpretation of the lower incidence of suicide among women suggests that male suicide results from the stresses inherent in men's roles and responsibilities, while female suicide occurs when women deviate from their less conflicted roles and status. Those women who kill themselves after a man deserts them do so, according to these analyses, because they can no longer fulfill their social functions as mothers and wives.

Kathryn Johnson's (1979) "Durkheim Revisited" is the only study that does not tie lower suicide rates for women to their allegedly less stressful situations. Johnson agrees that "compared to men, women do not appear to have a great 'suicide problem.'" Noting that women historically "participate differently from men" in what Durkheim called "collective life," Johnson endorses the arguments of those who see women inhabiting "different social worlds" from men. She finds, however, that "married employed women have lower suicide rates than unemployed housewives," and suggests that the highest female suicide rates are found among those women who are the most submerged in the family.[25]

Since most women historically have inhabited the "social sphere" of the family, we would expect a much greater incidence of suicide among women than Johnson describes. Indeed, if she were correct, we might anticipate a declining rate for women as social and economic barriers begin to fall. However, the opposite appears to be true.

On the other hand, it is difficult not to be sympathetic to Johnson's reluctance to accept the sexist ideology that seems to inform so many of these explanations for the differential between male and female suicide rates. In short, it seems absurd, in light of all the evidence amassed in the past two decades on "women's roles," to assume that women are "naturally" or "biologically" more content than men. Moreover, the corollary of this assumption—that the increase in suicide among women is the direct result of their abandonment of traditional roles, and its logical extension, that women can avoid suicide to the extent that they return to their "natural" roles—ought to make any researcher look more carefully at the data.

Attempted versus Completed Suicides

Explanations of why women kill themselves less frequently than men do are reinforced in large part by a bias built into official suicide statistics. That is, these data confine themselves to reporting only completed or "successful" suicides. Researchers naturally prefer to rely upon tabulated statistics that can be measured, compared, and grouped in quantifiable categories.[26] As a result, attempted suicides are often neglected when experts formulate their conclusions about the causes of suicide.

We can never know for certain the extent of attempted suicides, but most experts agree that for every completed suicide there are six to eight attempts.[27] Women attempt suicide at a rate approximately 2.3 times greater than do men. On the other hand, men demonstrate the opposite trend: they complete suicide at a rate 2.3 times greater than women.[28] If the numbers of those attempting and completing suicide are added together, the rate differential between genders collapses.

Some researchers, mindful of the exclusion of attempters from the data, justify it, claiming that completers and attempters are substantially distinct. Ronald Maris for instance focuses on the differences in intentions between the two, asserting that attempters expect to be discovered and saved, while completers are less likely to place themselves in a position that allows for intervention in their actions. These differences, argues Maris, demand that attempters and completers be studied separately.[29]

There are many examples that seem to support Maris's conclusion. Nevertheless, differences in intention are not always reflected in official suicide statistics. It is not always clear that a particular intention ends in a desired result. For instance, many persons intend to kill themselves, but by chance they survive. Because official statistics only measure results, these cases are not counted as suicides.*

The suicide attempt of Anna Brewster, a thirty-two-year-old single San Diego schoolteacher, in January 1898, is one among many cases that exemplify the limitations of official definitions. There was little question that when Brewster took a room at the Commercial Hotel and fired a pistol at pointblank range into her temple that she expected to die. But the outcome was different:

> Immediately afterward Miss Brewster burst from the room, holding a handkerchief to her right temple. . . . Miss Brewster pointed to a note lying on the table and said, "There are the directions, I have shot myself." To Mrs. Birdsall, who was immediately called, Miss Brewster said, "I am tired of life. I want to end it all. That's the only reason."[30]

Brewster's note was the type that experts such as Maris have identified as the kind left by individuals who intend to die:[31] "It is my earnest wish that my body be taken to the morgue and dispensed of from there—and not taken to my address. I wish the least possible expense and trouble. No funeral. No services." Both physicians who examined her "agreed that the bullet was imbedded in the brain . . . and that the chances for recovery were very dubious." Nevertheless, Brewster did not die, and thus her suicide attempt was ignored by official statistics.[32]

Others die from the complications of a botched attempt. Generally neither the coroner's report nor the death certificate will report the death as a suicide, because no matter how much the person's behavior had set up a chain of events leading to death, suicide was not the immediate cause of death. For instance, a person may not succumb to an intentional drug overdose, but die later of a cause such as pneumonia brought on by the attempt. This has special significance for women because they are more than twice as likely as men to employ poisons or drugs in suicide attempts.[33]

Clara Dudley, a thirty-four-year-old proprietor of "a house of ill-repute," attempted to commit suicide on 1 January 1899 "by swallowing a quantity of morphine." According to newspaper reports, Dudley had "made previous attempts to commit suicide, having on one occasion, several months ago, inhaled gas. She was almost dead

---

*Although the examples that follow are taken from nineteenth-century cases, they are parallel in every respect to contemporary cases.

when the door of her room was burst open, and it was with the greatest of difficulty that she was brought back to life." In her latest try, reported the *San Diego Union,* Dudley lost consciousness, but according to her doctor "she showed much improvement." Five days later Clara Dudley died of pneumonia brought on by her suicide attempt. Both the coroner's report and her death certificate list pneumonia as the cause of death. Officially, she and countless others like her are not recorded as suicides.[34]

Both of these scenarios, as exemplified by Brewster and Dudley, affect the reported differences in gender suicide because women tend to survive suicide attempts more frequently than men do and they also tend to die more often than men do of the prolonged effects of suicide attempts.

Additionally, official statistics cannot measure the difference between conscious and unconscious intentions. Who is to say that only conscious behavior constitutes a suicide? Dorcas Antle was a sixty-two-year-old widow who only two months previously had moved from Illinois to live with her son in Chula Vista, California. On 21 April 1895 Antle "took a dose of strychnine by mistake at 9 o'clock Saturday night and died in great agony twenty minutes later. She was in the habit of taking a sleeping powder upon retiring, but upon this occasion took a strychnine powder from the shelf and swallowed it." The county coroner ruled that the deceased died from "strychnine poisoning; the strychnine being administered by mistake." The coroner's evidence rested upon the deposition of Antle's son, a physician.[35] Of course, given the paucity of available information, we cannot possibly determine whether Dorcas Antle actually made an error. Nevertheless, as a recent widow and a new arrival in California who suffered from insomnia, she fits the category of those at high risk of taking their own lives.

The case of Dorcas Antle raises another issue about the reporting of suicide, especially as it relates to women. In this situation, the coroner relied upon the testimony of Antle's son, a physician, to determine whether her actions were suicidal or accidental. Children, even when they are physicians, have a strong inclination to cover up a parent's suicide.

Finally, many suicides, especially women's, are not reported.*

---

*Because it was almost immediately covered up by her husband, few are aware that America's first British suicide, Dorothy May Bradford (the wife of the Pilgrim leader William Brad-

Coroners, physicians, and others responsible for determining whether a particular death is a suicide are already tied to an ideology that differentiates women's motives from men's. Such preconceptions are bound to influence the collection of official statistics.

Jack Douglas found the impulse to misrepresent women's suicides to be endemic in the reporting of suicide because "the *meanings* of male suicides and of female suicides are different in Western societies." Social forces outside the family such as unemployment are generally perceived as the causes of men's suicides, while strains within the family are most often held responsible for women's. When a woman commits suicide, Douglas argues, her husband has "a much greater incentive . . . than a female in the same situation to attempt to conceal the suicidal action."[36]

All this suggests that official statistics provide an unreliable guide for the investigation of suicidal motivations. Even if these data presented an accurate accounting of completed suicides, they nevertheless offer an incomplete picture of suicidal intentions. What we are left with is a closed loop in which the assumptions that inform judgments about whether an individual act is a suicide are also presented as the reasons for the gender variations uncovered in rates of suicide. Ironically, the statistics that systematically exclude many women are employed as evidence to explain why women are more adjusted than men to their social roles.*

Lethality of Method

If men more often complete suicide than women do, the reason may be that men more often select more lethal methods.† In the United States this translates into the fact that the majority of

---

ford), was a woman. See William Bradford, *Of Plymouth Plantation, 1620–1647*, ed. by Samuel Eliot Morison (New York: Alfred A. Knopf, 1979), pp. xxix, 64.

*As we have seen, experts have found support for rather traditional views in the alleged maleness of suicide. Some have suggested that the way for women to guarantee their own mental health and to avoid self-destruction lies in the acceptance of traditional values, particularly those of the patriarchal family. The irony here of course is that this same data indicates that "traditional values" have contributed to a much higher rate of attempted suicide by women than by men. These statistics could be used to demonstrate that women are less content with their social roles than men are with theirs. Curiously, no suicide study has ever come to that conclusion.

†Maris, *Pathways to Suicide*, pp. 269–270 defines firearms, hanging, and jumping as highly lethal, and poisoning, cutting wrists, gassing, and most other methods as being of low lethality. There is, however, no necessary correlation between lethality and inflicted pain. An instantaneous death by firearms involves less pain to the victim than slow death by strychnine.

Table 4.2.
PERCENTAGES OF SUICIDE BY METHOD AND GENDER, SAN DIEGO COUNTY, 1880–1972

	Firearms		Poisons[a]		Hanging		Other	
	m	f	m	f	m	f	m	f
1880–1900	50.0	29.4	19.5	47.1	10.9	0	19.6	23.5
1911–1925	48.0	26.0	27.0	57.5	9.0	12.3	17.0	4.4
1938–1942	46.8	23.5	5.1	37.7	12.3	9.8	35.9	29.4
1948–1952	44.6	25.4	13.8	31.3	15.9	13.4	25.7	29.9
1967–1972	55.1	19.1	19.6	59.2	8.8	6.8	16.5	14.9

SOURCES: San Diego County, Coroner's Reports, 1870–1980, San Diego County Coroner's Office; Anita M. Muhl, "America's Greatest Suicide Problem: A Study of Over 500 Cases in San Diego," *Psychoanalytic Review* 14 (1927): 320; Aubrey Wendling, "Suicides in the City of San Diego, 1938–1942, 1948–1952," unpublished ms.
[a]Does not include asphyxiation by carbon monoxide, but includes other gases.

successful male suicides have employed firearms.[37] This is a trend that can be identified historically.

In what seems to have been the first systematic attempt to investigate suicide in the United States, E. K. Hunt found that women chose less lethal methods than men. Hunt reported that in 1843, 67.5 percent of male suicides selected highly lethal methods—the use of firearms, cutting their throats, or hanging themselves. On the other hand, only 36.6 percent of "successful" women suicides employed these means. None of the women used firearms, from which Hunt concluded that women had a "horror of guns or pistols."[38]

The *American Journal of Insanity*'s analysis of the incidence of suicide in New York State for 1848 concluded "that females rarely have recourse to firearms . . . as a means of committing suicide. Hanging, drowning, and poisoning are the modes which they most frequently employ."[39] According to Rhodes's 1876 study, men who killed themselves showed "a tendency toward violent methods," while women selected "pacific" means for suicide. "Drowning and poisoning are the favorite modes of getting rid of life in the case of women," Rhodes found, and "throat-cutting, hanging, and shooting those of the men."[40]

A century later, Alan Marks and Thomas Abernathy still found "that female attempters and completers most often use drugs-poison while male completers most often use firearms."[41] In San Diego County approximately one-half of all successful male suicides for the past one hundred years have relied upon firearms (see Table 4.2). National statistics reflect this same pattern.[42]

Table 4.3.
SUICIDE RATES FOR FIREARM USE BY GENDER, SAN DIEGO COUNTY, 1880–1972 (rates per 100,000)

	Firearms		All methods	
	m	f	m	f
1880–1900	21.3	1.9	42.5	6.7
1911–1925	32.6	3.1	67.3	12.0
1938–1942	17.3	3.0	36.5	12.6
1948–1952	13.4	2.8	29.8	10.7
1967–1972	13.1	2.7	23.8	14.4

SOURCES: San Diego County, Coroner's Reports, 1870–1980, San Diego County Coroner's Office; Anita M. Muhl, "America's Greatest Suicide Problem: A Study of Over 500 Cases in San Diego," *Psychoanalytic Review* 14 (1927): 320; Aubrey Wendling, "Suicides in the City of San Diego, 1938–1942, 1948–1952," unpublished ms.

Women tend to choose less lethal methods, particularly poisons. For instance, Hunt's 1843 study found that 63 percent of completed female suicides chose poisons.[43] The percentage of women who complete their suicides using firearms in San Diego County has varied, but it has remained well below the percentage of women who turn to poisons. At the same time, studies of the nation as a whole find "an increasing proportion of women who are suiciding by firearms."[44]

Percentages can be misleading. To be convincing statistically, suicide completion rates should be compared to rates that measure the use of firearms per one hundred thousand of the living population. When this is done for San Diego County, the results are striking. Table 4.3 demonstrates that over the last century, when the use of firearms by both men and women has increased, so has the rate of completed suicides. Of course, similar studies should be undertaken in other jurisdictions before such findings can be considered conclusive.

Most psychoanalysts would insist that the method chosen for suicide reveals a great deal about both the intention and fantasies that particular individuals have about suicide. Those who choose "less lethal" methods unconsciously may seek intervention or may hope to be saved at the last moment from the consequences of their acts.*

---

*The suicide of the poet Sylvia Plath is one of the most famous and tragic instances of an attempter who expected to be discovered and restrained from killing herself. Only a bizzare set of unforeseen circumstances transformed Plath's attempt into a completion. See A. A. Alvarez, *The Savage God: A Study of Suicide* (New York: Random House, 1972), pp. 3–42.

But as Robert Jay Lifton, Jean Baechler, and others have pointed out, all suicides (completed as well as attempted) have fantasy aims, not the least of which involve the imagination of others' reactions to their suicidal acts. Lifton describes this as a "quest for a future," while according to Baechler, suicide is a form of behavior or a strategy "that seeks and finds the solution to an existential problem."[45]

Moreover, we must not neglect the equally strong evidence that choices of method (as well as fantasies) are also determined by the material reality in which the suicidally inclined find themselves. "The relation of method," argues Herbert Hendin, "cannot be understood without reference to the cultural context in which suicide occurs." In New York City, jumping from buildings accounts for 50 percent of suicides completed by blacks. "So much of the life in Harlem is lived in and on top of these tenements," writes Hendin, "that they occupy the conscious and unconscious life of their inhabitants and come to provide a tragic setting for black suicide."[46]

He suggests that a similar analysis should be brought to bear on the relationship between firearms and female suicide completions. Because firearms historically have been less available to women than poisons, the fact that women more frequently employ poisons to kill themselves has a material as well as a fantasy content.* "The sociocultural acceptance of guns in the United States," Hendin believes, "is related to the frequency with which they are used for suicide."[47] This connection explains why men, whose use of firearms has greater social acceptance, generally are more likely than women to resort to guns. The exception that supports this view is found in the American South. In that region, "where guns are most accepted as a part of the household and where children are often introduced to their use by their parents," Marks and Abernathy found that "firearms are used by both sexes more frequently [for suicide completion] than in the rest of the country."[48]

In European countries, where suicide by firearms is far less frequent than in the United States, males, like their American counterparts, complete suicide at about two to three times the rate of females. Moreover, throughout Europe without exception, men

*A recent study has found that women chemists are five times more likely to complete suicide than other women. This provides substance to the claim that when women have easy access to lethal methods, their rate of suicide increases. See Malcom W. Browne, "Women in Chemistry: Higher Suicide Risk Seen," *New York Times*, 4 August 1987.

choose more lethal methods than women do and male use of firearms far exceeds that of women in every jurisdiction. Even in Denmark, where firearms are forbidden, 15 percent of male completers,
as compared with only one percent of females, used guns to kill
themselves.[49]

Real Differences

As we have seen, suicide among men generally has been portrayed as originating from economic and social conditions, while
both "successful" and attempted suicides by women were much
more likely to have been attributed to interpersonal or familial relations. Thus experts have concluded that the male suicide rate
serves as a barometer of social and economic well-being, but attempted suicide by women, because of its cause, is a private matter
requiring less public concern. One can, however, legitimately distinguish completed from attempted suicides without endorsing the
views of those suicide experts who have uncovered in women's
lower rates of completed suicide a justification for and an endorsement of the maintenance of traditional gender role separation.

Although it would be misleading not to point out the flaws in
official suicide statistics, it would be foolish to assume that we ought
to make no distinctions whatsoever between female and male suicides. Women are different from men. Women's history has taught
us that socialization to prescribed roles has been very effective. Both
men and women historically have internalized social roles and
gender-specific values and it would be absurd to contend that these
were not manifested also in self-destructive behaviors. Value-laden
as they are, the assumptions that suicide experts have projected onto
women's behavior do reflect a certain level of social reality. The fact
that increasing numbers of women have questioned these established norms may have heightened rather than diminished the ambivalence and guilt that necessarily accompany such challenges. It is
arguable that a nexus exists between alienation from traditional
roles and completed suicides by women. Attempting but not suc-
ceeding at suicide, on the other hand, meshes with perceived social
values.

One of the criticisms of official statistics offered by Douglas was
that husbands have more compelling reasons to hide a wife's suicide

than wives have to hide a husband's. According to Douglas, this is because when a woman kills herself, it is seen as a judgment on her husband, but when a husband kills himself, it is taken as a legitimate criticism of some particular social condition arising outside the family. What Douglas neglects to consider is the very great extent to which both women and men have internalized these values and the extent to which such internalization shapes behavior.[50]

In the Middle Ages strictures against suicide were based on the belief that a person's body was not her/his own, but God's or those above her/him in the hierarchy. Women, like serfs, have been and continue to be (as the current controversy over abortion indicates) socialized to the belief that their bodies are not theirs to dispose of.[51] Self-destruction must be preceded by a sense that a "self" exists. To the extent that women have internalized those patriarchal values that have defined women's role as "selflessness," we would expect suicide completion not to be a strategy as easily selected by women as by men. Carol Gilligan has found that when it comes to concepts of the self, women "reveal the existence of a distinct moral language . . . which defines the moral problem as one of obligation to exercise care and avoid hurt. The inflicting of hurt is considered selfish and immoral in its reflection of unconcern, while the expression of care is seen as the fulfillment of moral responsibility."[52] Thus one of the major restraints on mothers and wives taking their lives is their belief that they have a duty to live to care for their husbands and children. The idea that their children would be motherless seems to be a much greater restraining influence on women than the fear by men that their children would be fatherless.

Attempting suicide, on the other hand, has been viewed as a legitimate strategy for women to gain attention for their grievances. Since most women historically have been subsumed in the familial sphere (even when they work outside it), the issues that have informed their suicide attempts have revolved around familial matters. Moreover, to the extent that women have been taught that their intrinsic value can be reduced to their bodies, they have also learned to use their bodies to get what they want.[53] Thus, the threat to withhold their bodies (by threatening or attempting suicide) is a powerful (and often successful) strategy for women to deal with perceived loss.

When men, on the other hand, attempt, but fail to complete suicide, they often are viewed as weak and subject to ridicule (see Figures 4.3 and 4.4). Not only have experts assumed that men commit suicide when their careers fail or when they suffer public disgrace, but also such a reaction sometimes is tacitly encouraged, if not expected. To the extent that women internalize values that previously were prescribed for men, one would expect to find, as statistics seem to reflect, a growing rate of suicide completion among women.

Of course, the difference between suicide attempters and suicide completers is not genetically programmed by gender. Many men have used the threat of suicide to manipulate those around them and many women (most likely many more than official statistics report) intended to kill themselves because they believed they had exhausted alternative strategies.

THE TEENAGE SUICIDE EPIDEMIC

The analysis of gender suicide provides a context for exploring the claims that the United States is currently experiencing an epidemic of teenage suicides. As in the case of gender suicide, an historical view provides a useful perspective.

Beginning with the Puritans, successive generations of observers uncovered youth suicide epidemics that, like current analyses, invariably connected the rise in suicides to the tensions of contemporary life. In 1699 Cotton Mather announced the first in what was to become a series of alleged epidemics of teenage suicides. Mather attributed suicides among New England's youth to a deterioration of parental authority.[54] At the beginning of the nineteenth century, the Reverend Samuel Miller of New York published two widely distributed sermons that claimed "that the young are most apt to fall into the crime of suicide," which "has become alarmingly frequent in our land, and in our city." Miller attributed this epidemic to a breakdown in moral values that resulted from individual selfishness. Suicide, he explained, is inevitable when a society "sacrifices every thing on the altar of *individual feeling*. It is a practice which reverses all the doctrines of social benevolence, sets up as a principle of action the detestable maxim, that private caprice and private enjoyment

Noodles's Attempts at Suicide.

[A MODERN PATENT MEDICINE ADVERTISEMENT.]

Noodles, being tired of life, tries hanging.

Failing to accomplish his purpose in this,

Tries dashing brains out against paper imitation of Granite Wall.

Head penetrates wall. Is slashed at by Gent from Arkansas.

Narrow escape. Prepares to blow brains out.

Another failure—misses the mark,

And painfully disturbs quiet Gent above.

Attempts to cut throat with Bar of Soap.

VOL. XVIII.—No. 105.—D D*

Figures 4.3, 4.4 Noodles's Attempts at Suicide
SOURCE: *Harper's New Monthly Magazine* 18 (February 1859), 429–430.

HARPER'S NEW MONTHLY MAGAZINE.

Boot-black fortunately enters with Boots.

Noodles rushes down stairs—out of house—

Into Drug Store—demanding, from Small Boy, "Pint Laudanum, to kill rats."

Boy vanishes. Noodles frantically seizes bottle of something.

Swallows contents. Experiences a glorious reaction—instead of Death, Life!

Swallowed bottle Dr. Dipps's Eradicator. Saved! Once more himself!

Presents the Doctor with Certificate certifying to his Miraculous Cure.

Ever after, when depressed, drinks a bottle of Dr. Dipps, and Shoots his own Daguerreotype.

are to be regarded as more worthy objects of pursuit than public happiness."[55]

By mid-century physicians and the press had replaced ministers as producers of jeremiads on suicide. In 1859 the *New York Times* warned that "nocturnal dissipation and the infamous solitary vices that blazon themselves publicly in the shrunken, pale, and prematurely-aged faces of so many young men . . . are sowing for us a horrid harvest of suicides at an early day."[56] Two decades later, a respected New York physician attributed still another alleged outbreak of suicide among "young girls and men" to the "bad examples" that urban life presented to "the younger generation," who daily are exposed to "immorality, engendered by vice attendant upon civilization." Among youth in large cities, "it is much easier for a seed of sin to take root," he argued, "than one of virtue."[57]

Of course, these early pronouncements do not demonstrate that perceptions of a contemporary teenage epidemic are inaccurate nor should they be used to trivialize the tragic deaths of young people. Suicide (after accidents and homicide) is after all now the third greatest killer of teenagers. In large part this is because teenagers no longer die from other causes. With the eradication of childhood diseases and the decline of tuberculosis and cancer mortality among teenagers, accidents, homicides, and suicides have moved up as causes of death.

The much-publicized fact that the percentage of teenage suicides has increased dramatically is misleading because the base figure is low. The addition of only a few teenage suicides may translate into a very large percentage increase. On the other hand, because older males already constitute the largest group of suicides (see Figure 4.5), an even greater numerical increase among this group results in a much smaller percentage increase than for teenagers. In an investigation of suicides in Cook County, Illinois, from 1959 to 1979, Maris discovered that only 2 percent of all suicides were under age twenty.[58]

Rates, unlike percentages, are more accurate indicators of suicide incidence, but, as we have seen, the official statistics from which these rates are extracted are themselves suspect. The youth suicide rate has risen from 4.2 per 100,000 in 1955 to 12.5 per 100,000 in 1982. The current teenage rate (12 per 100,000) is relatively low compared to high risk groups like white males sixty-five to seventy-four,

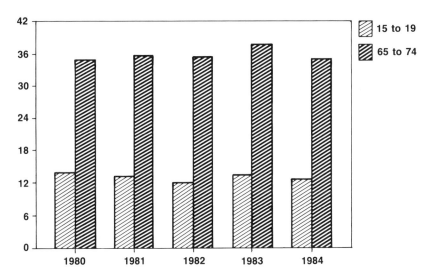

Figure 4.5 Youth versus Elder Suicides, California, 1980–1984 (males, rates per 100,000)
SOURCE: California Department of Health Services, *Suicides in California, 1980–1984*, prepared by Martin Green (Sacramento: Department of Health Services, 1986), p. 20.

for whom the incidence of suicide is approximately 35 per 100,000 (see Figure 4.5).*

While the teenage rate remains lower than the national rate for all ages (13.3), the twenty-year trend seems unmistakable.[59] However, most commentators seem to be unaware that these same data show that from 1900 to 1908, teenage suicide rose steadily from 8 per 100,000 to 13.9 and then declined slowly to 6 per 100,000 by 1924, remaining more or less at that level until 1960.[60] After studying these fluctuations, Paul C. Holinger of the University of Chicago concluded that "the rate of teenage suicides has risen whenever there was a large percentage of adolescents relative to the rest of the population." Rather than resulting from a breakdown in values, Holinger argued that "competition—in school, sports and jobs—

*This disparity has led Maris to suggest "that one of the keys to suicide prevention is not finding out why children and adolescents suicide; rather it is determining why they usually do *not* suicide." Although older Americans remain at greater risk of suicide than teenagers, "it is curious," writes Maris, "that so little interest is shown in suicide among the aged." *Pathways to Suicide*, pp. 42, 44– 45.

may be the trigger for some young people who don't make the grade."[61]

In November 1986, the National Centers for Disease Control issued a preliminary report that cautioned that reports of a youth suicide epidemic were based on a misreading of official data. The CDC explained that a "statistical quirk" in the 1984 data had misled suicide experts to conclude that the rate of teenage suicide was increasing when it actually was decreasing. Contrary to the much-publicized epidemic of the 1980s, the CDC found that suicide rates among fifteen- to twenty-four-year-old Americans had been dropping continuously since peaking in 1977. The upward drift in 1984 was, the center concluded, only a fleeting blip in a steady downward trend (see Figure 4.6).[62]

Proclamations of American youth suicide epidemics are at least as old as the earliest English settlements and as historically common as warnings that urban life breeds immorality. Because statistics reflect the values of those who collect them, historical comparisons are difficult and uncertain. Especially when it comes to suicide, claims of epidemics rest upon comparisons with past incidences. Even if the official statistics were to show that teenage suicides actually had increased, we should be restrained in extracting social meanings from this data.

One possible explanation of contemporary perceptions of a youth suicide epidemic suggests itself. After the First World War, as popularized versions of psychoanalysis captured the American imagination, suicide by young people became increasingly associated with "bad parenting." Seen as a judgment on parents, teenage suicide became a taboo subject and as a result it was largely hidden from public view. Because many physicians and coroners were sympathetic, they were willing to aid those families who wished to conceal a teenager's suicide. Since the early 1970s, a new biological paradigm has replaced bad parenting as the explanation of mental disorders, including suicide. This biological paradigm has been placed alongside vague but highly articulated pronouncements of the disintegration of social and moral values. Pitted against these two powerful forces—biology and impersonal social forces—parents increasingly perceive themselves as being powerless to influence their children's emotional lives.[63] As a result, parents are less frequently blamed by themselves and others for their children's suicides.[64] What we may

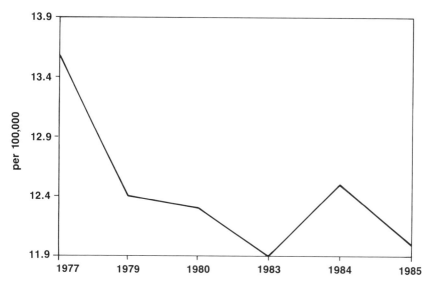

Figure 4.6 Youth Suicide (15–24 years old), United States, 1977–1985
SOURCE: U.S. National Center for Health Statistics, *Monthly Vital Statistics Report, Final Mortality Statistics* (Washington, D.C.: GPO, annual).

be experiencing as an epidemic more likely reflects a breakdown of an earlier reluctance to discuss or admit teenage suicide.

What all of this suggests is not that teenage suicides should be ignored. Like the rate for women, the rate for teenage suicide attempts far exceeds suicide completions. And importantly, a number of researchers have reported a significant increase in suicidal behavior among the young. "Mental health professionals," says James Selkin, president of the American Association of Suicidology, "are seeing a dramatic increase of depression and self-destructive behavior in adolescents. This includes alcohol and drug abuse, runaways, vandalism, teen-age pregnancy and violent crime."[65] "It is as important to see the suicidal intentions that may be hidden by homicide," writes Hendin, "as to see the homicidal intentions that may be concealed by suicide."[66]

CONCLUSION

The portrayal of suicide as a male behavior or the perception of a teenage suicide epidemic often tells us more about the assumptions that inform the collection of official statistics than it does about the etiology of suicide. The epidemiological conclusions about suicide are no more value free than the ideologies that inform them. The distortions found in official suicide statistics are not, of course, confined to gender and age. Rather, allegations about gender or youth suicide are symptomatic of the limitations inherent in all suicide statistics.

On the other hand, these statistics are not valueless, primarily because, like the values that inform them, they do reflect and reinforce social behavior. Men do complete suicide more frequently than women do. Women do attempt suicide more often than men do. And whenever social roles that historically have separated men from women begin to narrow, we can find alterations in suicide between the genders. Although warnings of a teen suicide epidemic may be exaggerated, evidence does suggest an increase in suicidal behavior, if not its completion, among America's youth.

In short, we must not ignore the fact that strategies that do not necessarily result in death can be as "suicidal" in terms of intention as those actions that do result in death. What we must do if we wish to understand the etiology of suicide is to expand our vision from completed suicide to include suicidal behavior. If we wish to examine suicide, insists British sociologist Steve Taylor, we "must widen the familiar question 'why do people kill themselves?' to include the broader question: 'why do so many people engage in acts of self damage which may result in death?'" For Taylor, the term "suicidal" must include "any deliberate act of self damage, or potential self damage, where the individual has to await an outcome, and cannot be sure of survival."[67] Perhaps Taylor throws his net too wide, but his general argument seems well-taken in light of the way in which an emphasis on suicide completion has distorted our view of gender suicide.

The goal of almost all investigations of suicide is to develop explanations for its etiology. Suicide completion is only one possible outcome of suicidal behavior. As long as studies continue to emphasize suicide completion instead of suicidal behavior, we will continue to be trapped in a maze of circular reasoning in which the result of some self-destructive behavior is relied upon to explain the causes for all self-destructive behavior. Certainly if we wish to understand why similar circumstances do not always result in suicide, we must examine suicidal behavior, not just outcome.

5

TWO STRATEGIES

THIS book began with a discussion of the suicide of a nineteen-year-old Hungarian immigrant, Max White. White's diary and suicide note provided ample evidence of his profound sense of unresolved loss. Testimony at his inquest revealed that White's mother had died when he was a child (some time before his twelfth birthday) and that when he was thirteen, young Max was sent by his father from his native Hungary to live with his maternal uncle in San Diego.[1] Although White had many legitimate complaints, including his inability to find employment, his diary also was filled with exaggerated ramblings about imagined enemies. He suspected conspiracies involving people with whom he had only a casual acquaintance. And he coupled his own suicide with threats of revenge against those he imagined had plotted his unhappy fate.

Both Durkheim and Freud would have agreed that, as in White's case, suicide is often accompanied by a combination of unresolved grief, an exaggerated belief in the hopelessness of one's condition, fear of conspiracies by others, and a wish for revenge. Both connected this behavior to loss. For Durkheim, the loss resulted from an individual's social and cultural alienation; for Freud, the loss resulted from disconnection from one's self. What neither explained to anyone's satisfaction was why the type of loss that they described did not always result in suicide.

Two case studies, those of Meriwether Lewis and of Abraham

Lincoln, speak to this issue. Both of these men experienced extreme loss; both reacted to it in ways that parallel Max White's response. But Lewis killed himself and Lincoln did not. These two examples illustrate that suicidal behavior* is both strategic and self-destructive. That is, anger, grief, a sense of hopelessness, risk-taking, and even threatening suicide ought to be viewed as strategies that individuals and groups adopt to help them master the social disorganization and ego disintegration that loss both brings about and exacerbates. We will look at these examples.

All strategies for dealing with loss, as Freud suggested, are reflective of mourning. What is crucial is not the material fact of loss itself but the success or failure of available strategies for "mourning." Lewis and Lincoln serve as compelling examples of the proposition that the success or failure of these strategies depends upon a confluence of historical possibilities and personal experience as both connect with psychological and constitutional factors.

Although neither Lewis nor Lincoln were "typical" Americans, their responses to loss are illustrative of the cultural bounds that inform suicidal behavior. The fact that both of these examples are taken from exceptional life histories does not diminish the argument, but rather magnifies it. I selected late eighteenth- and nineteenth-century rather than contemporary cases to demonstrate the importance of historical perspective for a psychocultural approach to suicide. Nevertheless, I employ historical examples here to shed light on the causes of suicide rather than to explain their significance in historical context.

THE SUICIDE OF MERIWETHER LEWIS

In November 1809 newspapers throughout the United States reported the startling news that Meriwether Lewis, the thirty-five-year-old governor of Upper Louisiana Territory and the hero of the Lewis and Clark Expedition, had committed suicide in a rude country inn in southcentral Tennessee.[2]

*Building on the discussion in the preceding chapter, I define suicidal behavior as a set of actions or strategies either intended or subintended that *sometimes, but not always*, results in death.

Three years earlier on 12 September 1806, Lewis, William Clark, and their "corps of discovery" had received a heroes' welcome as they reentered St. Louis, Missouri, after traversing the North American continent along the Missouri River over the Rockies to the Columbia's mouth at the Pacific and back again. At thirty-three, Lewis was a national hero without equal in the young republic.[3]

Rewarded with the governorship of the Upper Louisiana Territory, Lewis arrived in St. Louis in March 1808 to assume his new duties.[4] He soon discovered that it had been easier to guide forty-one men across a hostile continent than to satisfy the divergent demands converging on his executive office. The governor's authority and popularity were continually undercut by his chief assistant, Territorial Secretary Frederick Bates. Appointed to his position a month before Lewis's nomination, Bates administered the territory for over a year while Lewis procrastinated in the East. Lewis's early decisions to reverse some of Bates's Indian policies and to remove some of the secretary's appointees created tension between the two men. Mutual resentment grew into personal hostility, to the point where a duel was averted only by the intervention of Clark, now commander-in-chief of the territorial militia. Being not without influence and friends, Bates used both to circulate reports alleging the governor's incompetence. Moreover, Lewis's authoritarian manner undercut the initial popularity of his appointment in both St. Louis and Washington. Failing to establish a local political base, Lewis managed the territorial government like an army corps, lending credence to Bates's charge that he was "altogether military, and he never can . . . succeed in any other profession."[5]

The War Department seemed no better satisfied with the governor. Secretary of War William Eustis refused to honor the payment of various sums that Lewis had authorized without prior approval from the federal government, claiming that the governor had used public funds to support private commercial ventures. Adding to Lewis's personal financial plight were his extensive land speculations in and around St. Louis. These purchases created obligations that amounted to almost three times his annual salary, and by the fall of 1809 Lewis began selling off his holdings to cover his increasingly large debts. His plight was so extreme that he was forced to borrow money from Clark to pay a $49.00 medical bill; during his final months in St. Louis, he relied on loans from friends to meet daily expenses. The actions of the War Department pushed him to the verge of bankruptcy.[6]

The consequences of these political and financial troubles spilled over into Lewis's personal life. Desiring to bring his widowed mother Mary Marks from Virginia to live with him in St. Louis, he purchased land upon which he planned to build a residence for his mother and himself, but the project failed when the property had to be sold to satisfy his debts.[7] Depressed and angry, his political and personal integrity severely damaged, Lewis resolved to go to Washington to confront the secretary of war and the new president, James Madison. On 4 September 1809, having given power of attorney to his closest associates, he left St. Louis.[8]

On 11 September on the Mississippi south of St. Louis, the governor apparently for the first time in his life wrote a last will and testament, leaving his entire estate to his mother.[9] Lewis planned to go by river to New Orleans and then by sea to the nation's capital. While on route he reportedly made two attempts to kill himself. When he arrived at Fort Pickering near Memphis on 15 September, the commanding officer, Captain Gilbert C. Russell, found Lewis to be intoxicated and "in a state of mental derangement." Uncertain that the governor was emotionally fit to travel, Russell insisted that he rest at Fort Pickering until he recovered. Remaining there for two weeks, Lewis promised "never to drink any more spirits or use snuff again."[10]

Although Lewis's condition seemed to improve, he altered his plans and decided to travel overland to Washington. The British, he feared, might waylay him if he sailed from New Orleans.[11] On 29 September he departed with James Neelly, the federal agent for the Chickasaw nation, who was traveling to Nashville. Lewis's personal servant John Pernier and Neelly's slave Tom accompanied them. Soon Lewis began drinking heavily and he acted so strange that Neelly decided that the party should rest for two days.[12] By 8 October they reached the Tennessee River. The following day two of their horses escaped. Lewis and the two servants went ahead, agreeing to wait for Neelly at the first dwelling inhabited by whites, while he searched for the missing horses.

Lewis, Pernier, and Tom reached the homestead of Robert Grinder about sunset on the tenth. Grinder's Stand was a frequent resting place for travelers along the Nachez Trace. Grinder was away, but his wife took the party in and fed them supper. During and after dinner Lewis appeared incoherent and Mrs. Grinder remembered he was extremely agitated. Lewis retired to the room reserved for guests, while the servants stayed in the barn. Mrs. Grinder, her daughter, and their servants slept in the main house. According to Neelly, who arrived the next morning, Mrs. Grinder informed him that about three o'clock in the morning "she heard two pistols fire off in the Governor's room." She immediately awakened the servants, who found that Lewis "had shot himself in the head with one pistol, and a little below the breast with the other." Lewis, still alive, reportedly looked up at his servant Pernier and said, "I have done the business my good Servant give me some water." A short time later he died.[13]

In early Spring 1811, an ornithologist, Alexander Wilson, who was cataloguing birds for his *American Ornithology*, stopped at Grinder's Stand and interviewed Mrs. Grinder about the circumstances of Lewis's death. According to Wilson, Mrs. Grinder, "considerably alarmed" by Lewis's behavior, could not sleep and sat in the kitchen next to Lewis's room listening to him "walking backwards and forwards . . . for several hours talking aloud . . . like a lawyer." She then heard a pistol fire "and something heavy fall to the floor" and the words "Oh Lord." Immediately, "she heard another pistol" and a few minutes later outside the kitchen door Lewis called out, "O madam! give me some water and heal my wounds!" The walls of the Grinder's cabin were made of unplastered logs and the terrified woman watched through the cracks as Lewis staggered outside, "crawled for some distance, and raised himself by the side of a tree." Lewis returned to his room and again approached the kitchen door, wanting water. Mrs. Grinder waited petrified until daybreak when she roused the servants, who found Lewis "lying on the bed." The governor "uncovered his side, and showed them where the bullet had entered; a piece of his forehead was blown off, and had exposed his brains, without having bled much." Lewis "begged they take a rifle and blow out his brains." His last words, according to Wilson's report, were "I am no coward; but I am so strong, so hard to die."[14]

Although he was not a witness to the act, Captain Russell at Jefferson's request recounted what he had learned about the circumstances of Lewis's death. While Russell's version varied in details from Mrs. Grinder's, his conclusion confirmed hers. After everyone had retired, Lewis had loaded his pistols and "discharged one against his forehead without much effect." Then, "he discharged the other against his breast where the ball entered and passing downward thro' his body came out low near the backbone." He then staggered to Mrs. Grinder's door asking for water, but "her husband being absent and having heard the report of the pistols she was greatly alarmed and made no answer." When day broke, Lewis's servant found him "sitting up in his bed . . . busily engaged in cutting himself [with his razor] from head to foot." Before he died, Lewis said he wanted to kill himself and "to deprive his enemies the pleasure and honor of doing it." [15]

What led Lewis to take his life? As we have seen, by the early nineteenth century most Americans connected suicide with insanity or at the very least severe emotional distress. And like other diseases, suicide was assumed to result from a combination of constitutional and environmental factors.

Thomas Jefferson, who had known Lewis since Lewis's childhood, attributed the suicide to "a constitutional disposition" to "depressions of the mind" that was "inherited by him from his father." The pressures of urban life, Jefferson believed, exacerbated these tendencies. Whenever Lewis lived in a city, Jefferson noted, he exhibited symptoms of depression. The move to St. Louis in 1808 fit this pattern. "Lewis had from early life been subject to hypochondriac affections," Jefferson wrote. "While he lived with me in Washington, I observed at times sensible depressions of mind. During his Western expedition the constant exertion . . . suspended these distressing affections; but," Jefferson concluded, "after his establishment in sedentary occupations they returned upon him with redoubled vigor." [16]

When he learned of Lewis's suicide, his expedition collaborator William Clark proclaimed, "O! I fear the weight of his mind has overcome him." [17] Lewis's friend, the artist Charles Willson Peale, wrote to his son that Lewis had taken his life because "he had been sometime past in bad health and showed evident signs of disarrangement, & that having drawn bills for the payment of public services, which were protested because no specific funds had been provided, this mortification completed his despair." [18] Lewis's enemy, Louisiana Territorial Secretary Frederick Bates, whose actions others claimed had driven Lewis from office, likewise attributed the suicide to insanity. "Gov. Lewis," wrote Bates, "on his way to Washington became *insane*." "Mental derangement," Bates insisted, was at the root of both Lewis's "political miscarriages" and his subsequent suicide.[19]

The national press affirmed these explanations. Although Lewis recently had experienced severe financial and political reverses, *The National Intelligencer* rejected the possibility that these "alone, could have produced such deplorable consequences." Rather, it connected Lewis's suicide to physical deterioration: "Governor Lewis [was] . . . very weak, from a recent illness at Natchez, and showed signs of mental derangement."[20] Like the *Intelligencer*, newspapers throughout the country, reflecting the popular belief that suicide was connected with illness, reported Lewis's death with no hint of condemnation. *The Nashville Clarion* reported that Lewis "had been under the influence of a deranging malady for about six weeks" prior to his suicide.[21] *The Missouri Gazette* explained that Lewis had "been of late very much afflicted with fever, which never failed of depriving him of his reason; to this cause we may ascribe the fatal catastrophe!"[22]

A Life History

Meriwether Lewis was born on 14 August 1774 at Locust Hill, the family estate in Albemarle County, Virginia, about seven miles west of Charlottesville. He was the first son and second child of William Lewis (born ca. 1748) and Lucy Meriwether (born 1752). His sister Jane was born in 1770 and his brother Reuben in 1777. When Meriwether was not quite two years old, his father left home to join the revolutionary forces fighting in Virginia and, so far as we know, did not return until late October or early November 1779.[23]

Children tend to view absent parents in contradictory ways. They feel abandoned and resentful but simultaneously somehow responsible for the absence, believing that the parent left because of something the child did or wished to do. Children harbor these ambivalent feelings in part because of their inability to separate fantasies from actual events. A child may view his or her father as a competitor for the affections and time of the mother. Unconsciously and often consciously the child wishes the rival would disappear. Of course it also desires that the rival not disappear. When the father does go away, the child imagines that its own wishes have caused this event and—at some level—sees itself as responsible. To avoid the overwhelming guilt for such episodes, the child simultaneously externalizes these feelings and blames the absent parent for having abandoned him or her.[24]

Added to this general phenomenon is the idealization of fathers who go off to war and whose return from battle shatters the child's heroic vision.[25] There is of course nothing pathological about any of this; the circumstances are rather ordinary; most children adjust to them by one means or another. However, when an absent parent fails to return, the conflict for the child can be extreme. In Lewis's case the trauma was heightened by the fact that the syndrome repeated itself twice, each time with more permanent consequences. In November 1779, when Meriwether was not quite five, his father returned from the war and soon thereafter died of pneumonia. On 14 November 1779 he was buried on his wife's family estate at Cloverfield.[26] How Meriwether reacted to these events we can only imagine. Yet it would not be in the least farfetched to suppose that the father who returned after a three-year absence had not measured up to Meriwether's idealized expectations, and that the ambivalences and rivalries that are so common in these cases revived. William Lewis's death would thus have been viewed by his son as both the fulfillment of his own unconscious wishes and as the final abandonment and punishment of the son for those wishes.[27]

Moreover, the circumstances of the father's death suggest that these same wartime conditions restricted Meriwether's opportunity to participate fully in rituals of mourning. In May 1780, less than six months after her husband died, Lucy Meriwether married Captain John Marks. It was inevitable that the five-and-a-half-year-old boy would feel ambivalent about his stepfather. In contrast to William Lewis, who died while still in service of his country, Marks had been forced by poor health to retire from the revolutionary army in 1781. He immediately moved his new family from Virginia to his speculative landholdings along the Broad River in Georgia. Thus Meriwether was forced to leave not only his home but also the site of his father's grave. The following years brought the birth of two more siblings, John Hastings and Mary Marks, adding no doubt to the boy's already uncertain relationship with his new father. In any case, by 1785 eleven-year-old Meriwether was sent back to Virginia to live with his maternal uncles, Nicholas and William D. Meriwether. Whether he felt deserted or betrayed by his mother is impossible to determine. In 1791 Captain Marks died, leaving Meriwether father-less again. Marks's death had the effect of returning Meriwether's mother to Virginia and placing him at the head of the household. Thus at age seventeen he had lost and replaced both his father and stepfather. For the remainder of his life he would maintain an ex-tremely close relationship with his mother—so close, in fact, that his biographers concluded that Lewis never married because no women he ever met measured up to his vision of Lucy Marks.[28]

The pattern of Lewis's life suggests that these events troubled him intensely. All people develop strategies for coping with the stresses and contradictions of their lives. Although none of Lewis's strategies were unusual in themselves, in combination and interaction they are revealing. Moreover, the intensity with which they formed the pat-terns in his life is consistent with the case histories of those who take, or attempt to take, their own lives: a repeated failure to establish last-ing interpersonal relations, extreme risk-taking, and a compulsive desire for self-punishment.[29]

Like suicide itself, these modes of behavior are symptomatic of deeper conflicts and they should be viewed less as evidence of "men-tal disease" than as attempts to master underlying psychological conflicts. The repetition of these modes of behavior could be viewed as a ritualistic attempt to purge—once and for all—the guilt that in-forms the life of the incomplete mourner.

As a young man, Lewis was constantly in search of the ideal woman, falling in and out of love quickly and often. In each instance he discovered a reason or created a situation that made the contin-uation or culmination of the romantic relationship impossible. As Donald Jackson notes, "Lewis's search for a wife was dogged and inexplicitly futile."[30] Lewis never married, but he seemed always on the verge of matrimony. As a twenty-year-old soldier during the Whiskey Rebellion he wrote his mother from Pittsburgh that he would be bringing home "an insurgent girl . . . bearing the title of Mrs. Lewis." He didn't. When he was Jefferson's personal secretary and during the months before his departure on the expedition, he pursued several women and decided that he might marry his cousin Maria Wood. He named the north fork of the Missouri River after

her, but when he returned, his ardor cooled and Maria soon married another. Lewis then fell in love with a mysterious Miss "C,"
whom he described as rich and beautiful. When Clark announced
his own engagement to Julie Hancock, Lewis wrote that he had
definitely made up his mind to marry Miss "C," but after meeting
Letitia Brackenridge at the Hancock home, he told his brother Reuben that he meant to marry her instead. That notion, like all the
others, was soon abandoned.[31]

Past experience, object relations theory suggests, made Lewis cau-
tious in forming close emotional relationships in which he might
find himself once again abandoned as his father had abandoned
him. He unconsciously made the association between his ambiguous
pursuit of women and incomplete mourning when he wrote (and
underlined!) in 1807 after another failed love affair that he was
"now *a perfect widower with respect to love.*"[32] Throughout his life
Lewis created idealized visions of women that served the purpose of
avoiding marriage, thus saving himself from feared future desertion
by a love object.*

Moreover, Lewis had great difficulty maintaining many of his
personal relationships, including those with his mentor Jefferson
and his close friend Amos Stoddard.[33] The only exceptions to this
pattern seem to have occurred during the expedition, when risk-
taking, the second derivative of his personality conflict, predomi-
nated. This connection between avoiding love and risk-taking was
presented, though unintentionally, by Bakeless, who excused Lewis's inability to form lasting relationships with women in this fashion:
"What, after all, is a woman, compared to solitude in the wilderness,
Indians, the bright face of danger, the high adventure of the Rockies, canoes in foaming rapids, a grizzly hunt, or sword blades flash-
ing in the sun, a flag that flutters over steel-tipped columns, the
cadenced tramp of doughboys at your back, and polished brass and
bugles, calling, calling; and rifles crashing smartly to 'Present'?"[34]

What indeed? All Lewis's friends and all his biographers have

*Relating the story of these abortive courtships, John Bakeless concludes that "Meriwether
Lewis was no ladies' man, and—moody, solitary fellow that he was—[seemed] more in love
with wilderness adventure than anything else." Besides, adds Bakeless without intended irony,
"what mere girl could approach the grace, the charm, the intelligence, and the tremendous
vigor of his fascinating mother?" Bakeless, *Lewis and Clark,* pp. 385–386; Dillon, *Lewis,* pp.
284–286.

agreed that he was an extreme risk-taker. From earliest childhood he gambled with his life. Jefferson recalled that when Lewis was only eight years old, "he habitually went out in the dead of night alone . . . to hunt." Jefferson noted Lewis's compulsive pursuit of danger even at this young age: "no season or circumstance could obstruct his purpose, plunging thro' the winter's snows and frozen streams in pursuit of his object."[35] Lewis's biographers repeat the many stories of his boyhood bravado.[36] One of his schoolmates remembered him in his early teens as having an "obstinacy in pursuing . . . trifles" and "a martial temper; great steadiness of purpose, self-possession, and undaunted courage." Lewis's personal stiffness, "almost without flexibility," recalled to his classmate "a very strong resemblance to Buonaparte."[37]

This pattern continued throughout Lewis's early army career, including his reckless challenge of a superior officer to a duel in 1795.[38] His reputation as one who invited rather than avoided danger followed him to Washington. Attorney General Levi Lincoln, fearing Lewis's impulsiveness, urged Jefferson to modify the guidelines for the expedition: "From my ideas of Capt. Lewis he will be much more likely, in case of difficulty, to push too far, than to recede too soon. Would it not be well," Lincoln suggested, "to change the term, 'certain destruction' into probable destruction & to add— that these dangers are never to be encountered, which vigilance precaution & attention can secure against, at a reasonable expense."[39] Lewis's actions during the transcontinental explorations demonstrated both his extraordinary courage and his excessive inclination to gamble with his life. While no one ever doubted Clark's personal bravery, "Lewis had most of the narrow escapes."[40]

Placing one's life in constant danger is, as we have seen, a common trait of suicidal personalities. We can look at Lewis's excessive and repetitive risk-taking as repeated attempts to purge recurring self-destructive urges. That is why he seemed the least troubled when he was in the greatest danger.[41]

The third and in Lewis's case ultimate strategy was self-punishment. Suicide is of course the most extreme form of self-affliction, but Lewis also pursued other slower means, especially hard drink.[42] The evidence of his addiction to alcohol appears as early as his twentieth year, when Lewis, though ultimately found innocent, was court-martialed for drunkenness and "conduct unbecoming an officer."[43] Evidence from contemporary sources supports the view that he was a confirmed alcoholic. Jefferson, for example, noted that he "was much afflicted & habitually so with hypochondria. This was probably increased by the habit [intemperance] into which he had fallen & the painful reflections that would necessarily produce in a mind like his."[44] Gilbert Russell was convinced that Lewis's "untimely death may be attributed solely to the free use he made of liquor." Lewis admitted his dependence to Gilbert and promised to reform.[45] Yet by all accounts he was drinking heavily before and after his arrival at Grinder's Stand.[46] Only during the expedition does he seem to have lived without liquor.[47]

Lewis's actions as governor of Upper Louisiana Territory—including his suspicions of a conspiracy to damage his reputation and to remove him from office—are consistent with a deep-seated wish for punishment.[48] Given to fits of temper,* he was portrayed by one not-unbiased observer as behaving "like an overgrown baby[;] he began to think that everybody about the House must regulate their conduct by his caprices."[49]

From a psychological point of view, Lewis's suicide, then, was not merely a means of dying, but a grisly final self-punishment, even a self-execution. The reports about the manner of his death suggest that Lewis inflicted upon himself a punishment much worse than the "enemies" whom he imagined as desiring "the pleasure and the honor of doing it."[50]

A final thread in Lewis's psychological life remains dangling. It is impossible to ignore the important role that his relationship with and feelings toward his mother played in his life. The ambivalent child's wish to replace his father became a possibility early, and the fantasy grew into reality during his teenage years when his stepfather died and circumstances placed Meriwether at the head of his household. Lewis's inability to find a suitable mate, though marriage remained a central goal of his life and a topic of his letters, cannot be dismissed. Until the end of his days, he depended closely and constantly on his mother. While none of this is unusual, nor is it pathological, this relationship remained the anchor in his world of failed strategies.

*Lewis's inability to control his temper was evident when he served as Jefferson's secretary. See Rochonne Abrams, "Meriwether Lewis: Two Years with Jefferson, the Mentor," *Missouri Historical Society Bulletin* 36 (October 1979): 13.

His difficulties in St. Louis, however, made it impossible for Lewis finally to bring his mother under his own roof. This fact added to his despondency. His announced plan of action was to return to Washington to redeem himself, with a visit to his mother en route. He took all his worldly possessions with him, indicating that he did not intend to return to the West. Perhaps his impending reunion with his mother, with Jefferson, President Madison, and Secretary of War Eustis (father figures?) troubled him. Would they reject him as a failure? Would they judge him as his life history indicates he judged himself? In any case, the will he prepared a few days after departing from St. Louis left his estate to his mother. Only then did Lewis twice attempt, and fail, to take his life. He drank incessantly. Inexplicably, he altered his route, taking the more dangerous overland trail. Finally he succeeded in killing himself; though not before calling out for aid to another mother who was too frightened to answer his pleas and ignored his cries for help.

Different societies and different eras have dealt with death, mourning, and suicide in different ways; but to the extent that any society or set of circumstances restricts the mourning ritual for any of its members, one would expect to find evidence of alternative individual or social strategies that attempt to deal with earlier repressed loss.[51] Because the death of parents and siblings was more common in the late eighteenth- or early nineteenth-century America than it is today, we might suppose that people of Lewis's generation would not react to loss in the same way that we do. In fact, as recent studies have shown, during the early colonial period children generally were not separated from the mourning process and death rituals involved the participation of the entire community.[52] This is what makes Lewis's response so useful for our purposes. He seems to have responded to loss in a manner that appears to have been atypical of his generation, and this suggests that social parameters combined with constitutional and psychological problems to inform his behavior. The circumstances of the Revolutionary War restricted young Meriwether's mourning his father's death.[53] His mother's remarriage and subsequent migration to Georgia exacerbated this loss. Although he was a life-long depressive and alcoholic, historical circumstance in the form of the Lewis and Clark expedition provided a successful strategy—at least while it lasted—for Lewis to deal with his incomplete mourning.

Suicide emerges as an alternative of last resort for the incomplete mourner when other strategies prove either insufficient or unavailable. The life of Meriwether Lewis is suggestive of incomplete mourning, and a fuller understanding of his death should lead us to a more complete picture of his life. Admittedly, Lewis's suicide provides a sketch rather than a complete picture of how cultural and historical factors interact with psychological and organic factors in suicidal behavior. In a subsequent chapter this historical context for incomplete mourning will be elaborated. First, however, I want to explore more fully the relationship between loss and subsequent suicidal behavior by examining a successful strategy: the case of an individual who experienced severe early loss, but who nevertheless did not commit suicide.

THE STRATEGY OF ABRAHAM LINCOLN

All loss, as the case of Meriwether Lewis illustrates, calls forth personal strategies and socially defined rituals. It is the failure of these strategies that can eventually lead to suicide. Even suicide is not necessarily a denial of life. As Robert Jay Lifton explains, suicide often includes an attempt to live on, if only in the memory of those left behind. We shall examine Lincoln's early years from this point of view.[54]

The main argument here is that the goal of Lincoln's well-known depressive behavior was to avoid self-destruction.* As we shall see, his actions prior to 1842 fit this pattern. A threatened suicide in 1841 served as an extreme and partially successful attempt to purge the guilt, anger, and fears of desertion brought on by severe early loss and incomplete mourning.

Lincoln was born in Kentucky in 1809, the same year that Meriwether Lewis killed himself. Among Abraham Lincoln's earliest memories was the death of his infant brother Thomas when Abraham was between two and three years old. Thomas was buried in a small grave within sight of the family cabin.[55] In 1816, when Ab-

*I wish to emphasize the modest purposes of this section. The life of Abraham Lincoln is employed here only as an example of how early loss and later depressive episodes do not necessarily end in suicide. This discussion should not be confused with an explanation of why Lincoln was elected president or with the causes of the Civil War.

raham was seven, his father Thomas, his mother Nancy Hanks, and his nine-year-old sister Sarah moved to Little Pigeon Creek in Spencer County, Indiana. Soon they were joined by Nancy's uncle, Thomas Sparrow, his wife Elizabeth, and Nancy's illegitimate nineteen-year-old cousin, Dennis Hanks. Thomas Lincoln and his family lived in a one-room cabin, while the Sparrows and young Hanks lived close by in an even more primitive lean-to.[56]

In September 1818 Thomas Sparrow and his wife Elizabeth contracted brucellosis, a disease transmitted from cow's milk,* and within a week both died.[57] As her aunt and uncle lay dying, thirty-five-year-old Nancy Hanks Lincoln realized that she had contracted early signs of the illness. She called her children, Abraham, now nine, and Sarah, eleven, to her bedside. To her son, Nancy reportedly said, "I am going away from you, Abraham, and I shall not return. I know that you will be a good boy that you will be kind to Sarah and to your father." Nancy Lincoln died on 5 October 1818, one week after her uncle Thomas Sparrow. Abraham had watched his mother go through the course of the "milk sickness" in their one-room cabin and now he helped his father fashion a rude coffin. Father and son hauled it to a burial plot 1500 feet south of the cabin site, where a neighbor conducted a brief interment service.[58]

The next several years were bleak ones for Thomas Lincoln and his children. Young Sarah took over the duties of her mother until her father married the widow Sarah Bush Johnston of Elizabeth-Town, Kentucky, a year later. Sarah Johnston moved into the already crowded Lincoln cabin with her three children, Elizabeth, twelve, John D., ten, and Matilda, eight.[59]

Lincoln's relationship with his new stepmother seems to have been untroubled and affectionate—indeed, it remained closer than his relationship with his father. Charles B. Strozier writes that "Nowhere does Lincoln every say anything good about Thomas—a reticence that contrasts strikingly with his openly expressed idealization

*Brucellosis or undulant fever, which almost always proved fatal, was well known and sensibly feared by settlers in western Kentucky and southern Indiana. Its symptoms included "dizziness, nausea, vomiting, stomach pains, intense thirst, and a sickening odor of breath." Within a week, the victim would experience irregular respiration, an uneven pulse rate, below normal temperature, and "prostration . . . followed by a semi- to complete coma." See Wesley W. Spink, *The Nature of Brucellosis* (Minneapolis: University of Minnesota Press, 1956), pp. 145–170; B. M. Thimm, *Brucellosis: Distribution in Man, Domestic and Wild Animals* (New York: Springer-Verlag, 1982).

of Nancy and his deep affection for Sarah."[60] The portrait Lincoln left of his father in an 1848 letter to a relative is curt and unflattering: "Owing to my father being left an orphan at the age of six years, in poverty, and in a new country, he became a wholly uneducated man; which I suppose is the reason why . . . I can say nothing more that would interest you at all."[61] All evidence indicates that Lincoln shared William H. Herndon's characterization of Thomas Lincoln's "utter laziness and want of energy," which Herndon attributed to Thomas's loss of potency.[62] In 1851 Lincoln declined to visit Thomas, then on his deathbed, because, as he wrote to his stepbrother John D. Johnston, "Say to him that if we could meet now, it is doubtful whether it would not be more painful than pleasant."[63] At times Lincoln seems to have had the fantasy that Thomas Lincoln was not actually his father and that his mother Nancy Hanks was the illegitimate descendent of aristocratic Virginia planters.[64]

In any case, with his mother's death, Lincoln transferred his familial affections even more intensely to his sister Sarah. Her death at twenty-one during childbirth in January 1828 devastated the nineteen-year-old youth: "He sat down on the door of the smoke house and buried his face in his hands. The tears slowly trickled from between his bony fingers and his gaunt frame shook with sobs." One who remembered Lincoln in the years immediately following Sarah's death pictured him as "witty and sad and thoughtful by turns." His sister's death, according to Louis Warren, "left lasting marks deep within his mind and spirit, and he endured long periods of melancholic brooding and depression."[65]

Hearing of more promising opportunities in central Illinois, Thomas Lincoln led his family to a settlement about ten miles west of Decatur in the winter of 1830–1831. Within a year the Lincoln family moved to Coles County, Illinois, and twenty-two-year-old Abraham left his father's house to settle ultimately in New Salem along the Sangamon River where he worked as a clerk in a general store. Within six months Lincoln was an unsuccessful Whig candidate for the state legislature. In the middle of the campaign Lincoln served briefly as a militia captain in the Blackhawk War. By 1833 he was appointed as postmaster; he was a respected member of the community and a joint owner with William F. Berry of a general store. Even though that venture failed in 1834, twenty-five-year-old Abraham Lincoln was elected to the state legislature at Vandalia.[66]

Thus, in a relatively short period Lincoln had achieved what he had admitted candidly in 1832 was one of his primary motives for seeking political office: "Every man is said to have his peculiar ambition. Whether it be true or not, I can say for one that I have no other so great as that of being truly esteemed by my fellow men, by rendering myself worthy of their esteem. How far I shall succeed in gratifying this ambition, is yet to be developed."[67]

Electoral success, however, did not remove his recurrent depressive (or as he called them "hypochondria") episodes. The death of his friend Ann Rutledge in 1835 brought back memories of his earlier losses. Lincoln had become friends with Ann when he had first arrived in New Salem and had boarded at her father's tavern. No evidence exists to substantiate Herndon's claim that Lincoln and Ann were engaged. Lincoln's well-documented fears of rejection by women during this period suggests that he had sought out Ann's company because she was engaged and therefore Lincoln could maintain a friendship with her without the danger of commitment. Even after Ann broke off her engagement with John MacNamar, it is unlikely, because of Lincoln's internal conflicts, that he would have suggested marriage.[68] On the other hand, it cannot be doubted that he suffered greatly from her death. Lincoln's excessive public mourning at Ann Rutledge's death suggests to Robert V. Bruce "that the long repressed grief at the loss of his mother may have broken out again to swell Lincoln's grief at the similar death of Ann."[69]

All the women for whom Lincoln had cared most intensely had died. This fact provides an important context for understanding Lincoln's seemingly bizarre courtship of Mary Owens, which began in 1836, a little more than a year after Ann's death. Mary Owens, who lived in Kentucky, had met Lincoln briefly during an 1833 visit to her older sister, Mrs. Bennett Abell, in New Salem. Three years later Mrs. Abell suggested that she would bring Mary Owens back from Kentucky if Lincoln were interested in marrying her. Lincoln consented, but when Mary arrived, Lincoln's actions and words transformed his proposal into an offer no young woman could accept.[70]

In December 1836 Lincoln left for the legislative session meeting at the capitol in Vandalia. His letters to Mary Owens were filled with ambiguous messages. Although these were couched in terms of his continuing commitment to marriage, they seemed aimed at least unconsciously at obtaining a release from his promise. For instance, he wrote in December that "things I cannot account for, have conspired and have gotten my spirits so low, that I feel I would rather be any place in the world but here." He told Mary that he had "not been pleased since I left you." Yet he did not take the next step. Instead he ended, "This letter is so dry and stupid that I am ashamed to send it, but with my present feelings I can not do any better."[71]

Instead of returning to New Salem when the legislative session ended, Lincoln traveled to Springfield where he decided to settle. In May he wrote Mary that although he was "often thinking about what we said of your coming to live in Springfield. I am afraid you would not be satisfied." He informed her at great length and detail of the unpleasant living conditions that awaited her if she joined him. "My opinion," Lincoln offered, "is that you had better not do it." But, he promised, if she were inclined to insist on accepting his earlier offer of marriage, he would "most positively abide by it."[72]

If Mary Owens had not by then totally abandoned any ideas of marriage, Lincoln's letter of August must have provided the final reasons for that: "I want at this particular time, more than anything else, to do right with you, and if I *knew* it would be doing right, as I rather suspect it would, to let you alone, I would do it." It was up to her, Lincoln suggested, to make the next move: "And for the purpose of making the matter as plain as possible, I now say, that you can drop the subject, dismiss your thoughts (if you ever had any) from me forever, and leave this letter unanswered, without calling forth one accusing murmur from me." One cannot imagine how Mary Owens ever could have accepted Lincoln's "proposal." Certainly, politician and orator that he was, it is difficult to believe that Lincoln expected that Owens would have held him to his commitment. His closing lines could not be misunderstood: "If it suits you best not to answer this—farewell—a long life and merry one attend you."[73]

Nevertheless, one cannot read these letters without also sensing the pain that he felt. Lincoln was attracted to the idea of marrying Mary Owens, yet he maintained a genuine conscious fear that he could make no woman happy. This was no doubt a projection of his unconscious anxiety that previous experiences would be repeated; that Mary Owens, like the other women he had loved, would desert him.

Later Lincoln related his relationship with Owens to others in a humorous context; but humor, particularly Lincoln's, often obscured deeper ambivalences and harms. When he told Eliza Browning in 1838 that "when I beheld her [Owens], I could not for my life avoid thinking of my mother," Lincoln was revealing more of his inner conflicts than his caricature of Mary suggests.[74]

Lincoln unquestionably suffered from the loss of those he loved most intensely. His fear of further losses was acute—particularly when it came to women. It manifested itself in a reluctance to form attachments that surpassed nineteenth-century-frontier conventions of male shyness. In January 1841 Lincoln, not quite thirty-two, began a six-month-long severe episode of depression that included a threat to take his own life.

The Strategy of Depression

Lincoln characterized his behavior as "a discreditable exhibition of myself in the way of hypochondriaism." His actions led his friends "to remove all razors, knives, pistols, etc. from his room and presence," because they feared "that he might commit suicide." They described his behavior variously as "crazy as a loon," "deranged," and "that he had two Cat fits and a Duck fit." He described himself as "the most miserable man living. If what I feel were equally distributed to the whole human family, there would not be one cheerful face on earth." Lincoln wrote to a close friend that he could not go on living: "To remain as I am is impossible; I must die or be better."[75] Scholars generally agree with Strozier that although Lincoln was "subject to depression throughout his life," this was "his most severe bout."[76]

The precipitating incident was the threat of still another loss. Two important events preceded Lincoln's suicidal behavior. On 1 January 1841, Lincoln's most intimate friend, Joshua Speed, with whom Lincoln had shared a bed for the past four years, sold his store in preparation for leaving town to marry a woman in the neighboring state of Kentucky. On the same day, Lincoln broke his engagement to marry his fiancée, Mary Todd.[77]

One scholar, who studied these events intensively, concluded that the suicidal behavior resulted almost entirely from the broken engagement: "It is clear from his later references . . . to his ensuing

emotional chaos, that Lincoln underwent misery of no mild variety as a result, not merely of his own indecision and instability, but
also of his awareness that he was the cause of an injury . . . no less
severe and humiliating than his own."[78] Other investigators, however, have found Speed's imminent departure as the primary anxi-
ety-producing element. Speed was so concerned about his friend's
condition (and apparently so aware of his role in producing it) that
he deferred his plans to leave for Kentucky for almost six months.
Speed's father's death late that spring made his remaining in
Springfield impossible. Concluding that Lincoln was "emotionally
unfit to be alone," Speed took him to Kentucky where Lincoln lived
with Speed and his family for the next several months. At the end of
the summer, Speed returned to Springfield with Lincoln, where he
remained until December 1841.[79]

Having deferred his plans for almost a year, Joshua Speed finally
married Fanny Henning in February 1842. Prior to the wedding
Lincoln and Speed exchanged a series of letters in which Lincoln revealed quite explicitly his own anxieties about the connection between love and death. Speed had written that he feared for Fanny's
health and, ultimately, for her life. "Why Speed," Lincoln replied, "if
you did not love her, although you might not wish her death, you
would most calmly be resigned to it." Then Lincoln added, "Perhaps
this point is no longer a question with you, . . . [but] you must pardon me. You know the Hell I have suffered on that point."[80] With
Speed's assurance that married life was far from miserable, Lincoln
resumed his relationship with the jilted Mary Todd and on 4 November 1842 they were married. Lincoln was thirty-three.[81]

Although Lincoln would experience other depressive or melancholic episodes during his life, none reached the intensity of his
experience of 1841. A clinician encountering Lincoln in the early
months of 1841 would have taken seriously both Lincoln's threats
and his friends' judgments that he was a candidate for suicide. Lincoln's life history prior to 1841 provides compelling support for
such a view.

In Lincoln's case, those toward whom he had felt the closest—his
mother, his sister, and Ann Rutledge—all had deserted him by dying. His only brother died at the age of two or three and perhaps because of these events, Lincoln proved unable to form any positive
attachment to his father. Lincoln's experience made him anxious

about desertion by those (especially women) with whom he formed close relationships. His behavior toward Mary Owens provides a graphic example of these ambivalent feelings. When Joshua Speed, the closest friend he ever made, decided to leave Springfield (and Lincoln) to move to Kentucky to marry Fanny Henning, it was not surprising that Lincoln, feeling deserted by Speed, recalled his earlier losses and in panic deserted Mary Todd before she too might desert him.

In 1841, during the period when he contemplated suicide, Lincoln told Speed that "he had 'done nothing to make any human being remember that he had lived.'"[82] Suicide can be a form of revenge, like the child's threat to run away so it will be missed by those who have done it harm. In short, suicide may be imagined as a way of living on in other people's memories just as the lost object lives on in the memory of the potential suicide. After death, the suicide fantasizes, he too will become mourned (remembered). Abraham Lincoln's suicide threats fit this pattern.[83]

Speed's sensitive response to his friend's cry for help provided Lincoln with crucial therapeutic support. Although he continued to experience depressive episodes, Lincoln made no other threats to end his life. Like Meriwether Lewis, however, Lincoln remained troubled by the severe loss he had experienced and like Lewis he pursued strategies to alleviate his incomplete mourning. Unlike Lewis's, Lincoln's strategies proved to be sufficient, yet death and dying remained one of his central concerns. Throughout the rest of his life Lincoln mourned the early losses he had suffered and he continually seemed in search of an adequate way to resolve the guilt, anger, and anxiety that still accompanied them. What some writers have portrayed as Lincoln's obsession with death may be understood also as Lincoln's attempt to come to terms with these early losses.

Unlike Lewis, Lincoln seemed to have had a genuine opportunity to grieve both publicly and privately for the early losses he suffered. Like many of his literate nineteenth-century contemporaries, Lincoln rejected the existence of an afterlife.[84] One result, suggests Robert Bruce, was that Lincoln adopted the emerging "romanticism of death," which moved the survivor rather than the departed to the center of mourning rituals.[85] This reaction to death tended to downplay traditional communitarian participation in favor of private rites confined to family members. For isolated frontier families

like Lincoln's, the ideology of romanticized death often was reinforced by physical isolation. Thus, as death came to mean more to
survivors, the privacy of mourning rituals exacerbated loss, anger,
and guilt.[86]

Lincoln's romanticizing of death was evident in his repeated anxiety that those with whom he was closest were likely to die. He wrote
to Speed in 1842 that "the death scenes of those we love are surely
painful enough; but these we are prepared to, and expect to see."[87]
Moreover, he feared that his death was imminent. Two "romantic"
poems about death illustrate his response to these issues. The first
was written by William Knox, a Scot who died in 1825 at the age of
thirty-three, and the other by Lincoln himself.

In October 1844 Lincoln visited the graves of his mother and sister. This was Lincoln's first trip in fifteen years to "the neighbor-
hood . . . where my mother and only sister were buried." The
experience recalled a poem that he had "seen . . . once before, about
fifteen years ago," the author and title of which he did not learn until he was president. Knox's "Mortality" portrays life "Like a swift-
fleeting meteor, a fast-flying cloud, / A flash of lightening, a break in
the wave."[88] "I would give all I am worth, and go into debt," Lincoln wrote enclosing a copy to the editor of the *Quincy Whig* in 1846,
"to be able to write so fine a piece as I think that is."[89] Most scholars
concur with Bruce's assessment that the poem "possessed Lincoln's
mind throughout his adult life" with an "extraordinary . . . duration
and intensity."[90] Lincoln's first contact with the poem was in 1831
when he was twenty-two. Later he kept a newspaper clipping reproduction of the poem in his pocket until he had memorized it.[91] In
1850 Lincoln read Knox's lines as a eulogy on the death of President
Zachary Taylor. He quoted it to his relatives and to his fellow circuit-
riding lawyers in the 1850s. One of them recalled Lincoln often "sitting before the fire . . . with the saddest expression I have ever seen
in a human being's eyes." On these occasions, the companion remembered, Lincoln invariably would recite Knox's "Mortality."[92]
Toward the end of his life Lincoln explained that the poem "is my
almost constant companion; indeed, I may say it is continually present with me, as it crosses my mind whenever I have relief from
anxiety."[93]

Lincoln's extraordinary attachment to this poem went beyond its
expression of the brevity of life. The poem's most compelling im-
ages meshed with Lincoln's personal experiences and fantasies

about the death of a young woman—mother, sister, fiancée:

> The maid on whose cheek, on whose brow, in whose eye,
> Shone beauty and pleasure, her triumphs are by.
> And the memory of those that beloved her and praised,
> Are alike from the minds of the living erased.

At one level Lincoln's fascination with the piece rests upon its romantic portrayal of death and its refusal to seek relief from loss in an afterlife. However, it is less certain that Lincoln agreed with the poet's insistence that the goal of life is to "rest in the grave":

> So the multitude goes, like the flower or the weed,
> That withers away to let others succeed;
> So the multitude comes, even those we behold,
> To repeat every tale that has ever been told.

Lincoln's obsession with Knox's poem should not be confused with his endorsement of its sentiments. Rather its repetition may indicate Lincoln's search for an alternative meaning for his losses. Although the central theme speaks of the need to accept "the death we are shirking," Lincoln's own life history suggests less than total resignation to an end "To the thoughts we are thinking, . . . To the life we are clinging."

Lincoln's poem, "My Childhood-Home I See Again," was inspired by the same graveside visit that recalled Knox's "Mortality." Written from 1844 to 1846, "My Childhood-Home" implies a different response to Knox's opening and closing lines, "Oh! why should the spirit of mortal be proud?" Although Lincoln was saddened by the memories his visit recalled, he discovered also that "still, as memory crowds my brain, / There's pleasure in it too." If there were no actual life after death, "memory" might substitute:

> O Memory! thou midway world
> 'Twixt earth and paradise
> Where things decayed and loved one lost
> In dreamy shadows rise,[94]

Memory and Ambition

Lincoln's desire, as he had confided to Speed during the depressive episode of 1841, was "to connect his name with the events transpiring in his day and generation, and so impress himself upon them as to link his name with something that would redound to the interest of his fellow man." That, he informed Speed, "was what he desired to live for." [95] If there were no heaven, the only life after death, the only meaning for having lived would be in the memories one left behind. To live after death one's deeds must be truly memorable. Lincoln's recent biographers all have found him to be extremely ambitious. [96] Along with Bruce, they tie Lincoln's "almost obsessive ambition" to his fear of his own death: "Lincoln found the total annihilation of the self an intolerable prospect." Thus, Bruce finds, he "turned to the idea of survival by proxy in the minds of others. . . . Lincoln's antidote for numb despair was the concept of immortality through remembrance." [97] "Lincoln's ambition," argues Dwight Anderson, "was rooted in what can only be described as an obsession about death. . . . Ambition provided the means by which immortality could be attained." Lincoln's goal was "to win immortality . . . [and] to live on in the memory of subsequent generations." [98]

Although these same biographers' value judgments differ as to the quality of Lincoln's ambition, they concur with Strozier's evaluation that "Lincoln's driving ambition" was tied to his shame about his own father's "dull . . . character." [99] His fantasy that Thomas Lincoln was not his biological father, that he was descended on his mother's side from Virginia aristocracy, is similar to a common childhood regressive and nostalgic fantasy, which Otto Rank linked to all heroic mythic constructs:

> the substitution of both parents, or of the father alone, by more exalted personages—the discovery will be made that these new and highborn parents are invested throughout with the qualities which are derived from real memories of the true lowly parents. . . . The entire endeavor . . . is merely the expression of the child's longing for the vanished happy time, when his father still appeared to be the strongest and greatest man, and the mother seemed the dearest and most beautiful woman. [100]

By the time Lincoln was nine years old he had learned that his father Thomas could not protect him from loss, and subsequent events suggest that Lincoln might have found some solace in such a childhood fantasy.

According to Anderson this translates into Lincoln's conscious desire to transform the fantasy into reality by becoming father of himself and, ultimately, father of his country by replacing the Constitution of the Founding Fathers with the Declaration of Independence. Quoting Ernest Becker, Anderson compares Lincoln to the child who "wants to conquer death by becoming the *father of himself*, the creator and sustainer of his own life."[101] One does not have to go as far as Anderson to conclude that Lincoln's incomplete mourning led him to hope that fame rather than faith would bring life everlasting. Rather than viewing Lincoln's ambition to live in memory after death as a pathological response to the events of his early life, one might conceive of Lincoln's solution as therapeutic.

Lincoln's desires mesh with what Becker describes as the wish for "heroism" that springs from "the denial of death." The wish to be a hero, according to Becker, derives from the fear that after death one will be forgotten. Those that suffer the greatest from this anxiety are those who already have suffered desertion in their lives. Heroism shares with suicide a fantasy of remembrance. In both we uncover a wish to transcend death.[102] The most heroic act that one can imagine of course is to sacrifice one's life for social good—an act that Durkheim labeled "altruistic suicide."*

Lincoln, thanks to accident and design, achieved his goal to live on in the memory of others. Before he died he realized that he had approached the heroic, the self-made vision of national paternity. Those who knew him well in the 1860s attested to Lincoln's acceptance of death; some suggested that he welcomed it; others assert that Lincoln continually risked his own safety.[103] To the extent that these latter analyses are accurate, one might conclude that Lincoln's strategies for dealing with his early losses never surrendered all of their suicidal content. Unique historical circumstances allowed Lincoln to deal with his depressive disorders on the national stage.

---

*Lincoln, who often questioned his own sanity, dreaded insanity, not least of all because he connected it with anonymity. Juxtaposed to the memories of his dead kin in his poem "My Childhood-Home" was "an object of more dread/ Than ought the grave contains—/ A human form with reason fled." The poem also related the story of a childhood acquaintance, Matthew Gentry, who, "At the age of nineteen . . . unaccountably became furiously mad," attempting to kill his parents and himself. During the 1844 visit, Lincoln found Matthew "still lingering in this wretched condition. . . . I could not forget the impressions his case made upon me." Like Matthew Gentry, the insane, although avoiding death, are forgotten: "O death! Thou awe-inspiring prince,/ That keepst the world in fear;/ Why dost thou tear more blest ones hence/ And leave him ling'ring here?" Also see Abraham Lincoln to Andrew Johnston, 6 September 1846, *Collected Works*, 1: 384–386.

Unlike many others who have experienced incomplete mourning, Lincoln's strategy allowed him to live out his fantasies and for the most part to transform his self-destructive urges into socially acceptable behavior.

CONCLUSION

The life history of Abraham Lincoln provides an example of why the experience of severe early loss does not automatically result in a suicide. To put it another way, although loss often may bring on suicidal behavior, the aim of that behavior is not necessarily self-destruction, rather it is a search for a strategy to deal with guilt, anger, and the desire for revenge so that life can continue.* Completed or "successful" suicide occurs only when alternative strategies fail.

The issues raised by the self-destructive behavior of both Meriwether Lewis and Abraham Lincoln are emblematic of the psychocultural etiology of suicide in America. The strategies each man pursued, while typical of suicidal behavior, were nevertheless shaped by personal circumstances and by the possibilities offered in the larger world that each inhabited. This larger world was, of course, the historically specific world of late eighteenth- and early nineteenth-century America. Thus, the early and subsequent losses that Lewis and Lincoln sustained did not make suicide inevitable; rather it led each man to seek strategies whose possibilities of success were to a great extent determined by forces beyond his control.

---

*Of course, as Freud demonstrated, all neurotic behavior is "overdetermined" and thus suicidal behavior may be informed both by unconscious self-destructive urges *and* by adaptive/manipulative strategies.

6

THE PSYCHOCULTURAL
MEANING OF SUICIDE

Cᴀʟɪꜰᴏʀɴɪᴀ, Max White's promised land, had failed to measure up to his expectations. Instead of self-transformation and wealth, White found unemployment and loneliness in what he mockingly referred to as "this land of the free." His hopes dashed, he cursed imagined enemies whose greatest sin seems to have been indifference to his plight. He lamented that he had fled his native Hungary and that he ever had been born. Whether or not White exaggerated his predicament, he could no longer imagine a future worth living. A local newspaper labeled him "The Victim of Despair." [1]

White was not only a victim of despair, he was also a social statistic of the Depression of 1893. One of the most devastating economic collapses in America's history, the Depression of 1893 challenged opinion-makers both to explain its causes and to warn of its probable effects. One month after White's suicide, the historian Frederick Jackson Turner, formulating what turned out to be the most influential of these explanations, located the etiology of the disorder in the closing of the American frontier. With the 1890 federal census as his source, Turner's "Frontier Thesis" (1893) claimed that the nation had last its traditional "safety-valve" of cheap western lands for its surplus migrant population. [2]

One corollary hypothesis of Turner's analysis was that the great influx of immigrants who had arrived in the past decade would out

Table 6.1.
REPORTED SUICIDE RATES IN SELECTED CITIES,
1891–1895

Place	Rate per 100,000
Philadelphia	10.2
Boston	13.1[a]
Chicago	16.8[a]
New York City	19.8[a]
California (state)	22.9[a]
San Diego	28.6
San Francisco	41.3[a]

SOURCE: U.S. Census, 11th Census, 1890, 4: pt. 1, cvi–cvii; 12th Census, 1900, 3: pt. 1, Table 19, 285–555; Census of 1900 4: pt. 2, Table 7, 115–226; San Diego County Coroner's Office; Lane, *Violent Death in the City*, p. 12. For rates for selected countries, 1891–1895, see Table 6.4.
[a] Average rate for period 1890–1900

of frustration turn either to political and social rebellion or to self-destruction. Evidence supporting both alternatives already filled the pages of American newspapers. Labor unrest had punctuated the last half-decade. Throughout 1892 editorial writers alternated giving warnings of an impending social revolution with dire predictions of a national suicide epidemic.

Like other American newspapers in the 1890s, the *San Diego Union's* pages were saturated with reports of suicides from throughout the nation. "Day after day," lamented the *San Diego Union* in February 1893, "the rehearsal of these crimes goes on in the daily press." Its claim that "suicide has become so frequent as to attract comparatively little attention" seemed particularly true in San Diego.* In California, which boasted the highest suicide rates in the nation, San Diego's official suicide rate for the period from 1891 to 1895 of 28.6 per 100,000 was second only to San Francisco's (see Table 6.1).

*On the page following its editorial, the *Union* reported the suicide of a forty-seven-year-old woman, Elizabeth George, who was discovered lying across her bed in St. Joseph's hospital "with her throat cut from ear to ear . . . dressed only in her night clothes." Using a piece of window glass, "she had cut deeply into her throat, severing both jugular veins and the windpipe." A widow with three children, George had migrated to San Diego from her native Scotland. In 1886 she met and married her current husband, who turned out to be a compulsive gambler. The man soon lost his wife's property and savings and then abandoned Elizabeth George and her children. Increasingly "moody and despondent," George threatened suicide and was admitted to the hospital where on 22 February she killed herself. *San Diego Union*, 28 February 1893; San Diego County Coroner's Office, Coroner's Report, "Elizabeth George," 28 February 1893; Coroner's Inquest File, 28 February 1893, San Diego Historical Society, Manuscript Collections.

The Depression of 1893 seemed only to exacerbate a wave of apparently economically motivated suicides that received notoriety for almost a year. The suicide of Judge James A. Dillar, a forty-five-year-old real estate agent and notary public, was typical of these. On 18 March 1892 he placed "the muzzle of a revolver in his mouth," literally blowing out his brains. Dillar had come to San Diego in 1886, the height of the great San Diego property boom, from Wellington, Kansas. He had brought his wife and three children and what the press reported to have been "quite a sum of ready cash." Dreams of instant wealth attracted Dillar and thousands of other speculators who hoped to make their fortunes in the expected rapid increase in land prices. Because of San Diego's outstanding natural harbor, rumors that the city would be chosen as the national southwestern railroad terminus translated into hopes that San Diego would become the key transfer point of trade between the East Coast and the Orient. Overnight San Diego grew from a village of a few thousand to a teeming boom town of over thirty-five thousand.[3]

Like so many others, Dillar invested all of his savings in real estate and then, as speculators were apt to do, he borrowed against what he had purchased to buy even more. Los Angeles, not San Diego, won the battle to become the southwestern port to the Far East. Dillar's financial world collapsed. The crash came in April 1888, and within six months the city's population fell by more than half to sixteen thousand. Dillar's investments followed a pattern that the press reported was "the same old story familiar to thousands." As property values plummeted, income from Dillar's rental property ceased, leaving him "unable to pay the interest on his mortgage, and that went with the rest." Dillar had also invested his widowed mother's life savings of five thousand dollars, the loss of which, according to the *Union*, "drove him into a spirit of melancholia culminating in the tragedy of yesterday." At the coroner's inquest, a physician testified that Diller had been under his care "for nervous prostration and general debility." According to the doctor, Dillar was so distressed by his financial condition that he planned to kill his wife and then himself because "he dreaded to leave her to battle with poverty alone." Unlike the editorials, which condemned suicide in general, individual news stories ordinarily displayed more sympathy: Dillar's "only error," concluded a reporter, was "that of judgment in choosing his investments, but in that he had plenty of sympathizers."[4]

Nine days prior to Dillar's death, George Golden, a sixty-six-year-old retired railroad worker and Civil War veteran, shot himself through the head. Golden, born in Ireland, had arrived in San Diego five months earlier with his life savings of fourteen hundred dollars. At the suggestion of a local Wells-Fargo clerk, Golden deposited thirteen hundred dollars in the First National Bank. On the following day the bank suspended business and subsequently the owner, J. W. Collins, was indicted for embezzling more than two hundred thousand dollars of the bank's deposits. Enraged at this turn of events, Golden threatened to shoot the Wells-Fargo clerk but was turned back by others who assured him that Collins would soon make restitution to his depositors. Unable to find work, Golden pawned his few remaining possessions while he waited for Collins to make good on his public promises. On 3 March 1892, Golden, along with the rest of San Diego, learned that J. W. Collins had committed suicide. With evaporated hopes of retrieving his money, George Golden killed himself six days later. He left a bitter note: "San Diego is a good place to stay away from, nothing but swindlers are of any use in this cursed place."[5]

In the same month that Max White killed himself, another immigrant, Carl Creutzenberg, a forty-four-year-old native of Germany, arrived in San Diego from San Bernardino, looking for work. An alcoholic whose wife had divorced him "on account of his dissolute habits," Creutzenberg "had lately become despondent because he could not find work." On 17 December, after several days of heavy drinking, Creutzenberg took strychnine in sufficient quantity to kill himself.[6]

Ever since the 1890s experts have warned that one of the prices society pays for an economic crisis is an increase in the suicide rate, and the suicides of White, Dillar, Golden, Collins, and Creutzenberg seem to provide evidence for that view. Nevertheless, explanations that link suicide to economic crises, while they are appealing, are superficial. Many people suffered equally severe losses in the 1888 collapse and in the 1893 depression, but only a few committed suicide. What any theory of suicide worth considering must explain is not only why these events often lead to suicide, but also why more often they do not.

In 1897 Émile Durkheim supplied an answer. Durkheim concluded that specific factors like war, poverty, or economic depression were not in themselves responsible for fluctuations in the suicide rate. Rather, suicide increased whenever the members of a particular group or subculture could no longer find solutions for these distresses in traditional institutions and values. A particular crisis served only to exacerbate an already deteriorated situation. Social crises, like economic depressions, were important only insofar as they forced those who had already experienced social disintegration and personal alienation to privatize their losses and their solutions.

What Durkheim's sociology did not do was to explain why only some but not all members of a particular group or subculture experience social disorganization. Implicit in Durkheim's theory was the admission that cultural (moral) disintegration is informed as much by individual perception as it is by measurable material conditions. In other words, for Durkheim a moral crisis was both a cultural and a psychological condition.*

Ever since 1897, sociologists have assumed that by refining Durkheim's methodology they would be able to explain (if not predict) differences in group behavior. In terms of suicide, that translated into a series of studies whose object was to identify and analyze variations in the incidence of suicide among different groups—people united by gender, age, common experience, ethnicity, religion, residency, and so forth. These studies have been more successful in developing a sophisticated methodology for identifying differences in suicide completion rates among specified groups than they have been in constructing convincing explanations for the differences they have identified. The reason for this is that like Durkheim these researchers have not paid sufficient attention to behavioral variations within the groups. Sociology without psychology, Durkheim without Freud, seems unable to uncover a satisfactory answer to the question that sociology was founded to answer.

The discussion of the life histories of Meriwether Lewis and Abraham Lincoln that I presented in the preceding chapter provides a partial explanation of why seemingly similar experiences of severe early object loss do not always result similarly in a completed suicide. Loss itself matters less than the relative success or failure of the strategies each individual pursues to deal with his or her losses. Although

*Durkheim, as I have already pointed out, investigated suicide because he believed that its incidence could provide an objective scale by means of which social scientists could measure the level of cultural (moral, for Durkheim) health or pathology. His goal was to establish sociology as a science. His study of suicide would provide a model.

individual psychology provided meaning for these strategies, their success or failure was also informed by specific cultural and historical circumstances.

The limitation of individual cases studies is of course that they are always idiosyncratic. The limitation of group investigations is that while they often suggest plausible theories for differences in suicide rates among specified groups, they tend to ignore variations of behavior within the groups. A convincing theory must explain both group and individual differences. Although neither emphasized the point, both Durkheim and Freud ultimately agreed that suicidal behavior was always informed by an intersection of intrapsychic distress and cultural conflict.

A psychocultural approach seems essential if we wish to understand both differences between and within groups. In what follows I will build on the psychocultural model I applied to Lewis and Lincoln as we look at those American groups that social science methodology has identified as having the highest incidences of suicide: migrants and immigrants.

SUICIDE AMONG MIGRANTS AND IMMIGRANTS

In the early nineteenth century, when statistics on suicide were first collected systematically in the United States, they revealed that people who migrated were the population at greatest risk of killing themselves.[7] On a superficial level this is reflected by the fact that wherever the levels of in-migration have been the greatest, so has the incidence of suicide. The three maps that follow present a graphic example of this phenomenon over the past one hundred years. The suicide rate seems to mirror American migrations, presenting perhaps another side of the "Frontier Thesis." Since the 1850s, San Francisco generally has reported the highest suicide rate among urban areas. Although some might attribute this solely to that city's unique reputation and attraction for the off-beat, such an explanation will not suffice for other western cities like San Diego. Today, among the states California's suicide supremacy has been superseded by Alaska, Arizona, Colorado, Nevada, and New Mexico. Miami, Florida, is closing in fast on San Francisco, which has fallen behind Las Vegas. It is a historical rule of thumb that wherever the

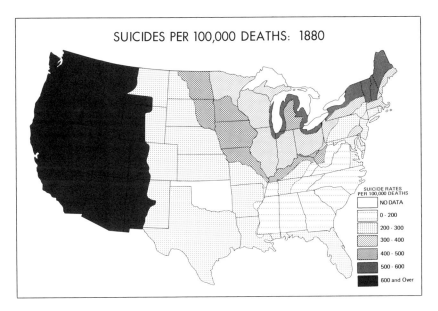

Map 6.1 Suicide by Region in the United States, 1880

in-migration is the greatest as a percentage of the total population, so is the overall suicide rate. This has recently been reflected in the South with its massive new Sun Belt migration; it has changed from its traditional last place to being presently second among regions in terms of the incidence of suicide.[8]

It would be an ecological fallacy, however, to conclude that migration itself causes high suicide rates unless it also can be demonstrated that those who migrate are actually the ones killing themselves. Such evidence exists in abundance and it can be found uniformly and historically in all suicide returns collected in the United States.[9] This connection, particularly as it relates to immigrants, has been commented upon by many of those who have analyzed the incidence and distribution of suicide in the nineteenth century.

In New York City, suicide statistics were first collected in 1805 and beginning in the 1840s they were published yearly for the entire state in the *American Journal of Insanity*.[10] By midcentury New York City was experiencing the greatest proportional inflow of immigration in its history and its suicide rate reached record levels. In 1861 the *New York Times* reported that "The last decade . . . shows an

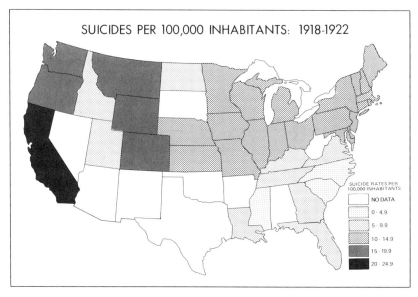

Map 6.2 Suicide by Region in the United States, 1918–1922

extraordinary increase of the suicidal mania among us. . . . This increase," the *Times* found, "may be attributable, in part at least, to the great German and Irish emigration of the decade." Indeed, the newspaper reported, in those cities with even higher percentages of in-migrations, such "as New Orleans, San Francisco, etc., the proportion [of suicides] is even larger than with us." Reviewing the statistics, the *Times* concluded that

> Of the whole number of suicides, one-quarter were Germans, another quarter Irish, a third quarter were natives of the United States, and the remaining fourth credited to various European nations. This gives an enormous disproportion of suicides to the foreign as compared with the native-born population; for while the proportion of foreigners of all nations in New York is only about one-third, the rate of foreign to native suicides is three to one.[11]

Federal census returns affirmed these conclusions. By 1890 the census reported that the suicide rate for foreign-born Americans was almost three times greater than for the native-born. These figures were consistent with the statistics reported in earlier census returns.[12]

Roger Lane's investigation of violence in nineteenth-century Philadelphia concluded that "The [suicide] figures for foreign born

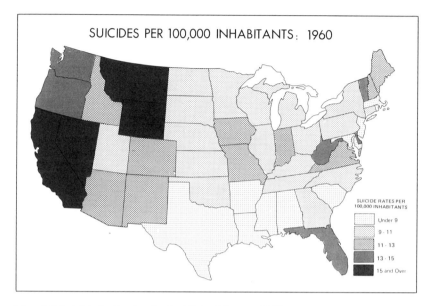

Map 6.3 Suicide by Region in the United States, 1960

are dramatic." For instance, in 1870 there were 184,000 immigrants living in Philadelphia, accounting for about 27 percent of the total population. "Their age-standardized rate of suicide during the five years 1868–1872," Lane found, "was 7.4 per 100,000, markedly higher than the 5.5 among natives." By 1900, the percentage of foreign born had dropped to 23 percent, but "for 1899–1901 their suicide rate . . . had climbed to 14.6, compared to 11.8 among natives."[13]

In 1927 Anita M. Muhl, a psychiatrist who had retired to San Diego, investigated coroners' reports beginning in 1911 and discovered that "the city of San Diego has the highest suicide rate in the United States and has held that questionable distinction for the past fifteen years." Muhl attributed this to "The symbolic significance of the Southwest corner of the United States. . . . The regression which it typifies attracts regressives, who express this destructive tendency by indulging in the most primitive form of regression which is known—suicide."[14] Muhl's study did not distinguish between native-born and foreign-born migrants. Reconstitution of suicide rates in San Diego since 1880 confirms Muhl's conclusions about that city's high rate of suicide in general and the rate among immigrants in particular.[15] From 1880 to 1900, 88 percent of all suicides in San

Table 6.2.
SUICIDE RATES IN SELECTED CITIES, ACCORDING TO NATIVITY
(rates per 100,000)

Place of birth	New York 1911–20	Chicago 1919–21	Philadelphia 1919–24	Boston 1911–15 1918–19
Total rate	15.4	15.2	no data	17.0
United States	8.1	9.4	9.3	12.7
All foreign	no data	28.8	20.1	21.3
Canada	no data	27.9	23.8	21.5
England	30.6	17.7	23.5	31.5
Ireland	15.3	8.1	10.3	15.3
France	33.8	no data	18.4	no data
Italy	10.5	15.8	10.5	10.9
Russia	17.8	19.3	16.1	16.0
Austria	no data	56.9	no data	no data
Hungary	no data	47.3	no data	no data
Germany	64.2	43.4	53.2	68.9
Scandinavia	no data	37.4	25.6	57.5
Poland	no data	11.3	11.2	no data

SOURCE: Ruth S. Cavan, *Suicide* (Chicago, 1928), p. 3.

Diego were born outside of California and 52 percent were born outside the United States.* The disproportional immigrant rate is reflected in the fact that in 1900 only 11.8 percent of San Diego's population was foreign-born.[16]

Ruth Cavan's classic study of suicide at the turn of the century found that immigrant suicides in New York City, Chicago, Philadelphia, and Boston far exceeded those of the native-born population (see Table 6.2). Moreover, Cavan discovered that "In all cases the rates for immigrants are two or three times as high as the rates for their brethren in Europe." Aubrey Wendling's investigation of San Francisco for the period 1938 to 1952 demonstrated the same thing—the foreign-born in the United States have a much greater risk of killing themselves than the native-born (see Table 6.3). Recent national statistics continue to confirm these earlier trends (see Figure 6.1).[17]

Nevertheless, analyzing the link between high suicide rates and immigration indicates that it is not "foreignness" per se that leads to

*For instance, all of the five suicides—White, Dillar, Golden, Creutzenberg and the embezzler Collins—that I introduced in this chapter were migrants; three of the five were immigrants.

Table 6.3.
SUICIDE RATES BY COUNTRY OF BIRTH, SAN FRANCISCO,
1938–1942 AND 1948–1952

Country	1938–1942	1948–1952
Native-born	25.3	20.7
Foreign-born	48.5	44.0
Germany	65.4	53.3
Italy	37.4	24.9
Russia	59.6	33.2
Ireland	34.9	20.0
England, Wales	36.4	39.3
China	42.2	no data
Canada	32.5	38.2
Denmark	94.2	94.3
Sweden	49.3	45.3
Norway	81.3	91.6
Austria	67.3	34.7
Finland	61.7	90.0
France	20.5	67.4
Poland	32.8	57.8

SOURCE: Aubrey Wendling, "Suicide in the San Francisco Bay Region, 1938–1942, 1948–1952," Ph.D. diss., University of Washington, Seattle, 1954, p. 81.
NOTE: Countries listed in order of number of suicides; rates per 100,000

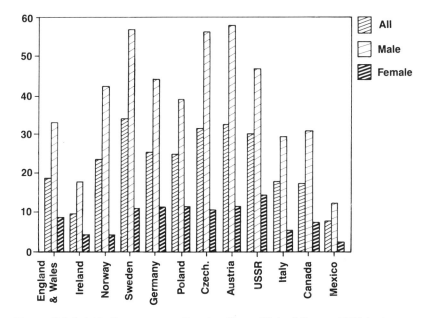

Figure 6.1 Suicide Rates among Foreign Born, United States, 1959 (rates per 100,000)
SOURCE: Louis Dublin, *Suicide: A Sociological and Statistical Study* (New York: The Ronald Press, 1963), p. 31.

Table 6.4.
SUICIDE RATES IN SELECTED COUNTRIES, SINCE 1880 (rates per 100,000)

Country	1881–85	1891–95	1910–14	1926–30	1960	1978
Ireland	2.2	2.9	3.2	3.3	3.0	5.7[b]
Italy	4.9	5.7	8.5	9.6	3.0	5.8[c]
Norway	6.7	6.5	8.5	9.6	6.3	11.4[d]
United States	5.6	6.7	15.4	15.0	10.6	13.5[d]
England, Wales	7.5	8.9	9.9	12.3	11.2	8.0[d]
Australia	9.7	11.9	12.8	12.2	10.6	11.1[d]
Sweden	9.7	14.4	17.6	14.5	17.4	19.0
Japan	14.6	17.9	19.0	20.6	21.3	17.7
Austria	16.2	15.9	25.7	35.3	23.0	24.8
France	19.4	24.1	14.0	15.8	14.6	16.5[d]
Germany	21.1	21.1	21.9	25.9	18.8[a]	22.2[a]
Switzerland	23.2	22.2	23.7	25.3	19.0	23.9
Denmark	24.8	25.0	18.6	16.8	20.3	23.2

SOURCES: U.S. Census, *10th Census, 1880*, 11:civ, table 10; *11th Census, 1980*, 4:1, 463; *12th Census, 1900*, 3:1, cclv; Ruth S. Cavan, *Suicide* (Chicago, University of Chicago Press 1928), p. 9; Louis I. Dubin, *Suicide: A Sociological and Statistical Study* (New York, 1963), p. 211; United Nations, *Demographic Yearbook* (New York, 1980), Table 21.
[a]West Germany, [b]1976, [c]1972, [d]1977

suicide, but rather that among immigrants, some particular groups have a much higher incidence than others. The distribution of suicide among immigrants reflects in an inflated fashion the suicide rates in their homelands. Beginning in the mid-nineteenth century, Germans and Danes recorded the greatest incidence of suicide, while Irish, Italians, and Norwegians continued to have among the lowest rates (see Table 6.4 and Figure 6.2). European immigrants to the United States had higher incidences of suicide than those who remained in their native countries. Thus Germans, Danes, and Austrians have had the highest rates in both the old and new worlds, while Irish and Italians have had consistently lower rates.[18]

These ethnic distinctions were reported and commented upon by the press. For instance, in an August 1859 editorial warning of an "Alarming Increase of Suicides," the *New York Times* pointed out that six of the twenty-six suicides that had been reported in its pages during the previous two weeks were German immigrants.[19] By 1861, the *Times* had concluded that "of all the peoples of Europe the Germans . . . furnished by far the largest proportion of deaths from this cause—as the Italians do the least; thus while the proportion of registered suicides in Naples and Palermo to the whole population is but 1 in 175,000 annually, in Berlin it reaches the terrific figure of

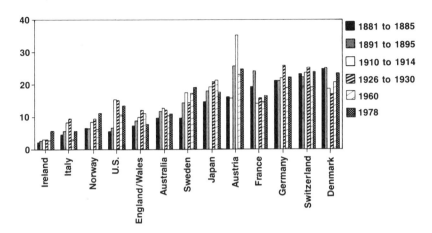

Figure 6.2 Suicide Rates in Selected Countries, 1880–1978 (rates per 100,000)
SOURCE: Same as Table 6.4

about 1 to 1,000." In New York City, the *Times* reported, one out of every four suicides was a German.[20]

By the mid-nineteenth century Germans and Danes seemed to make up a disproportionately large part of the American suicide rate.[21] This did not go unnoticed. Throughout the 1870s and 1880s those who investigated suicide in America were struck by this statistic. Writing in *Popular Science Monthly* in 1875 the respected neurologist Allan M. Hamilton pointed out that "Among immigrants, particularly the Germans, there is a great disposition to suicide."[22] Albert Rhodes informed readers of *The Galaxy* in 1876 of "the extraordinary preponderance" of suicides among those from Germany and Denmark. "This," he suggested, "has a particular interest to Americans, as the inhabitants of Northern Germany and Denmark emigrate to the United States in greater numbers than those of any other lands, with the exception of the Irish."[23] "It is interesting to note," wrote Thomas Masaryk in 1881, "that the Germans in America also show the largest number of suicides."[24] And the *American Journal of Insanity* reported that in 1883 German nationals accounted for 43 percent of all suicides in New York City.[25]

These nineteenth-century observations have been confirmed in twentieth-century studies. For instance, Lane discovered that "those born in Germany tended to be several times more suicidal than those born in Ireland." Although the German and Danish immigrant suicide rates were high, recent investigations demonstrate that this phenomenon was not exclusively limited to Germans and Danes. "In general," Lane found, "some ethnic groups had very high rates, and others had low ones." In 1890 Irish and Italian immigrants had "relatively low" rates, while Bohemians, Hungarians, Austrians, and Germans had very high ones.[26]

Ruth Cavan's study, which reviewed suicide in the United States from the 1880s through the 1920s, also discovered that "German immigrants in the United States have high rates; Scandinavian [with the exception of Norwegians], Austrian, and English come next; the Irish and the Russian groups follow, while the Italian immigrants have almost as low a rate as native-born Americans."[27] What is most surprising is that even today the incidence of suicide among European ethnic groups in America continues to reflect the patterns first noticed in the mid-nineteenth century.†

HISTORY AND MOURNING

Why have particular ethnic groups historically had much higher suicide rates than others and why has the incidence of suicide among European immigrants been greater than among native-born Americans?* In *Suicide and Scandinavia* (1964) Herbert Hendin suggested

---

*The evidence for these findings comes from sources similar to those for the gender rates discussed earlier and therefore it is liable to similar criticisms. In the case of women, the inherent bias in official statistics led to a substantial underreporting of women's suicides. This same bias seems to have worked against the underreporting of migrant and immigrant suicides. For instance, because migrants and immigrants had less social and political influence than most citizens, their families could exert only minimal influence on officials charged with determining if a particular death was a suicide. Nevertheless, both statistical and theoretical evidence indicates that immigrants and migrants killed themselves in greater proportions than did the rest of the population. The fact that the rate differentials among specific immigrant groups in the United States reflects in an inflated fashion the difference among suicide rates in Europe is persuasive evidence of the general reliability of immigrant suicide data. Although I do not claim that reported rates for migrants and immigrants are exact, I am persuaded that they reflect a certain statistical reality—that is, that suicides by migrants and immigrants have and continue to exceed significantly those of native-born Americans.

†Tied to the assumption that suicides resulted from individual psychological dysfunctions, early twentieth-century psychiatrists assumed that rates of insanity were ethnic-specific. As a result their discussions of ethnic variations often devolved into generalizations about national character and heredity. "Indifference to life is quite pronounced not only among certain individuals, but even in nationalities," reported Dr. Charles Pilgrim to the Sixty-second Annual

that differences in suicide rates among Danes, Swedes, and Norwegians could be understood in relation to the "different fantasies and attitudes toward death" found in each of those societies.[28] A historical review of attitudes toward mourning provides substance for Hendin's insights.*

The way that a society or subculture deals with death serves as an indicator of how its members cope with other losses. All losses—loss of employment, loss of self-worth, the loss of physical limbs or functions, or of material possessions—are "mourned." The way death is mourned is only an extreme illustration of the mechanisms available to any group at any time to deal with loss.

Philippe Ariès's impressive volume *The Hour of Our Death* identifies five consecutive western attitudes toward death spanning the past one thousand years. He labels these: "the tame death, the death of the self, remote and imminent death, the death of the other, and the invisible death." In each mode, Ariès describes profoundly different mourning rituals. In the early Middle Ages, he finds that "Death is not a purely individual act, any more than life is. Like every great milestone in life," Ariès writes, "death is celebrated by a ceremony that is always more or less solemn and whose purpose is to express the individual's solidarity with his family and community." That and Ariès's description of the intervening stages pose a stark contrast to contemporary practices of ignoring (repressing) death. In the modern era the community "forbid the mourning which (previously) it was responsible for imposing."[29]

Meeting of the American Medico-Psychological Association in 1906. "The ratio of suicides," he explained, "is very high among the Germans, Scandinavians, Bohemians, Russians, and French, while it is very low among the Irish, English, Canadians, Scotch, and Italians." Pilgrim attributed this fact to "inborn traits of character and mind" among some national groups that "make the act of suicide easy to embrace when a few clouds obscure the brightness of their lives." Given such tendencies, "those who are born with this craving for death," Pilgrim argued, "should no more be blamed for commiting the act than the man who is color blind should be blamed because he cannot distinguish the spectrum's rays." Charles W. Pilgrim, "Insanity and Suicide," *AJI* 63 (January 1907): 356–357.

*Almost two decades later these suggestions appear to have been largely ignored by those who have investigated American suicides. What is needed still, Hendin argued recently, is "a truly psychosocial approach, not an amalgam of Freud and Durkheim, but an approach that includes the examination of the psychodynamics of suicide of differing social groups . . . for any deeper understanding of the significance of suicide in a society." Only then, Hendin concluded, will we be able to "deal with the challenge of integrating psychological and social knowledge with our burgeoning, but still fragmented, psychobiological knowledge of suicide." Herbert Hendin, "Suicide: A Review of New Directions in Research," *Hospital and Community Psychiatry* 37 (February 1986): 153.

Ariès's history of mourning helps us to understand why the relationship between early loss and later suicide is qualitative and not quantitative. For instance, if the connection were merely causal, we would expect to uncover a greater incidence of suicide in early America than exists today, because high mortality rates increased the risk of loss. "Few people in the colonial period," Charles Jackson points out, "could have got very far along in life without losing more than one person in their immediate circle of relatives and friends." Nevertheless, this early loss did not lead to a high incidence of suicide because "the great majority of inhabitants . . . lived in small communities where mutual dependency between individuals was the norm." As a result, "the death of even a single individual was experienced as a community loss. In turn, the community rallied in a variety of ways to assist the bereaved family." This increased the likelihood of effective mourning.[30]

By the late nineteenth century, attitudes toward death and mourning in the West underwent profound alterations. For some, migration from rural areas or to different countries disrupted traditional patterns of social life. This in turn led to a decline in religious practice, which carried with it an increasing skepticism about the certainty of an afterlife, causing a new fear of death. "As death became less and less acceptable, not merely for self, but especially for close 'others,' it was domesticated and beautified," explains Jackson. Ariès suggests that "what the survivor mourned was no longer the fact of dying but the physical separation from the deceased." However, this "romanticism" of death was now confined to the nuclear family, which had "replaced both the traditional community and the individual of the late Middle Ages and early modern times." Migration and immigration exacerbated this process for many. Thus while the fear of loss moved to the center of mourning rituals, the increasing privatization of these rituals intensified individual feelings of loss, anger, and guilt.[31] According to Ariès, none of these general trends completely displaced earlier ones. Moreover, for specific historical reasons, some individuals and cultures remained tied to earlier modes of mourning.[32]

Evidence suggests that different national, ethnic, and religious groups often developed different ritual responses to loss. Hendin's study of suicide in Scandinavia concluded that "Differences in the fantasies about suicide, death, and afterlife . . . reflect differences in the psychosocial character of the respective countries." For instance, the Danes, whose response to death was similar to those of the Germans and Austrians, disposed of their dead with little ceremony. "The Danes," Hendin discovered, "do not use funerals as an occasion for grief or mourning; they find them painful and want them to be over as soon as possible. Being uncomfortable around a bereaved person, they aim at shortening the period of grieving and then wish the subject to be dropped." In Norway, on the other hand, which consistently reported the lowest suicide rates in Scandinavia, "one does not see those extremely rapid funerals with a brief period of mourning and a general 'get it over quickly' attitude toward death, which are common in Denmark and apparently reflect the widespread separation anxieties of the Danes."[33]

Like the Norwegians, the Irish and Italians in both the old world and new continued more traditional communal mourning practices, which included the participation of children. Settlement in large cities, the immediate establishment of burial societies and community support organizations as well as residential persistence all served to encourage continuity among the Italians and Irish.[34] On the other hand, migration to the United States greatly exacerbated the already high rates of suicide among Germans. Like Italians, German immigrants even earlier "had founded a rich array of voluntary associations supported by a sophisticated German language press and extensive systems of parochial and private German language schools." However, Kathleen Neils Conzen shows that unlike the Irish and Italians in the late nineteenth century, Germans' "assimilation, however defined, was high." As a result, "German language usage diminished rapidly, association membership fell off." By 1910, according to Conzen, "ward level segregation indices . . . for the 20 cities with the largest German populations [were] well below the . . . cutoff often accepted as indicative of segregation."[35] Ethnic groups with the highest incidence of suicide were less successful on the whole than the Italians and Irish in recreating the world they had left in Europe in their new American homeland. Not only were the cultural practices of some groups less effective for mourning than others, but these same groups had less holding power for transplanting communal supports.

What is crucial, however, is not German or Italian ethnicity as such, but the fact that among these immigrants who have experienced loss, Germans and Danes historically seem less likely than Irish or Italians to ritualize loss in effective ways. Nevertheless, those Italians who proved unable to deal adequately with severe loss also risked self-destructive behavior. As a generalization, we may conclude that Irish and Italian immigrants to the United States historically have provided themselves more opportunities for communal rituals for mourning loss than have German and Danish immigrants.

Of course to some extent all of these issues are informed by particular religious beliefs about and proscriptions against suicide.[36] Durkheim, for instance, found that Protestants were more apt to kill themselves than either Roman Catholics or Jews.[37] Nevertheless, even though some Roman Catholic groups such as the Irish and Italians report low suicide rates, other Catholics, among them Austrians, Southern Germans, and French, have among the highest rates. Norwegians, whose incidence of suicide was almost as low as Irish and Italians, are almost all Protestants. Even among Jews, whose suicide rates were the lowest of European religious groups in the nineteenth century, Austrian, German, and Hungarian Jews reported much higher incidences than Polish and Russian Jews.[38] Thus the incidence of suicide seems to be cultural rather than specific to religion.

In the end, what seems to separate Roman Catholics, Protestants, and Jews is less their particular religion's doctrines concerning suicide and more the intensity of the individual's or group's religious beliefs. As so many studies have shown, that intensity seems to result as much from idiosyncratic factors as from religious doctrines themselves. Moreover, as the evidence presented in earlier chapters has suggested, as many suicides may result from religious motives as are restrained by them.[39]

CONCLUSION

Migrants are both deserting and deserted. Migration itself may be a strategy of risk-taking pursued by some who feel particularly self-destructive. Those who migrate inevitably face major losses. Losses result not only from the material fact that others have been left behind, but also because the ritual structures that enable people to deal with loss frequently have been abandoned and cannot be reestablished. The more incompletely an early loss is mourned, the greater the chance that later losses will result in self-destructive strategies. When a subsequent loss (for instance, unemployment) occurs, earlier unresolved losses are recalled and these memories exacerbate the current crisis.*

Migrants tended and tend to be people in search of self-transformation. The centrality of the ideology of self-transformation in modernizing societies helps us understand why a general decline in mortality does not necessarily lead to a reduction in suicidal behavior. In a bourgeois society, an individual is no longer measured by status alone but by material possessions. Status and self-esteem become a function of these objects. In such a world, social relations become object relations. Spouses, children, parents, and friendships become objectified and symbolic of self-worth in a capitalist society. Objects owned (and the value of them)—automobiles, dwellings, clothing—also become equated with one's self; the possession of material objects merges with identity. Loss (of any of these) means more in the modern world than ever before. For many people the measure of success toward the goal of self-transformation remains lodged in these symbols. However, to achieve such a goal, modernization also demands a denial of the past (parents, traditional values, and so forth). Because the goal of self-transformation is tied to the repudiation of past values, social failure cannot be diffused by falling back on those traditional values that have been rejected both individually and culturally. Any loss comes to mean more to those who have failed at the goal of self-transformation (that is, who have suffered real or imagined material losses).

To the extent that transformation is either restricted or impossible, the guilt for having rejected past values and rituals intensifies as the dream of self-transformation fades. In any case, fantasies of self-transformation always carry with them a burden of self-rejection

*At least four of the five suicides that I discussed at the beginning of this chapter had experienced an earlier loss (desertion) of a loved one. White's mother died when he was a child, and when he was thirteen his father sent him from Hungary to live with his maternal uncle in San Diego. The *Union* reported that about a year before he took his own life, Dillar's "little daughter died, which seemed to have a lasting and depressing effect on his mind." Creutzenberg's wife and three children had left him, and Collins's wife and children had drowned two years before.

and to a certain extent a level of self-hate.[40] Immigration and migration exacerbate all of these problems.

One exception, which may prove this rule, seems to be evident in migration to Utah and Idaho. These two Mormon-dominated states, which have consciously recreated community structures and rituals, have had and continue to report the lowest suicide rates among jurisdictions with high levels of in-migration.[41] Not only does Mormonism encourage community participation in mourning, but also Mormons view death as a form of personal progress toward an afterlife in which the believing departed are immediately and literally resurrected.[42] Thus, although all migration creates object loss, those migrants who reconnect with meaningful rituals and social support face a lower risk of suicide than those who cannot do so.

A psychocultural approach forms part of the explanation of why similar experiences sometimes but not always result in suicide. Completed suicide is, after all, only one possible outcome of the strategies that individuals pursue as they mourn loss. Some cultures provide more effective mechanisms than others for dealing with loss. Nevertheless, the values and rituals that any group may provide as a restraining element against self-destructive behaviors always are limited by the extent of a member's sense of connection to and identification with those values. Assimilation, modernization, and migration all serve to lessen those ties. And as a general proposition the more any culture or ethnic group truncates mourning or demands the privitization of loss, the greater the possibility becomes that any of its members will pursue strategies that involve risk-taking that may result in the death of the actor.

Unemployment had a different meaning for Max White than for others. His failure to find work came to be synonymous with the loss of his "self." Earlier White had lost his family, his culture, and his country. As an immigrant in a strange land, cut off from whatever security he attached to his earlier life, White could find no effective strategy to deal with his current sense of loss. In desperation he called upon his memory of the childhood home he had left behind. Angry at a society that could offer him none of the strategies that he fantasized would have protected him in Hungary (though he must have realized that these too had failed him because of his mother's death and his father's desertion), White envisioned nonexistence as the only possible solution to his existential problem. He also fantasized that his death would serve as revenge on the enemies that he imagined had conspired to bring his life to its unhappy conclusion. Cultural circumstances informed the psychic conflict and limited the strategies that were available to Max White. Like White's, all suicidal behavior is informed by the psychocultural meaning that individuals and groups attach to earlier losses. Memory or, to put it more accurately, the way in which things are remembered, underpins this process. Thus, suicide and suicidal behavior are always informed by memory and spurred on by the hope of remembrance. It is more than coincidence that both Freud and Durkheim, whose writings laid the foundations for modern theories of suicide, assumed that memory held the key to any deeper understanding of human processes. While Freud laid bare the intrapsychic contents and power of memory and its distortions, Durkheim and his followers explicated the power of cultural memory. But, as the followers of Kraepelin have demonstrated, the mechanisms of memory extend beyond psychology and culture to biology. For the way that we remember things depends as well on an intricate series of neuronal connections stimulated by the release and transmission of specific neurochemicals. If memory has a biological component, so must suicide.

7

TOWARD A
PSYCHOCULTURAL BIOLOGY

LIKE so many others, Max White's case history revealed recurrent bouts of depression and evidence of somatic disorders that suggested neurological involvement.* These facts serve to reinforce the view, first articulated by Emil Kraepelin, that the causes of depression and suicide are to be found in biology rather than in culture or psychology. Abnormalities in brain function and physiology, Kraepelin insisted, separated the suicidal from those with similar life experiences who exhibited no suicidal behavior. Although he had not identified the specific pathological conditions that led to depression and suicide, Kraepelin was convinced that neurobiological science ultimately would yield the evidence he sought. Durkheimian and Freudian explanations were for Kraepelin and his followers no more convincing or scientific than late medieval pronouncements that Satan's temptations underlay suicidal impulses.

Were he alive today, Kraepelin would have reason to believe that his faith in neuroscience had been vindicated. Indeed, recent discoveries in neuroscience appear to contradict a psychocultural approach to suicide in two significant areas. First, pathological studies

---

*White had experienced frequent fainting spells. San Diego County, "Inquisition by Coroner's Jury," "Max White," 16 November 1893. See the testimonies of Marcus Schiller and I. C. Ulrich.

have revealed the remarkable plasticity of the brain in early childhood. These investigations have found that connections between
neurons (dendrites, axons, and synapses) are not fully developed at
birth and increase dramatically in length and synaptic complexity
during the first two years of life, continuing to develop at a more
modest rate until approximately the twelfth year. Because memory
transmission and storage appear to depend upon these neuronal
connections, we are unprepared, according to some neurobiologists,
to remember early childhood experiences. As a result, several neuroscientists have argued that early object loss, rather than being repressed, as psychoanalytic theory assumes, more likely is not even
recorded in memory. Second, as outlined in chapter 3, biochemical
investigations have connected suicide to low concentrations of the
neurotransmitter serotonin. This research has convinced many psychiatrists that depressive behavior, which often precedes suicide, has
a chemical rather than a psychological or social etiology.

   It is my thesis that these two neurobiological issues—the significance of early brain plasticity and the link between serotonin and
suicide—complement rather than contradict the psychocultural analysis offered in this book. Let us begin with brain plasticity.

Brain Plasticity

At a cellular level, memory is accomplished via the electrochemical
interaction of neurons and may involve their physical alteration.
The neurons of the phylogenetically older structures of the brain,
the brain stem, the cerebellum, and diencephalon are relatively prepared at birth to manage those internal bodily actions necessary for
an infant's survival: temperature control, blood pressure, breathing,
sleep, heart rate, and so forth. But the neurons of the newborn's
cerebral cortex, where neuroscientists believe that long-term memories are eventually stored, lack the extensive branching and intercon-
nection of dendrites and axons that characterize the adult brain.
The most rapid neuronal development takes place within the first
two years of life, but growth continues until puberty marks the end
of the critical period of human brain plasticity (see Figure 7.1).[1]

   Richard Restak observes that "the difficulty we all have retrieving
memories of earliest childhood has traditionally been attributed to

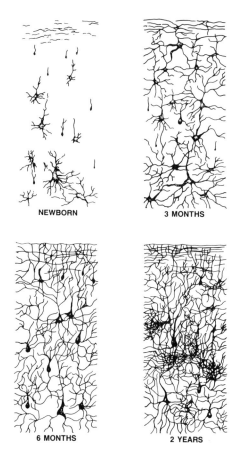

Figure 7.1 Early Neuronal Growth

'repression' . . . difficult, negative, or traumatic events were re-pressed so that painful experiences of the past would not be relived in the present." In view of the immaturity and plasticity of the infant brain, Restak suggests an alternative explanation: "It is likely that during our earliest childhood we simply hadn't yet developed those portions of our brain that would be responsible for recording memory events."[2]

But early childhood experiences, even if not completely encoded in memory, do play a crucial role in developing those neural connections available for future assemblies. "Learning and the exercise of

memory," Restak explains, "lead to enhancement of brain functioning."[3] Sensory experience prompts the multiplication of neural
synapses.[4] And strong circuits of such synapses facilitate the establishment, storage, and retrieval of memories. Thus, early experiences, even if they are not completely imprinted, play a crucial role
in developing the physical connections necessary for future experiences to be stored in the brain's long-term memory.

Neuroscientists are only beginning to untangle the vast neural
network that enables the memory system. But there is general
agreement on the importance of certain brain structures to that system and of the pathways taken by sensory information on its way to
memory formation. Normally, daily experiences are sent along neural paths through the thalamus while simultaneously being analyzed
in specialized neocortical areas. The resulting refined data converge
in the hippocampus, and, if not discarded, are eventually gated
from the hippocampus into long-term memory in the neocortex.[5]

There is, moreover, strong evidence that events that occasion
highly emotional responses are encoded more rapidly and lastingly
in memory. When an event triggers an emotional response, stress-
related hormones are released into the bloodstream. Under such
conditions, sensory information is apparently sent in parallel not
only to the hippocampus but also to the amygdala,* which "makes
an immediate connection with the memory structures" (see Figure
7.2).[6] The neural processing of emotion-laden experience appears
then to promote the rapid growth of lasting synaptic connections
within the memory system. And, as memory is state-dependent, its
retrieval is encouraged if the conditions under which it was first
encoded are replicated.

In contrast to the assertion that early childhood memories like the
death of a parent or a sibling simply do not exist, it seems more
accurate to assume that traumatic experiences of childhood are
encoded incompletely, but powerfully, into memory. These memories, or the memory assemblies that contain them, may be elicited
by psychically similar trauma later in life. But the imperfect nature of the original encoding condemns their recall to a kind of

---

*Like emotional experiences, sensations of smell also are routed directly to the amygdala,
accounting for the powerful effect of smell in stimulating memory.

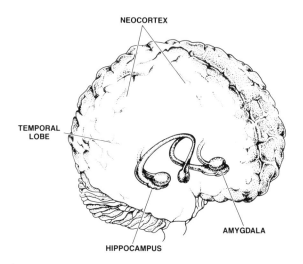

Figure 7.2 Hippocampus and Amygdala

"repression" unimagined by Freud.* That is, these incomplete memories may resurface during later periods of stress and emotional trauma. What is remembered will always be distorted and what is retrieved will remain disturbing, compelling, and incomplete. Early loss, therefore, may always remain "repressed," though not in the precise manner that Freudian theory suggests. Nevertheless, studies of early memory formation underscore a powerful connection between early losses and later behavior.

SEROTONIN AND SUICIDE

Neuroscientists have been unable to explain the functional relationship between serotonin and depressive disorders. Rather, they have relied upon the effects of antidepressants on serotonin and norepinephrine concentrations as evidence for the conclusion that depression has a biological rather than a psychocultural etiology.[7] Clinical

*On the other hand, as Israel Rosenfield reminds us, Freud assumed that "neurotic symptoms . . . are only recognized as 'memories' when linked to emotions. Crucial to the Freudian view is the idea that emotions structure recollections and perceptions." Israel Rosenfield, *The Invention of Memory: A New View of the Brain* (Basic Books: New York, 1988), p. 6.

treatment depends on pharmacological interventions because depressive episodes often may be alleviated or controlled by raising the available levels of these neurotransmitters in the brain.[8] While brain levels of both serotonin and norepinephrine have been associated with depressive disorders, serotonin has been particularly identified with suicidal behavior.

Although neuroscientists have investigated the transmission of serotonin extensively, until recently they have not concerned themselves with its synthesis or production. Yet once we understand how serotonin is produced in the brain we will be able to move a step closer toward a nexus between psychocultural and biochemical explanations of the etiology of suicide.

Chemically, many neurotransmitters are indistinguishable from hormones. Like hormones, neurotransmitters are made up of amino acids, which coordinate cell activity. Hormones are released through the circulatory system and travel in minutes or hours toward their goals. Neurotransmitters, on the other hand, transmit their messages in microseconds to brain cells.[9]

The impact of the social environment upon hormone operations is well known. For instance, social and medical historians have been aware for some time that the age of onset of menarche depends upon the relative body weight and height of young women.[10] The dramatic decline of the age of menarche from the late Middle Ages until the early twentieth century has been tied directly to changing diets, particularly to increased carbohydrate consumption among young women. Although researchers disagree about the significance of lower ages of menarche to fertility rates, all seem to agree that menarche itself is dependent upon nutritional levels.[11]

Some neurotransmitter production, like that of hormones, is linked to the ingestion of foods. In particular, brain levels of serotonin are coupled with the consumption of serotonin's chemical precursor, the amino acid tryptophan. One of the eight "essential" amino acids, tryptophan cannot be manufactured by the body itself and must be supplied by diet. Tryptophan also serves as a precursor for niacin, a coenzyme that is vital for the breakdown and utilization of proteins, fats, and carbohydrates. Lean meats, poultry, fish, and peanuts are rich in tryptophan. Approximately 1080 milligrams of tryptophan are needed to synthesize eighteen milligrams of niacin, the minimum daily requirement for a 160-pound adult male. How much additional tryptophan, if any, is required for serotonin synthesis has not been established.[12]

The ingestion of a particular quantity of tryptophan, however, does not automatically translate into a specific level of brain serotonin. Once tryptophan enters the blood plasma, it must compete with other amino acids in order to cross the blood-brain barrier for brain uptake. If the blood plasma contains high levels of competing amino acids, the ultimate amount of tryptophan reaching the brain will be lowered. When some carbohydrates such as potatoes are consumed, insulin is secreted, lowering the levels of other amino acids in the blood. This allows more tryptophan to travel to the brain. Although carbohydrate consumption itself adds nothing to the levels of tryptophan in the body, it does have a significant impact on how much tryptophan ultimately is synthesized as serotonin.[13]

Dietary habits are gender-, ethnic-, and class-specific. Evidence suggests that suicide completion has been historically lowest among specific populations such as women, the Irish, and the Italians, whereas it has been highest among white males, Danes, Austrians, and Germans. Recent social-historical investigations are beginning to provide us with surprisingly detailed information about diet and nutrition covering the past four hundred years.[14] Future research in both biochemistry and history might explore the relationship between changing diets and neurotransmitter activity among specified groups. Such an investigation would be difficult, but its potential results could be valuable.

Applying what is known about serotonin synthesis to groups with varied dietary habits is of course complex. For instance, those Western European groups with the highest suicide rates—Germans, Austrians, and Danes—appear to have diets that contain higher concentrations of tryptophan than those of the Irish and Italians. Moreover, some scholars have shown that the diets of women differed significantly from those of men in the same household. The evidence from these studies suggests that women's diets contain foods with lower concentrations of protein than men's diets.[15] However, serotonin synthesis is dependent on carbohydrate consumption because carbohydrates cause a release of insulin. Insulin lowers the blood levels of those amino acids that normally compete with tryptophan to enter the brain. Thus, a meal that contains relatively large amounts of tryptophan can also include even larger concentrations of competing amino acids. Such a meal actually lowers brain tryptophan and serotonin levels because the other competing amino acids are far more abundant than tryptophan in dietary protein. On the other hand, a meal low in protein but high in carbohydrates causes a maximal elevation of brain serotonin levels. Consequently, Germans, Austrians, and Danes, who appear to have diets higher in protein than do the Irish and Italians, may in fact have lower concentrations of serotonin and therefore be more vulnerable to depression and suicide.

It would be ecologically fallacious, however, to transform such observations into firm conclusions, because reported diets of specific populations tell us nothing absolute about the habits of individual members of a group. However, many of those who experience severe object loss often react by altering their dietary habits in ways that logically could affect their production of serotonin. Future investigations ought to consider the metabolic impact of loss as carefully as they have its psychological aspects.

THE PROBLEM OF CAUSATION

This review of the dietary connections between serotonin synthesis and depressive disorders may at first glance appear to contradict the psychocultural analysis offered in the preceding chapters. But a fuller understanding of the way neurotransmitters appear to operate suggests a complementary rather than contradictory explanation.

The relation between serotonin and depressive disorders is invariably explained in terms of cause and effect. That is, most biochemical researchers assume that a lower-than-normal level of brain serotonin (as evidenced by a low level of the metabolite 5–HIAA) is the cause of patient's depressive disorder. To put it another way, suicide has been tied to not having enough brain serotonin. Many psychopharmacologically oriented psychiatrists assume that low concentrations of serotonin result from physical or chemical deficiencies rather than from psychological conflicts. In a recent book aptly entitled *The Broken Brain* (1985), psychiatrist Nancy C. Andreasen heralds "the biological revolution in psychiatry" that has uncovered the chemical causes of depressive disorders. "While episodes of [mental] illness are sometimes triggered by unfortunate life events," Andreasen insists that "the basic causes lie in the biology of the brain."[16] Recent research and the arguments made in this book, however, suggest that the association of low concentrations of serotonin with suicide is more complex than that.

Speaking to this issue, psychiatrist Morton F. Reiser writes, "The fact that the clinical manifestations may be so profoundly influenced by drugs does not mean that the disorder is primarily and entirely 'organic' or 'biochemical'; it clearly does not justify patently incomplete conceptualizations of psychiatric illness—conceptualizations that fail to include mental processes (the realm of meanings, of subjective mental distress, and of conflicted motives)."[17] When pressed to explain causation, even Herman van Praag, whose pathbreaking work first connected serotonin with depression, admits that "whether the 5HT [serotonin] disorders are related to instability of mood regulation or to other personality characteristics remains obscure."[18] "Some basic dimensions of personality," writes Marie Åsberg, the principal investigator for most of the Karolinska Institute serotonin studies, "have a biological foundation and are under genetic control. The realm of personality is one of the possible targets for serotonin influence." But, Åsberg concedes, suicide

> may occur when an individual finds himself in a situation which he conceives as desperate, or when he has no hope for the future. Adverse life events may have created this situation, and the individual's perception of it may be coloured by a depressive illness. Whether this state of affairs leads to a suicide attempt or not is partially determined by the quality of the person's social support net. . . . Previous experiences of adverse events, e.g., childhood loss or repeated defeats during adult life may render the interpretation of current adversities more ominous.

Thus, specific psychological and social conditions as well as biological propensities underlie all suicides.[19]

Let us start with the possibility that Åsberg suggests, that many depressive episodes have external stimuli, such as the death of a loved one or the loss of employment. These traumata might excite the serotonergic system causing excessive or abnormal depletion of the supply of serotonin. If we remember that neurotransmitters are messengers, not messages, we will uncover a possible synergistic relationship between biochemical and psychocultural explanations.

Earlier we examined the relation between the feelings expressed in mourning a loss and the symptoms of a depressive disorder. Konrad Lorenz long ago found a parallel in animal behavior. When one of a pair of geese or ducks dies, the other begins a search for its missing partner that may last for days. During this search, the surviving animal manifests abnormal behavior that mirrors in many respects what we label as a depressive disorder.[20] Drawing on Lorenz's studies, Israel Rosenfield has suggested that "some of the symptoms of depression may derive from search procedures within the brain. Such procedures," writes Rosenfield, "are well known to computer scientists, and the brain performs analogous operations." For instance, the studies have shown that when some individuals fail to solve puzzles, they react as if they had suffered a mild depression. When they are shown the solution, the depression disappears. This suggests to Rosenfield that "depression during time of loss (of a job, of friends, prestige, and so forth) may be a period during which the brain is looking (searching) for a solution to problems that cannot be solved, at least in a relatively brief period of time." In some cases, like the loss of a loved one, the search may require the "reorganization of our patterns of thought." The time consumed in such a search "may involve trial and error" and the experience of "the hopeless feeling associated with depression."[21]

How serotonin acts on the brain is unclear, but it is possible that this neurotransmitter is necessary to the sort of search procedure proposed by Rosenfield. Current research suggests that serotonin is implicated in memory retrieval because serotonin relays messages to the hippocampus and the amygdala, both of which are intimately connected with memory formation and retrieval (see Figure 7.3).[22] The hippocampus has been identified as the seat of short-term memory. From the hippocampus, messages are relayed to areas of the brain associated with long-term memory storage.[23] The amygdala, on the other hand, directly transmits emotionally laden memories to long term storage in the neocortex.[24]

The ease and speed with which an individual's search for ways to deal with loss are accomplished depends to a great extent on the nature of his or her memories. When some individuals experience a loss, their search for answers to this puzzle becomes more difficult because they lack the long-term memories—either mourning has been truncated or their culture frowns on public displays of grief—

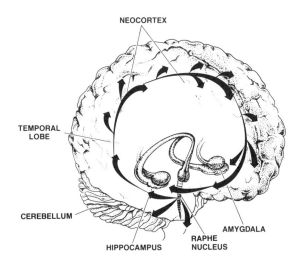

Figure 7.3 Likely Circuitry of Serotonin

which would enable them to deal with their loss. Those who search for ways to deal with loss but who find no systematic, cultural, or historical answers to their questions would logically deplete particular neurotransmitters more than those who more quickly uncover satisfactory solutions. Extreme traumata during early childhood would of course exacerbate these conditions, especially if they were incompletely mourned, because an individual would later find it even more difficult to assemble (remember) behavioral strategies to deal successfully with current loss. Additionally, if a person's diet is also low in tryptophan or inhibits tryptophan from traveling to the brain, serotonin's searching functions would be further impeded.

These speculations may help to explain the differences in suicide incidences among ethnic groups. Germans and Danes who truncate mourning rituals coincidentally appear to favor diets of the variety least favorable to brain serotonin synthesis. Moreover, one would expect that mourners in general would evidence lower concentrations of brain serotonin for similar psychocultural and biologic reasons; i.e., mourning would cause an increased demand on their serotonergic systems at a time when dietary irregularities may have hampered normal serotonin synthesis.

Although the evidence is far from complete, what we do know

suggests an interaction between psychocultural and biochemical factors in the etiology of suicidal behavior. The precise nature of that interaction must await a fuller elucidation of the serotonergic and other neurotransmitter systems. One thing, however, seems certain. The more we learn about how neurotransmitter systems operate, the more likely we are to uncover links between psychocultural and biochemical explanations for the etiology of suicide.

CONCLUSION

Suicide is such an immense and complex topic that no one study can ever claim to have "explained" its causes or even to have conveyed its history. The psychocultural biology of suicide that *Self-Destruction in the Promised Land* has offered is not intended to be the final word or *the* comprehensive explanation of the etiology of suicide. Rather, it serves as an argument for an interdisciplinary approach to topics like the social and medical histories of suicide. Much remains to be done; I hope others will find in these pages material on which they may build their arguments and explanations.

If I have insisted on anything in the preceding pages, it is that we only can begin to understand suicide by integrating social, psychological, and biological factors. In that sense, my sympathies lie with those nineteenth-century asylum psychiatrists whose lack of specialized training gave rise to what they called "moral treatment," but what we might better label holistic therapy. Although, or perhaps because, they lacked the specific knowledge that specialization has provided us since the last century, they reasoned that suicide resulted from a combination of organic, social, and psychological causes. I am convinced that these assumptions about the psychocultural and organic etiology of suicide will be vindicated. It would be a tragedy if we who are armed with information unavailable to them continue to be misled down paths of specialization that deny the validity of other approaches and other insights.

one study also must combine all three perspectives

ditto on onanism — now regarded as normal and, perhaps, in the age of Aids and narcissism, about to become the safest (and sanest) sex of all.

Epilogue

FROM JAMESTOWN TO JONESTOWN: SOME SPECULATIONS ON AMERICAN SUICIDE

T HE goal of *Self-Destruction in the Promised Land* is to make a case for an integrated interdisciplinary approach to the study of suicide. Throughout this work, history, or more properly historical perspective, was used as a tool in an arsenal of methodologies and arguments. It is beyond the scope and ambition of this work to provide a social or cultural history of American suicide. But some speculations are possible.

What follows is not a final or even a fully articulated outline for a social and cultural history of American suicide. Rather, I offer a series of reflections informed by the psychocultural biology I have elaborated in the preceding pages. Although my book must stand or fall without these conjectures, they could not be offered outside the context of the text that preceded them.

In recent years, the "new social history" has provided models for historians who wish to write socially based historical studies. Concentrating variously on quantitative analyses and studies of "mentalité," it has elaborated methodologies for historians to approach topics that were previously the property of the social sciences. Beginning with family and mobility studies, social history has moved in many directions. Subjects such as childrearing, family structure, sexuality, demography, and patterns of violence, heretofore investigated only by sociologists and anthropologists, have become legitimate areas for historical research. The sources for a history of suicide are similar to those used in many other social-historical investigations: census returns, medical records, coroners' reports, death certificates, newspaper stories, wills, and so forth. Indeed, one might wonder why a social history of American suicide has not yet been produced.

In part, the reason lies in the competition between sociological and psychoanalytic theories of the causes of suicide. Moreover, historians themselves are divided over methodological approaches. Social historians, even those who prefer explanations of "mentalité" to quantification, are suspicious of psychological approaches to history and especially have resisted psychoanalytic models, characterizing them as unscientific.[1] The issues that separate psychological from social history are similar to those that divide psychiatry from sociology. Social historians have accused psychohistorians of a tendency to emphasize internal conflict at the expense of social forces, while psychohistorians claim that social historians have ignored the psychological dimension of historical issues.

Historian Don E. Fehrenbacher summarized the objections to psychohistory in this way: "For the chronic weakness of his evidence, the psychohistorian compensates with elaborate theory, most of it drawn from psychoanalysis. But psychoanalytic theory . . . remains largely unauthenticated and highly controversial. Its generalizations are essentially a body of speculative lore rather than scientific knowledge." Psychohistory, argued Fehrenbacher, "habitually converts biography into mental diagnosis, almost always with derogatory effects." Its greatest "methodological difficulty" is "demonstrating causal connections between . . . a person's private life and the public events in which he or she participates."[2]

The uniformity and repetition of reactions like this one to psychohistory are surprising because they neglect the responses made by psychohistory's defenders.[3] Most of Fehrenbacher's allegations, for instance, had already been answered by Peter Loewenberg and Saul Friedlander.[4] As Dorothy Ross has pointed out, "historians are frequently warned off psychological theories, particulary psychoanalytic ones, because they are not truly scientific. Yet none of the social sciences," she reminds us, "meets the positivistic test of science established by the physical sciences. At a time when many social and behavioral scientists, and most psychoanalysts, have given up the claim to science in that sense, it seems inappropriate for historians, of all people, to uphold the positivistic canon."[5] Thus, in an ironic disciplinary twist, social science historians have accused psychoanalytic historians of a lack of scientific specificity, while psychiatrists have made the same charge concerning sociological explanations of behavior.* Nevertheless, historians cannot approach a topic that is as tied to individual psychodynamics as suicide seems to be while simultaneously ignoring its psychological aspects. Nor can they attempt to explain suicide's historical significance while neglecting its social context.

Beyond these issues of course lies the more troubling problem of integrating the biological aspects of suicidal behavior into a comprehensible social and cultural history of suicide. Overcoming this obstacle requires not only data that often are unavailable in most historical sources, but also it demands a familiarity with, if not mastery of, fields with which few historians are conversant.

In the preceding pages I have offered a psychocultural and biological model that I believe avoids both the reductionism and the pathological pitfalls that have angered so many critics of psychohistorical studies. Such an approach informs this essay.

DEATH IN JAMESTOWN

Jonestown, Guyana, where 912 Americans killed themselves in 1978, has become synonymous with mass suicide. Three hundred and fifty years earlier, the first permanent English colony in America experienced an even greater loss of life. Of the six thousand settlers who arrived in Jamestown, Virginia, between 1607 and 1625, forty-eight hundred died. Historians who have investigated the high mortality rate at Jamestown attribute most of these deaths to diseases incident to starvation. Contemporary and current observers agree that sufficient food was available to the settlers, if they had made a minimum effort to obtain it. However, Jamestown's colonists

---

*The two issues raised by both the critics and the advocates of psychohistory are coincidentally the same issues that have separated sociologists from psychoanalysts and neuropsychiatrists over the causes of suicide. First, as Ross admits, "A persistent feature of . . . most psychohistorical literature is . . . concentration on pathological aspects of personality." Second, as Fehrenbacher contends, these studies overestimate the effects of individual pathological behavior as an explanation for wider historical events.

resisted work; they were lethargic and apathetic. They failed especially to contribute to their food supply by their refusal to pursue ag-
riculture. Descriptions of the settlers' behavior indicate that most of
the deaths also were preceded by what today we would label as clinical depression. Many of the colonists acted in ways that mirror what
we have come to view as suicidal behavior.[6]

Like many immigrants since, those who settled in Jamestown in
the early seventeenth century had a distorted vision of what life
would offer on a new frontier. Their views about the new world
came in large part from translations of Spanish accounts originally
written to gain support for transatlantic expeditions. "The land that
emerged from these writings was," according to historian Edmund
Morgan, "an Eden, teeming with gentle and generous people who,
before the Spanish conquest, had lived without labor, or with very
little, from the fruits of a bountiful nature." These accounts were reinforced by reports of English visitors like the late sixteenth-century
explorer Arthur Barlowe, who proclaimed about the land that
would become North Carolina: there "the earth bringeth foorth all
things in abundance, as in the first creation, without toile or la-
bour." The natives, Barlowe wrote, were "most gentle, loving, and
faithfull, void of all guile, and treason, and such as lived after the
manner of the golden age."[7]

Jamestown's first settlers found a far different world. The Indians
often proved to be hostile and food had to be cultivated rather than
gathered from an Edenic garden. Within a year, seventy of the original 108 colonists had died. Four hundred and sixty-two new settlers
arrived in 1608, but during the winter of 1609, 440 were dead. And
so the story went, year after year. From 1619 to 1622 the Virginia
Company recruited 3,570 additional colonists, raising the population to almost five thousand. Three thousand of them died within
three years. By 1625, 80 percent of the first six thousand colonists
had perished. Although wars with the Indians accounted for a few
hundred deaths, the vast majority died from what appeared to be a
combination of starvation and disease.[8]

Morgan has explained this behavior as being consistent with a
feudal mentality that strictly defined and limited occupational pursuits.[9] Other investigators, however, have insisted that the idleness
and laziness of the colonists exceeded anything found in contemporary England. "Why," asks Karen Kupperman, "was not staying

alive sufficient incentive?" Seventeenth-century witnesses found the settlers' idleness and laziness extraordinary and "inexplicable." They described the colonists as "distracted and forlorne" individuals who died "shameful" deaths. The settlers' refusal to eat even the foods available to them can best be described as anorexia. They appeared to give up living. They refused to make even minimal attempts to stave off starvation and seemed willingly to submit to death.[10]

Kupperman discovered that the diet of early Jamestown settlers was based almost entirely on Indian corn.[11] Maize-exclusive diets, because they are deficient in niacin, often lead to pellagra. Depression is one of the symptoms of pellagra because maize, which lacks tryptophan and contains high concentrations of the competing amino acid, leucine, inhibits serotonin synthesis.[12] This imbalance suggests another factor that may have contributed to the settlers' widespread depressive behavior.[13] Thus we have another example of how the psychocultural components of suicidal behavior seem to have been exacerbated by biological factors.

Only the introduction of slave labor to plant and harvest the to-bacco crop rescued the Virginia colony and ensured its ultimate survival.[14] Ironically, the Jamestown settlement succeeded in large measure due to its reinstitution of a traditional caste society. The heirs of Jamestown's first settlers became English gentlemen land-holders, not self-transforming "new men."

Of course, the history of America's first permanent English settle-ment has not been portrayed this way. Beginning in grammar school American children are taught that the settlers at Jamestown persevered in the face of adversity. America's first frontier is pre-sented as having been demanding and dangerous, but brave men and women supposedly transformed it into a garden through hard work and self-denial. In the process, we learn, they also transformed themselves from people with traditional values and habits into mod-ern pragmatic Americans. This portrayal meshed with what has emerged from the eighteenth century to the present as America's frontier myth. Indeed, the story is represented much the same way in many university courses. For instance, the following is found in a highly respected and widely assigned college textbook:

The Virginia Company of London, in December 1606, sent over its first set-tlers, a hundred men and four boys crammed aboard three small ships, the

Susan Constant, the *Godspeed*, and the *Discovery*. In May 1607 they sailed up a river they called the James and landed on a peninsula they called Jamestown. Swampy and forested, the site was well situated for defense but a haven for mosquitoes and microbes. The colonists made almost every possible mistake in their new environment, but they also corrected their mistakes; and they had the vision, the courage, or the foolhardiness to stick it out.[15]

Although three-and-a-half centuries separate the immigrants of Jamestown from those of Jonestown, they shared some striking similarities. And, as we have seen, to some extent these elements are found in all suicidal behavior. Both groups sought a new life in a promised land and paradoxically both migrated in large measure to escape the modernizing societies in which they found themselves. When the vision they sought fell short of its promise, they became depressed and lethargic. Unable to return to a rejected past, they found in self-destruction a viable alternative.

THE FRONTIER MYTH

While the experiences at Jamestown were later distorted and incorporated into the frontier myth, the settlers at Jonestown, attempting to relive this mythic vision, rediscovered the truth about life and death on the frontier. Although the story of Jamestown was merged into the frontier myth, the underside of its history—the self-destruction that accompanies all self-transformation—was never fully submerged.

To the degree that migration itself is destructive of strategies for dealing with loss, it contributes to depression and to self-destructive behavior. Given the extent of migration in American history, one might wonder why the incidence of suicide in the United States is not higher than it is. Certainly migrants and their children appear to be particularly vulnerable to those elements of self-transformation that we have connected to suicide. Several possibilities are worth considering. First, as I attempted to demonstrate, official suicide statistics are at best unreliable and at worst misleading measures. Most experts agree that the actual incidence of suicide is from three to four times greater than the reported rate.[16] Second, as I have suggested throughout this book, by concentrating on completed suicides, we run the risk of misperceiving the nature and extent of suicidal behavior, only some of which results in what authorities officially label as suicide.

Nevertheless, it would be unreasonable to conclude that the belief in or striving for self-transformation results inevitably in self-destruction. No persistent ideology can be devoid of life-affirming aspects. Like all idea systems, self-transformation operates dialectically. Although it can be destructive of traditional values and rituals, it also offers a substitute value structure that speaks directly to the issues I have raised about the relationship between migration and self-destructive behavior. This alternative value system is informed in large part by the myth of the American frontier.

The frontier myth is presented to children and to immigrants as a substitute for those traditional values that have been or ought to have been discarded. Migrants with traditional old world habits and values, the story goes, were transformed by the wilderness experience into pragmatic individualists. And the lesson learned from this encounter with nature is that anyone willing to expend the energy and to sacrifice old or outworn ideas can transform *himself* into anything *he* wants to be. As a general proposition, I suggest that the retelling of this myth seems to be therapeutic, but acting it out, as was attempted in Jonestown, Guyana in 1978, can lead to self-destruction.

Like the events at Jamestown, the epic tale of the American frontier contains both manifest and latent elements similar to those found in suicidal behavior. Overtly, these appear in the hero's inadvertent contribution to his demise as a result of the success of his quest. On a covert level, the story describes a dynamic often associated with suicide. Repetition of these myths is not equivalent to suicidal behavior. Rather, the myth may serve a ritual function that acts therapeutically to blunt self-destructive urges.*

Whenever folklore or fiction is employed as a vehicle for understanding group consciousness, two objections need to be raised. First, to what extent should the writings of individuals be relied upon to explicate popular culture? Second, to what degree may universal stories be called upon to analyze particular national or cultural attitudes?

---

*Here and in what follows I adopt Roland Barthes's notion that modern myth functions as a distinctly ideological system that serves to contain cultural tensions. Roland Barthes, *Mythologies* (London: Jonathan Cape, 1972), pp. 115–120.

When a tale is repeated and imitated with its essential form and plot intact by a variety of writers and by the press for more than two centuries, and when the public at large continues to provide a wide audience, that story tells us something important about popular values. In fact, the authors who continue to produce these tales seem to be pandering to popular taste rather than leading it.[17]

All mythic stories, because they tell us psychological rather than factual truth, are universal in content. Nevertheless, certain aspects of universal mythic tales may be emphasized in some cultures at the expense of others. Particular national forms of archetypal stories do emerge and it would be as foolish to ignore these features as it would be to deny the universality of myth.[18] Scholarship on the American frontier hero and the cowboy, from Henry Nash Smith's *Virgin Land* (1950) to Richard Slotkin's *The Fatal Environment* (1985), has convincingly established this point.[19]

National myths do not manifest themselves all at once. It took a century and three-quarters from the founding of Jamestown for the American frontier hero to emerge in John Filson's 1784 *Adventures of Col. Daniel Boon.*[20] In this classic account, the trail-blazer feels an uncontrollable urge to move whenever his neighbors come too close. Eventually the American press imitated art in its portrayal of Daniel Boone. "This singular man," proclaimed *Niles Register* in 1816, "could not live in Kentucky when it became settled . . . but prefers the woods where you see him in the dress of the roughest, poorest, hunter."[21] "As civilization advanced," reported the *New York American*, Boone, "from time to time," retreated."[22] In 1833, in the first of fourteen editions spanning thirty-six years, Timothy Flint's *Life and Adventures of Daniel Boone* explained that "go where he would," Boone found that "American enterprise seemed doomed to follow him and thwart all his schemes of backwoods retirement. He found himself . . . surrounded by this rapid march of improvement . . . which he could not prevent."[23] Thus, by the time that James Fenimore Cooper enshrined Boone as Hawkeye in the *Leatherstocking Tales*, few were surprised to read that the hero was "driven by the unparalleled advance of population, to seek a final refuge in the broad and tenantless plains of the West."[24]

Paradoxically, the force of civilization that pushed the hero ever westward was of his own creation. Filson's *Adventures of Col. Daniel Boon,* for instance, appeared as an appendix to a property prospectus assuring investors that Kentucky was a safe place to purchase land, thanks to the labors of Daniel Boone who had pacified the local Indian tribes. "The account of my adventures," Filson has Boone say, "will inform the reader . . . that I now live in peace and safety . . . in this delightful country, which I have purchased with a vast expense of blood and treasure, delighting in the prospect of its being, in a short time, one of the most opulent and powerful states on the continent."[25] This was hardly a message aimed at discouraging settlement. While a captive of the Indians, Boone, according to an 1813 account, lectured Chief Montour on the superiority of white civilization, which soon would transport culture, refinement, and "social love" to the "heathen frontier."[26] Timothy Flint understood that Boone's actions brought about the conditions that impelled him westward: Boone "saw . . . that the great valley must soon become the abode of millions of freemen, and his heart swelled with joy, and warmed."[27] Cooper related, if he failed to explore, the hero's dilemma: "The sound of the ax has driven him from his beloved forests to seek refuge, by a species of desperate resignation, on the denuded plains that stretch to the Rocky Mountains. Here he passes the few closing years of his life, dying as he had lived."[28] Thus, the Boone-type, whether he appeared as Davy Crockett, Leatherstocking, or as the scout in repeated American folklore, opened the paths that forced him westward until his success set the stage for his disappearance.

The manifest content of these tales does not represent an actual suicide. Rather, the hero's overt behavior resembles the life histories of those groups of Americans, migrants and immigrants, who have shown themselves to have a very high potential for suicide. This suggests a possible connection between the unconscious dynamic of actual suicidal behavior and the latent content of American frontier epics.

Fictional frontiersmen seem to pursue strategies found among incomplete mourners—the pursuit of risk-taking activities and a difficulty in forming stable object relations. Moreover, as migrants they fit the epidemiological category of those who historically have run a greater risk of suicide. In the Boone and frontiersman stories, problems concerning object relations often are tied to risk-taking. Cooper's deerslayer, for instance, proclaimed that, although he would risk his life for her, he could not marry Judith. Curiously, the deerslayer tied his decision to his dead parents: "Everything in the way of fri'ndship Judith—even to sarvices and life itself. Yes, I risk as much for you." But, he cannot marry her because "I do not think I feel . . . as if I wished *to quit father and mother—if father and mother was livin'; which however neither is* —but, if both was livin'; I do not feel towards any woman as if I wished to quit 'em in order to cleave unto *her*."[29]

These heroes tied their rejection of marriage to risk-taking, to migration, and, as in Leatherstocking's case, to earlier object loss. Unwilling to form enduring object relations, the heroes are migrants, moving further and further west in search of some undefined and often mysterious goal. The frontiersman is of course a hunter, but what he is hunting for remains obscure to us and to him. "Leatherstocking," notes Slotkin, "is doomed to wander until his end on a fruitless quest for faith and identity."[30] The quest may point to incomplete mourning as a fundamental element of American culture.

The uncritical incorporation of the frontier hero tale into an historical explanation of American society reached its apotheosis with Frederick Jackson Turner's announcement of the "Frontier Thesis" in 1893.[31] As with the myth of the frontiersman from whose roots it sprang, the power of the thesis lay not in its novelty but in Turner's use of a traditional tale to explain the origins of America's crisis of the 1890s. This fact explains the almost instant popular appeal of the "Frontier Thesis."[32]

It is no coincidence that the same national crises of economic depression and massive immigration that informed Turner's explanation also fueled widespread fears about a suicide epidemic. If individual frontier heroes were symbolic of the ontogenetic content of American suicide, the "Frontier Thesis" provided a phylogenic context. Turner's arguments that the frontier West provided an escape valve for recurrent eastern urban instability proved attractive because it seemed to affirm the truths of the repeated tale as that reflected a seeming repetition of the national experience. The nation of migrants and immigrants kept moving west to escape its own civilizing force. "American social development has been continually beginning over again," wrote Turner. "This perennial rebirth, this fluidity of American life, this expansion westward with its . . . continuous touch with the simplicity of primitive society furnish the forces dominating American character."[33] Yet, like the frontiersman, the expanding nation continually recreated the very civilization that it sought so desperately to escape: "a new society . . . emerged from its contact with the backwoods. Gradually this society loses its primitive conditions, and assimilates itself to the type of older social conditions of the East."[34]

For Turner, as for most Americans, the East symbolized parental authority. On a superficial level, the attraction to the wilderness seems to grow, as the *North American Review* suggested in 1846, out of "a love of nature, *of perfect freedom*, and of the adventurous life in the woods."[35] However, if Turner's thesis is understood in psychological terms, the East is rejected, not, as Alan Beckman suggested, because it is overbearing, but rather because it appears particularly powerless.* Turner pictured the East as unable to provide justice because "an aggregation of property and vested rights are in the foreground." But in the West, "the frontiersman was impatient with restraints. He knew how to preserve order even in the absence of legal authority."[36] The West, on the other hand, offers the anxious child a harsh, but protecting environment; one that promises a mythic reunion with an all-powerful nature. In the West "there was a reproduction of the primitive idea of the personality of law," Turner argued. "A crime was more an offense against the victim than a violation of the law of the land. Substantial justice, secured in the most direct way, was the ideal of the backwoodsman. He had little patience with finely drawn distinctions or scruples of the method." In the West, "complex society is precipitated by the wilderness into a kind of primitive organization based on the family."[37] Thus, the attraction of the "Frontier Thesis" lies in its unconscious contents of infantile revenge, justice, and reunion and not in its alleged vision of freedom.

Whatever else the Turner thesis had done, it contributed to the decline of the mythic frontiersman as a literary type. Yet Boone's

*Beckman argued that the frontiersman desires "to dominate, to be destructive, to be masterful, and to use the West and its resources in a destructive way." He saw the hero "in a state of rebellion against authority." Although Beckman has identified the overt content of the story, he missed the repressive nature of the Oedipus Complex. Thus, he confused the frontiersman's actual domination of the West with his nostalgic wish to merge with nature. Beckman, in an otherwise imaginative essay, clings to a literal vision of the parent complex that even Freud rejected. Alan Beckman, "Hidden Themes in the Frontier Thesis: An Application of Psychoanalysis to Historiography," *Comparative Studies in Society and History* 8 (1966): 368–370. For Freud's view of the parent complex, see Sigmund Freud, *New Introductory Lectures on Psychoanalysis* [1933] (New York: W. W. Norton, 1964), pp. 63–65.

successor, the cowboy, who first emerged in Owen Wister's *The Virginian* in 1902, retained the symbolic power and cultural meaning of his predecessor.[38] Like Filson's Boone, Wister's cowboy tale* evolved over the years until later authors and the public settled upon a final, stock formula.[39] The countless repetitions of this plot in novels, films, radio, and television hardly vary. Arriving in a town beset with evil, the cowboy destroys the serpents that infest the American garden, only to put an end to his own usefulness. "The ideal cowboy," suggested David Brian Davis, "fights for justice, risks his life to make a dismal little cowtown safe for law abiding, respectable citizens, but in doing so he destroys the very environment which made him a heroic figure."[40] A modern Moses, the cowboy may never inhabit the promised land that he has pacified, and he too is destined to wander in the American desert, bringing the order that condemns the necessity for his existence.

We should not assign these heroes to America's more primitive past. Their basic outlines remain alive in Louis L'Amour's ever-popular novels, in endless television shows, and in contemporary films such as *Star Wars*, *Raiders of the Lost Ark*, and *The Electric Horseman*.[41]

Like the frontier hero, the cowboy seldom married and seemed capable only of adolescent attachments to women. Hopalong Cassidy, a cowboy hero whose resilience was evident in his long career in novels, films, and finally on television, remained the representative type from 1910 until the 1950s. Hopalong's explanation of why he could never marry fits the classic American hero mold:

> "But you can't always move on Hoppy!" Lenny protested. "Someday you must settle down! Don't you ever think of marriage?" "Uh-huh, and whenever I think of it I saddle Topper and ride. I am not a marrying man, Lenny. Sometimes I get to thinkin' about a poem a feller wrote, about how a woman is only a woman—" "The open road is my fate!" she finished. "That's it. But can you imagine any woman raised outside a tepee livin' in the same house with a restless man?"[42]

The cowboy, according to Kenneth Munden, "shields women but he does not marry them. . . . When given the choice, the hero chooses his horse or gun instead of the woman."[43] Their refusals to

---

*We are concerned here with what emerged as the popular, heroic version and not with the actual, historical cowboy.

marry, according to Richard Slotkin, suggest that American heroes "never attain the final prize of heroism, which is to become . . . the founder of a people or a dynasty."[44] Such men leave no progeny and in a symbolic sense commit race suicide. As D. H. Lawrence pointed out, the American frontier hero rejects sex in favor of violence: "he lives by death, by killing the wild things of air and earth."[45]

The archetypal cowboy tale was offered in the 1953 film classic *Shane*, based on Jack Shafer's novel.[46] Like Leatherstocking, in whose costume he literally first appears, Shane hasn't—nor will he ever have—a woman of his own. Instead, he risks his life to save another man's family. The homesteaders of the valley are locked in a deadly struggle to preserve their nuclear family structure from the intimidations of the family-less cattlemen of the Ryker gang. Shane, who owns no property save his horse, has abandoned whatever family he may once have had. Although the hero never will have a wife, child, or home of his own, he fights the sodbusters' battle to preserve their families, property, and dignity. As the young narrator proclaims: "He was the man who rode into our little valley out of the heart of the great glowing West and when his work was done rode back whence he had come and he was Shane."[47]

In the tales, the heroes have no living parents. "The hero of *The Virginian* is nameless. A child of the best stock of the East," David Noble points out, " he has fled its complexity, decadence, and materialism while only a youth to find freedom in the West." The cowboy was "a self-made orphan . . . the archetypical American; . . . he represented all the people who left Europe and families and history behind."[48]

"The cowboy hero's arrival from nowhere at the beginning of each adventure," writes Warren Barker, "suggests the child's feeling of mystery and confusion about its own origin."[49] The cowboy "often lacks a family," and according to Harry Schein, he "is one of those exceptional human beings who seem never to have had a mother."[50] These stories* are similar to the common childhood nostalgic fantasy of "the substitution of both parents . . . by more exalted personages" that Otto Rank linked to mythic heroic tales.

*Two points deserve emphasis. First, in most cases these are tales told to or by adolescents. Second, the issues raised in these stories focus on adolescent conflicts with parents, with members of the opposite sex, and with issues of identity.

"These new and highborn parents," Rank explained, "are invested throughout with the qualities which are derived from real memories of the true lowly parents. . . . The entire endeavor . . . is merely the expression of the child's longing for the vanished happy time, when his father still appeared to be the strongest and greatest man, and the mother seemed the dearest and most beautiful woman."[51]

Like Boone or the Virginian, these orphaned heroes are self-made men who help to complete in storybook form the fantasy of becoming the father of oneself. They abandon in order to avoid being abandoned—another childhood fantasy with suicidal contents. As with all tragic figures, their actions of course are shaped by a destiny beyond their control. When young Joey pleads with Shane to remain, the hero explains, "A man has to be what he is Joey, you can't break the mold."[52] Yet, by rejecting the parents they may have had, these heroes choose the ultimate, all-powerful parent, nature. The code of the wilderness is harsh and arbitrary, but paradoxically, if obeyed nature provides total nurture for her children. Therefore, the goal of the mythic hero is regressive and homeostatic—a time and place without conflict, located in the recesses of early unrecallable memory.

It is not surprising that the frontiersman and the cowboy helped to create the conditions for their own demise; for the frontier never could provide an adequate substitute for the lost parents it symbolized. The impetus for the hero's quest was located in his primitive past. Try as he might to find reunion through the repetition compulsion of migration, only death offered the respite he sought. Often, at the end of the tale, the hero admits as much:

> "Your days are over!" Shane warns the ruthless cattle-baron. "Mine?" he replies. "What about yours, gunslinger?" "The difference is," laments Shane, "I know it."[53]

Like the suicide, the fantasy is not death, but rather, as Robert Jay Lifton suggests, a quest for a less troubled existence, one that includes as all suicides do at the unconscious level revenge, guilt, and nostalgia.[54]

The latent content of the American frontier myth is similar to the unconscious dynamic of suicidal behavior. Through a series of strategies, many of which contain elements of repetition compulsion, both the suicide and the hero seek reunion with lost love objects. For an actual suicide, the available alternative strategies may prove unsatisfactory because the object sought has been lost forever and the rituals available have proved inadequate. The mythic hero desires reunion with once-rejected and rejecting parents and in the end the frontier fails to provide an adequate substitute. Of course, the hero does not actually kill himself. The parallel between the hero and the suicide lies in their motivations, goals, and strategies rather than in their method of dying.

JONESTOWN, THE FINAL FRONTIER

The suicide of 912 Americans in Jonestown, Guyana, in November 1978 provides an extreme example of how acting out the frontier myth rather than merely believing in it can lead to self-destruction. The followers of the Reverend Jim Jones migrated to Jonestown on the edge of a South American jungle in the hopes of attaining the self-transformation explicitly promised in Turner's Frontier Thesis. Jones's "Perspectives from Guyana" portrayed Jonestown as a peaceful "Promised Land." There was nothing, Jones wrote, "so fulfilling anywhere as living this country life. . . . I work in the fields whenever I can. . . . It strikes me as immensely sad that the vast majority of people submit to the regimentation and extreme tension of a highly technological society. They pay such a high price in strokes, hypertension, physical diseases, and mental stress." But in Jonestown, "by sharing and living the highest ideals," its pioneers "have passed beyond alienation and have found a way of living that nurtures trust—one that could speak to a society grown cynical and cold." Yet, this "cooperative living provides such security" that "it provides the structure to see that everyone's needs are met. It maximizes everyone's own individual creativity and allows time for pursuit of individual interest."[55]

His colony, Jones explained to San Francisco columnist Herb Caen, functioned as a safety valve for urban discontent. "Many of the young people who came here were alienated, angry, and frustrated. They were tired of the hypocrisy that cried over 'human rights' while they were being buried alive." Like the promise of the frontier, "the society we are building here in Guyana," Jones wrote, "has given people who were considered refuse in urban America a new sense of pride, self-worth, and dignity."[56]

In fact, Jonestown had more in common with a slave plantation than with Turner's portrayal of the frontier. While a white minority led by Jones formed the governing body, the majority of settlers, who were black, labored in the fields eleven hours a day, six days a week and seven hours on Sunday.* Minor infractions of the rules or reasonable complaints were met with severe public corporal punishments. While Jones and a favored few dined on meat, the field hands were fed "rice for breakfast, rice water soup for lunch, and rice and beans for dinner." Only on Sunday was this diet supplemented with "an egg and a cookie."[57]

James Warren Jones, born in Lynn, Indiana, in 1931, was the only child of James T. and Lynetta Jones. Unable to hold full-time employment as a result of injuries sustained during the First World War, James T. Jones contributed to his family's support with monthly government disability checks, while Lynetta Jones, whose marriage had dashed her young fantasies of life as an anthropologist, took factory work whenever it was available. As a young child Jones was often left in the care of neighbors. Later in life, Jim Jones would insist that his mother was a Cherokee Indian, although this claim appears to have been a complete fabrication. Like many others in Lynn, Jim's father James T. Jones joined the Ku Klux Klan and espoused its racist views. Jim Jones's reputation as a childhood bully and his later extensive use of corporal punishment and other forms of humiliation at his People's Temple suggest that Jim was beaten as a child.[58]

When Jim Jones was fourteen his parents separated. The subsequent divorce forced Lynetta and Jim to leave segregated Lynn and move to a bigger town with a large black population. Jim Jones apparently never saw his father again. In 1951 the elder Jones, now despised by his son, died alone and in poverty. Whatever deeper ambivalences informed Jones's relationship to his father remained submerged until the son emerged as the all-powerful punishing and forgiving "father" of his People's Temple. As a youth Jones attempted to deal with his early losses in a variety of ways. He looked

---

*After the mass suicide, almost half-a-million dollars of uncashed social security checks were found in Jones's cabin. Millions more deposited in banks throughout the world have yet to be recovered.

after stray animals and held funerals for dead pets. He organized mock religious services for other children, which he led with dictatorial seriousness. His early fantasies of heroism were reinforced by his mother's often repeated belief that she had borne "a messiah," a son "who would right the wrongs of the world."[59]

Remembered as a mediocre student who displayed some intellectual promise, Jones attended the University of Indiana for one year, but dropped out in 1949 to marry a nurse four years his senior. For the next decade Jones, an unordained minister, moved from one religious denomination to another. In 1956 he founded the People's Temple in Indianapolis and aimed his ministry at a poor, mainly black congregation. Contrary to his father's example, Jones became a prominent local advocate of racial desegregation. Yet his father's lifelong illness may have provided some of Jones's impetus to protect the weak and dependent from injustice. "Dad" to his new-found followers, Jones became the protecting father he never had. And believing his own fantasies, he became a self-made American Indian who set out to avenge centuries of injustice. For a while, it seemed to work. Jones attracted a wide following of poor and idealistic parishioners and a reputation as a spokesman for civil rights in Indianapolis. Then, inexplicably, he decided to move to a new frontier.

In 1966 Jones informed his congregation that an article he had read in *Esquire* had convinced him that a nuclear attack would destroy Indiana. There were only two safe havens, the jungles of Brazil or the redwood forest near Ukiah in northern California. That year Jones led one hundred disciples to what he called the "promised land," in Ukiah, California. Again, he established himself as a spokesman for the oppressed and in 1971, apparently no longer concerned about nuclear vulnerability, he moved his People's Temple to San Francisco. Advocating a variety of social causes supportive of the poor and of blacks, Jones also turned out voters. By the mid-1970s, Jim Jones had become a politically influential figure in the Bay Area.

Jones portrayed himself as the embodiment of the martyred hero, unappreciated by his contemporaries. At times he claimed to be the incarnation of Christ, literally healing the sick and raising the dead. At other times he asserted that he was the reincarnation of Lenin, presenting arguments for social justice based upon a vaguely socialist rhetoric. He also compared himself to Martin Luther King, Malcolm X, and Eugene Debs. "No one," Jones wrote of himself, "could be more fearless or principled."[60]

While appearing publicly as a champion of the oppressed, Jones tightened his emotional stranglehold on the already vulnerable members of the People's Temple. Playing on alleged enemies who threatened his congregation's existence, Jones heightened his demands for loyalty, praise, donations, confessions, and obedience from his followers. The more that Jones's wishes for total devotion were fulfilled, the less satisfied he became. He began to project with even greater intensity the anger that resulted from his early object losses. Jones, whose parents' marriage had failed and whose own marriage had been a sham of semi-public unfaithfulness, sought to destroy his followers' marriages:

> Jones appointed a marriage committee that attempted to regulate courtship, marriage, and intercourse. Couples were told to change partners. Extramarital liaisons were encouraged. The living quarters discouraged privacy. Family members were encouraged to spy on one another. In many of his six-hour sermons, Jones dwelled on sex. He forced others to concede his heterosexual supremacy and insisted that all cult members confess their homosexuality. As the group's influence grew, mature personal relationships not only were destroyed but were replaced with the kind of primitive, part-object, poorly differentiated, polymorphous impersonal relationships.[61]

Psychiatrist Hugo Zee concluded that Jones displayed the "major features" of "paranoid personalities," especially the "need to betray important attachments—people, ideals, or causes." Jones demonstrated an "inability to establish enduring relationships. After a period of expressing devotion to a person, cause, or group, paranoid individuals have an irresistible urge to betray that alliance and to espouse another object." Often, they "betray former allies by playing them against each other. Jones," according to Zee, "clearly met these criteria by betraying his father, his hometown, his Methodist affiliation, and later his wife, his religion, his government, his country, and even his own followers." Paranoia is often accompanied by narcissism. Jones constantly "devalue[d] the idealized object he once craved in order to maintain his grandiose illusion, to avoid feelings of shame about his neediness or inferiority." Moreover, "on a number of occasions, Jones defiled the Bible by spitting on it or throwing it on the floor, telling his followers that they paid too much attention to it and not enough to him. His urge for 'narcissistic repair' consumed itself, revealing the underlying depravity, greed, ruthlessness, and exploitativeness of the dissociated 'bad' self-representation."[62]

Even if we do not go as far as Zee in characterizing Jones's symptomatology, Jones certainly pursued strategies that indicated severe unresolved object conflicts, especially with regard to his parents. Whenever his attempts at object reunion failed, Jones sought his next frontier. He had called Ukiah the promised land, but abandoned it for San Francisco. Within two years of migrating to San Francisco, Jones laid plans for finding a utopian frontier in the South American nation of Guyana. Prompted by the belief that a fire in his San Francisco temple was set by sinister forces who planned to destroy him, Jones sent a mission of twenty of his followers to Guyana in 1973 to negotiate a lease for twenty-seven thousand acres in a jungle on the outskirts of Port Kaituma. The settlement, Jones announced, would be used as "an agricultural mission for ghetto youths and others whose spirits could benefit from exposure to rural life."[63]

Also in 1973, the year that Jones began his plans for his Guyana "promised land," he informed his followers that they might have to die for their cause. During the next five years, the talks about group suicide increased. On Memorial Day 1977 Jones spoke at an anti-suicide rally held on the Golden Gate Bridge, a structure that since its opening in the 1930s had been the symbol and vehicle for hundreds of suicides. It was a curious talk, at once condemning suicide while also justifying it as a reasonable response to an uncaring world. Suicides, Jones explained, were "casualties of society. For, in the final analysis, we have to bear collective responsibility for those individuals who could not find a place to go with their burdens, who came to that place of total helplessness, total despondency." A suicide, Jones insisted, "is a victim of conditions which we cannot tolerate, and I guess that was a Freudian slip because I meant to say which *he* cannot tolerate, which overwhelm him for which there is no recourse." Jones began to ramble. He asserted that "several thousand" of his followers had been so depressed lately, because "there are those elements in the society," especially "one magazine in particular," which was attempting to discredit the People's Temple, that they had considered suicide. His son, Jones revealed, told him that he "felt like committing suicide" because "maybe it might cause people to care if I jumped off the bridge while you were speaking." Even he, Jones confessed, had been considering suicide: "I think the despair got to me yesterday. If it hadn't been for an academy award winning actress joining our church . . . I think I would have been in a suicidal mood myself today for the first time in my life."[64] Jones presented the adolescent's fantasy of revenge: if criticism of the People's Temple and Jim Jones did not desist, Jones and his followers would kill themselves and then everyone would be sorry.

In July 1977, *The New West* magazine published an article detailing the sexual practices, violence, and fraud practiced by Jones and the People's Temple. Jones immediately fled to Guyana and within months approximately one thousand church members had followed. In June 1978, a defector from Jonestown, Deborah Layton Blakey, prepared and signed an affidavit asserting that Jones planned to lead his followers in a mass suicide. "There was constant talk of death," wrote Blakey:

> In the early days of the People's Temple, general rhetoric about dying for principles was sometimes heard. In Jonestown, the concept of mass suicide for socialism arose. . . . At least once a week, Rev. Jones would declare a "white night," or a state of emergency. The entire population of Jonestown would be awakened by blaring sirens. Designated persons, approximately fifty in number, would arm themselves with rifles, move from cabin to cabin, and make certain that all members were responding. A mass meeting would ensue. Frequently, during these crises, we would be told that the jungle was teeming with mercenaries and that death could be expected at any minute.[65]

During one of the "white nights," Blakey reported that "everyone, including all children, was told to line up. As we passed through the line, we were given a small glass of red liquid to drink. We were told that the liquid contained poison and that we would die within 45 minutes. When the time came that we should have dropped dead, Rev. Jones explained that the poison was not real and that we had just been through a loyalty test. He warned us that the time was not far off when it would become necessary to die by our own hands."[66] That time came five months later on 17 November 1978, approximately one year after the death of Jones's mother Lynetta. After he gave the order for a "white night," Jones took a revolver and shot himself. Among his final words, recorded on tape, were "Mother, Mother, we are going to meet in another place."[67]

The question that remains is why did almost a thousand people follow Jones's order to self-destruct in their promised land? Many of course were children who had no choice and little idea of the consequences of their actions. Others no doubt were coerced. Yet a substantial number of people willingly followed Jones's orders. A comprehensive explanation of their motives may never be possible, but some tentative conclusions are possible. As Zee pointed out, "many were apparently in a state of unresolved separation from their families, and the impression is that a sizable number of them were people who were disillusioned with themselves and with society." Added to this was the fact that "more than half of Jones's followers were in a transitional phase of life, concerned with belonging and with the identity struggles that accompany such a phase: more than twenty-five percent were over sixty years old, and twenty-five percent were young adults between the ages of seventeen and twenty-five."[68]

Like those of Jamestown, the colonists in Jonestown consumed a diet that most likely exacerbated their communal depression. The majority lived on rice supplemented weekly by an egg, a cookie, and unspecified vegetables.[69] Such systematic malnutrition could lead to a variety of disorders tied to vitamin deficiencies, such as beriberi and scurvy, among whose symptoms are depressive behavior. Additionally, such a diet could result in anorexia, which would of course exacerbate vitamin deficiencies and depression. Finally, the general malnutrition, when added to Jonestown's jungle climate, suggests that Jonestown's population was subject to a variety of other diseases, especially the gastrointestinal disorders that are often encountered by migrants to such regions.[70]

Equally important as this factor, many of the unresolved issues that informed Jones's suicidal tendencies had been successfully projected on his followers. As they prepared to swallow cyanide, Jones raised the frontier analogy once again. Now he portrayed his pioneers as encircled Cherokees, driven mercilessly to their last frontier: "They robbed us of our land and they've taken us and driven us and we tried to find ourselves. We tried to find a new beginning. But it's too late."[71] By playing on the contradictions inherent in the ideology of self-transformation and the myth of the frontier, Jones exacerbated whatever object losses this group of displaced persons had brought with them when they joined the People's Temple. He had purposely separated husbands from wives, children from parents, and followers from one another. And then, demanding total allegiance, he periodically withdrew his support from those who identified with him as the sole object of value. Physically exhausted, emotionally drained, and weakened by hunger, the colonists were left only an identification with an oppressor. In the end, Jonestown was transformed from a slave plantation into a death camp.

Jonestown, of course, was not the embodiment of the American migrant experience, but an extreme perversion of it. Nevertheless, its story serves as a cautionary tale for those who attempt to transform myth into reality.

CONCLUSION

The frontier myth has been offered to migrants and immigrants as a substitute for the cultures and values that they have abandoned as they integrated themselves into a modernizing industrial society. In part, the myth owes its resilience to the fact that on a fantasy level it speaks to the cultural tensions of a society of deserters and deserted. As the social rituals of mourning and community were weakened, the frontier myth grew into an unchallenged national dogma. It was sustained because in the United States, more than in other western cultures, assimilation of new populations was and continues to be a central feature of everyday life. As a result, the mythic frontier hero evolved from Filson's Daniel Boone to *Star Wars'* Luke Skywalker without any serious mutations. The tale's repetition in popular literature and mass entertainment serves as a symbolic reenactment of real and fantasized object loss for a nation of migrants.

It is not surprising that the largest audience for these repetitious morality plays has become the nation's adolescent population. Perhaps what attracts them to these these stories can be traced to the great sense of emotional dislocation that so many commentators have found in the lives of young Americans. Yet, values and myths often seem strongest at the very moment when new realities begin to call them into question. The repetition compulsion sought in popular entertainment may symbolize one last desperate attempt to recapture a world that has been lost. For the evidence of increased suicidal behavior by America's youth suggests that the frontier myth may no longer provide a therapeutic fantasy for a generation that has grown up after the Vietnam experience called into question the validity of so much of American myth.

Like all fantasies, the power of the frontier remains symbolic. Those who attempt to live the fantasy often find themselves, like the settlers in Jamestown and Jonestown, alone and afraid in the promised land. Those who reject the fantasy must construct alternative myths that help them make sense of the object loss that accompanies the promise of modern bourgeois culture. Or they too may become lost, like the love objects they crave.

NOTES

Introduction

1. San Diego County Coroner's Office, California, Coroner's Reports, "Max E. White," 8 November 1893; "Inquisition by Coroner's Jury," M. E. White, 8 November 1893, San Diego Historical Society, Library and Manuscript Collection; *San Diego Union*, 8 November 1893, 5:3.

2. "Self-Murder," *San Diego Union*, 28 February 1893, 4:2.

3. *San Diego Union*, 9 November 1893, 5:3.

4. Émile Durkheim, *Suicide: A Study in Sociology* [1897], trans. John A. Spaulding and George Simpson (Glencoe, Ill.: The Free Press, 1951), pp. 284–286.

5. Ibid., pp. 241–258, esp. 246, 252, 258.

6. Sigmund Freud, "Mourning and Melancholia," *Standard Edition of the Complete Psychological Works of Sigmund Freud*, ed. and trans. James Strachey et al., vol. 14 (London: The Hogarth Press, 1957), pp. 239–258.

7. Ibid., pp. 244–246, 252.

8. San Diego County, "Inquisition by Coroner's Jury," "Max White," 16 November 1893, see testimony of Marcus Schiller.

9. Durkheim, *Suicide*, pp. 167–168. Durkheim was more interested in developing a model for the prediction of a society's suicide rate than in explaining the probable suicide of any one of its members. "Suicide was of primary interest to Durkheim," Dominick LaCapra reminds us, "not as an isolated tragedy in the lives of discrete individuals, but as an index of a more widespread pathology in society as a whole." His thesis was that variations in suicide statistics were distinct from the factors determining which particular individuals kill themselves. Therefore, while suicide rates were a barometer of "disturbances of the collective order," they did not necessarily explain why any individual committed suicide. Dominick LaCapra, *Emile Durkheim: Sociologist and Philosopher* (Ithaca: Cornell University Press, 1972), p. 144. LaCapra's study remains one of the very few that places Durkheim's *Suicide* in the context of his other works. Much has been written on Durkheim's sociology of suicide. Aside from LaCapra's, those studies that have most informed my understanding of Durkheim's concept of suicide include Jack D. Douglas, *The Social Meanings of Suicide* (Princeton: Princeton University Press, 1967), pp. 13–76; Anthony Giddens, "The Suicide Problem in French Sociology," *British Journal of Sociology* 16 (March 1965): 3–18; Whitney Pope, *Durkheim's Suicide: A Classic Analyzed* (Chicago: University of Chicago Press, 1976); J. Maxwell Atkinson, *Discovering Suicide* (London: Macmillan, 1978); and Steve Taylor, *Durkheim and the Study of Suicide* (New York: St. Martin's, 1982), esp. pp. 3–21.

10. There have been attempts to bridge this gap by bringing Durkheimian and Freudian variables together to explain variations in official statistics. However, because these studies continue to offer eclectic concatenations that try to merge the arguments of psychology with those of sociology rather than to formulate systematic integrated approaches, they are not wholly successful. "Most work on suicide," argues Herbert Hendin, "has become an unsynthesized mixture of Durkheim and Freud." Anthony Giddens seems correct in asserting that "A systematic theory of suicide cannot be developed through an *ad hoc* combination of sociological and psychological concepts, but only in the context of a generalized understanding of relationships between social structure and personality." Herbert Hendin, *Suicide in America* (New York: W. W. Norton & Co., 1982), pp. 17–19; Giddens, "The Suicide Problem in French Sociology," p. 13.

11. For useful discussions of Kraepelin's psychiatry, see Stanley W. Jackson, *Melancholia and Depression: From Hippocratic Times to Modern Times* (New Haven: Yale University Press, 1986), pp. 188–195; Gerald N. Grob, *Mental Illness and American Society, 1875–1940* (Princeton: Princeton University Press, 1983), p. 114. Also see Nancy C. Andreasen, *The Broken Brain: The Biological Revolution in Psychiatry* (New York: Harper and Row, 1984), pp. 13–17. Nathan G. Hale, Jr., *Freud and the Americans: The Beginnings of Psychoanalysis in the United States, 1876–1917* (New York: Oxford University Press, 1971), pp. 83–86.

12. Emil Kraepelin, *Lecture on Clinical Psychiatry* (1904), rev. and ed. Thomas Johnstone (New York: Hafner Publishing Company, 1968), pp. 6–20.

13. San Diego County, "Inquisition by Coroner's Jury," "Max White," 16 November 1893, see testimony of Marcus Schiller and I. C. Ulrich.

14. For a discussion of these studies, see Howard I. Kushner, "Biochemistry, Suicide, and History: Possibilities and Problems," *Journal of Interdisciplinary History* 16 (Summer 1985):69–85.

15. For a general discussion of these issues, see: Jonathan Winson, *Brain & Psyche: The Biology of the Unconscious* (New York: Anchor Press, 1985), pp. 163–179; Richard Restak, *The Brain* (New York: Bantam Books, 1984), pp. 221, 235; Floyd E. Bloom, Arlyne Lazerson, and Laura Hofstadter, *Brain, Mind, and Behavior* (New York: W. H. Freeman, 1985), pp. 201–203.

Chapter 1. From Crime to Disease

1. Andrew McFarland Davis, "Valentine-Vans Currency Pamphlets," *Massachusetts Historical Society, Proceedings* 43 (March 1910):439–440; Samuel Sewall, *The Diary of Samuel Sewall, 1674–1729*, ed. M. Halsey Thomas, 2 vols. (New York: Farrar, Straus, & Co., 1973), 2:1012. Also see "Sewall Papers," *Massachusetts Historical Society, Collections*, 5th ser. (1878–1882), 7:329–330.

2. Sewall, *Diary*, 2:1012; "Valentine-Vans Pamphlets," p. 441. Jeremiah Bumstead, a Boston mechanic, recorded these events in his diary: "February 1. On ye 1. Mr. Valintine, ye lawyer, hanged himself, att home, in his upper chamber, with his sash. Mr. Harris, minister, & Mr. Auchmutty, giving oath of his distraction, he had a funerall, and was buryed in ye Church yard on ye 4 day of ye month." "Diary of Jeremiah Bumstead of Boston, 1722–1727," ed. S. F. Haven, *New England Historical and Genealogical Register* 15 (July 1861):200.

3. *The Colonial Laws of Massachusetts*, reprinted from the edition of 1672, ed. William H. Whitmore (Boston, 1889), p. 137; *Commonwealth v. Mink*, 123 Mass. 422, 428–429 (1877). For the role of the coroner in colonial Massachusetts, see Paul F.

Mellen, "Coroner's Inquests in Colonial Massachusetts," *Journal of the History of Medicine and Allied Sciences* 40 (October 1985):462–472.

4. Sewall, *Diary*, 2:1012; "Sewall Papers," *MHS, Collections*, 5th ser., 7:330.

5. In 1700, Sewall wrote the first antislavery tract in America, *The Selling of Joseph*. For a good brief biographical sketch of Sewall, see M. Halsey Thomas's "Preface" to *Diary of Samuel Sewall*, pp. v–xiii. See also David D. Hall, "The Mental World of Samuel Sewall," in *Saints and Revolutionaries: Essays on Early American History*, ed. David D. Hall, John M. Murrin, and Thad W. Tate (New York: Norton, 1984), pp. 75–95.

6. Sewall, *Diary*, 2:1012–1013; Davis, "Valentine-Vans Pamphlets," pp. 440–444.

7. *The Boston News-Letter*, No. 1045, 30 January to 6 February 1724; In Latin: "Quid valet innumeras scire, atque evolvere causas; Si facienda fugis, si fugienda facis." Sewall, *Diary*, 2:1013.

8. *The New England Courant*, No. 132, 3 February to 10 February 1724; *The Boston News-Letter*, No. 1046, 6 February to 13 February 1724; Davis, "Valentine-Vans Pamphlets," p. 441.

9. Cotton Mather, *Diary of Cotton Mather*, ed. Worthington Chauncey Ford, 2 vols. (Boston, 1911, reprinted New York: Frederick Unger, 1957), 2:701–702.

10. Increase Mather, *A Call to the Tempted. A Sermon on the Horrid Crime of Self-Murder*, Evans, *Early American Imprints, 1639–1800* (Worcester, Mass.: American Antiquarian Society, 1963), No. 2563, emphasis added. See also *The New England Courant*, No. 140, 30 March to 6 April 1724.

11. Davis, "Valentine-Vans Pamphlets," pp. 438–441. See John M. Murrin, "The Legal Transformation: The Bench and Bar of Eighteenth-Century Massachusetts," in *Colonial America: Essays in Politics and Social Development*, ed. Stanley N. Katz & John M. Murrin (New York: Alfred A. Knopf, 1983), pp. 546–547; see also Henry Wilder Foote, *Annals of King's Chapel, from the Puritan Age of New England to the Present Day*, 2 vols. (Boston: Little, Brown and Company, 1882), 2:247–248.

12. For a discussion of the medical definition of melancholia in the eighteenth century, see Stanley W. Jackson, "Melancholia and Mechanical Explanation in Eighteenth-Century Medicine," *Journal of the History of Medicine and Allied Sciences* 38 (July 1983): 298–319.

13. Henry de Bracton, *On the Laws and Customs of England*, trans. Samuel E. Thorne, 2 vols. (Cambridge, Mass.: Harvard University Press, 1968), 2:423–424.

14. *Hales v. Petit*, 1 Plowden 253, 75 Eng. Rep. 387, 399–400 (1562). For a discussion of suicide in the Elizabethan period, see Richard L. Greaves, *Society and Religion in Elizabethan England* (Minneapolis: University of Minnesota Press, 1981), pp. 531–537.

15. Dalton's handbook, which was used widely, went through several editions, each of which varied slightly in language but not in substance. See Michael Dalton, *The Countrey Justice, 1619*, ed. P. M. Glazerbrook (London: Professional Books, 1973), pp. 216–217; Michael Dalton, *The Countrey Justice*, 3d ed. (London: Societie of Stationers, 1626), pp. 234–235, 243. The fullest treatment of suicide in early modern England is found in Michael MacDonald, "The Inner Side of Wisdom: Suicide in Early Modern England," *Psychological Medicine* 7 (1977):567–568 and "The Secularization of Suicide in England, 1660–1800," *Past and Present* 111 (May 1986):52–57.

16. Edmund Wingate, *Justice Revived, Being the Whole Office of a Countrey Justice of the Peace* (London: Thomas Williams, 1661), pp. 68–69, 100–101.

17. William Blackstone, *Commentaries on the Law of England*, 4 vols. (London: T. Cadell and W. Davies, 1809), 4:189–190.

18. Although Alvarez claims that suicide attempters were executed as felons until the nineteenth century, his one example rests upon the report of a foreign traveller who witnessed the execution of a murderer who attempted to cheat the gallows by committing suicide. See A. A. Alvarez, *The Savage God, A Study in Suicide* (New York: Random House, 1972), p. 45. I know of no cases in early modern England where an attempted suicide was executed. In Massachusetts, suicide attempters could be and were tried and punished. See "Records of the Suffolk County Court, 1671–1680," *Publications of the Colonial Society of Massachusetts* 29 (Boston, 1933):189.

19. Thomas Rogers Forbes, *Chronicle from Aldgate, Life and Death in Shakespeare's London* (New Haven: Yale University Press, 1971), pp. 164–165; Leon Radzinowicz, *A History of English Criminal Law and its Administration from 1750*, 4 vols. (London: Stevens & Sons, 1948), 1:195–199. For a general discussion of burial practices, see Henry Romilly Fedden, *Suicide, a Social and Historical Study* (New York: Benjamin Blom, 1972), pp. 32–48; Alvarez, *The Savage God*, pp. 45–51; Louis I. Dublin, *Suicide: A Sociological and Statistical Study* (New York: The Ronald Press, 1963), pp. 120–122; George Rosen, "History," in *A Handbook for the Study of Suicide*, ed. Seymour Perlin (New York: Oxford University Press, 1975), pp. 13–14.

20. MacDonald, "The Inner Side of Wisdom," pp. 567–570.

21. Dalton, *The Countrey Justice, 1619*, p. 216; Dalton, 3d ed, pp. 234–235, 243; Wingate, *Justice Revived*, pp. 68–69.

22. MacDonald, "The Inner Side of Wisdom," pp. 569–571.

23. Dalton, *The Countrey Justice, 1619*, pp. 216–217.

24. Michael MacDonald, *Mystical Bedlam, Madness, Anxiety, and Healing in Seventeenth-Century England* (New York: Cambridge University Press, 1981), pp. 135–138, 171. Robert Burton, *Anatomy of Melancholy*, ed. Floyd Dell & Paul Jordan-Smith (New York: Tudor Publishing Co., 1927), pp. 357–366. For an analysis of the increase in *non compos mentis* verdicts in early modern England, see MacDonald, "The Secularization of Suicide in England," pp. 60–93. See also Fedden, *Suicide: A Social and Historical Study*, pp. 178–181. For a general history of the insanity plea in England, see Nigel Walker, *Crime and Insanity in England, Volume One: the Historical Perspective* (Edinburgh: Edinburgh University Press, 1968).

25. Forbes, *Chronicle from Aldgate*, p. 31.

26. John Sym, *Lifes Preservatives Against Self-Killing. or, an Useful Treatise Concerning Life and Self-Murder* (London: R. Dawlman and L. Fawne, 1637), pp. 172–174.

27. Richard Capel, *Tentations*, 4th ed. (London, 1650), p. 327. William Gouge, an influential Puritan minister, wrote in 1637 that "scarce an age since the beginning of the world hath afforded more examples of this desperate inhumanity [suicide], than this our present age." According to Gouge, the increase in suicide included "all sorts of people, clergy, laity, learned, unlearned, noble, mean, rich, poor, free, bond, male, female, young and old." See S. E. Sprott, *The English Debate on Suicide: from Donne to Hume* (La Salle, Illinois: Open Court, 1961), pp. 32–34, 45–46, 48, and MacDonald, "The Inner Side of Wisdom," p. 566.

28. Sym, *Lifes Preservatives*, pp. 217–219, 166–167.

29. William Denny, *Pelecanicidium: or the Christian Adviser against Self-Murder* (London: Thomas Hucklescott, 1653), the quotation is from Book 1, p. 1. For a discussion of the incidence of suicide in seventeenth-century England, see Peter Laslett, *The World We Have Lost, Further Explored: England Before the Industrial Age*, 3rd ed. (New York: Scribner's, 1984), pp. 175–177.

30. Sprott, *English Debate on Suicide*, pp. 120–121.

31. See *The Body of Liberties* (1641), in *The Colonial Laws of Massachusetts*, ed. William H. Whitmore, reprinted from the edition of 1660 (Boston: City Council of Boston, 1889), pp. 34–35. On the other hand, in Providence Plantations the General Assembly's Code of Laws of 1647 retained forfeiture of goods: If guilty of self-murder, a man's "good and chattels are the kings custom, but not his debts nor lands." *The Earliest Acts and Laws of the Colony of Rhode Island and Providence Plantations, 1647–1719*, ed. John D. Cushing (Wilmington, Del.: Michael Glazier, 1977), p. 19. A general account of the legal aspects of colonial suicide is found in Keith Burgess-Jackson, "The Legal Status of Suicide in Early America: A Comparison with the English Experience," *Wayne Law Review* 29 (Fall 1982):57–87. Although Burgess-Jackson attempts to deal with suicide in a historical framework, he neglects the fact that different jurisdictions defined suicide in different ways.

32. For a complete discussion of the issues surrounding the doctrine of preparation, see Norman Pettit, *The Heart Prepared: Grace and Conversion in Puritan Spiritual Life* (New Haven, Conn.: Yale University Press, 1966). See also Samuel Willard, *Covenant-Keeping the Way to Blessedness* (Boston, 1682); Philip Greven, *The Protestant Temperament: Patterns of Child-Rearing, Religious Experience, and The Self in Early America* (New York: New American Library, 1977), pp. 6–12; Emory Elliott, *Power and the Pulpit in Puritan New England* (Princeton: Princeton University Press, 1975), pp. 164–166.

33. "Inquest on the Body of William Richards [15 September 1640]," *Winthrop Papers*, 4 vols. (Boston: Massachusetts Historical Society, 1944), 4:285–286; *Colonial Laws of Massachusetts*, 1672 edition, p. 137. The first suicide in New England seems to have been that of Dorothy May Bradford, the wife of the Pilgrim leader William Bradford, who, according to Samuel Eliot Morison, "took her own life, [in December 1620] after gazing for six weeks at the barren sand dunes of Cape Cod," by jumping off the Mayflower into the freezing bay. See William Bradford, *Of Plymouth Plantation, 1620–1647*, ed. Samuel Eliot Morison (New York: Alfred A. Knopf, 1979), pp. xxix, 64.

34. Most criminal cases fell to the jurisdiction of the Court of Assistants. Why Citterne was tried by the Suffolk County Court is unclear. In any case, his is the only surviving example of punishment for an attempted suicide in seventeenth-century Boston. Successful suicides, coming under the jurisdiction of the coroner, would not be reported in either the County Court or The Records of the Court of Assistants. "Records of the Suffolk County Court, 1671–1680," *Publications of the Colonial Society of Massachusetts* 29 (Boston 1933):189. See "Records of the Suffolk County Court, 1671–1680," p. xxvii; *Records of the Court of Assistants of the Colony of Massachusetts Bay, 1630–1692*, 3 vols., ed. John Noble and John Cronin (Boston: The County of Suffolk, 1901–1928); and "Notes on the Trial and Punishment of Crimes in the Court of Assistants in the Time of the Colony, and in the Superior Court of Judicature in the First Years of the Province," *Publications of the Colonial Society of Massachusetts, Transactions* 3 (1895–1897):51–66. Attempted suicide continued to be a crime in some jurisdictions until the early twentieth century. See *May v. Pennell*, 101 Me. 516; *The American and English Annotated Cases*, ed. William M. McKinney, David S. Garland, and H. Noyes Greene (Northport, New York: Edward Thompson Co., 1908), 8:351–354.

35. Most seventeenth-century Massachusetts coroners' inquests of suicides appear to have been lost or destroyed. A handful are housed in the "Collection of Essex Inquisitions" at the Essex Institute in Salem. Seventeen coroners' reports for the years 1731 through 1744, including those for five suicides, are in the possession

of the Judicial Preservation Project of the Supreme Judicial Court of Massachusetts at the New Suffolk County Court House in Boston. A few others are scattered throughout Suffolk Court files. Additionally, a number of late-eighteenth-century coroners' inquest bills are found in the Boston Public Library's Rare Book and Manuscript Collections. See "Inquest Records and Other Material Pertaining to the Suffolk County Coroners, 1775 to 1860," and "Suffolk County Bills, 1770–1822," in the Adlow Collection, Boston Public Library, Rare Books and Manuscripts Collection.

36. Lawrence Hammond, *Diary of Lawrence Hammond, MHS, Proceedings* 7 (January 1892):168–169.

37. In addition to those sermons discussed in this chapter, see Increase Mather, *The Wicked Mans Portion. Or a Sermon* (Boston: John Foster, 1675); Cotton Mather, *Memorable Provinces Relating to Witchcrafts and Possessions* (1689; reprinted, Boston: Andrew Anderson, 1697), *A Family Well-Ordered or an Essay to Render Parents and Children Happy in One Another*, (Boston: B. Green and J. Allen, 1699) in Thomas J. Holmes, *Cotton Mather, A Bibliography*, 3 vols. (Newton, Mass.: Crofton Publishing Co., 1974), 1:378–301; and "Propositions Concerning Self-Killing," in *Thirty Important Cases, Resolved with Evidence of Scripture and Reason* (Boston, 1699) in ibid., 3:1090–1091. For research on population, see Jay Mack Holbrook, *Boston Beginnings, 1630–1699* (Oxford, Mass.: Holbrook Research Institute, 1980), p. vii.

38. Elliott, *Power and the Pulpit*, pp. 41–42.

39. Increase Mather, *The Wicked Mans Portion*, pp. 19–20. A recent study argues that suicide among children and adolescents in early modern England "exceeded modern percentages considerably." See Terence R. Murphy, "'Woful Childe of Parents Rage': Suicide of Children and Adolescents in Early Modern England, 1507–1710," *The Sixteenth Century Journal* 17 (Fall 1986):259–270.

40. *Colonial Laws of Massachusetts*, 1672 edition, p. 137; *Commonwealth v. Mink*, 123 Mass. 422, 428–429 (1877); see also John Noble, "A Glance at Suicide in the Colony and Province of Massachusetts," *Massachusetts Historical Society, Proceedings* 2nd Series, 16 (December 1902):524.

41. *Earliest Laws of Rhode Island*, p. 19.

42. Sewall, *Diary*, 1:163; *MHS Collections*, 5th ser., 5:208–209; see also Edwin Powers, *Crime and Punishment in Early Massachusetts, 1620–1692* (Boston: Beacon Press, 1966), pp. 439–442.

43. *Records of the Court of Assistants*, 2:78; John Winthrop, *Winthrop's Journal, "History of New England," 1630–1648*, ed. James Kendall Hosmer, 2 vols. (New York: Charles Scribner's Sons, 1908), 1:282–283.

44. Peter C. Hoffer and N. E. H. Hull, *Murdering Mothers: Infanticide in England and New England, 1588–1803* (New York: New York University Press, 1981), pp. 40–41.

45. John Putnam Demos, *Entertaining Satan, Witchcraft and the Culture of Early New England* (New York: Oxford University Press, 1982), pp. 99–131, esp. 99–103; Samuel Willard, "A Brief Account of a Strange and Unusual Providence of God Befallen to Elizabeth Knapp of Groton" (1672) in *Remarkable Providences, 1600–1760*, ed. John Demos (New York: George Braziller, 1972), pp. 358–371, esp. p. 360.

46. Like Valentine's body, Taylor's body was discovered kneeling as if in prayer. See "Diary of Noadiah Russell," *The New England Historical and Geneological Register*, 7 (January 1853):56; Sewall, *Diary*, 1:52.

47. Increase Mather, *A Call to the Tempted* (1682).

48. Powers, *Crime and Punishment in Early Massachusetts*, pp. 186–187, 303–308; David Thomas Konig, *Law and Society in Puritan Massachusetts, Essex County, 1629–1692* (Chapel Hill: University of North Carolina Press, 1979), pp. 158–168, 186–192.

49. Cotton Mather, *The Cause and Cure of a Wounded Spirit* (Boston: B. Greene and J. Allen, 1692); S. A. Green, ed., *Early American Imprints*, 3d Supplementary List, pp. 58–59; according to Thomas J. Holmes, in *Cotton Mather, a Bibliography*, 1:65, this sermon is incorrectly identified as having been published in December 1691 instead of December 1692.

50. *Laws of the Province of Massachusetts, 1700–1701*, 1:429, quoted in Noble, "A Glance at Suicide," p. 527 (emphasis added).

51. For changes in English suicide verdicts after the Glorious Revolution, see MacDonald, "The Secularization of Suicide", pp. 69–76; Sprott, *The English Debate on Suicide*, pp. 120–121.

52. Noble, "A Glance at Suicide," pp. 521–522.

53. "Diary of Jeremiah Bumstead," 21 April 1724, p. 201; Sewell, *Diary*, 2:1015; *MHS Collections*, 5th ser., 7:333–334.

54. *Cotton Mather Bibliography*, 2:833, italics in original.

55. Kenneth Silverman, *The Life and Times of Cotton Mather* (New York: Harper & Row, 1984), pp. 11–13.

56. Greven, *The Protestant Temperament*, pp. 82–83.

57. Michael J. Crawford, "The Spiritual Travels of Nathan Cole," *William and Mary Quarterly* 3rd Series, 33 (January 1976):101–103.

58. William Blackstone, *Commentaries on the Laws of England*, 4 vols. (London: T. Cadell and W. Davies, 1809), 4:189–190.

59. MacDonald, "The Secularization of Suicide in England, 1600–1800," pp. 69–75, 98–99. Also see Sprott, *English Debate on Suicide*, pp. 160–161. Sprott finds a decrease in the incidence of suicide after the 1640s. He compares the number of suicides listed in official mortality bills to the recorded incidence of death because of the difficulty of procuring accurate figures for the living population in seventeenth-century England. Sprott's rates have been justly criticized by P. E. H. Hair because comparisons based on death rates ignore the impact of epidemics, and so forth on the incidence of death. P. E. H. Hair, "A Note on the Incidence of Tudor Suicide," *Local Population Studies* 5 (1970): 42n.

60. Sprott, *English Debate on Suicide*, pp. 120–122; Anonymous, *A Discourse Upon Self-Murder* (London, 1754), pp. 15–16; Courtney Stanhope Kenny, *Kenny's Outlines of Criminal Law*, 19th ed., ed. J. W. Cecil Turner (Cambridge: Cambridge University Press, 1966), p. 184; MacDonald, "The Secularization of Suicide in England," pp. 75–77.

61. See Lester G. Crocker, "The Discussion of Suicide in the Eighteenth Century," *The Journal of the History of Ideas* 13 (January 1952):47–52; Henry Romilly Fedden, *Suicide, a Social and Historical Study*, pp. 204–246.

62. In a recent essay, Michael MacDonald attributes the secularization of suicide in England to a convergence of factors that he divides roughly into three chronological phases from the Restoration to the end of the eighteenth century. During the first phase (from the Restoration to the end of the seventeenth century), coroners' juries, sharing local hostility to forfeiture, "increasingly flouted the crown's claims to the goods of suicides." From the Glorious Revolution to the accession of George III, juries employed *non compos mentis* in over 50 percent of their verdicts in order to mitigate the effects of forfeiture. Finally, from 1760 to 1800, led by edu-

210   NOTES TO PAGES 29–30

cated laymen, coroners' juries, now composed of literate middling classes, began to share the belief that "philosophical and medical arguments condoning suicide were more compelling than the religious and folkloric traditions condemning it." At first, this attitude was reflected in a "selective enforcement," with most leniency extended to those of higher rank. Ultimately, however, this attitude filtered down to include suicides by "men and women of very humble social standing," until *non compos mentis* became "the usual verdict in almost all cases of suicide." See MacDonald, "The Secularization of Suicide in England," esp. pp. 70–97. Although Mac-Donald's argument seems convincing when applied to England alone, it does not fully fit the Massachusetts experience for several reasons. First, as I have pointed out, there never was forfeiture of goods in Massachusetts because its Puritan leaders, consistent with their belief that suicide resulted from individual free choice, concluded that families of suicides should not be punished for others' having succumbed to Satan's temptations. This view was codified in *The Body of Liberties* (1641), which specifically protected a person's property not only from the unlawful acts of others but also from his own unlawful acts. Thus, the reasons for an increase in *non compos mentis* verdicts in Massachusetts could not have been motivated by a desire to avoid forfeiture, as MacDonald argues for England. It is true that punishment was increasingly selective, as the dispute over Valentine's verdict indicates. But, in contrast to England, it was the educated elite (the Mathers, Sewall, and others) who resisted *non compos mentis* verdicts. Also in Massachusetts coroners' juries in the seventeenth century appear to have been more literate than their English counterparts and to have played a more important role in accepting the medical view that most suicides were insane, earlier than English jurors initially did. All this suggests that it might be useful to explore attitudes among English colonials toward suicide as a way to test MacDonald's interesting analysis of the secularization of English suicide.

63. Solomon Williams, "The Frailty and Misery of Man's Life," 9 July 1740 (Boston: Draper, 1740), Evans, No. 4469. For a discussion of how these changes were reflected more generally in attitudes toward madness, see Mary Ann Jimenez, "Madness in Early American History," *Journal of Social History* 19 (Fall 1986):25–44.

64. Samuel Phillips, *The Sin of Suicide Contrary to Nature*, 7 July 1767 (Boston: Kneeland & Adams, 1767), Evans, No. 10740.

65. See *Commonwealth v. Bowen*, 13 Mass. 356, 358 (1816); *Commonwealth v. Mink*, 123 Mass. 425, 25 Am. Rep. 109. See also Donald Wright, "Criminal Aspects of Suicide in the United States," *North Carolina Central Law Review* 7 (Fall 1975): 156–163; David S. Markson, "The Punishment of Suicide—A Need for a Change," *Villanova Law Review* 14 (Spring 1969):463–483.

66. "Coroner's Reports, 1731–1744," Judicial Preservation Project of the Supreme Judicial Court of Massachusetts, New Suffolk County Court House, Boston; "Inquest Records and Other Material Pertaining to the Suffolk County Coroners, 1775 to 1860," and "Suffolk County Bills, 1770–1822," Adlow Collection, Boston Public Library, Rare Books and Manuscripts Collection.

67. Arthur P. Scott, *Criminal Law in Colonial Virginia* (Chicago: The University of Chicago Press, 1930), pp. 107–109, 198–199. There are several examples in Virginia court records of property forfeitures, one as late as 1782, but in that case the deceased Robert Williams was a bastard who died intestate having no wife or issue. Also, Virginia courts held that neither slaves nor real property were subject to forfeiture. See William P. Palmer, ed., *Calendar of State Papers and Other Manuscripts Preserved in the Capital at Richmond*, 14 vols. (Richmond, Va., 1883), 3:125. For two early

eighteenth-century cases in which goods and chattels of suicides were forfeit, see ibid., 1:117, 119. I thank Ms. Sandra R. Maddox, a graduate student at the College of William and Mary, who graciously provided me a copy of her unpublished paper, "A Crime and A Sin: Self-Murder in Colonial Massachusetts and Virginia," which drew my attention to these examples.

68. "A Bill for Proportioning Crimes and Punishments in Cases Heretofore Capital," in Thomas Jefferson, *The Papers of Thomas Jefferson*, 18 vols., ed. Julian P. Boyd (Princeton: Princeton University Press, 1950), 2:496.

69. "Plan Agreed upon by the Committee of Revisors at Fredericksburg," 13 January 1777, *Papers of Thomas Jefferson*, 2:325.

70. *The Federal and State Constitutions, Colonial Charters, and Other Organic Laws of the States, Territories, and Colonies Now or Heretofore Forming the United States of America*, ed. Francis Newton Thorpe (Washington, D.C.: GPO, 1909), 5:2597, 3101, 3081; *The State Records of North Carolina*, ed. W. Clark, 24 (1905):927; also see Burgess-Jackson, "The Legal Status of Suicide in Early America," p. 66.

71. Louis P. Masur, "The Revision of the Criminal Law in Post-Revolutionary America," paper presented at the Conference on Law in America, 1607–1861, New York Historical Society, 17 and 18 May 1985.

72. Charles Brockden Brown, *Wieland or the Transformation* ((1799) New York: Doubleday & Co., 1962); David Lee Clark, *Charles Brockden Brown* (Durham: Duke University Press, 1952), pp. 162–163; Norman S. Grabo, *The Coincidental Art of Charles Brockden Brown* (Chapel Hill, The University of North Carolina Press, 1981), pp. 3–29, esp. 8–10.

73. Samuel Miller, *The Guilt, Folly, and Sources of Suicide: Two Discourses* (New York: T. and J. Swords, 1805), pp. 44–45, 13, 15, 25, 36, 37, 68–69.

74. Joseph Lathrop, *Two Sermons on the Atrocity of Suicide, and the Causes Which Lead to It* (Springfield, Mass.: Henry Brewer, Printer, 1805), p. 6.

75. See "Inquest Records Pertaining to the Suffolk County Coroner Coroners, 1810–1860." Adlow Collection.

76. "Coroner's Inquisition," Michael Boling, Jr., 3 August 1827, Inquest Records, Adlow 118.

77. "Coroner's Inquisition," Hannah Andrews Winslow, October 1, 1827, Inquest Records, Adlow 127.

78. "Coroner's Inquest," William Bond, 28 March 1828, Inquest Records, Adlow 137.

79. "Coroner's Inquest," Jacob Wilson, 8 November 1828, Inquest Records, Adlow 176. Other examples include John Skelton, who hanged himself, but was not determined a suicide because at the time of his death he was "in a state of mental derangement." Ibid., 28 May 1828, Adlow 142; Nathaniel Hopkins hanged himself, but was not counted a suicide because the inquest determined that he had previously attended a funeral and, as a result, was "not in his right mind." Ibid., 6 July 1828, Adlow 155. Joseph Gee, who hanged himself in August 1828 while "in a state of mental insanity," also was not considered a suicide. Ibid., 19 August 1828, Adlow 163.

80. "Coroner's Inquest," George Duffett, 15 April 1843, Adlow 611.

81. See "Statistics of the Suicides," *American Journal of Insanity* 3 (April 1847):352; "Homicides-Suicides, &c.,—By the Insane," *American Journal of Insanity* 4 (October 1847): 170–178.

82. Alexis de Tocqueville, *Democracy in America*, 2 vols., ed. Phillips Bradley (New York: Alfred A. Knopf, 1966), 2:134.

83. Ibid., 2:139.

Chapter 2. Rise and Decline of Moral Treatment

1. Gerald N. Grob, *Mental Institutions in America, Social Policy to 1875* (New York: The Free Press, 1973), pp. 137–139.

2. "Cases of Insanity—Illustrating the Importance of Early Treatment in Preventing Suicide," *American Journal of Insanity* (hereafter cited as *AJI*), 1 (January 1845):243–244.

3. Ibid., pp. 246–249.

4. "Millerism," *AJI* 1 (January 1845):249–253.

5. A useful discussion of the founding of the Association of Medical Superintendents of American Institutions for the Insane is provided in Constance M. McGovern, *Masters of Madness: Social Origins of the American Psychiatric Profession* (Hanover, N.H.: University Press of New England, 1985), pp. 62–85.

6. For more on this point, see Michael P. Rogin, "The Market Revolution and the Reconstruction of Paternal Authority," in *Fathers and Children: Andrew Jackson and the Subjugation of the American Indian* (New York: Alfred A. Knopf, 1975), pp. 251–279; and Herbert Gutman, "Work, Culture, and Society in Industrializing America, 1818–1919," *American Historical Review* 78 (June 1973):531–588.

7. Andrew Scull, "Moral Treatment Reconsidered: Some Sociological Comments on an Episode in the History of British Psychiatry," in *Madhouses, Mad-Doctors, and Madmen: The Social History of Psychiatry in the Victorian Era*, ed. Andrew Scull (Philadelphia: University of Pennsylvania Press, 1981), pp. 108, 114–115.

8. Charles E. Rosenberg, "The Therapeutic Revolution: Medicine, Meaning, and Social Change in Nineteenth-Century America," in *The Therapeutic Revolution: Essays in the Social History of Medicine*, ed. Morris J. Vogel and Charles E. Rosenberg (Philadelphia: University of Pennsylvania Press, 1979), pp. 5–6; Charles E. Rosenberg, "The Cause of Cholera: Aspects of Etiological Thought in 19th-Century America," *Bulletin of the History of Medicine* 34 (July/August 1960):331–333.

9. Edward Jarvis, M.D., "On the Supposed Increase of Insanity," *AJI*, 8 (April 1852): 333–364, esp. p. 364; Norman Dain, *Concepts of Insanity in the United States, 1789–1865* (New Brunswick, N.J.: Rutgers University Press, 1964), pp. 88–91; David Rothman, *The Discovery of the Asylum, Social Order and Disorder in the New Republic* (Boston: Little, Brown, 1971), pp. 112–113.

10. "Cases of Insanity—Illustrating the Importance of Early Treatment in Preventing Suicide," *AJI*, 1 (January 1845):243–245.

11. See Benjamin Rush to Ashton Alexander, 21 December 1795, *Letters of Benjamin Rush*, ed. L. H. Butterfield, 2 vols. (Princeton: Princeton University Press, 1951), 2:766–767. For Rush's views on melancholia, see his *Medical Inquiries and Observations Upon the Diseases of the Mind* (1812 ed.), pp. 98–134.

12. For a discussion of the interplay between theoretical considerations and clinical experience in antebellum therapeutics for insanity, see Samuel B. Thielman, "Madness and Medicine: Trends in American Medical Therapeutics for Insanity, 1820–1860," *Bulletin of the History of Medicine* 61 (Spring 1987):25–46.

13. Rush, *Medical Inquiries and Observations*, pp. 27–28.

14. Roger Cooter, "Phrenology and British Alienists, ca. 1825–1845," in Scull, *Madhouses, Mad-Doctors, and Madmen*, pp. 58–90.

15. "Cases of Insanity," p. 245.

16. "Miscellany," *AJI* 1 (April 1845):383.

17. For a discussion of nosology in American psychiatry, see Gerald N. Grob, "Rediscovering Asylums: The Unhistorical History of the Mental Hospital," in

Vogel and Rosenberg, *The Therapeutic Revolution,* pp. 140–141; James H. Cassedy, *American Medicine and Statistical Thinking, 1800–1860* (Cambridge, Harvard University Press, 1984), pp. 157–168. See also Lester F. King, *The Medical World of the Eighteenth Century* (Chicago: University of Chicago Press, 1958), pp. 193–226; Gerald N. Grob, *Edward Jarvis and the Medical World of Nineteenth-Century America* (Knoxville: The University of Tennessee Press, 1978), pp. 83–137.

18. "Statistics of Suicides in the United States," *AJI* 1 (January 1845):225–234. At the beginning of the nineteenth century both in Europe and in the United States government agencies at various levels began to collect statistics concerning all types of human endeavors, including the distribution and rate of mortality. By the time that the United States Federal Census began the systematic collection and analysis of mortality statistics in 1850, many local and state jurisdictions already had more than a century's experience in doing that. For instance, beginning in 1805 New York City's Inspector, John Pintard, began a compilation of annual mortality returns, which included the annual number of suicides for the city. See "Reports of the City Inspectors of New York, 1805–1843," in *AJI* 1 (January 1845):232–233; Cassedy, *American Medicine and Statistical Thinking,* pp. 18–19; see also James H. Cassedy, *Demography in Early America: Beginnings of the Statistical Mind, 1600–1800* (Cambridge, Mass.: Harvard University Press, 1969), esp. pp. 274–304. For Western Europe, see Theodore M. Porter, *The Rise of Statistical Thinking, 1820–1900* (Princeton: Princeton University Press, 1986).

19. "Statistics of Suicides in the United States," *AJI* I (January 1845):232–234.

20. "Statistics of the Suicides," *AJI* 3 (April 1847):352.

21. "Statistics of Suicides," *AJI* 4 (January 1848):247–249.

22. "A Chapter of Suicides," *New York Times,* 3 August 1859. "The Alarming Increase of Suicides," *New York Times,* 3 August 1859.

23. "Statistics of Suicides in the United States," *AJI* 1 (January 1845):234. See also "On Monomania Induced Through Imitation," ibid. (October 1844): 119–121.

24. "Statistics of Suicides," *AJI* 5 (April 1849):308–309.

25. A Southern Physician, "Suicide," *The American Whig Review* 6 (August 1847): 137–145, esp. 137–138. This essay was reprinted in several journals, including *The Democratic Review* 34 (November 1854): 405–417.

26. John Ordroneaux, M.D., "On Suicide: A Lecture Delivered Before the Students of Columbia College," *AJI* 20 (April 1864):369–401, esp. 390–391.

27. "Statistics of Suicides," *AJI* 4 (January 1848):252.

28. "Homicides-Suicides, &c.,—By the Insane," *AJI* 4 (October 1847):170–178.

29. [John P. Gray], "Bertrand on Suicide," *AJI* 14 (October 1857):210. The American asylum movement reflected similar developments in Britain and on the continent. See Andrew Scull, "The Discovery of the Asylum Revisited: Lunacy Reform in the New Republic," in *Madhouses, Mad-Doctors, and Madness: The Social History of Psychiatry in the Victorian Era,* ed. Andrew Scull (Philadelphia: University of Pennsylvania Press, 1981), pp. 144–165.

30. H. T., "Suicide and Suicidal Insanity," *AJI* 12 (April 1856):351–354.

31. Allan McLane Hamilton, M.D., "Suicide in Large Cities", *Popular Science Monthly* 8 (November 1875):88–93. From 1871 to 1880 Hamilton was connected with the New York City Health Department. In the 1880s Hamilton practiced neurology and abandoned many of his earlier environmentalist positions. See his autobiography, *Recollections of an Alienist, Personal and Professional* (New York: George H. Doran Company, 1916), pp. 375–376; Charles E. Rosenberg, *The Trail of the Assassin Guiteau: Psychiatry and Law in the Gilded Age* (Chicago: University of Chicago

Press, 1968), 172–173. See also Allan McLane Hamilton, *Nervous Diseases: Their Description and Treatment* (Philadelphia: Henry C. Lea, 1878); *The Dictionary of American Biography*, 10 vols. (New York: Charles Scribner's Sons, 1931), 4:179–180.

32. Hamilton, "Suicide in Large Cities," 94–95. Also see Émile Durkheim, *The Division of Labor in Society*, trans. George Simpson (Glencoe, Ill.: The Free Press, 1960), esp. pp. 241–251, 396–409.

33. Isaac Ray, *A Treatise on The Medical Jurisprudence of Insanity*, 5th ed. (Boston, 1871, reprinted New York: Arno Press, 1976), pp. 209–237. Occasionally *The American Journal of Insanity* would reprint notes on case studies that seemed to lend credence to such claims. A postmortem examination of a suicide who believed himself to be "the Son of God and Elijah," *The Journal* reported, "showed a diseased state of the brain, sufficient to account for the mental aberration." See "Delusion and Suicide," *AJI* 13 (April 1857):401–402. Support for such views also was reflected in the press. For instance, an editorial in the *New York Times* in 1861 claimed that "modern investigation has demonstrated the fact that suicide" was "the result of bodily disease, and moreover, is amenable to the same laws of treatment and cure as ordinary maladies." See "Suicides in New York City in 1860," *New York Times*, 17 January 1861.

34. Isaac Ray, *Medical Jurisprudence of Insanity*, 3d ed. (Boston: Charles C. Little and James Brown, 1853), pp. 69, 129–130; Ray consistently maintained these views in all five editions of this work: see the 5th edition, 1871, pp. 148–151, 487–488, 490–491, 493–496; Jean-Pierre Falret, *De l'Hypochondrie et du Suicide* (Paris, 1822).

35. Gray's dogmatism, coupled with his increasingly rigid control of the contents of the *American Journal of Insanity*, often aroused the ire of his colleagues. For more on Gray see Dain, *Concepts of Insanity*, pp. 56–57, 77–79, 86; Grob, *Mental Institutions in America*, p. 147; Gerald N. Grob, *Mental Illness and American Society, 1875–1940* (Princeton: Princeton Univerity Press, 1983), pp. 33–34, 40; Barbara Sicherman, *The Quest For Mental Health in America, 1880–1917* (New York: Arno Press, 1980), 161–166.

36. John P. Gray, "Thoughts on the Causation of Insanity," *AJI* 29 (October 1872):264–283, esp. 272–273; John P. Gray, "Suicide, A Lecture Delivered at Bellevue Medical College, March 1878," *AJI* 35 (July 1878):44–45; see also John P. Gray "Insanity and Its Relation to Medicine," *AJI* 25 (October 1868):145–172, esp. 162–163. For a discussion of the debate over the existence of "moral insanity," see S. P. Fullinwider, "Insanity As the Loss of Self: The Moral Insanity Controversy Revisited," *Bulletin of the History of Medicine* 49 (Spring 1975):87–101; and Rosenberg, *Trial of the Assassin Guiteau*, pp. 192–194.

37. Gray, "Suicide," 37–73, esp. pp. 52, 57–58.

38. Gray, "Suicide," pp. 63–66.

39. Barbara Sicherman, "The Uses of Diagnosis: Doctors, Patients, and Neurasthenia," in *Sickness and Health in America: Readings in the History of Medicine and Public Health*, ed. Judith Walzer Levitt and Ronald Numbers (Madison: The University of Wisconsin Press, 1978), pp. 25–26. Grob, *Mental Illness*, pp. 41, 44, 46–71; Charles E. Rosenberg, "The Therapeutic Revolution: Medicine, Meaning, and Social Change in Nineteenth-Century America," in Morris Vogel and Charles Rosenberg, eds., *The Therapeutic Revolution*, pp. 3–25; see also Rosenberg, *Trial of the Assassin Guiteau*, pp. 244–245, 248–249; also see Gerald N. Grob, *The Inner World of American Psychiatry, 1890–1940, Selected Correspondence* (New Brunswick, N.J.: Rutgers University Press, 1985), pp. 1–18.

40. Bonnie Ellen Blustein, "'A Hollow Square of Psychological Science': American Neurologists and Psychiatrists in Conflict," in Scull, *Madhouses, Mad-Doctors, and Madmen*, pp. 244–270; Rosenberg, *Trial of the Assassin Guiteau*, pp. 155–179.

41. McGovern, *Masters of Madness*, pp. 149–172.

42. Grob, *Mental Illness and America*, pp. 69–71; Barbara Sicherman, *The Quest for Mental Health in America, 1880–1917* (New York: Arno Press, 1980), 231–256; David J. Rothman, *Conscience and Convenience: The Asylum and its Alternatives in Progressive America* (Boston: Little, Brown, & Co., 1980), 293–297; S. Weir Mitchell, "Address Before the Fiftieth Anniversary Meeting of the American Medico-Psychological Association, Held in Philadelphia, 16 May 1894," *Journal of Nervous and Mental Diseases* 21 (July 1894):422–424; see also Barbara Sicherman, "The Paradox of Prudence: Mental Health in the Gilded Age," *Journal of American History* 62 (March 1976):890–912.

43. Edward Cowles, "The Relation of Mental Diseases to General Medicine," *The Boston Medical and Surgical Journal* 137 (September 1897):277–278.

44. Rothman, *Conscience and Convenience*, pp. 294–309.

45. See David Noble, "The Paradox of Progressive Thought," *American Quarterly* 5 (Fall 1953):201–212.

46. For a discussion of the decline of neurology and the growth of psychological psychiatry in America, see Elliott S. Valenstein, *Great and Desperate Cures: The Rise and Decline of Psychosurgery and Other Radical Treatments for Mental Illness* (New York: Basic Books, 1986), pp. 16–20; Nathan G. Hale, Jr., *Freud and the Americans: The Beginnings of Psychoanalysis in the United States, 1876–1917* (New York: Oxford University Press, 1971), pp. 47–115; Rothman, *Conscience and Convenience*, pp. 302–309. See also Sicherman, "The Uses of Diagnosis," in Leavitt and Numbers, *Sickness and Health in America*, pp. 26–28; Henri F. Ellenberger, *The Discovery of the Unconscious: The History and Evolution of Dynamic Psychiatry* (New York: Basic Books, 1970), pp. 254–330. For an analysis of the impact of these developments on medical practice, see Paul Starr, *The Social Transformation of American Medicine* (New York: Basic Books, 1983), esp. pp. 79–144.

47. See John Chynoweth Burnham, *Psychoanalysis and American Medicine, 1894–1918: Medicine, Science, and Culture* (New York: International Universities Press, 1967), pp. 13–30; Hale, *Freud and the Americans*, pp. 200–224, 379–380; Rothman, *Conscience and Convenience*, pp. 302–309; Grob, *Mental Illness and American Society*, pp. 112–121; Sicherman, *The Quest For Mental Health in America*, pp. 203–227.

48. J. W. Wherry, M.D., "Melancholia, The Psychical Expression of Organic Fear," *AJI* 62 (January 1906): 370–371, 397–406.

49. Charles W. Pilgrim, M.D., "Insanity and Suicide," *AJI* 63 (January 1907): 349–360, esp. pp. 349–351, 358–359.

50. Ibid., pp. 351–359.

51. Tom A. Williams, M.B., C.M., "The Prevention of Suicide," *AJI* 71 (January 1915):559–571, esp. 561–562, 570.

52. Ibid., pp. 562–565.

53. Two excellent discussions of masturbation as a disease are in Robert P. Neuman, "Masturbation, Madness, and the Modern Concepts of Childhood and Adolescence," *Journal of Social History* 8 (Spring 1975):1–27; and H. Tristram Engelhart, Jr., "The Disease of Masturbation: Values and the Concept of Disease," *Bulletin of the History of Medicine* 48 (Summer 1974):234–248.

54. Williams, "The Prevention of Suicide," pp. 564–565. Williams includes several other cases in this presentation, see pp. 559–562, 565–570.

55. Burnham, *Psychoanalysis and American Medicine*, pp. 27–29; Hale, *Freud and the Americans*, pp. 138–147, 462–463; Grob, *Mental Illness and American Society*, pp. 120–122.

56. Sigmund Freud, "Mourning and Melancholia," *The Standard Edition of the Complete Psychological Works of Sigmund Freud*, ed. and trans. James Strachey, 23 vols. (London: The Hogarth Press, 1957), 14:239–258.

57. Ibid., 14:244–246, 252.

58. For a discussion of Durkheim's reception in the United States, see Roscoe C. Hinkle, Jr., "Durkheim in American Sociology," in *Emile Durkheim 1858–1917*, ed. Kurt H. Wolf (Columbus, Ohio: Ohio State University Press, 1960), pp. 267–295. I have found only one semi-contemporary reference to Durkheim in American psychiatric literature and that in an essay written by a lay person. See G. Styles, "Suicide and Its Increase," *AJI* 57 (July 1900):100.

59. Robert N. Reeves, "Suicide and the Environment," *Popular Science Monthly* 51 (June 1897): 186–191.

60. Theodore Dreiser, *Sister Carrie* (New York: W. W. Norton, 1970). For a useful discussion of suicide in turn-of-the-century American fiction, see George M. Spangler, "Suicide and Social Criticism: Durkheim, Dreiser, Wharton, and London," *American Quarterly* 31 (Fall 1979):496–516. Given the lack of reception to Durkheim's work in the United States at the turn of the century, I am skeptical that these novelists were influenced by Durkheim. More likely they shared the social values of the editorial writers of the *San Diego Union* and other publicists such as Robert Reeves.

61. Edith Wharton, *The House of Mirth* (New York: Charles Scribner's Sons, 1905).

62. Jack London, *Martin Eden* (New York: Holt, Rinehart, & Winston, 1967).

63. Maurice de Fleury, *l'Angiosse Humaine* (Paris: Editions de France, 1924), pp. 110–126, 145–150.

64. François Achilles-Delmas, *Psychologie Pathologique du Suicide* (Paris: Alcan, 1932), pp. 47–53, 234. For a discussion of this debate in France, see Anthony Giddens, "The Suicide Problem in French Sociology," *British Journal of Sociology* 16 (March 1965):3–18.

65. In many ways the changes in psychiatry mirrored the transformations of general medical practice. See Starr, *The Social Transformation of American Medicine*, esp. pp. 79–144.

Chapter 3. Specialization and Its Causalities

1. Émile Durkheim, *Suicide: A Study in Sociology*, trans. John A. Spalding and George Simpson (Glencoe, Ill.: The Free Press, 1951), pp. 277–278. Durkheim's study was sometimes ambiguous on this issue. For instance, later in his text he asserted that "There is nothing which cannot serve as an occasion for suicide. It all depends on the intensity with which suicidogenetic causes have affected the individual" (p. 300). See Dominick LaCapra, *Emile Durkheim: Sociologist and Philosopher* (Ithaca: Cornell University Press, 1972), pp. 144–154 and Jack D. Douglas, *The Social Meanings of Suicide* (Princeton: Princeton University Press, 1967), pp. 45–76. Contrary to many views, Whitney Pope argued that "the way in which Durkheim marshalled confirmatory empirical evidence" was *Suicide's* "major weakness." "By contemporary standards," Pope wrote, "neither the data nor the methods of analysis are satisfactory." Like LaCapra and Douglas, Pope concluded that *Suicide* did not

reject psychological explanations for the etiology of suicide. See Whitney Pope, *Durkheim's Suicide: A Classic Analyzed* (Chicago: University of Chicago Press, 1976), pp. 201–202.

2. See Andrew F. Henry and James F. Short, *Suicide and Homicide* (Glencoe, Ill.: The Free Press, 1954); Jack P. Gibbs and Walter T. Martin, *Status Integration and Suicide* (Eugene, Ore.: University of Oregon Books, 1964); Brian MacMahon, Samuel Johnson, and Thomas F. Pugh, "Relations of Suicide Rates to Social Conditions," *Public Health Reports* 78 (April 1963):285–293; Albert Pierce, "The Economic Cycle and the Social Suicide Rate," *American Sociological Review* 74 (June 1967):457–462; and Julian Simon, "The Effect of Income on the Suicide Rate," *American Journal of Sociology* 74 (November 1968):302–303. The only major American sociological interpretation of suicide that rejects a statistical approach is Douglas, *The Social Meanings of Suicide*. For two British studies that extend Douglas's analysis, see J. Maxwell Atkinson, *Discovering Suicide* (London: Macmillan, 1978) and Steve Taylor, *Durkheim and the Study of Suicide* (New York: St. Martin's Press, 1982).

3. Mary Monk, "Epidemiology," in *A Handbook for the Study of Suicide*, ed. Seymour Perlin (New York: Oxford University Press, 1975), pp. 185–187.

4. For an extended discussion of the limitations of official data, see Howard I. Kushner, "Women and Suicide in Historical Perspective," *Signs: Journal of Women and Culture in Society*, 10 (Spring 1985):537–552. See also Jack D. Douglas, *The Social Meanings of Suicide* (Princeton: Princeton University Press, 1967), pp. 163–231.

5. Some scholars, while acknowledging the limitations of official statistics, nevertheless insist that these data are valid indicators of the relative incidence of suicide. Conceding that suicide statistics "are very often to be said to throw more light on collection procedures than on the happenings they purport to enumerate," Olive Anderson, nevertheless, insists that the "softness" of suicide statistics presents a greater problem for sociologists than for historians. "To a historian," Anderson argues, "these doubts and criticisms do not seem particularly disconcerting," because the "underlying weakness" of suicide statistics "are all weaknesses which a historian is accustomed to find in any body of returns, *mutatis mutandis*. So far as a historian of suicide is concerned, their existence dictates not that the statistical evidence should be ignored, but that it should be used for appropriate purposes, and with care." Olive Anderson, *Suicide in Victorian and Edwardian England* (Oxford: Oxford University Press, 1987), pp. 13–14.

6. Jack D. Douglas, *The Social Meanings of Suicide* (Princeton: Princeton University Press, 1967), pp. 163–231; Roger Lane, *Violent Death in the City: Suicide, Accident, and Murder in Nineteenth Century Philadelphia* (Cambridge, Mass.: Harvard University Press, 1979), pp. 2–4.

7. See also Robert E. L. Faris, *Chicago Sociology, 1920–1932* (Chicago: University of Chicago Press, 1979); Martin Bulmer, *The Chicago School of Sociology: Institutionalization, Diversity, and the Rise of Sociological Research* (Chicago: University of Chicago Press, 1984).

8. Ernest Burgess, "The Growth of the City: An Introduction to a Research Project," in *The City*, ed. Robert E. Park, Ernest Burgess, Roderick McKenzie (Chicago: University of Chicago Press, 1925), pp. 46–62.

9. Ruth Shonle Cavan, *Suicide* (New York: Russell & Russell, 1965), preface, pp. 3–11, 100–102. For more on Cavan see Faris, *Chicago Sociology*, p. 84.

10. Cavan, *Suicide*, pp. 45–55, 325–327.

11. One prominent contemporary sociologist of suicide dismissed Cavan's study

as "more descriptive than analytic. The conspicuous lack of rigorous logical examination of her data has made Cavan's theory of suicide rather superficial." Ronald
W. Maris, *Social Forces in Urban Suicide* (Homewood, Ill.: The Dorsey Press, 1969),
p. 58.

12. Sociologists who eschew statistical methodologies often are viewed with a mixture of suspicion and contempt by their more quantitatively-minded colleagues.
This emphasis on statistical rigor seems now stronger than ever. In 1985, a sociologist at Harvard was denied tenure largely on the ground that his research was not
considered scientifically rigorous, even though he had been awarded the Pulitzer
Prize in 1984 for his sociological study of American medicine. Indeed, he was the
first sociologist ever to have won the Pulitzer Prize. See Colin Campbell, "Harvard
Tenure Ruling Stirs Debate," *New York Times,* 22 April 1985.

13. Louis I. Dublin and Bessie Bunzel, *To Be or Not To Be: A Study of Suicide* (New
York: Harrison Smith and Robert Hass, 1933), revised as Louis I. Dublin, *Suicide: A
Sociological and Statistical Study* (New York: The Ronald Press Co., 1963). For more
on Dublin, see his autobiography, *After Eighty Years: The Impact of Life Insurance on the
Public Health* (Gainesville: University of Florida Press, 1966).

14. Dublin, *Suicide,* p. 153.

15. Ibid., pp. 205–206. Maris, who characterized Cavan's work as superficial,
praised Dublin's work because "it serves the very valuable function of providing up-
to-date information." An additional virtue was the fact that "strictly speaking Dublin has no theory of suicide but rather has materials . . . for a theory of suicide."
Maris, *Social Forces in Urban Suicide,* pp. 57–58.

16. Dublin, *Suicide,* pp. 205–206.

17. Henry and Short, *Suicide and Homicide,* esp. pp. 54–65.

18. Maris, *Social Forces in Urban Suicide,* pp. 118–121. Similar criticisms can and
have been made of Martin Gold's "Suicide, Homicide, and the Socialization of
Aggression," *American Journal of Sociology* 63 (1958):651–661. See Douglas, *Social
Meanings of Suicide,* pp. 132–151.

19. Douglas, *Social Meanings of Suicide,* pp. 271–283, 155.

20. Taylor, *Durkheim and the Study of Suicide,* p. 62.

21. Maris, *Social Forces in Urban Suicide,* pp. 168–169.

22. The production of Norman L. Farberow and Edwin S. Shneidman is impressive if measured only by its bulk. Typical of their approach is their edited volume,
Clues to Suicide (New York: McGraw-Hill, 1957). See also Shneidman's edited volume, *Essays in Self-Destruction* (New York: Science House, Inc., 1967).

23. Ronald W. Maris, *Pathways to Suicide: A Survey of Self-Destructive Behaviors*
(Baltimore: Johns Hopkins University Press, 1981), pp. 8, 16–19.

24. Ibid., pp. 8, 292–294.

25. Ibid., p. 294 (italics in original). Maris adds that if distinct elements cannot be
identified, "a science of suicide would be impossible and we would be reduced to
the mysticism and magic many suicide scholars seem eager to embrace." Another of
Maris's major conclusions is that "individuals who *complete* suicide are very different
from those who 'merely' attempt suicide." (p. 264).

26. Maris, *Pathways to Suicide,* p. 17 (italics added).

27. For Black suicide rates see Robert Davis, "Black Suicide in the Seventies: Current Trends," *Suicide and Life-Threatening Behavior* 9 (Fall 1979):131–140.

28. Maris, *Pathways to Suicide,* p. 18.

29. Another sociological approach that has provoked a great deal of interest is
that of David P. Phillips, who in a series of interesting articles has argued that pub-

licity about suicides has a profound effect on subsequent suicidal incidence in the United States. See David P. Phillips, "The Influence of Suggestion on Suicide: Substance and Theoretical Implications of the Werther Effect," *American Sociological Review* 34 (June 1974):340–354; and with Lundie L. Carstensen, "Clustering of Teenage Suicides After Television News Stories About Suicide," *New England Journal of Medicine* 315 (September 1986):685–689.

30. Sigmund Freud, *Beyond the Pleasure Principle* (1920), trans. and ed. James Strachey (New York, W. W. Norton, 1961), pp. 23–31 (italics in original). For a useful discussion of Freud's views on childhood memories, see Edward S. Casey, "Freud on Emotion and Memory," forthcoming in *The International Philosophical Quarterly*.

31. Sigmund Freud, "Freud's Psychoanalytic Procedure" (1904), *Standard Edition of the Complete Psychological Works of Sigmund Freud*, ed. and trans. James Strachey, 23 vols. (London: The Hogarth Press, 1957), 7:253. Freud to James Jackson Putnam, 5 December 1909, in *James Jackson Putnam and Psychoanalysis: Letters Between Putnam and Sigmund Freud, Ernest Jones, William James, Sandor Ferenczi, and Morton Prince, 1877–1917*, ed. Nathan G. Hale, Jr. (Cambridge, Mass.: Harvard University Press, 1971), pp. 90–91. As early as *Studies in Hysteria* (1895), coauthored with Joseph Breuer, Freud wrote that the goal of psychoanalysis was to transform "hysterical misery into everyday unhappiness."

32. Russell Jacoby, *Social Amnesia: A Critique of Conformist Psychology from Adler to Laing* (Boston: Beacon Press, 1974), pp. 120–121. "Psychoanalysis," Jacoby argues, "is a theory of society and civilization as a whole, as well as immediate practice, therapy for the individual. . . . Yet this is not to indicate that there is no relationship between general theory and the individual therapy. . . . Rather the relationship is dialectical. Individual therapy must necessarily forget the whole so as to aid its individual victim; how exactly it does this is, *in part* irrelevant to theory." Also see Howard I. Kushner, "Pathology and Adjustment in Psychohistory: A Critique of the Erikson Model," *Psychocultural Review* 1 (Fall, 1977):493–506.

33. See Paul Roazen, *Freud and His Followers* (New York: Alfred A. Knopf, 1974), pp. 323–324.

34. Gregory Zilboorg, "Considerations on Suicide, With Particular Reference to that of the Young," *Journal of Orthopsychiatry* 17 (1937):18–19. See also Gregory Zilboorg, "Suicide Among Civilized and Primitive Races," *American Journal of Psychiatry* 92 (May 1936):1347–1369.

35. Zilboorg, "Considerations on Suicide," pp. 17, 21–23. See also Gregory Zilboorg, "Differential Diagnostic Types of Suicide," *Archives of Neurology and Psychiatry* 35 (1936):270–291.

36. For biographical material on Menninger, see Karl Menninger, *A Psychiatrist's World: The Selected Papers of Karl Menninger, M.D.*, ed. Bernard D. Hall (New York: The Viking Press, 1959), esp. pp. 5–103.

37. Karl Menninger, *Man Against Himself* (New York: Harcourt, Brace, & World, 1938), pp. 400–406. See also Karl Menninger, "Psychoanalytic Aspects of Suicide," *International Journal of Psycho-Analysis* 14 (July 1933):376–390; idem, "A Psychoanalytic Study of the Significance of Self-Mutilations," *Psychoanalytic Quarterly* 4 (July 1935):408–466; idem, "Purposeful Accidents as an Expression of Self-Destructive Tendencies," *International Journal of Psycho-Analysis* 17 (January 1936):6–16.

38. Menninger, *Man Against Himself*, pp. 10–73, esp. 23, 37, 43, 72–73.

39. Anthony Giddens, "The Suicide Problem in French Sociology," *British Journal of Sociology* 16 (March 1965): p. 13.

40. Freud, "Mourning and Melancholia," pp. 239–258.

41. See John Bowlby, "Separation Anxiety," *Interpretational Journal of Psycho-Analysis* 41 (1960):105–109; D. W. Winnicott, *The Maturational Processes and the Facilitating Environment: Studies in the Theory of Emotional Development* (New York: International Universities Press, 1965).

42. See John Bowlby, "Separation Anxiety," esp. pp. 105–109; Kurt R. Eissler, *The Psychiatrist and the Dying Patient* (New York: International Universities Press, 1955); Robert J. Lifton, *The Broken Connection: On Death and the Continuity of Life* (New York: Simon & Schuster, 1979); Margaret S. Mahler, "Symbiosis and Individuation: The Psychological Birth of the Human Infant," *Psychoanalytic Study of the Child* 29 (1974):89–106; George H. Pollock, "Childhood Parent and Sibling Loss in Adult Patients: A Comparative Study," *Archives of General Psychiatry* 7 (1962): 295–305; idem, "On Childhood Sibling Loss and Adult Functioning," *Annual of Psychoanalysis* 6 (1978), whole volume; Martha Wolfenstein, "Effects on Adults of Object Loss in the First Five Years," *Journal of the American Psychoanalytic Association* 24 (1976):659–668.

43. Freud, "Mourning and Melancholia," pp. 256–258.

44. Pollock, "Childhood Parent and Sibling Loss," pp. 295–305; Pollock, "On Childhood Sibling Loss." Martha Wolfenstein, "Effects on Adults of Object Loss," pp. 659–668; Gilbert C. Morrison and Jenny G. Collier, "Family Treatment Approaches of Suicidal Children and Adolescents," *Journal of the American Academy of Child Psychiatry* 8 (1969):143–152. See also Vern R. Andress and David M. Corey, "Survivor-Victims: Who Discovers or Witnesses Suicide?" *Psychological Reports* 43 (June 1978):759–764.

45. Martha Wolfenstein, "Effects on Adults of Object Loss," and her earlier "How is Mourning Possible?" *The Psychoanalytic Study of the Child* 21 (1966):93–112; John Bowlby, "Grief and Mourning in Infancy and Early Childhood," *The Psychoanalytic Study of the Child* 15 (1960):9–51. The correlation between parent or sibling death and suicide was first suggested by Gregory Zilboorg in "Considerations on Suicide, With Particular Reference to that of the Young," *Journal of Orthopsychiatry* 17 (1937):15–31, esp. 22–23; Pollock, "Childhood Parent and Sibling Loss." See also Robert A. Furman, "Death and the Young Child: Some Preliminary Considerations," *The Psychoanalytic Study of the Child* 19 (1964):321–333; Marjorie McDonald, "A Study of the Reactions of Nursery School Children to the Death of a Child's Mother," *The Psychoanalytic Study of the Child* (1964), 358–364; and Marion J. Barnes, "Reactions to the Death of a Mother," *The Psychoanalytic Study of the Child* (1964), 334–357; George R. Bach, "Father-Fantasies and Father-Typing in Father-Separated Children," *Child Development* 17 (1946):71–77. Useful historical studies that have employed this theory include Alexander Mitscherlich, *Society Without the Father: A Contribution to Social Psychology*, trans. Eric Mosbacher (New York: Schocken Books, 1970), and Peter Loewenberg, "The Psychohistorical Origin of the Nazi Youth Cohort," *American Historical Review* 76 (December 1971): 1457–1502.

46. Cf. to Freud, "Mourning and Melancholia," pp. 247–252. A useful summary of the dynamics of this response is provided by Alvin Alvarez, *The Savage; God: A Study of Suicide* (New York: Random House, 1972), pp. 91–118, esp. pp. 102–104.

47. Lifton, *The Broken Connection*, pp. 248–249; Eissler, *The Psychiatrist and the Dying Patient*, p. 66.

48. George H. Pollock, "Manifestations of Abnormal Mourning: Homicide and Suicide Following the Death of Another," *Annual of Psychoanalysis* 4 (1976):246–247. Freud made a similar argument in "Mourning and Melancholia," pp. 248–250.

49. Pollock, "Manifestations of Abnormal Mourning," esp. pp. 241–247.

50. Herbert Hendin, *Suicide and Scandinavia* (New York: Anchor Books 1964), pp. 29–30, 144.

51. Herbert Hendin, *Suicide in America* (New York: W. W. Norton, 1982), pp. 17–19.

52. This is not of course a recent criticism; see for instance, Sidney Hook, ed., *Psychoanalysis, Scientific Method and Philosophy* (New York: Grove Press, 1959), p. 44; Karl R. Popper, *Conjectures and Refutations: The Growth of Scientific Knowledge* (New York: Basic Books, 1962), p. 37.

53. See Jonathan Winson, *Brain & Psyche: The Biology of the Unconscious* (Garden City, New York: Anchor Press, 1985), pp. 163–179; Richard Restak, *The Brain* (New York: Bantam Books, 1984), pp. 221, 235; Floyd E. Bloom, Arlyne Lazerson, and Laura Hofstadter, *Brain, Mind, and Behavior* (New York: W. H. Freeman, 1985), pp. 201–203.

54. Adolf Meyer, "A Review of Recent Problems in Psychiatry," in *Nervous and Mental Disorders*, 4th ed., ed. A. Church and F. Peterson (Philadelphia: Saunders, 1904), pp. 650–688; Gerald N. Grob, *Mental Illness and American Society, 1875–1940* (Princeton: Princeton University Press, 1983), 112–115; John Chynoweth Burnham, *Psychoanalysis and American Medicine, 1894–1918: Medicine, Science, and Culture* (New York, International Universities Press, 1967), pp. 163–164.

55. Nancy C. Andreasen, *The Broken Brain: The Biological Revolution in Psychiatry* (New York: Harper and Row, 1984), p. 14. For Kraepelin's views on suicide, see his *Lectures on Clinical Psychiatry* rev. and ed. Thomas Johnstone (London, 1904, reprint New York: Hafner Publishing Co., 1968), 6–20.

56. Elliot S. Valenstein, *Great and Desperate Cures: The Rise and Decline of Psychosurgery and Other Radical Treatments for Mental Illness* (New York: Basic Books, Inc., 1986), p. 27.

57. Cotton also studied with Alois Alzheimer. Valenstein, *Great and Desperate Cures*, pp. 39–43.

58. Valenstein, *Great and Desperate Cures*, pp. 45–48.

59. Ibid., pp. 48–61.

60. In a recent article on the effects of antidepressants, a team of authors from Sweden's Karolinska Institute claimed that ECT "still remains the most effective antidepressant therapy." See Anna Wägner, et al. "Effects of Antidepressant Treatments on Platelet Tritiated Imipramine Binding in Major Depressive Disorder," *Archives of General Psychiatry* 44 (October 1987):871. Also see Susan Squire, "Shock Therapy's Return to Respectability," *The New York Times Magazine*, 22 November 1987; Charles L. Rich, "Electroconvulsive Therapy," in *Psychobiological Foundations of Clinical Psychiatry*, ed. Lewis L. Judd and Philip M. Groves (New York: Basic Books, 1986), pp. 335–344.

61. For an introduction to neurotransmitters see: Solomon H. Snyder, "Brain Peptides as Neurotransmitters," *Science* 209 (August 1980):976–983; and Floyd E. Bloom, "Neuropeptides," *Scientific American* 245 (October 1981):148–168. For an overview of the relation between suicide and neurotransmitters, see Solomon H. Snyder, "Biology," in *A Handbook for the Study of Suicide*, ed. Seymour Perlin (New York, 1975), 113–129.

62. See D. W. Wooley and E. Shaw, "A Biochemical and Pharmacological Suggestion about Certain Mental Disorders," *Proceedings of the National Academy of Sciences, USA* 40 (1954):228–231. Debates on these theories continued into the mid-1970s. For instance, see Malcolm B. Bowers, Jr., "Serotonin Systems in Psychotic States," in "Proceedings of the 1975 Intra-Science Symposium," published as *New Vistas in the*

Biochemistry of Mental Disorders, ed. Earl Usdin and Arnold J. Mandell (New York: Marcel Dekker, 1978), pp. 198–204.

63. Winson, *Brain & Psyche,* p. 194; Dennis L. Murphy, Iain C. Campbell, and Jonathan L. Costa, "The Brain Serotonergic System in Affective Disorders," *Progress in Neuro-Psychopharmacology* 2 (1978):11.

64. For a review of the explanations of how MAOs work, see Herman van Praag, "Central Monoamines and the Pathogenesis of Depression," in *Handbook of Biological Psychiatry,* ed. Van Praag, et al. Part 4: *Brain Mechanisms and Abnormal Behavior—Chemistry* (New York: Marcel Dekker, 1981), pp. 159–205. Van Praag also discussed the possibility that an oversupply of monoamine oxidase may play a role in low concentrations of serotonin (pp. 193–197). Also see Jeffrey L. Raush, "The Neuropsychopharmacology of Serotonin Function in Psychiatric Illness," in *Psychobiological Foundations of Clinical Psychiatry,* ed. Lewis L. Judd and Philip M. Groves, pp. 189–205; Murphy, "The Brain Serotonergic System," pp. 1–11, 16–19; Winson, *Brain & Psyche,* pp. 194–195; and Synder, "Biology," pp. 122–125.

65. Marie Åsberg, Lil Träskman, and Peter Thoren, "5–HIAA in the Cerebrospinal Fluid—A Biochemical Suicide Predictor?" *Archives of General Psychiatry* 33 (October 1976):1193–1197; and Åsberg, et al., "'Serotonin Depression': A Biochemical Subgroup Within the Affective Disorders?" *Science,* 191 (February 1976): 478–480. The most comprehensive survey of studies dealing with the relationship between biochemistry and affective disorders is Murphy, "The Brain Serotonergic System," pp. 1–31.

66. Herman van Praag, "Evidence of Serotonin-Deficient Depression," *Neuropsychobiology* 3 (1977):56–63; "Significance of Biochemical Parameters in the Diagnosis, Treatment, and Prevention of Depressive Disorders," *Biological Psychiatry* 12 (1977):101–131. Van Praag's 1962 Ph.D. dissertation at the University of Utrecht was entitled "A Critical Investigation of MAO Inhibition as a Therapeutic Principle in the Treatment of Depressions."

67. Snyder, "Biology," pp. 113–129, serves as a clear overview to studies of biochemistry and suicide. See Murphy, "The Brain Serotonergic System," pp. 11, 20–22; see also Kenneth G. Hoyd, et al., "Serotonin and 5–Hydroxyindoleacetic Acid in Discrete Areas of the Brainstem of Suicide Victims and Control Patients," *Advances in Biochemical Psychopharmacology* 11 (1974):387–397; Gerald L. Brown, et al., "Aggression in Humans Correlates With Cerebrospinal Fluid Amine Metabolites," *Psychiatry Research* 1 (1979):131–139; Lars Oreland, et al., "Platelet MAO Activity and Monoamine Metabolites in Cerebrospinal Fluid in Depressed and Suicidal Patients and in Healthy Controls," *Psychiatry Research* 4 (1981):21–29; Stephen H. Koslow, et al., "CSF and Urinary Biogenic Amines and Metabolites in Depression and Mania," *Archives of General Psychiatry* 40 (September 1983):999–1010.

68. Van Praag, "Central Monoamines and the Pathogenesis of Depression," pp. 185–197. See also David S. Janowsky, S. Craig Risch, and Robert Neborsky, "Strategies for Studying Neurotransmitter Hypotheses of Affective Disorders," in Judd and Groves, *Psychobiological Foundations,* pp. 179–188, esp. pp. 183–184, 186.

69. Recent studies have shown that antidepressives act with much less specificity than was earlier believed. For instance, desiprimine hydrochloride (norpramin), a norepinephrine uptake inhibitor, reduces 5–HIAA as well as the norepinephrine metabolite, MHPG. Zimeldine hydrochloride, a serotonin uptake inhibitor, reduces MHPG as well as 5–HIAA. Clorgyline, a MAO inhibitor, which was predicted to affect 5–HIAA, had a much more dramatic impact on MHPG concentrations, while it mod-

erately affected levels of the dopamine metabolite, homovanillic acid (HVA). See William Z. Potter, et al., "Selective Antidepressants and Cerebrospinal Fluid: Lack of Specificity on Norepinephrine and Serotonin Metabolites," *Archives of General Psychiatry* 42 (December 1985):1171–1177.

70. Lois Timnick, "Researchers Think Suicide Factor Test May Save Lives," *Los Angeles Times*, 11 July 1981; Lil Träskman, et al., "Monoamine Metabolites in CSF and Suicidal Behavior," *Archives of General Psychiatry* 38 (June 1981): 631–636. A supplement to this study is Marie Åsberg and Lil Träskman, "Studies of CSF 5–HIAA in Depression and Suicidal Behavior," *Advances in Experimental Medical Biology* 133 (1981):739–752.

71. Träskman, "Monoamine Metabolites," p. 635. Träskman had worked with Åsberg on her earlier studies and Åsberg was a collaborator on the 1981 Träskman study. For a useful overview of these studies, see Marie Åsberg, et al., "Suicide and Serotonin," in *Depression et Suicide: Aspects Medicaux, Psychologiques, et Socio-Culturels,* ed. J. P. Soubrier & J. Vedrinne (Paris: Pergamon Press, 1983), pp. 367–404.

72. Daniel Goleman, "Clues to Suicide: A Brain Chemical is Implicated," *New York Times*, 8 October 1985. Also see J. John Mann, et al., "Increased Serotonin[2] and β–Andrenergic Receptor Binding in the Frontal Cortices of Suicide Victims," *Archives of General Psychiatry* 43 (October 1986):954–959.

73. See Michael Stanley, et al., "Neurochemical Findings in Suicide Completers and Suicide Attempters," in *Biology of Suicide*, ed. Ronald Maris (New York: The Guilford Press, 1986), 204–218, esp. 215.

74. U.S. Department of Commerce, Bureau of the Census, *Historical Statistics of the United States, Colonial Times to 1970*, 2 vols. (Washington, D. C.: GPO, 1975) 1: 414; Morton Kramer, et al., *Mental Disorders/Suicide* (Cambridge, Mass.: Harvard University Press, 1972), pp. 216–217.

75. Between "7 to 21 percent of all alcoholics die from suicide in countries where suicide is the cause of death for from 1 to 2 percent of the total population." See Herbert Hendin, *Suicide in America* (New York: W. W. Norton, 1982), pp. 124–125; Donald W. Goodwin, "Alcohol in Suicide and Homicide," *Quarterly Studies in Alcohol* 34 (1973):144–156. Some studies downplay the role of alcoholism in the etiology of suicide, but even among these authors, alcoholics are shown to have a higher risk of suicide than nonalcoholics. See Ronald W. Maris, *Pathways to Suicide*, pp. 172–180. Also see Alec Roy and Markku Linnoila, "Alcoholism and Suicide," in Maris, *Biology of Suicide*, pp. 162–191.

76. Charles L. Rich, Deborah Young, and Richard C. Fowler, "San Diego Suicide Study," *Archives of General Psychiatry* 43 (June 1986):577–582; Nathan S. Kline, "Pharmacotherapy of the Depressed Suicidal Patient," in *Suicidal Behaviors: Diagnosis and Management*, ed. H. L. P. Resnik (Boston: Little, Brown, 1968), 314; Maris, *Pathways to Suicide*, pp. 184–188.

77. National Center for Health Statistics. "Advance Report of Final Mortality Statistics, 1984," *Monthly Vital Statistics Report* 35 (September 1986), Tables D, 10.

78. Träskman, "Monoamine Metabolites and Suicidal Behavior," pp. 631–632.

79. Edwin S. Shneidman and Norman L. Farberow, "Statistical Comparisons Between Attempted and Committed Suicides," in *The Cry for Help*, ed. Norman L. Farberow and Edwin S. Shneidman (New York, 1961), 28; Maris, *Pathways to Suicide*, p. 243. For a fuller discussion of this subject see Kushner, "Women and Suicide in Historical Perspective," esp. pp. 538–539.

80. Träskman, "Monoamine Metabolites and Suicidal Behavior," p. 635.

81. Maris, *Pathways to Suicide*, pp. 264, 267, 275–279.

82. The reluctance to employ the findings of epidemiology is not limited to psychopharmacology. As Rogers Hollingsworth points out, "the medical profession [historically] has . . . been reluctant to accept epidemiological evidence until there is definitive laboratory confirmation of findings." See Rogers Hollingsworth, "Causes and Consequences of the American Medical System," *Reviews in American History* 11 (September 1983):326–327.

83. See Kushner, "Women and Suicide," pp. 538–539.

84. Hendin, *Suicide and Scandanavia.* See also Howard I. Kushner, "Immigrant Suicide in the United States: Toward A Psycho-Social History," *Journal of Social History* 18 (Fall 1984):6–15.

85. This point of view is presented by Stanton Peele, "Reductionism in the Psychology of the Eighties: Can Biochemistry Eliminate Addiction, Mental Illness, and Pain?" *American Psychologist* 36 (August 1981):807–818. There are some notable exceptions to this resistance. In particular, see Winson, *Brain & Psyche;* and Morton F. Reiser, *Mind, Brain, Body: Toward A Convergence of Psychoanalysis and Neurobiology* (New York: Basic Books, 1984).

Chapter 4. Official Statistics and Cultural Meaning

1. "Youthful Suicides on the Rise; Experts Point to Reasons," *Atlanta Constitution* story reprinted in the *San Diego Union,* 12 December 1981; Douglas D. Palmer, "Youth Suicide Rises Fivefold," *Deseret News,* 3 April 1982; *Los Angeles Times,* 19 August 1984.

2. Jane Brody, "The Haunting Specter of Teenage Suicide," *New York Times,* 4 March 1984.

3. Mike Granberry, "San Diego Doctor Deals With Teen-Agers on Brink of Suicide," *Los Angeles Times,* 23 November 1981; *San Diego Union,* 12 December 1981; *Los Angeles Times,* 27 May 1982; James Barron, "Youth Suicides: Are Their Lives Harder to Live?" *New York Times,* 15 April 1987.

4. Quoted in Jane Brody, "The Haunting Specter of Teenage Suicide," *New York Times,* 4 March 1984; see also Mary Griffen and Carol Felsenthal, "A Cry for Help: Teen Suicide," *Family Circle,* 8 March 1983, pp. 28–34, 68–69, 154; David Gelman, "Teenage Suicide in the Sun Belt," *Newsweek,* 15 August 1983, pp. 70–74; Allan Parachini, "An Alarming Picture of Youthful Suicides," *Los Angeles Times,* 19 August 1984.

5. Ruth S. Cavan, *Suicide* (Chicago: The University of Chicago Press, 1928), pp. 307–310.

6. U.S. Census Office, 7th Census, 1850. *Mortality Statistics of the Seventh Census of the United States, 1850* (Washington, D.C.: A. O. P. Nicholson, Printer, 1855).

7. E. K. Hunt, M.D., "Statistics of Suicide in the U. S." [for 1843], *American Journal of Insanity* 1 (January 1845):225, 229–232; George P. Cook, "Statistics of Suicide, Which Have Occurred in the State of New York from Dec. 1st 1847 to Dec. 1 1848," *American Journal of Insanity* 5 (April 1849):308–309.

8. Morton Kramer et al., *Mental Disorders/Suicide* (Cambridge, Mass.: Harvard University Press, 1972), p. 205.

9. Jay Mathews, "Darker Side of Sunny California, A High Suicide Rate Under Study," *The Washington Post,* 26 December 1981.

10. Roger Lane, *Violent Death in the City: Suicide, Accident, and Murder in Nineteenth Century Philadelphia* (Cambridge, Mass.: Harvard University Press, 1979), p. 29.

11. Charles P. Hellon and Mark I. Solomon, "Suicide and Age in Alberta, Can-

ada, 1951 to 1977: The Changing Profile," *Archives of General Psychiatry* 37 (May 1980):508–509.

12. A Southern Physician, "Suicide," *The American Whig Review* 6 (August 1847): 142.

13. A Southern Physician, "Suicide," *The Democratic Review* 34 (November 1854): 405–417; C. Nordhoff, "A Matter of Life And Death," *Harper's New Monthly Magazine* 18 (March 1859):516–520.

14. "Suicides in New York City in 1860," *New York Times*, 17 January 1861.

15. Barbara Welter, "The Cult of True Womanhood: 1820–1860," *American Quarterly* 18 (Summer 1966):151–155.

16. Nathaniel Hawthorne, *The Blithedale Romance* [1852], Laurel ed. (New York: Dell Publishing Company, 1960), pp. 269–270, 274–275.

17. *The Alta California*, 2 January 1890; *New York Times*, 2 January 1890.

18. Albert Rhodes, "Suicide," *The Galaxy* 21 (February 1876):192, 194.

19. William Knighton, "Suicidal Mania," *Littel's Living Age* 148 (February 1881): 376.

20. Robert N. Reeves, "Suicide and the Environment," *Popular Science Monthly* 51 (June 1897):189–190.

21. Louis I. Dublin, *Suicide: A Sociological and Statistical Study* (New York: The Ronald Press, 1963), pp. 23–25, 27–28.

22. Peter Sainsbury, *Suicide in London, An Ecological Study* (London: Chapman & Hall, 1955), p. 80.

23. Kramer, *Mental Disorders/Suicide*, pp. 176–178.

24. Richard A. Davis, "Female Labor Force Participation, Status Integration and Suicide, 1950–1969," *Suicide and Life-Threatening Behavior* 11 (Summer 1981):123.

25. Kathryn K. Johnson, "Durkheim Revisited: Why Do Women Kill Themselves?" *Suicide and Life-Threatening Behavior* 9 (Fall 1979):145.

26. Monk, "Epidemiology," pp. 206–207; Douglas, *The Social Meanings of Suicide*, pp. 164–171.

27. Edwin S. Shneidman and Norman L. Farberow, "Statistical Comparisons Between Attempted and Committed Suicides," in *The Cry for Help*, ed. Norman L. Farberow and Edwin S. Shneidman (New York: McGraw-Hill, 1961), pp. 24–37; Ronald Maris, *Pathways to Suicide: A Survey of Self-Destructive Behavior* (Baltimore: Johns Hopkins University Press, 1981), p. 268; Dublin, *Suicide*, p. 3; Herbert Hendin, *Suicide in America* (New York: Norton, 1982), p. 49. Hendin sees the ratio as 10:1.

28. Shneidman and Farberow, "Statistical Comparisons Between Attempted and Committed Suicide," p. 28; Maris, *Pathways to Suicide*, p. 243.

29. Maris, *Pathways to Suicide*, pp. 264–286.

30. *San Diego Union*, 10 January 1898.

31. Maris, *Pathways to Suicide*, pp. 275–279.

32. *San Diego Union*, 10 January 1898.

33. Alan Marks and Thomas Abernathy, "Toward A Sociocultural Perspective on Means of Self-Destruction," *Suicide and Life-Threatening Behavior* 4 (Spring 1974): 14.

34. *San Diego Union*, 2 January 1899; 7 January 1899; San Diego County, California, Coroner's Reports, "Clara Dudley," 6 January 1899.

35. *San Diego Union*, 22 April 1895; San Diego County Coroner's Reports, "Dorcas Antle," 22 April 1895.

36. Douglas, *The Social Meanings of Suicide*, p. 215. The problem of intention as it

relates to the reporting of homicide is discussed in Kathleen Jones, "Homicide in Nineteenth Century America: San Diego, A Case Study, 1870-1900," a paper presented to the Pacific Coast Branch Meeting of The American Historical Association, San Francisco, August 1982.

37. Dublin, *Suicide*, p. 41.

38. E. K. Hunt, M.D., "Statistics of Suicide in the U. S." [for 1843], *American Journal of Insanity* 1 (January 1845):225, 229–232.

39. George P. Cook, "Statistics of Suicide, Which Have Occurred in the State of New York from Dec. 1st 1847 to Dec. 1 1848," *American Journal of Insanity* 5 (April 1849):308–309.

40. Rhodes, "Suicide," pp. 192, 194.

41. Marks and Abernathy, "Toward A Sociocultural Perspective," p. 11.

42. Kramer, *Mental Disorders/Suicide*, pp. 216–217.

43. Hunt, "Statistics of Suicide in the U. S.," p. 229.

44. Marks and Abernathy, "Toward A Sociocultural Perspective," p. 15; John L. McIntosh and John F. Santos, "Changing Patterns in Methods of Suicide by Race and Sex," *Suicide and Life-Threatening Behavior* 12 (Winter 1982):221–233.

45. See Robert Jay Lifton, *The Broken Connection: On Death and the Continuity of Life* (New York: Simon and Schuster, 1979), pp. 248–249; Jean Baechler, *Suicides*, trans. Barry Cooper, (New York: Basic Books, 1979), pp. 11, 217.

46. Hendin, *Suicide in America*, pp. 148–149.

47. Hendin, *Suicide in America*, p. 145. See also Maurice Taylor and Jerry Wicks, "The Choice of Weapons, A Study of Suicide by Sex, Race, and Religion," *Suicide and Life-Threatening Behavior* 10 (Fall 1980):142–149; Paul Friedman, "Suicide Among Police: A Study of 93 Suicides Among New York City Policemen, 1934–1940," in *Essays in Self-Destruction*, ed. Edwin Shneidman (New York: Science House, 1967), pp. 414–449.

48. Marks and Abernathy, "Toward A Sociocultural Perspective," p. 15.

49. Grethe Paerregaard, "Suicide in Denmark: A Statistical Review for the Past 150 Years," *Suicide and Life-Threatening Behavior* 10 (Fall 1980):150–157; for methods by gender for Europe and North America, see *World Health Statistics Report* (Geneva: United Nations, 1968), 21:6, Table 2; see also, Kramer, *Mental Disorders/Suicide*, Table 7.20, p. 220.

50. The literature on this subject is vast. Among the most useful studies are Welter, "The Cult of True Womanhood"; Juliet Mitchell, *The Woman's Estate* (New York: Pantheon Books, 1971), esp. pp. 153–158; Carroll Smith-Rosenberg, "Beauty, the Beast, and the Militant Woman: A Case Study in Sex Roles and Social Stress in Jacksonian America," *American Quarterly* 23 (October 1971):562–584; Charles E. Rosenberg, "Sexuality, Class and Role in Nineteenth-Century America," *American Quarterly* 25 (May 1973): 131–154; Carroll Smith-Rosenberg and Charles E. Rosenberg, "The Female Animal: Medical and Biological Views of Woman and Her Role in Nineteenth-Century America," *Journal of American History* 60 (September 1973):332–356; Linda Gordon, *Woman's Body, Woman's Right* (New York: Penguin Books, 1977), esp. pp. 95–115.

51. See Rosalind Pollack Petchesky, *Abortion and Women's Choice: the State Sexuality, and Reproductive Freedom* (New York: Longman, 1984), pp. 328–330. Also see Kristen Luker, *Abortion and the Politics of Motherhood* (Berkeley and Los Angeles: University of California Press, 1984).

52. Carol Gilligan, *In A Different Voice: Psychological Theory and Women's Development* (Cambridge, Mass.: Harvard University Press, 1982), pp. 73, 149–150.

53. See esp. Gordon, *Woman's Body, Woman's Right*, pp. 95–115.

54. Cotton Mather, *A Family Well-Ordered. Or An Essay to Render Parents and Children Happy in one Another* (Boston: Greene and Allen, 1699). Historians of early America have affirmed Mather's claim, noting that "nervous breakdowns and suicides were not uncommon" among seventeenth- and eighteenth-century youths. These youth suicides, according to one scholar, resulted from the pressures of everyday life in colonial New England, which bred an "uncertainty of outcome" and often led "to an inner tension and agony of soul disruptive in a new society." See Emory Elliott, *Power and the Pulpit in Puritan New England* (Princeton: Princeton University Press, 1975), pp. 41–42. A recent study suggests that "the suicide rate for children and adolescents in early modern England exceeded modern percentages considerably." See Terence R. Murphy, "'Woful Childe of Parents Rage': Suicide of Children and Adolescents in Early Modern England, 1507–1710," *The Sixteenth Century Journal* 17 (Fall 1986):259–270; Norman Petit, *The Heart Prepared: Grace and Conversion in Puritan Spiritual Life* (New Haven: Yale University Press, 1966), p. 19.

55. Samuel Miller, *The Guilt Folly, and Sources of Suicide* (New York: T. and J. Swords, 1805), pp. 5, 13, 26.

56. "The Alarming Increase of Suicides," *New York Times*, 3 August 1859. See also Amariah Brigham, "Statistics of Suicides in the United States," *American Journal of Insanity* 1 (January 1845):232–234.

57. Allan McLane Hamilton, "Suicide in Large Cities," *Popular Science Monthly* 8 (November 1875):92, 94.

58. Maris, *Pathways to Suicide*, p. 42.

59. Brody, "The Haunting Specter of Teenage Suicide."

60. Hendin, *Suicide in America*, p. 31. Also see Hendin, "Youth Suicide: A Psychosocial Perspective," *Suicide & Life-Threatening Behavior* 17 (Summer 1987): 160–162.

61. Brody, "The Haunting Specter of Teenage Suicide." Paul C. Holinger, *Violent Deaths in the United States: An Epidemiological Study of Suicide, Homicide, and Accidents* (New York: The Guilford Press, 1987). For a comprehensive review of youth suicide see Hendin, "Youth Suicide: A Psychosocial Perspective," pp. 151–165.

62. For a discussion of preliminary analysis of the Centers for Disease Control as reported to a national meeting on youth suicide in November 1986, see Allan Parachini, " '84 Youth Suicides a Blip in 7-Year Drop, Report Says," *Los Angeles Times*, 19 November 1986. Also see Steven Stack, "Youth Suicide Rates," *Newslink of the American Association of Suicidology* 12 (December 1986):6. The most recent statistics for California confirm these trends. See California Department of Health Services, "Suicides in California, 1980–1984" (Sacramento: Department of Health Services, November 1987), esp. pp. 2, 8.

63. Allan Bloom finds "a tendency in the social sciences to prefer deterministic explanations of events to those that see them as results of human deliberation or choice." Building on Tocqueville, Bloom remarks on the irony that in democracies more than in autocracies, "men turn out to be more willing to accept doctrines that tell them that they are determined, that is, not free. No one by himself seems to be able, or have the right, to control events, which appear to be moved by impersonal forces." Allan Bloom, *The Closing of the American Mind: How Higher Education Has Failed Democracy and Impoverished the Souls of Today's Students* (New York: Simon and Schuster, 1987), p. 255.

64. Hendin, *Suicide in America*, pp. 59–60; Kramer, *Mental Disorders/Suicide*, p. 176.

65. Joyce Jurnovoy, "Shaken by Teen Suicides, School District Seeks a Cure for 'the Hidden Epidemic,'" *Los Angeles Times*, 27 May 1982.

66. Hendin, "Youth Suicide," p. 157.

67. Steve Taylor, *Durkheim and the Study of Suicide* (New York: St. Martin's Press, 1982), pp. 144–145; see also pp. 163–166.

Chapter 5. Two Strategies

1. San Diego County Coroner's Office, "Inquisition by Coroner's Jury: In the Matter of the Body of Max E. White, 16 November 1893 [testimony of Marcus Schiller].

2. *The National Intelligencer*, 15 November 1809.

3. The Jeffersonian poet Joel Barlow attempted to immortalize Lewis with a poem "On the Discoveries of Lewis." Comparing the explorer to Columbus, Barlow proclaimed his "soaring genius" and urged the nation to rename the Columbia River in his honor: "Let our Occident Stream bear the young hero's name/ Who taught him his path to the sea." Joel Barlow, "On the Discoveries of Lewis," *National Intelligencer* and *Washington Advertiser*, 16 January 1807. See also Joel Barlow to Thomas Jefferson, 13 January 1807, in *Letters of the Lewis and Clark Expedition, with Related Documents, 1783–1854*, 2 vols., 2d ed. rev., ed. Donald Jackson (Urbana, Ill.: University of Illinois Press, 1978), 1:361–363 (hereafter cited as *Letters*).

4. Lewis's journey from St. Louis to Washington took on the aspects of a triumphal tour. When he reached the capital in December 1807, he asked his mentor, President Thomas Jefferson, in true hero's fashion only for "a just reward for all" his men and insisted that no distinction in award or in compensation be made between him and William Clark. Jefferson to Senate, 28 February 1807, in *Letters*, 1: 376; *Annals of Congress, Debates and Proceedings in the Congress of the United States, 1789–1824* (Washington, D.C., 1834–1856), 9 Cong., 2d sess., 1278; "The Act Compensating Lewis and Clark," 3 March 1807, *Letters* 2:377–380. "Messrs. Lewis & Clarke's Donation Lands," 6 March 1807, *Letters*, 2:380–382. See also John Bakeless, *Lewis and Clark: Partners in Discovery* (New York: William Morrow & Co., 1947), pp. 380–381, and Richard Dillon, *Meriwether Lewis: A Biography* (New York: Coward-McCann, Inc., 1965), pp. 270–271.

5. Frederick Bates to Richard Bates, 15 April 1809, in *The Life and Papers of Frederick Bates*, 2 vols., ed. Thomas Maitland Marshall (St. Louis, Mo.: Missouri Historical Society, 1926) 2:69; F. Bates to R. Bates, 14 July 1809, ibid., 63–73, esp. 68–70; Dillon, *Lewis*, pp. 289–316, quotation on p. 314; Bakeless, *Lewis and Clark*, pp. 392–411, 426–427.

6. William Eustis to Lewis, 15 July 1809, in *Letters*, 2:456–457; Lewis to Eustis, 18 August 1809, *Letters*, 2:459–461; John H. Marks on Lewis's debts, 1811, *Letters*, 2: 728–730; "The Lewis Estate," *Letters*, 2:730–732; Gilbert C. Russell to William D. Meriwether, 18 April 1813, *Letters*, 2:732.

7. Lewis to Lucy Marks, 1 December 1808, Lewis Collection, Missouri Historical Society, St. Louis; Bakeless, *Lewis and Clark*, p. 401. Lewis also planned to bring his half-sister Mary and her husband to St. Louis.

8. Lewis to Eustis, 18 August 1809, in *Letters*, 2: 459–461; Lewis to James Madison, 16 September 1809, *Letters*, 2: 464; Dillon, *Lewis*, pp. 325–327; Bakeless, *Lewis and Clark*, pp. 410–411.

9. William D. Meriwether to John Marks, 5 January 1810, in *Letters*, 2:487–488; "Abstract Copy of the Will of Meriwether Lewis," in *Virginia Soldiers of 1776*, 7 vols.,

ed. Louis A. Burgess (Virginia State Library: Richmond, Va., 1927), 2:739. See also "Memorandum of Lewis's Personal Effects," in *Letters*, 2:471, 473.

10. James House to Frederick Bates, 28 September 1809, Lewis Collection, Missouri Historical Society; "Statement of Russell," 26 November 1811, in *Letters*, 2: 573. Russell to Jefferson, 31 January 1810, Jefferson Papers, Library of Congress. See also Vardis Fisher, *Suicide or Murder? the Strange Death of Governor Meriwether Lewis* (Denver, Colo.: Alan Swallow, 1962), pp. 87, 115–166, 134, and *Letters*, 2: 748.

11. Neelly to Jefferson, 18 October 1809, in *Letters*, 2:467–468; Lewis to Amos Stoddard, 22 September 1809, *Letters*, 2:466–467.

12. Russell to Jefferson, 31 January 1810, Jefferson Papers; Neelly to Jefferson, 18 October 1809, in *Letters*, 2:467–468. See also Dawson A. Phelps, "The Tragic Death of Meriwether Lewis," *William and Mary Quarterly*, 3d Series, 13 (1956):314.

13. Neelly to Jefferson, 18 October 1809, in *Letters*, 2:467–468.

14. Alexander Wilson to Joseph Dennis, 28 May 1811, in *The Port Folio*, 3d Ser. (Philadelphia, 1811), 9:34–47; reproduced in Fisher, *Suicide or Murder?* pp. 147–149.

15. "Statement of Russell," 26 November 1811, in *Letters*, 2:573–574. Dillon, *Lewis*, 336–337. See also Capt. John Brahan to Jefferson, 18 October 1809, Jefferson Papers, Library of Congress and Charles Wilson Peale to Rembrandt Peale, 17 November 1809, in *Letters*, 2: 469–470; Phelps, "Tragic Death of Lewis," pp. 314–318; see also, Jefferson to Paul Allen, 18 August 1813, *Letters*, 2:586–593, esp. 592; William Clark to Jonathan Clark, 28 October 1809, *Letters*, 2:726–727; John Brahan to Amos Stoddard, 18 October 1809, in *Original Journals of the Lewis and Clark Expedition, 1804–1806*, 8 vols., ed. Reuben G. Thwaites (New York, 1904–1905), 7:389. Mrs. Grinder's accounts remain the only eyewitness reports of Lewis's death. Although Pernier was present at the end, neither he nor anyone else ever recorded the events from his perspective. Pernier, however, met with Jefferson soon after Lewis's death, and as a result of that encounter Jefferson remained satisfied that Lewis had died by his own hand. All other contemporary letters and documents conclude that Lewis took his own life. Nevertheless, some writers have concluded on rather insubstantial evidence that Lewis was murdered. A discussion of these arguments appears in my essay "The Suicide of Meriwether Lewis: A Psychoanalytic Inquiry," *William and Mary Quarterly* 3d Series, 38 (July 1981):465–481, esp. 468–470. See also Phelps, "The Tragic Death of Lewis."

16. Jefferson to Paul Allen, 18 August 1813, in Donald Jackson, *Letters*, 2:591–592; Jefferson's views on the causes of insanity were similar to those of his friend, Dr. Benjamin Rush. See Benjamin Rush, *Medical Inquiries and Observations Upon the Diseases of the Mind*, 4th ed. (Philadelphia, 1830), pp. 46, 142–143, 173, 191, 246–247; Norman Dain, *Concepts of Insanity in the United States, 1789–1865* (New Brunswick, N.J.: Rutgers University Press, 1964), pp. 19–20.

17. William Clark to Jonathan Clark, 28 October 1809, *Letters*, 2:575.

18. Charles Willson Peale to Rembrandt Peale, 17 November 1809, *Letters*, 2: 469–470.

19. Frederick Bates to Richard Bates, 9 November 1809 in *The Life and Papers of Bates*, 2:110–111.

20. *National Intelligencer*, 15 November 1809.

21. *Nashville Clarion*, 20 October 1809, reprinted in *National Intelligencer*, 15 November 1809.

22. *Missouri Gazette*, 2 November 1809. Also see *The Farmer's Friend* (Russellville),

which repeated that "The governor had been in a bad state of health," which caused him to appear "at times considerably deranged." Quoted in Fisher, *Suicide or Murder?* pp. 186–187.

23. For information on the Lewis family, see Sarah Travers Lewis (Scott) Anderson, *Lewises, Meriwethers and Their Kin . . .* (Richmond, Va.: The Dietz Press, 1938), 115–116, 180–181, 302–303, 500–505. The outline of Lewis's childhood is covered by Bakeless, *Lewis and Clark,* pp. 11–12; Dillon, *Lewis,* pp. 6–17; and Rochonne Abrams, "The Colonial Childhood of Meriwether Lewis," *Missouri Historical Society Bulletin* 34 (1978):218–227. Curiously, each author offers a different birth year for William Lewis: Bakeless offers 1748 *(Lewis and Clark,* p. 11); Dillon offers 1733 *(Lewis,* p. 8); Abrams offers 1738 ("Colonial Childhood of Lewis," p. 218). Abrams apparently relied upon Lewis's grave marker, which Bakeless warned his readers in 1947 was incorrect *(Lewis and Clark,* p. 13), while Dillon relied upon Anderson *(Lewises, Meriwethers and Their Kin,* p. 115).

24. On separation anxiety, see John Bowlby, "Separation Anxiety," *Interpretational Journal of Psycho-Analysis* 41 (1960):105–109. D. W. Winnicott, *The Maturational Processes and the Facilitating Environment: Studies in the Theory of Emotional Development* (New York: International Universities Press, 1965); and Margaret S. Mahler, "Symbiosis and Individuation: The Psychological Birth of the Human Infant," *Psychoanalytic Study of the Child* 29 (1974):102. Useful historical studies that have employed this theory include Alexander Mitscherlich, *Society Without the Father: A Contribution to Social Psychology,* trans. Eric Mosbacher (New York: Schocken Books, 1970), and Peter Loewenberg, "The Psychohistorical Origin of the Nazi Youth Cohort," *American Historical Review* 76 (December 1971):1457–1502. The classic psychoanalytic discussion of this topic appears in Sigmund Freud, *Totem and Taboo: Some Points of Agreement Between the Mental Lives of Savages and Neurotics* (New York: W. W. Norton, 1950), pp. 83–84; See also Otto Rank, *Myth of the Birth of the Hero: A Psychological Interpretation of Mythology* (New York: Alfred A. Knopf, 1964), pp. 65–72.

25. See Loewenberg, "Psychohistorical Origin of the Nazi Youth Cohort," esp. pp. 1480–1489, and George R. Bach, "Father-Fantasies and Father-Typing in Father-Separated Children," *Child Development* 17 (1946):71–77.

26. For more on William Lewis, see Burgess, *Virginia Soldiers,* 2:738–740; Anderson, *Lewises, Meriwethers and Their Kin,* pp. 115–116; Bakeless, *Lewis and Clark,* pp. 12–18; and Abrams, "Colonial Childhood of Lewis," pp. 221–227.

27. Erik H. Erikson, *Childhood and Society* (New York: W. W. Norton, 1963), pp. 238–241; Mitscherlich, *Society Without the Father,* pp. 150–159; Loewenberg, "Psychohistorical Origin of the Nazi Youth Cohort," pp. 1483–1484.

28. Bakeless, *Lewis and Clark,* pp. 13–21; Dillon, *Lewis,* pp. 12–17; Abrams, "Colonial Childhood of Lewis," pp. 221–227.

29. A. A. Alvarez, *The Savage God: A Study of Suicide* (New York: Random House, 1972), pp. 113–139.

30. Lewis, *Letters,* 2:721.

31. Dillon, *Lewis,* p. 20; Bakeless, *Lewis and Clark,* pp, 77–79, 114, 383–386; Reuben Lewis to Mary Marks, 29 November 1807, Lewis Collection, Missouri Historical Society.

32. Lewis to Mahlon Dickerson, 3 November 1807, in *Letters,* 2:720.

33. Thomas Jefferson to Meriwether Lewis, 17 July 1808, *Letters,* 2:444–445; Lewis to Stoddard, 22 September 1809, *Letters,* 2:466–467.

34. Bakeless, *Lewis and Clark,* p. 386.

35. Thomas Jefferson to Paul Allen, 18 August 1813, in *Letters*, 2:587, 591–592.

36. Anderson, *Lewises, Meriwethers and Their Kin*, p. 501; Bakeless, *Lewis and Clark*, p. 14; Dillon, *Lewis*, p. 12; Abrams, "Colonial Childhood of Lewis," p. 226.

37. Richard Beale Davis, *Francis Walker Gilmore: Life and Learning in Jefferson's Virginia* (Richmond, Va.: The Dietz Press, 1939), p. 361; Bakeless, *Lewis and Clark*, p. 20; Dillon, *Lewis*, p. 15; Abrams, "Colonial Childhood of Lewis," p. 226.

38. Dillon, *Lewis*, p. 21.

39. Levi Lincoln to Thomas Jefferson, 17 April 1803, in *Letters*, 1:35.

40. Bakeless, *Lewis and Clark*, p. 117.

41. Thomas Jefferson to Paul Allen, 18 August 1813, in *Letters*, 2:591–592.

42. The relationship between suicidal personalities and alcoholism is discussed in detail by Karl Menninger, *Man Against Himself* (New York, Harcourt, Brace, & World, 1938), pp. 140–161. See also Herbert Hendin, *Suicide in America*, pp. 124–125; Nathan Adler and Daniel Goleman, "Gambling and Alcoholism: Symptom Substitution and Functional Equivalents," *Quarterly Journal of Studies on Alcohol* 30 (1969):733–736; Donald W. Goodwin, "Alcohol in Suicide and Homicide," *Quarterly Journal of Studies on Alcohol* 34 (1973):144–156.

43. Gilbert C. Russell to Thomas Jefferson, 31 January 1810, Jefferson Papers, Library of Congress; Fisher, *Suicide or Murder?* pp. 115–116; Dillon, *Lewis*, p. 21.

44. Thomas Jefferson to Gilbert C. Russell, 18 April 1810, in *Letters*, 2: 728.

45. Gilbert C. Russell to Thomas Jefferson, 31 January 1810, Jefferson Papers.

46. Lewis *Letters*, 2:575; "Statement of Russell," 26 November 1811, *Letters*, 2:573–574.

47. For information concerning Lewis's alcoholism, see Gilbert C. Russell to Thomas Jefferson, 31 January 1810, Jefferson Papers; Thomas Jefferson to Gilbert C. Russell, 18 April 1810, in *Letters*, 2:728; "Statement of Gilbert C. Russell," 26 November 1811, *Letters*, 2:573–575. See also Jackson's discussion in notes, *Letters*, 2:575, 578, and Paul Russell Cutright, *A History of the Lewis and Clark Journals* (Norman, Okla.: University of Oklahoma Press, 1976), pp. 49–50.

48. Bakeless, *Lewis and Clark*, pp. 387–407; Dillon, *Lewis*, pp. 288–316, esp. 313–316; Lewis, *Letters*, 1:134, 2: 575; Phelps, "Tragic Death of Lewis," pp. 310–312.

49. Frederick Bates to Richard Bates, 9 November 1809, in *Life and Papers of Bates*, 2:108–109.

50. "Statement of Russell," 26 November 1811, in *Letters*, 2:573–574.

51. Philippe Ariès, *The Hour of Our Death*, trans. Helen Weaver (New York: Random House, 1982), 603–613; Ariès, *Western Attitudes Toward Death, from the Middle Ages to the Present*, trans. Patricia M. Ranum (Baltimore: Johns Hopkins University Press, 1974), pp. 100–101; for a discussion of changing attitudes toward suicide, see Alvarez, *The Savage God*, pp. 63–109. The cultural relativity of suicide is discussed by George De Vos, *Socialization for Achievement: Essays on the Cultural Psychology of the Japanese* (Berkeley and Los Angeles: University of California Press, 1973), pp. 438–485; Lee A. Headley, *Suicide in Asia and the Near East* (Berkeley and Los Angeles: University of California Press, 1983); and Norman L. Farberow, ed., *Suicide in Different Cultures* (Baltimore: University Park Press, 1975).

52. Maris A. Vinovskis, "Angels' Heads and Weeping Willows: Death in Early America," *Proceedings of the American Antiquarian Society* 86, pt. 2 (1977):273–302; Charles O. Jackson, "American Attitudes to Death," *Journal of American Studies* 11 (December 1877): 297–312.

53. While the need for mourning rituals intensifies during periods of social

turmoil, social disruptions make traditional forms of mourning more difficult. See David E. Stannard, *The Puritan Way of Death: A Study in Religion, Culture, and Social Change* (New York: Oxford University Press, 1977), pp. 96–134, 137–139.

54. Robert Jay Lifton, *The Broken Connection: On Death and The Continuity of Life* (New York: Simon & Schuster, 1979), pp. 248–249.

55. Abraham Lincoln, "Autobiography Written for J. L. Scripps," June 1860, in *The Collected Works of Abraham Lincoln*, 8 vols., ed. Roy B. Balser (New Brunswick, N.J.: Rutgers University Press, 1953), 4:61; Louis A. Warren, *Lincoln's Youth, Indiana Years, Seven to Twenty-one, 1816–1830* (Indianapolis: Indiana Historical Society, 1959), pp. 10, 18; Charles B. Strozier, *Lincoln's Quest for Union, Public and Private Meanings* (New York: Basic Books, 1982), p. 18.

56. Lincoln, "Autobiography," *Collected Works*, 4:61–62; Warren, *Lincoln's Youth*, pp. 51–55; Strozier, *Lincoln's Quest for Union*, pp. 18–20.

57. Philip D. Jordan, "The Death of Nancy Hanks Lincoln," *Indiana Magazine of History* 40 (June 1944):103–110; Warren, *Lincoln's Youth*, pp. 52–53.

58. Warren, *Lincoln's Youth*, pp. 54–55.

59. Ibid., pp. 59–66.

60. Strozier, *Lincoln's Quest for Union*, p. 14.

61. Abraham Lincoln to Solomon Lincoln, 6 March 1848, *Collected Works*, I: 455–456.

62. Emanuel Hertz, *The Hidden Lincoln, From the Letters and Papers of William H. Herndon* (New York: The Viking Press, 1938), pp. 393, 204–207.

63. Lincoln to John D. Johnston, January 12, 1851, *Collected Works*, 2:96–97.

64. Hertz, *The Hidden Lincoln*, pp. 204–205; Strozier, *Lincoln's Quest for Union*, pp. 7–8. Lincoln's paternal ancestors were more distinguished than mythic portrayals of Lincoln's roots often suggest. The possibility that Lincoln was aware of the high social standing of some of his ancestors does not of course contradict his ambivalence toward his father, Thomas Lincoln. See Thomas L. Purvis, "The Making of A Myth: Abraham Lincoln's Family Background in the Perspective of Jacksonian Politics," *Journal of the Illinois State Historical Society* 75 (Summer 1982):149–162.

65. Warren, *Lincoln's Youth*, pp. 173–175.

66. Benjamin P. Thomas, *Lincoln's New Salem* (Chicago: Americana House, 1961), pp. 63–116; see Stephen B. Oates, *With Malice Toward None: The Life of Abraham Lincoln* (New York: Harper & Row, 1977), pp. 17–31, for a general discussion of these years.

67. "Communication to the People of Sangamon County," 9 March 1832, *Complete Works*, 1:8.

68. Thomas, *Lincoln's New Salem*, pp. 121–126; David Donald, *Lincoln's Herndon* (New York: Alfred A. Knopf, 1948), pp. 352–354; Oates, *With Malice Toward None*, pp. 19–20, 30–31, 57.

69. Robert V. Bruce, *Lincoln and the Riddle of Death* (Fort Wayne, Indiana: Fourth Annual Gerald McMurtry Lecture, 1981), p. 7; Oates, *With Malice Toward None*, pp. 19–20, 30–31, 57.

70. Lincoln's relationship with Owens is discussed by all his biographers. See Benjamin P. Thomas, *Abraham Lincoln, A Biography* (New York: Alfred A. Knopf, 1952), pp. 56–57, 69–71. The story is presented accurately, but with an added fictionalized dialogue in Olive Carruthers and R. Gerald McMurtry, *Lincoln's Other Mary* (Chicago: Ziff Davis Publishing Co., 1946). The appendix reproduces Lincoln's and Owens's correspondence on the subject.

71. Abraham Lincoln to Mary S. Owens, 13 December 1836, *Collected Works*, 1: 54–55.

72. Abraham Lincoln to Mary S. Owens, 7 May 1837, *Collected Works*, 1: 78–79.

73. Abraham Lincoln to Mary S. Owens, August 16, 1837, *Collected Works*, 1: 94–95.

74. Abraham Lincoln to Mrs. Orville H. Browning, 1 April 1838, *Collected Works*, 1: 117–118.

75. Abraham Lincoln to John Stuart, 20 January & 23 January 1841, *Collected Works*, 1:228–229; Martin McKee to John Hardin, 22 January 1841, *Collected Works*, 2:229n; Abraham Lincoln to Joshua Speed, 27 March 1842, *Collected Works*, 1:282–283; William H. Herndon and Jesse W. Weik, *Abraham Lincoln: The True Story of a Great Life*, 2 vols. (New York: D. Appleton & Co., 1892), 1: 200–204; Hertz, *The Hidden Lincoln*, p. 374; Paul Simon, *Lincoln's Preparation for Greatness: The Illinois Legislative Years* (Norman, Okla., University of Oklahoma Press, 1965), pp. 236–241.

76. Strozier, *Lincoln's Quest for Union*, pp. 44–45; see Balser's comments in *Collected Works*, 1: 228–229n.

77. For a discussion of the Lincoln-Speed relationship, see Strozier, *Lincoln's Quest for Union*, pp. 42–48.

78. Balser, *Collected Works*, 1: 229n.

79. Lincoln to Joshua Speed, 19 June 1841, *Collected Works*, 1:258; Lincoln to Mary Speed, 27 September 1841, *Collected Works*, 1:259–261.

80. Abraham Lincoln to Joshua Speed, 3 February 1842, *Collected Works*, 1: 267–268; see also Abraham Lincoln to Joshua Speed, 3 January 1843, *Collected Works*, 1:265–266; idem, 13 February 1842, *Collected Works*, 1:269–270.

81. Abraham Lincoln to Joshua Speed (2 letters), 25 February 1842, *Collected Works*, 1:280–281; and 27 March 1842, *Collected Works*, 1:282–283.

82. Herndon and Weik, *Abraham Lincoln*, 1:203.

83. A. A. Alvarez, *The Savage God: A Study of Suicide* (New York: Random House, 1972), pp. 108–109; Gregory Zilboorg, "Differential Diagnostic Types of Suicide," *Archives of Neurology and Psychiatry* 35 (1936):282–284; Kurt R. Eissler, *The Psychiatrist and the Dying Patient* (New York: International Universities Press, 1955), p. 66; Sigmund Freud, "Mourning and Melancholia," *The Standard Edition of the Complete Works of Sigmund Freud*, ed. trans. James Strachey, 23 vols. (London: Hogarth Press, 1957), 14:248–250. John Baechler, *Suicides*, trans. Barry Cooper (New York: Basic Books, 1978), pp. 248–249.

84. Bruce, *Lincoln and the Riddle of Death*, pp. 14–15.

85. Philippe Ariès, *The Hour of Our Death*, trans. Helen Weaver (New York: Vintage Books, 1982), pp. 609–611; Philippe Ariès, *Western Attitudes Toward Death, From the Middle Ages to the Present*, trans. Patricia M. Ranum (Baltimore: Johns Hopkins University Press, 1974), pp. 55–82. For Bruce's discussion of Lincoln's attitudes, see Bruce, *Lincoln and the Riddle of Death*, pp. 14–18.

86. Charles Jackson finds that as the death of "close 'others'" became increasingly unacceptable to the survivors, they responded by domesticating and beautifying funerals. See Charles O. Jackson, "American Attitudes to Death." *Journal of American Studies* 11 (December 1977):301, 305–306.

87. Abraham Lincoln to Joshua Speed, 3 February 1842, *Complete Works*, 1:267.

88. A complete version of Knox's "Mortality" can be found in Maurice Boyd, "Lincoln and the Influence of William Knox," *Lincoln Herald* 60 (Spring 1958):

14−15; also see Boyd, "Knox's Poems: A Legacy to Lincoln," *Lincoln Herald* 60 (Fall 1958):82−86.

89. Abraham Lincoln to Andrew Johnston, 18 April 1846, *Complete Works*, 1:378.

90. Bruce, *Lincoln and the Riddle of Death*, pp. 9−10; Boyd, "Lincoln and the Influence of Knox," pp. 12−14; David J. Harkness and R. Gerald McMurtry, *Lincoln's Favorite Poets* (Knoxville, Tenn.: University of Tennesse Press, 1959), pp. 15−16. Dwight G. Anderson, *Abraham Lincoln: Quest for Immortality* (New York, Alfred A. Knopf, 1982), p. 82.

91. Boyd, "Lincoln and the Influence of Knox," pp. 12−14.

92. Boyd, "Lincoln and the Influence of Knox," pp. 12−15; Boyd, *William Knox and Abraham Lincoln: The Story of a Poetic Legacy* (Denver: Sage Books, 1966), pp. xiv−xvii; "Eulogy on Zachary Taylor, 25 July 1850, *Collected Works*, 2:90; Henry C. Whitney, *Life on the Circuit with Lincoln*, intoduction and notes by Paul M. Angle (Caldwell, Idaho: The Caxton Printers, Ltd., 1940), pp. 68−69, 146−147, 425−426, 428−429; Hertz, *The Hidden Lincoln*, pp. 110−111, 121−122, 204; Albert J. Beveridge, *Abraham Lincoln, 1809−1858*, 2 vols. (Cambridge, Mass.: Houghton Mifflin Co., 1928), 1:523−524.

93. Bruce, *Lincoln and the Riddle of Death*, p. 11.

94. Abraham Lincoln to Andrew Johnston, 24 February 1846, 18 April 1816, & 6 September 1846, *Collected Works*, 1:367−370, 378-379, 384−386.

95. Herndon and Weik, *Abraham Lincoln*, 1:203.

96. Strozier, *Lincoln's Quest for Union*, p. 15; Bruce, *Lincoln and the Riddle of Death*, p. 20; Anderson, *Abraham Lincoln*, pp. 97−99; George B. Forgie, *Patricide in the House Divided: A Psychological Interpretation of Lincoln and His Age* (New York: W. W. Norton, 1979), pp. 55−87.

97. Bruce, *Lincoln and the Riddle of Death*, pp. 20, 18, 23.

98. Anderson, *Abraham Lincoln*, p. 79, 95.

99. Strozier, *Lincoln's Quest for Union*, pp. 14−16.

100. Otto Rank, *The Myth of the Birth of the Hero: A Psychological Interpretation of Mythology* (1914, reprint, New York: Vintage Books, 1964), p. 71.

101. Anderson, *Abraham Lincoln*, pp. 78, 99, 79.

102. Ernest Becker, *The Denial of Death* (New York: The Free Press, 1973), p. 4.

103. See Anderson, *Abraham Lincoln*, p. 207.

Chapter 6. Psychocultural Meaning of Suicide

1. *San Diego Union*, 8 November 1893.

2. Frederick Jackson Turner, "The Significance of the Frontier in American History," *Annual Report of the American Historical Association for the Year 1893* (Chicago, 1893).

3. Elizabeth C. MacPhail, *The Story of New San Diego and its Founder, Alonzo E. Horton* (San Diego Historical Society: San Diego, 1979), pp. 88−101.

4. *San Diego Union*, 19 March 1892; *San Diego Union*, 20 March 1892; San Diego County Coroner's Office, Coroner's Report, "James A. Dillar," 19 March 1892 [hereafter cited as sDCCO, CR]; Coroner's Inquest File, 19 March 1892, San Diego Historical Society, Manuscript Collections [hereafter cited as CIF:SDHS].

5. *San Diego Union*, 3 March 1892; 4 March 1892; 5 March 1892; sDCCO, CR, "J. W. Collins," 4 March 1892; CIF:SDHS. Collins was born in Pennsylvania and had

moved to San Diego in 1886 from Cheyenne, Wyoming. For Golden see *San Diego Union*, 10 March 1892; SDCCO, CR, "George Golden," 10 March 1892; CIF:SDHS.

6. *San Diego Union*, 18 December 1893; SDCCO, CR, "Carl Creutzenberg," 18 December 1893; CIF:SDHS.

7. Peter Sainsbury and Brian Barraclough, "Differences Between Suicide Rates," *Nature* 220 (December 1968): 1252; Ruth S. Cavan, *Suicide* (Chicago: University of Chicago Press, 1928), pp. 9, 34, 49, 52; Calvin F. Schmid, "Suicide in Minneapolis," *American Journal of Sociology* 39 (July 1933):30–48; Morton Kramer, et al., *Mental Disorders/Suicide* (Cambridge, Mass.: Harvard University Press, 1972), pp. 181–185. See also Roger Lane, *Violent Death in the City: Suicide, Accident, and Murder in Nineteenth Century Philadelphia* (Cambridge, Mass.: Harvard University Press, 1979); Aubrey Wendling, "Suicide in the San Francisco Bay Region, 1938–1942 and 1948–1952," Ph.D. dissertation, University of Washington, Seattle, 1954.

8. National Center for Health Statistics, *Monthly Vital Statistics Report, Advanced Report, Final Mortality Statistics, 1984* 35 (6, Supplement(2)) (Washington, D.C.: GPO, 1986) for the latest comprehensive figures.

9. On the other hand, Olive Anderson has found that migrants from rural to industrial areas in nineteenth-century England and Wales had a lower incidence of suicide than many who remained in their native villages. Anderson attributes this to the fact that many industrial migrants were able to join networks of co-villagers both in their selection of lodging and of work places. Thus Anderson questions "the classic association of the advent of urban industrialization with the breakdown of controls over behavior and hence with increased collective violence, millenarianism, revolutionary movements, and individual deviance." Olive Anderson, "Did Suicide Increase with Industrialism in Victorian England?" *Past & Present* 86 (February 1980):166. Also see Olive Anderson, *Suicide in Victorian and Edwardian England* (Oxford: Oxford University Press, 1987), pp. 54, 84–93, 418–426. This contrasts somewhat with Louis Chevalier's conclusion that migrants were the most likely suicide victims in nineteenth-century Paris, though Chevalier attributed this to the fact that migrants in Paris (apparently unlike Anderson's migrants) were unable to form social networks and instead became part of "an anonymous mass." Chevalier, *Labouring Classes and Dangerous Classes in Paris During the First Half of the Nineteenth Century*, trans. Frank Jellinek (London: Routlege & Kegan Paul, 1973), pp. 290–292.

10. K. Hunt, "Statistics of Suicide in the United States," *American Journal of Insanity* 1 (January 1845):225–234, which includes statistics on suicides for New York City, 1805–1843. For New York State, 1844–1849, see "Statistics of the Suicides," *American Journal of Insanity* 3 (April 1847):349–352; "Statistics of Suicides," *American Journal of Insanity* 4 (January 1848): 247–253; and *American Journal of Insanity* 5 (April 1849):303–310.

11. "Suicide in New York City, 1860," *New York Times*, 17 January 1861.

12. *11th Census of the U.S., 1890*, "Vital and Social Statistics," 4: 466; see also *10th Census of the U.S., 1880*, "Mortality and Vital Statistics," 12: C. The Federal Census in the nineteenth century underreported mortality rates and thus must be used with caution. For instance, the authors of the 1880 census admitted "enumerators did not obtain and record more than 60 to 70 percent of the actual number of deaths." U.S. Census Office, *10th Census of the United States, 1880* (Washington, D.C., 1883–1888), 11:1, p. xi. The 1890 census reported that its mortality returns were deficient in "from 20 to 50 percent in different localities." *11th Census of the U.S., 1890* (Washington, D.C., 1892–1897), 4:pt. 1, p. 1. See also *Abstract of the Elev-*

enth Census: 1890, 2nd ed. (Washington, 1896), p. 264. See also John B. Shayless and Roy M. Shortridge, "Biased Underenumeration in Census Manuscripts: Methodological Implications," *Journal of Urban History* 1 (1975):409–439. For a discussion of nineteenth-century mortality returns as they relate to homicide, see Kathleen Bulmash [Jones], "Homicide in Nineteenth-Century America: San Diego, A Case Study, 1870–1900," Paper presented at the Annual Meeting of the Pacific Coast Branch of the American Historical Association, San Francisco, 11–14 August 1982.

13. Lane, *Violent Death in the City,* p. 24.

14. Anita M. Muhl, "America's Greatest Suicide Problem: A Study of Over 500 Cases in San Diego," *Psychoanalytic Review* 14 (1927):317–325, esp. pp. 322–323.

15. For a published report of this work, see Jay Mathews, "Darker Side of Sunny California, A High Suicide Rate Under Study," *Washington Post,* 26 December 1981; see also Nancy Ray, "Reasons for High Suicide Rate Questioned," *Los Angeles Times* (San Diego Edition), 14 October 1981; Muriel Dobbin, "3-Year California Study Seeks Whys of Suicide," *Baltimore Sun,* 9 November 1981.

16. San Diego County Coroner's Office, *Coroners' Reports,* 1870–1900; the rates of foreign versus native-born suicides for San Diego County were computed by relying on immigration figures supplied in *12th Census of the U.S., 1900* (Washington. D.C.: GPO, 1901), Population, Part 1, Table 18. "Male and Female and Native and Foreign Born Population by Counties: 1880–1900," p. 495. Rates for San Diego were adjusted with 95 percent confidence intervals. See also Francis H. Mead, "The Suicide Rate in San Diego," *American Medical Association Journal* 61 (November 1913):1999–2000.

17. Cavan, *Suicide,* pp. 33–36; Kramer, *Mental Disorders/Suicide,* pp. 181–187, 208–215; Mary Monk, "Epidemiology," in *A Handbook for the Study of Suicide,* ed. Seymour Perlin (New York: Oxford University Press, 1975), pp. 192–200; Louis Dublin, *Suicide, A Sociological and Statistical Study* (New York: Ronald Press, 1963), 30–35; Lane, *Violent Death in the City,* pp. 26–28; Wendling, "Suicide in San Francisco," pp. 76–87.

18. Grethe Paerregaard, "Suicide in Denmark: A Statistical Review for the Past 150 Years," *Suicide and Life Threatening Behavior* 10 (Fall 1980):150–156. The cultural relativity of suicide is discussed by George De Vos, *Socialization for Achievement: Essays on the Cultural Psychology of the Japanese* (Berkeley and Los Angeles: University of California Press, 1973), pp. 438–485, and Norman L. Farberow, ed., *Suicide in Different Cultures* (Baltimore: University Park Press, 1975); Lee A. Headley, ed., *Suicide in Asia And the Near East* (Berkeley and Los Angeles: University of California Press, 1983); see also A. Alvarez, *The Savage God: A Study In Suicide* (New York: Random House, 1972), pp. 47–75.

19. "The Alarming Increase of Suicides," *New York Times,* 3 August 1859; "A Chapter of Suicides," *New York Times,* 3 August 1859.

20. "Suicides in New York City in 1860," *New York Times,* 17 January 1861.

21. *11th Census of the U.S., 1890,* 4:pt. 1, p. 465.

22. Allan McLane Hamilton, M.D., "Suicide in Large Cities," *Popular Science Monthly* 8 (November 1875):93, 89.

23. Albert Rhodes, "Suicide," *The Galaxy* 21 (February 1876):194.

24. Thomas G. Masaryk, *Suicide and the Meaning of Civilization* (1881), trans. William B. Weist and Robert G. Batson (Chicago: University of Chicago Press, 1970), p. 210.

25. *AJI* 40 (April 1884):522; see also *AJI* 39 (April 1883):471.

26. Lane, *Violent Death in the City,* p. 27.

27. Cavan, *Suicide*, pp. 34–35, 46.

28. Herbert Hendin, *Suicide and Scandinavia* (New York: Anchor Books, 1964), pp. 29–30, 144; Hendin, *Suicide in America*, 17–19.

29. Philippe Ariès, *The Hour of Our Death*, trans. Helen Weaver (New York: Basic Books, 1982), pp. 603–613. Philippe Ariès, *Western Attitudes Toward Death, from the Middle Ages to the Present*, trans. Patricia M. Ranum (Baltimore: Johns Hopkins University Press, 1974), pp. 100–101. For a study of early modern English attitudes that affirms Ariès's arguments, see Clare Gittings, *Death, Burial, and the Individual in Early Modern England* (Dover, N.H.: Croom Helm, 1984).

30. Maris A. Vinovskis, "Angels' Heads and Weeping Willows: Death in Early America," *Proceedings of the American Antiquarian Society* 86, pt. 2 (1977):273–302; Charles O. Jackson, "American Attitudes to Death," *Journal of American Studies* 11 (December 1977):297–312; David E. Stannard, *The Puritan Way of Death: A Study in Religion, Culture, and Social Change* (New York: Oxford University Press, 1977), pp. 96–134, 137–139.

31. Jackson, "American Attitudes to Death," pp. 301, 305–306; Ariès, *Hour of Our Death*, pp. 609–611; Ariès, *Western Attitudes Toward Death*, pp. 55–82. A similar point is made in Arthur E. Imhof, "From the Old Mortality Pattern to the New: Implications of a Radical Change from the Sixteenth to the Twentieth Century," *Bulletin of the History of Medicine* 59 (Spring 1985):1–29, esp. 24–29.

32. Ariès, *Western Attitudes Toward Death*, pp. 100–101. For a useful review of the literature on cultural variations toward death and mourning, see Phyllis Palgi and Henry Abramovitch, "Death: A Cross-Cultural Perspective," *Annual Review of Anthropology* 13 (1984):385–417.

33. Hendin, *Suicide and Scandinavia*, pp. 30, 45, 144; Leonard Dinnerstein and David M. Reimers, *Ethnic Americans: A History of Immigration and Assimilation* (New York: Dodd, Mead & Co., 1975), pp. 33–35. Eugene Boe, "Norwegians on the Prairie," in *Uncertain Americans: Readings in Ethnic History*, ed. Leonard Dinnerstein and Frederic Cople Jaher (New York: Oxford University Press, 1977). p. 193

34. Thomas Kessner, *The Golden Door: Italian and Jewish Immigrant Mobility in New York City, 1880–1915* (New York: Oxford University Press, 1977), pp. 93–96, 150–151; Herbert Gans, *The Urban Villagers* (New York: Free Press, 1962), pp. 197–225, 289–291; Virginia Yans McLaughlin, "Patterns of Work and Family Organization: Buffalo's Italians," *Journal of Interdisciplinary History* 2 (Autumn 1971): 302–303; Alan M. Kraut, *The Huddled Masses: The Immigrant in American Society, 1880–1921* (Arlington Heights, Ill.: Harlan Davidson, 1982), pp. 101, 132–133. For an argument that Italian immigrants faced more conflict than the suicide rates seem to indicate, see Andrew Rolle, *The Italian Americans: Troubled Roots* (New York: The Free Press, 1980).

35. Kathleen Neils Conzen, "Immigrants, Immigrant Neighborhoods, and Ethnic Identity: Historical Issues," *Journal of American History* 66 (December 1979): 603-615, esp. 609.

36. Cavan, *Suicide*, pp. 35–45; see also Dr. Hans Rost, "Suicide in Cities," *American Journal of Sociology* 10 (January 1905):562; Ronald W. Maris, *Pathways to Suicide: A Survey of Self-Destructive Behaviors* (Baltimore: Johns Hopkins University Press, 1981), pp. 253–255.

37. Émile Durkheim, *Suicide: A Study in Sociology* [1897], trans. John A. Spaulding and George Simpson (Glencoe, Ill.: The Free Press, 1951), pp. 167–168. Durkheim of course was not the first to make this connection. See for instance, "Suicide in Bavaria," *AJI* 16 (October 1863):246–247.

38. Cavan, *Suicide*, pp. 38–42.

39. See Maris, *Pathways to Suicide*, pp. 250–260, esp. 254–255; John Baechler, *Suicides*, trans. Barry Cooper (New York: Basic Books, 1979), pp. 303–308; Herbert Hendin, *Suicide in America* (New York: W. W. Norton & Co., 1982), p. 17; Jack D. Douglas, *The Social Meanings of Suicide* (Princeton: Princeton University Press, 1967), pp. 286–287.

40. Ernest Becker, *The Denial of Death* (New York: The Free Press, 1973), pp. 1–8, 17–19. For a discussion of self-transformation in relation to identity, see Erik H. Erikson, *Identity: Youth and Crisis* (New York: W. W. Norton, 1968), pp. 165–207.

41. Cavan, *Suicide*, pp. 27–28; *Monthly Vital Statistics Report, 1984*, Table 17, pp. 40–41.

42. Mary Ann Meyers, "Death in Swedenborgian and Mormon Eschatology," *Dialogue* 14, 1 (1981):58–64.

Chapter 7. Toward a Psychocultural Biology

1. Jonathan Winson, *Brain & Psyche: The Biology of the Unconscious* (New York: Anchor Press, 1985), pp. 163–179; Richard Restak, *The Brain* (New York: Bantam Books, 1984), pp. 221, 235; Floyd E. Bloom, Arlyne Lazerson, and Laura Hofstadter, *Brain, Mind, and Behavior* (New York: W. H. Freeman, 1985), pp. 201–203.

2. Restak, *The Brain*, p. 221.

3. Restak, *The Brain*, p. 235.

4. Mortimer Mishkin and Tim Appenzeller, "The Anatomy of Memory," *Scientific American* 256 (June 1987):80–89, esp. pp. 82–85; Bloom, Lazerson, & Hofstadter, *Brain, Mind and Behavior*, pp. 202–203.

5. Of course, the process of memory formation, storage, and retrieval is very complicated and not fully understood. See Larry R. Squire, "Mechanisms of Memory," *Science* 232 (June 1986):1612–1619; Richard F. Thompson, "The Neurobiology of Learning and Memory," *Science* 233 (August 1986):941–947.

6. Restak, *The Brain*, p. 212. For detailed discussions of the role of the amygdala in memory processing, see Martin Sarter and Hans J. Markowitsch, "The Amygdala's Role in Human Mnemonic Processing," *Cortex* 21 (1985):7–24; E. Halgren, "The Amygdala Contribution to Emotions and Memory: Current Studies in Humans," in *The Amygdaloid Complex*, ed. Y. Ben-Ari (Amsterdam: Elsevier/North Holland Biomedical Press, 1981), pp. 395–408.

7. Jeffrey L. Rausch, "The Neuropsychopharmacolgy of Serotonin Function in Psychiatric Illness," in *Psychobiological Foundations of Clinical Psychiatry*, ed. Lewis Judd and Philip Groves (New York: Basic Books, 1986), esp. pp. 199–202; Herman van Praag, "Central Monoamines and the Pathogenesis of Depression," in *Handbook of Biological Psychiatry, Part IV: Brain Mechanisms and Abnormal Behavior—Chemistry*, ed. Van Praag, et al. (New York: Marcel Dekker, 1981), pp. 185–197.

8. Recent studies have shown that antidepressives act with much less specificity than was earlier believed. For instance, desiprimine hydrochloride (norpramin), a norepinephrine uptake inhibitor, reduces 5–HIAA as well as the norepinephrine metabolite, MHPG. Zimeldine hydrochloride, a serotonin uptake inhibitor, reduces MHPG as well as 5–HIAA. Clorgyline, a MAO inhibitor, which was predicted to affect 5–HIAA, had a much more dramatic impact on MHPG concentrations, while it moderately affected levels of the dopamine metabolite, homovanillic acid (HVA). See William Z. Potter, et al., "Selective Antidepressants and Cerebrospinal Fluid: Lack of Specificity on Norepinephrine and Serotonin Metabolites," *Archives of Gen-*

eral Psychiatry 42 (December 1985):1171–1177. Also see John K. Hsiao, et al., "Monoamine Neurotransmitter Interactions and the Prediction of Antidepressant Response," *Archives of General Psychiatry* 44 (December 1987):1078–1083.

9. Floyd E. Bloom, "Neuropeptides," *Scientific American* 245 (October 1981): 148–168.

10. Edward Shorter, "L'âge des premières règles en France, 1750–1950," *Annales* 36 (Mai-Juin 1981):495–511; Peter Laslett, "The Age of Menarche in Europe Since the Eighteenth Century," in *The Family in History: Interdisciplinary Essays,* ed. Theodore K. Rabb and Robert I. Rotberg (New York, Harper and Row, 1973), pp. 28–47.

11. For the case for the centrality of nutrition to fertility rates, see Rose E. Frisch, "Population, Food Intake, and Fertility," *Science* 199 (January 1978):22–30. Also see Alfred W. Crosby, Jr., *The Columbian Exchange: Biological and Cultural Consequences of 1492* (Westport, Conn., Greenwood Press, 1972), pp. 165–207; Thomas McKeown, "Food, Infection, and Population," *Journal of Interdisciplinary History* 14 (Autumn 1983):227–247, esp. 244. For a critique of Frisch's conclusions, see Jane Menkin, James Trussell, and Susan Cotts Watkins, "The Nutrition Fertility Link: An Evaluation of Evidence," *Journal of Interdisciplinary History* 11 (Winter 1981): 425–441. Menkin, Trussell, and Watkins agree that "the age of ménarche might be affected by the level of nutrition," but they argue that "this hypothesis is of little use in explaining the variations of marital fertility in Western Europe" (pp. 430–431). See also Susan Cotts Watkins and Etienne van de Walle, "Nutrition, Mortality, and Population Size: Malthus' Court of Last Resort," *Journal of Interdisciplinary History* 14 (Autumn 1983):210–224. In any case, my point is simply to use the variations in the age onset of ménarche as an example of how nutrition affects hormone production. On that, all researchers agree.

12. Richard J. Wurtman and John H. Growdon, "Dietary Enhancement of CNS Neurotransmitters," *Hospital Practice* 13 (March 1978):71–77; John D. Fernstrom and Richard J. Wurtman, "Control of Brain Serotonin Levels by the Diet," *Advances in Biochemical Psychopharmacology* 11 (1974):133–142. The most comprehensive recent overview is to be found in Herschel Sidransky, "Tryptophan: Unique Action by an Essential Amino Acid," in *Nutritional Pathology: Pathochemistry of Dietary Imbalances,* ed. Herschel Sidransky (New York: Marcel Dekker, 1985), pp. 1–62. A useful discussion of various aspects of tryptophan for the general reader is found in John D. Kirschman, *Nutrition Almanac,* rev. ed. (New York: McGraw-Hill, 1979), pp. 36–37, 235–243.

13. Wurtman and Growdon, "Dietary Enhancement of CNS Neurotransmitters," pp. 71–72; John D. Fernstrom and Jacob H. Jacoby, "The Interaction of Diet and Drugs in Modifying Brain Serotonin Metabolism," *General Pharmacology* 6 (1975): 253–258; Fernstrom and Wurtman, "Control of Brain Serotonin Levels by the Diet," pp. 140–141; Fernstrom and Wurtman, "Brain Serotonin Content: Increase Following Ingestion of Carbohydrate Diet," *Science* 174 (December 1971):1023–1025. See also "Scientists Ponder Diet's Behavioral Effects," *JAMA,* 254 (December 1985):3407–3408.

14. There are several studies concerning differing diets over time among different classes and ethnic groups, including Andrew B. Appleby, "Diet in Sixteenth-Century England: Sources, Problems, Possibilities," in *Health, Medicine, and Mortality in the Sixteenth Century,* ed. Charles Webster (Cambridge, England: Cambridge University Press, 1979), pp. 97–116. Essential reading is a recent collection of essays edited by Robert I. Rotberg, entitled "Hunger and History: The Impact of

Changing Food Production and Consumption Patterns on Society," *The Journal of Interdisciplinary History* 14 (Autumn 1983). See also D. J. Oddy, "Working Class Diets in Late Nineteenth Century Britain," *Economic History Review* 23 (1970):314–323. Another direction of recent historical research is the relationship suggested by J. M. Tanner between nutrition and height. An issue of *Social Science History* 6 (Fall 1982) edited by Robert W. Fogel and Stanley L. Engerman entitled "Trends in Nutrition, Labor Welfare, and Labor Productivity" contains a collection of articles employing Tanner's approach. Also see James M. Tanner, *A History of the Study of Human Growth* (Cambridge, England: Cambridge University Press 1981).

15. Frisch, "Population, Food Intake, and Fertility," pp. 26–27.

16. Nancy C. Andreasen, *The Broken Brain: The Biological Revolution in Psychiatry* (New York: Harper and Row, 1984), pp. 8, 231–237, 249.

17. Morton F. Reiser, *Mind, Brain, Body: Toward A Convergence of Psychoanalysis and Neurobiology* (New York: Basic Books, 1984), pp. 180–181.

18. Van Praag, "Central Monoamines," p. 197.

19. M. Åsberg, D. Schalling, E. Rydin, and L. Träskman-Bendz, "Suicide and Serotonin," in *Depression & Suicide, Aspects Medicaux, Psychologiques, et Socio-Culturels*, ed. J. P. Soubrier & J. Vedrinne (Pergamon Press: Paris, 1981), p. 381.

20. Israel Rosenfield, "The New Brain," *The New York Review of Books*, 14 March 1985, pp. 36–37.

21. Rosenfield, "The New Brain," pp. 36–37.

22. See Gary Wenk, et al., "Neurotransmitters and Memory: Role of Cholinergic, Serotonergic, and Noradrenergic Systems," *Behavioral Neuroscience* 101 (1987): 325–332. Also see Gary Lynch and Michael Baudry, "The Biochemistry of Memory: A New and Specific Hypothesis," *Science* 234 (June 1984):1057–1063.

23. Bloom, Lazerson, & Hofstadter, *Brain, Mind, & Behavior*, pp. 184–188, 192–194; Winson, *Brain & Psyche*, pp. 201–202, 211–213, 236–237, 241–242; Reiser, *Mind, Brain, Body*, pp. 122–124. Also see Squire, "Mechanisms of Memory," pp. 1612–1613; Mishkin and Apenzeller, "The Anatomy of Memory," pp. 80–89.

24. Sarter and Markowitsch, "The Amygdala's Role in Human Mnemonic Processing," *Cortex* 21 (1985):15–18; Halgren, "The Amygdala Contribution to Emotions and Memory," pp. 395–408; Hans J. Markowitsch, "Thalamic Mediodorsal Nucleae and Memory: A Critical Evaluation of Studies in Animals and Man," *Neuroscience and Biobehavioral Reviews* 6 (1982):351–380.

Epilogue

1. For an attempt to combine the history of mentalities with a psychohistorical approach, see Patrick H. Hutton, "The Psychohistory of Erik Erikson from the Perspective of Collective Mentalities," *The Psychohistory Review* 12 (Fall 1983):18–25.

2. Don E. Fehrenbacher, "In Quest of the Psychohistorical Lincoln," *Reviews in American History* 11 (March 1983):12–13. For some of the most outspoken of these criticisms, see Jacques Barzun, *Clio and the Doctors: Psycho-History, Quanto-History, and History* (Chicago: University of Chicago Press, 1974) David E. Stannard, *Shrinking History: On Freud and the Failure of Psychohistory* (New York: Oxford University Press, 1980).

3. Stannard's *Shrinking History* is an example of this. See *The Psychohistory Review* 9 (Winter 1980):136–161, for a "Symposium" on this book along with the author's response.

4. Peter Loewenberg, "Psychohistorical Perspectives on Modern German His-

tory," *Journal of Modern History* 47 (June 1975), 229–279, esp. 247–251; Loewenberg, "Psychohistory," in *The Past Before Us*, ed. Michael Kammen (Ithaca: Cornell University Press, 1980), pp. 408–432; Saul Friedlander, *History and Psychoanalysis: An Inquiry into the Possibilities and Limits of Psychohistory*, trans. Susan Suleiman (New York: Holmes & Meier, 1978), pp. 12–16.

5. Dorothy Ross, "Woodrow Wilson and the Case for Psychohistory," *Journal of American History* 69 (December 1982):659–660.

6. Edmund S. Morgan, "The Labor Problem at Jamestown, 1607–18," *American Historical Review* 76 (June 1971):596–611; Karen Ordahl Kupperman, "Apathy and Death in Early Jamestown," *Journal of American History* 66 (June 1979):24–28; Carville V. Earle, "Environment, Disease, and Mortality in Early Virginia," in *The Chesapeake in the Seventeenth Century: Essays on Anglo-American Society*, ed. Thad W. Tate and David L. Ammerman (Chapel Hill: University of North Carolina Press, 1979), pp. 96–125.

7. Morgan, "Labor Problem at Jamestown," pp. 597–598.

8. Edmund S. Morgan, *American Slavery, American Freedom: The Ordeal of Colonial Virginia* (New York: W. W. Norton, 1975), p. 101; Kupperman, "Apathy and Death in Jamestown," pp. 24.

9. Ibid., pp. 27–28, 35–36.

10. Morgan, "Labor Problem at Jamestown," pp. 610–611.

11. Karen Ordahl Kupperman, "Apathy and Death in Early Jamestown," *Journal of American History* 66 (June 1979):32–33.

12. Coluthur Gopalan and Kamala S. Jaya Rao, "Pellagra and Amino Acid Imbalance," *Vitamins and Hormones: Advances in Research and Applications* 33 (1975):508, 516; John D. Fernstrom and Loy D. Lytle, "Corn Malnutrition, Brain Serotonin and Behavior," *Nutrition Reviews* 34 (September 1976):257–262; Mark D. Altschule, *Nutritional Factors in General Medicine: Effects of Stress and Distorted Diets* (Springfield, Ill.: Charles C. Thomas, 1978), pp. 104–107. Also see Daphne A. Roe, *A Plague of Corn: The Social History of Pellagra* (Ithaca, Cornell University Press, 1973).

13. Not all historians accept Kupperman's interpretation. In an interesting essay published simultaneously to Kupperman's, Carville V. Earle argued that a brackish water supply was the cause of Jamestown's high mortality rate. See Carville V. Earle, "Environment, Disease, and Mortality in Early Virginia," in *The Chesapeake in the Seventeenth Century: Essays on Anglo-American Society*, ed. Thad W. Tate and David L. Ammerman (Chapel Hill: University of North Carolina Press, 1979), pp. 96–125.

14. Morgan, "Labor Problem at Jamestown," pp. 610–611.

15. John Morton Blum, et al., *The National Experience: A History of the United States*, 4th ed. (New York: Harcourt, Brace, 1977), p. 14.

16. Louis I. Dublin, *Suicide: A Sociological and Statistical Study* (New York: The Ronald Press, 1963), p. 3.

17. For more on this point see Robert G. Athearn, *The Mythic West in Twentieth Century America*, foreword by Elliott West (Lawrence, Kansas: University of Kansas Press, 1986), pp. 160–189.

18. For a useful discussion of how archetypal tales also develop distinctly national characteristics, see Robert Darnton, *The Great Cat Massacre and Other Episodes in French Cultural History* (New York: Basic Books, 1984), pp. 21–24, 50–51.

19. Henry Nash Smith, *Virgin Land, The American West as Symbol and Myth* (Cambridge, Mass.: Harvard University Press, 1950); Richard Slotkin, *The Fatal*

Environment: The Myth of the Frontier in the Age of Industrialism, 1800–1890 (New York: Atheneum, 1985), pp. 13–32. See also Richard Slotkin, *Regeneration Through Violence, The Mythology of the American Frontier, 1600–1860* (Middletown, Conn.: Wesleyan University Press, 1973).

20. John Filson, *The Discovery, Settlement and Present State of Kentucke* (1784, reprint, New York: Corinth House, 1962). For a discussion of Boone and the Boone myth, see Smith, *Virgin Land*, pp. 54–63; Marshall W. Fishwick, "Daniel Boone and the Pattern of the Western Hero," *Filson Club Historical Quarterly* 27 (1953):119–138; and Slotkin, *Regeneration Through Violence*, pp. 268–312.

21. *Niles Register* 10 (15 June 1816):361.

22. *New York Monthly Magazine and Critical Review* 3 (June 1818) 152; see also Smith, *Virgin Land*, p. 58.

23. Timothy Flint, *The Life and Adventures of Daniel Boone, the First Settler of Kentucky, Interspersed with Incidents in the Early Annals of the Country* (1833, reprinted New Haven: Yale University Press, 1967), pp. 226–227.

24. James Fenimore Cooper, *The Prairie: A Tale*, quoted from the rev. ed. (New York, n.d.) in Smith, *Virgin Land*, p. 65.

25. Filson, *Kentucke*, pp. 80–81.

26. Daniel Bryan, *The Mountain Muse: Comprising the Adventures of Daniel Boone; and the Power of Virtuous and Refined Beauty* (Harrisonburg, Va., 1813), pp. 42–43.

27. Flint, *Life and Adventures of Boone*, pp. 226–227.

28. Cooper, *The Prairie* (New York: New American Library, 1964), p. vii.

29. James Fenimore Cooper, *The Deerslayer or the First War-Path* (1841, reprint, New York: Collier Books, 1962), p. 474 (italics added).

30. Slotkin, *Regeneration Through Violence*, p. 493.

31. Frederick Jackson Turner, "The Significance of the Frontier in American History," *Annual Report of the American Historical Association for the Year 1893* (Chicago, 1893), pp. 200, 227.

32. Smith, *Virgin Land*, pp. 291–305. Also see Richard J. Ellis and Alun Munslow, "Narrative, Myth, and the Turner Thesis," *Journal of American Culture* 9 (Summer 1986): 9–16, esp. pp. 12–13.

33. Turner, "Significance of the Frontier," pp. 200, 227.

34. Ibid., p. 207; Turner, *The Frontier in American History* (New York: Holt, Rinehard, & Winston, 1963), p. 205.

35. James H. Perkins, *North American Review* 72 (January 1846): pp. 86–87, 97.

36. Turner, *Frontier in History*, p. 210; Turner, "Significance of the Frontier," pp. 213, 224–225.

37. Turner, *Frontier in History*, p. 212; Turner, "Significance of the Frontier," pp. 221–223.

38. Owen Wister, *The Virginian* (New York: Macmillan, 1904). The book went through seventeen printings in its first year and became one of the ten bestsellers among American novels.

39. For a discussion of the mythic versus the actual cowboy, see William W. Savage, Jr. *The Cowboy Hero: His Image in American History and Culture* (Norman, Okla.: University of Oklahoma Press, 1979), esp. pp. 3–48.

40. David Bryan Davis, "Ten-Gallon Hero," *American Quarterly* 6 (Summer 1954): 78; Harry Schein, "The Olympian Cowboy," *American Scholar* 24 (Summer 1955): 309–320; see also David Noble, *The Progressive Mind, 1890–1917* (Chicago: Rand McNally, 1970), pp. 154–156, for a discussion of Wister's *Virginian*; and see James

Oliver Robertson, *American Myth, American Reality* (New York: Hill and Wang, 1980), pp. 164–165.

41. Athearn, *The Mythic West*, pp. 188–189.

42. Tex Burns (pseud. Louis L'Amour), *Hopalong Cassidy and the Trail to Seven Pines* (New York: Bantam, 1951), p. 187.

43. Kenneth J. Munden, "A Contribution to the Psychological Understanding of the Origin of the Cowboy and His Myth," *American Imago* 15 (Summer 1958): 115, 124–125; Schein, "The Olympian Cowboy," pp. 310–312.

44. Slotkin, *Regeneration Through Violence*, p. 498.

45. D. H. Lawrence, *Studies in Classic American Literature* (New York: Viking Press, 1975), p. 62.

46. Jack Schaeffer, *Shane* (1949) in *The Short Novels of Jack Schaeffer*, intro. Dorothy M. Johnson (Boston: Houghton Mifflin, 1976), pp. 5–111. The 1953 movie screenplay written by A. B. Guthrie, Jr., did not deviate significantly from Schaeffer's novel. See William R. Meyer, *The Making of Great Westerns* (New Rochelle, N.Y.: Arlington House, 1979), pp. 221–234; Schein, "The Olympian Cowboy," pp. 317–320.

47. Schaeffer, *Shane*, p. 111.

48. Noble, *The Progressive Mind*, p. 154.

49. Warren J. Barker, "The Stereotyped Western Story: Its Latent Meaning and Psychoeconomic Function," *Psychoanalytic Quarterly* 24 (June 1955): 276.

50. Schein, "The Olympian Cowboy," p. 311; Munden, "A Contribution to Understanding the Cowboy," pp. 128–129. Although Munden's exposition of the mythic elements is comprehensive, his interpretation of them is less satisfactory. In order to fit the cowboy into a too-literal Oedipal mold, Munden reduces history to its symbolic content. In doing so, we learn less rather than more about American society; esp. see pp. 138–139.

51. Otto Rank, *The Myth of the Birth of the Hero: A Psychological Interpretation of Mythology* (1914, reprint, New York: Vintage Books, 1964), p. 71.

52. Schaefer, *Shane*, p. 106. The dialogue quoted in the text is from the screenplay and varies only slightly from that in the novel.

53. Meyer, *Making the Great Westerns*, p. 222.

54. Robert Jay Lifton, *The Broken Connection: On Death and the Continuity of Life* (New York: Simon and Schuster, 1979), pp. 248–252.

55. Jim Jones, "Perspectives From Guyana," reprinted in Charles A. Krause, *Guyana Massacre: The Eyewitness Account* (New York: Berkeley Books, 1978), p. 205.

56. Jim Jones to Herb Caen, 3 April 1978, in Herb Caen, "Epilogue," in *Suicide Cult: The Inside Story of the Peoples Temple Sect and the Massacre in Guyana*, ed. Marshall Kilduff and Ron Javers (New York, Bantam Books, 1978), p. 199.

57. "Affidavit of Deborah Layton Blakey," 15 June 1978, reprinted in Krause, *Guyana Massacre*, p. 191; see also Tom Mathews, et al., "The Cult of Death," *Newsweek*, 4 December 1978; Richard Steele, et al., "Life in Jonestown," *Newsweek*, 4 December 1978. For Jones's financial holdings, see Krause, *Guyana Massacre*, pp. 139–140; Kildoff and Javers, *Suicide Cult*, pp. 78–90.

58. Useful accounts of Jones's life are to be found in James Reston, Jr., *Our Father Who Art in Hell* (New York: Times Books, 1981); Judith Mary Weightman, *Making Sense of the Jonestown Suicides: A Sociological History of Peoples Temple* (New York: Edwin Mellon Press, 1983); Tim Reiterman, *Raven: The Untold Story of the Rev. Jim Jones and His People* (New York: E. P. Dutton, 1982); Pete Axthelm et al., "The

Emperor Jones," *Newsweek*, 4 December 1978; Kilduff and Javers, *The Suicide Cult*, pp. 8–26, and Krause, *Guyana Massacre*, pp. 25–34. Also see Jeanne Mills, *Six Years With God: Life Inside Jim Jones's People's Temple* (New York: A&W Publishers, 1979); John Peer Nugent, *White Night* (New York: Rawson, Wade, 1979), pp. 7–15; Mark Lane, *The Strongest Poison* (New York: Hawthorn Books, 1980), pp. 43–52.

59. Nugent, *White Nights*, p. 8; Axthelm, "The Emperor Jones," pp. 54–60.

60. Jones, "Perspectives From Guyana," p. 208; Affidavit of Deborah Blakey," in Krause, *Guyana Massacre*, p. 188; Kilduff and Javers, *Suicide Cult*, p. 117; Krause, *Guyana Massacre*, p. 25; Nugent, *White Nights*, pp. 12–16; Weightman, *Making Sense of Jonestown*, p. 25.

61. Hugo J. Zee, "The Guyana Incident: Some Psychoanalytic Considerations," *Bulletin of the Menninger Clinic* 44 (July 1980):361. There is evidence that by the mid-1970s Jones had become dependent on a variety of prescription drugs. See also Reston, *Our Father Who Art in Hell*, pp. 281–285; Kilduff and Javers, *The Suicide Cult*, pp. 57–58; Steele, "Life in Jonestown," pp. 62–66.

62. Zee, "The Guyana Incident," pp. 348–350.

63. Krause, *Guyana Massacre*, p. 32; Weightman, *Making Sense of Jonestown*, pp. 51–54.

64. Reverend Jim Jones, "Extemporaneous Speech, 31 May 1977," edited by Richard H. Seiden and reprinted in *Suicide and Life-Threatening Behavior* 9 (Summer 1979):117–119.

65. "Affidavit of Deborah Blakey," in Krause, *Guyana Massacre*, pp. 192–3.

66. Ibid.

67. Kilduff and Javers, *The Suicide Cult*, p. 179; Mathews, "The Cult of Death," p. 40; Weightman, *Making Sense of Jonestown*, p. 63.

68. Zee, "The Guyana Incident," p. 355.

69. "Affidavit of Deborah Layton Blakey," 15 June 1978, in Charles A. Krause, *Guyana Massacre: The Eyewitness Account* (New York: Berkeley Books, 1978), p. 191.

70. Vicky Rippere, "Diet and Mental Illness," in Stephen Seely, David L. J. Freed, Gerald A. Silverstone, and Vicky Rippere, eds., *Diet-Related Diseases: The Modern Epidemic* (London: Croom Helm, 1985), pp. 241–244; Altschule, *Nutritional Factors in General Medicine*, pp. 130–144; Harold H. Sandstead, "Clinical Manifestations of Certain Vitamin Deficiencies," in *Modern Nutrition in Health and Disease: Dietotherapy*, ed. Robert S. Goodhart and Maurice E. Shils (Philadelphia: Lea & Febiger, 1973), pp. 594–603.

71. "Excerpts From Transcript of Final Moments at Jonestown," in Steve Rose, *Jesus and Jim Jones* (New York, The Pilgrim Press, 1979), p. 224.

BIBLIOGRAPHY

Abrams, Rochonne. "The Colonial Childhood of Meriwether Lewis." *Missouri Historical Society Bulletin* 34 (July 1978):218–227.

――――― . "Meriwether Lewis: Two Years with Jefferson, the Mentor." *Missouri Historical Society Bulletin* 36 (October 1979):3–18.

Achilles-Delmas, François. *Psychologie Pathologique du Suicide*. Paris: Alcan, 1932.

Adams, William. "Memoir of the Rev. William Adams, of Dedham, Mass." *Massachusetts Historical Society, Collections*. 4th ser. Boston, 1852, 1:1–18.

Adler, Nathan, and Goleman, Daniel. "Gambling and Alcoholism: Symptom Substitution and Functional Equivalents." *Quarterly Journal of Studies on Alcohol* 30 (1969):733–736.

"The Alarming Increase of Suicides." *New York Times*, 3 August 1859.

Altschule, Mark D. *Nutritional Factors in General Medicine: Effects of Stress and Distorted Diets*. Springfield Ill.: Charles C. Thomas, 1978.

Alvarez, Alvin A. *The Savage God: A Study in Suicide*. New York: Random House, 1972.

Anderson, Dwight G. *Abraham Lincoln: The Quest for Immortality*. New York: Alfred A. Knopf, 1982.

Anderson, Olive. "Did Suicide Increase with Industrialization in Victorian England?" *Past & Present* 8 (February 1986):149–173.

――――― . *Suicide in Victorian and Edwardian England*. Oxford: Oxford University Press, 1987.

Anderson, Sarah Travers Lewis (Scott). *Lewises, Meriwethers and Their Kin . . .* Richmond, Va.: The Dietz Press, 1938.

Andreasen, Nancy C. *The Broken Brain: The Biological Revolution in Psychiatry*. New York: Harper and Row, 1984.

Andress, Vern R., and Corey, David M. "Survivor-Victims: Who Discovers or Witnesses Suicide?" *Psychological Reports* 43 (June 1978):759–764.

Annals of Congress. Debates and Proceedings in the Congress of the United States, 1789–1824. Washington, D.C., 1834–1856.

Anonymous, *A Discourse Upon Self-Murder*. London, 1754.

Appleby, Andrew B. "Diet in Sixteenth-Century England: Sources, Problems, Possibilities." In *Health, Medicine, and Mortality in the Sixteenth Century*. Edited by Charles Webster. Cambridge, England: Cambridge University Press, 1979:97–116.

Ariès, Philippe. *Western Attitudes Toward Death, from the Middle Ages to the Present*.

Translated by Patricia M. Ranum. Baltimore: Johns Hopkins University Press, 1974.

————. *The Hour of Our Death.* Translated by Helen Weaver. New York: Random House, 1982.

Athearn, Robert G. *The Mythic West in Twentieth Century America.* Foreword by Elliott West. Lawrence, Kansas: University of Kansas Press, 1986.

Atkinson, J. Maxwell. *Discovering Suicide.* London: Macmillan, 1978.

Åsberg, Marie; Schalling, Daisy; Rydin, E.; and Träskman-Benz, Lil. "Suicide and Serotonin." in *Depression et Suicide: Aspects Medicaux, Psychologiques, et Socio-Culturels.* Edited by J. P. Soubrier and J. Vedrinne. Paris: Pergamon Press, 1983, pp. 367–404.

————; Thoren, Peter; Träskman, Lil; Bertilsson, Leif; and Ringverger, V. "'Serotonin Depression': A Biochemical Subgroup Within the Affective Disorders?" *Science* 191 (February 1976):478–480.

————, and Träskman, Lil. "Studies of CSF 5–HIAA in Depression and Suicidal Behavior." *Advances in Experimental Medical Biology* 133 (1981):739–752.

————; Träskman, Lil; and Thoren, Peter. "5–HIAA in the Cerebrospinal Fluid—A Biochemical Suicide Predictor?" *Archives of General Psychiatry* 33 (October 1976):1193–1197.

Axthelm, Pete, et al., "The Emperor Jones." *Newsweek* 4 December 1978.

Baechler, John. *Suicides.* Translated by Barry Cooper. New York: Basic Books, 1979.

Bach, George R. "Father-Fantasies and Father-Typing in Father-Separated Children." *Child Development* 17 (1946):71–77.

Bakeless, John. *Lewis and Clark: Partners in Discovery.* New York: William Morrow & Co., 1947.

Balser, Roy B. ed. *The Collected Works of Abraham Lincoln.* 8 vols. New Brunswick, N.J.: Rutgers University Press, 1953.

Barker, Warren J. "The Stereotyped Western Story: Its Latent Meaning and Psychoeconmic Function." *Psychoanalytic Quarterly* 24 (June 1955):270–280.

Barnes, Marion J. "Reactions to the Death of a Mother." *The Psychoanalytic Study of the Child* 19 (1964):334–357.

Barron, James. "Youth Suicides: Are Their Lives Harder to Live?" *New York Times.* 15 April 1987.

Bartel, Roland. "Suicide in Eighteenth-Century England: The Myth of A Reputation." *The Huntington Library Quarterly* 23 (February 1960):145–158.

Barthes, Roland. *Mythologies.* London: Jonathan Cape, 1972.

Barzun, Jacques. *Clio and the Doctors: Psycho-History, Quanto-History, and History.* Chicago: University of Chicago Press, 1974.

Basch, Michael Franz. et al. "Symposium on David E. Stannard's *Shrinking History.*" *The Psychohistory Review* 9 (Winter 1980):136–161.

Becker, Ernest. *The Denial of Death.* New York: The Free Press, 1973.

Beckman, Alan. "Hidden Themes in the Frontier Thesis: An Application of Psychoanalysis to Historiography." *Comparative Studies in Society and History* 8 (1966): 361–376.

Beveridge, Albert, J. *Abraham Lincoln 1809–1858.* 2 vols. Cambridge, Mass.: Houghton Mifflin Co., 1928.

Bigelow, L. J. "The Aesthetics of Suicide," *The Galaxy* 1 November 1866:471–476.

Blackstone, William. *Commentaries on the Law of England.* 4 vols. London, 1809.

Bloom, Allan. *The Closing of the American Mind: How Higher Education Has Failed Democracy and Impoverished the Souls of Today's Students*. New York: Simon and Schuster, 1987.

Bloom, Floyd E. "Neuropeptides," *Scientific American* 245 (October 1981):148–168.

Bloom, Floyd E.; Lazerson, Arlyne; and Hofstadter, Laura. *Brain, Mind, and Behavior*. New York: W. H. Freeman, 1985.

Blum, John Morton, et al., *The National Experience: A History of the United States*. 4th ed. New York: Harcourt, Brace, 1977.

Blustein, Bonnie Ellen. "'A Hollow Square of Psychological Science': American Neurologists and Psychiatrists in Conflict." In *Madhouses, Mad-Doctors, and Madness: The Social History of Psychiatry in the Victorian Era*. Edited by Andrew Scull. Philadelphia: University of Pennsylvania Press, 1981, pp. 244–270.

Boe, Eugene. "Norwegians on the Prairie." In *Uncertain Americans: Readings in Ethnic History*. Edited by Leonard Dinnerstein and Frederic Cople Jaher. New York: Oxford University Press, 1977, pp. 181–200.

The Boston News-Letter. No. 1045. 30 January to 6 February 1724.

Boyd, Maurice. "Lincoln and the Influence of William Knox." *Lincoln Herald* 60 (Spring 1958):14–15.

———. "Knox's Poems: A Legacy to Lincoln." *Lincoln Herald*, 60 (Fall 1958): 82–86.

———. *William Knox and Abraham Lincoln: The Story of a Poetic Legacy*. Denver: Sage Books, 1966.

Bowers, Malcolm B. Jr. "Serotonin Systems in Psychotic States." In *New Vistas in the Biochemistry of Mental Disorders*. Edited by Earl Usdin and Arnold J. Mandell. New York: Marcel Dekker, 1978, pp. 198–205.

Bowlby, John. *Attachment and Loss*. 3 vols. New York: Basic Books, 1969–1980.

———. "Grief and Mourning in Infancy and Early Childhood." *The Psychoanalytic Study of the Child*. 15 (1960):9–52.

———. "Separation Anxiety." *Interpretational Journal of Psycho-Analysis*. 41 (1960):89–113.

Bracton, Henry de. *On the Laws and Customs of England*. Translated by Samuel E. Thorne. 2 vols. Cambridge, Mass.: Harvard University Press, 1968.

Bradford, William. *Of Plymouth Plantation, 1620–1647*. Edited by Samuel Eliot Morison. New York: Alfred A. Knopf, 1979.

Brigham, Amariah. "Statistics of Suicides in the United States." *American Journal of Insanity* 1 (January 1845):232–234.

Brody, Jane. "The Haunting Specter of Teenage Suicide." *New York Times*. 4 March 1984.

Brown, Charles Brockden. *Wieland or the Transformation*. 1799. Reprint. New York: Doubleday & Co., 1962.

Brown, Gerald L.; Goodwin, Frederick K.; Ballenger, James C.; Goyer, Peter F.; and Major, Leslie F. "Aggression in Humans Correlates With Cerebrospinal Fluid Amine Metabolites." *Psychiatry Research* I (1979):131–139.

Browne, Malcom W. "Women in Chemistry: Higher Suicide Risk Seen." *New York Times*. 4 August 1987.

Bruce, Robert V. *Lincoln and the Riddle of Death*. Fort Wayne, Indiana: Fourth Annual Gerald McMurtry Lecture, 1981.

Bryan, Daniel. *The Mountain Muse: Comprising the Adventures of Daniel Boone; and the Power of Virtuous and Refined Beauty*. Harrisonburg, Va., 1813.

Bulmer, Martin. *The Chicago School of Sociology: Institutionalization, Diversity, and the Rise of Sociological Research*. Chicago: University of Chicago Press, 1984.

Bumstead, Jeremiah. "Diary of Jeremiah Bumstead of Boston, 1722–1727." Edited by S. F. Haven. *New England Historical and Genealogical Register* 15 (July 1861):180–210.

Burgess, Ernest. "The Growth of the City: An Introduction to a Research Project." In *The City*. Edited by Robert E. Park, Ernest Burgess, Roderick McKenzie. Chicago: University of Chicago Press, 1925, pp. 46–62.

Burgess, Louis A., ed. *Virginia Soldiers of 1776*. 3 vols. Virginia State Library: Richmond, Va., 1927.

Burgess-Jackson, Keith. "The Legal Status of Suicide in Early America: A Comparison with the English Experience." *Wayne Law Review* 29 (Fall 1982):57–87.

Burnham, John Chynoweth. *Psychoanalysis and American Medicine, 1894–1918: Medicine, Science, and Culture*. New York: International Universities Press, 1967.

Burns, Tex. [pseud. Louis L'Amour]. *Hopalong Cassidy and the Trail to Seven Pines*. New York: Bantam Books, 1951.

Burton, Robert. *Anatomy of Melancholy*. Edited by Floyd Dell & Paul Jordan-Smith. New York: Tudor Publishing Co., 1927.

California Department of Health Services, *Suicides in California, 1980–1984*. Prepared by Martin Green. Sacramento: Department of Health Services, 1986.

Campbell, Colin. "Harvard Tenure Ruling Stirs Debate." *New York Times*. 22 April 1985.

Capel, Richard. *Tentations*. 4th ed. London, 1650.

Carruthers, Olive, and McMurtry, R. Gerald. *Lincoln's Other Mary*. Chicago: Ziff Davis Publishing Co., 1946.

"Cases of Insanity—Illustrating the Importance of Early Treatment in Preventing Suicide." *American Journal of Insanity* 1 (January 1845):243–249.

Casey, Edward S. "Freud on Emotion and Memory." Forthcoming in *The International Philosophical Quarterly*.

Cassedy, James H. *Demography in Early America: Beginnings of the Statistical Mind, 1600–1800*. Cambridge, Mass.: Harvard University Press, 1969.

———. *American Medicine and Statistical Thinking, 1800–1860*. Cambridge, Mass.: Harvard University Press, 1984.

———. *Medicine and American Growth, 1800–1860*. Madison, Wisc.: University of Wisconsin Press, 1986.

Cavan, Ruth S. *Suicide*. Chicago: University of Chicago Press, 1928. Reprinted New York: Russell & Russell, 1965.

"A Chapter of Suicides." *New York Times*. 3 August 1859.

Chevalier, Louis. *Labouring Classes and Dangerous Classes in Paris During the First Half of the Nineteenth Century*. Translated by Frank Jellinek. London: Routledge & Kegan Paul, 1973.

Clark, David Lee. *Charles Brockden Brown*. Durham: Duke University Press, 1952.

Clark, W., ed., *The State Records of North Carolina*. 24 vols. (1905).

Cohen, Patricia Cline. *A Calculating People: The Spread of Numeracy in Early America*. Chicago: University of Chicago Press, 1982.

"Collection of Essex Inquisitions." Essex Institute, Salem, Massachusetts.

Colony of Massachusetts. *Records of The Court of Assistants of the Colony of Massachusetts Bay, 1630–1692*. 3 vols. Edited by John Noble and John Cronin. Boston: The County of Suffolk, 1901–1928.

Colony of Massachusetts. "Notes on the Trial and Punishment of Crimes in the Court of Assistants in the Time of the Colony, and in the Superior Court of Judicature in the First Years of the Province." *Publications of the Colonial Society of Massachusetts, Transactions* 3 (1895–1897):51–66.

Commonwealth v. Bowen, 13 Mass. 356 (1816).

Commonwealth v. Mink, 123 Mass. 425, (1877) 25 Amer. Rep. 109.

Cook, George P. "Statistics of Suicide, Which Have Occurred in the State of New York from Dec. 1st 1847 to Dec. 1 1848." *American Journal of Insanity* 5 (April 1849):303–310.

Conzen, Kathleen Neils. "Immigrants, Immigrant Neighborhoods, and Ethnic Identity: Historical Issues." *Journal of American History* 66 (December 1979):603–615.

"Coroner's Inquests, 1731–1744," Judicial Preservation Project of the Supreme Judicial Court of Massachusetts, New Suffolk County Court House, Boston.

Cooper, James Fenimore. *The Deerslayer or the First War-Path*. [1841] New York: Collier Books, 1962.

———. *The Prairie: A Tale*. [1827] New York: New American Library, 1964.

Cooter, Roger. "Phrenology and British Alienists, ca. 1825–1845," in *Madhouses, Mad-Doctors, and Madmen: The Social History of Psychiatry in the Victorian Era*, edited by Andrew Scull. (Philadelphia: University of Pennsylvania Press, 1981), 58–90.

Cowles, Edward. "The Relation of Mental Diseases to General Medicine." *The Boston Medical and Surgical Journal* 137 (September 1897):277–282.

Crawford, Michael J. "The Spiritual Travels of Nathan Cole." *William and Mary Quarterly* 3d ser. 33 (January 1976):89–126.

Crocker, Lester G. "The Discussion of Suicide in the Eighteenth Century." *The Journal of the History of Ideas* 13 (January 1952):47–72.

Crosby, Alfred W. Jr. *The Columbian Exchange: Biological and Cultural Consequences of 1492*. Westport, Conn.: Greenwood Press, 1972.

Cushing, John D., ed. *The Earliest Acts and Laws of the Colony of Rhode Island and Province Plantations, 1647–1719*. Wilmington, Del.: Michael Glazier, 1977.

———. *The Earliest Printed Laws of Pennsylvania, 1681–1713*. Wilmington, Del.: Michael Glazier, 1978.

Cutright, Paul Russell. *A History of the Lewis and Clark Journals*. Norman: University of Oklahoma Press, 1976.

Dain, Norman. *Concepts of Insanity in the United States, 1789–1865*. New Brunswick, N. J.: Rutgers University Press, 1964.

Darnton, Robert. *The Great Cat Massacre and Other Episodes in French Cultural History*. New York: Basic Books, 1984.

Davis, Andrew McFarland. "Valentine-Vans Currency Pamphlets." *Massachusetts Historical Society, Proceedings* 43 (March 1910):428–447.

Davis, David Bryan. "Ten-Gallon Hero," *American Quarterly* 6 (Summer 1954): 111–125.

Davis, Richard A. "Female Labor Force Participation, Status Integration and Suicide, 1950–1969." *Suicide and Life-Threatening Behavior* 11 (Summer 1981): 111–123.

Davis, Richard Beale. *Francis Walker Gilmore: Life and Learning in Jefferson's Virginia*. Richmond, Va.: The Dietz Press, 1939.

Davis, Robert. "Black Suicide in the Seventies: Current Trends." *Suicide and Life-Threatening Behavior* 9 (Fall 1979):131–140.

Dalton, Michael. *The Countrey Justice.* 3d ed. London, 1626.

———. *The Countrey Justice, 1619.* Edited by P. M. Glazerbrook. London: Professional Books, 1973.

"Delusion and Suicide," *American Journal of Insanity* 13 (April 1857):401–402.

Demos, John Putnam. *Entertaining Satan: Witchcraft and the Culture of Early New England.* New York: Oxford University Press, 1982.

Denny, William. *Pelecanicidium: or the Christian Adviser against Self-Murder.* London, 1653.

De Vos, George. *Socialization for Achievement: Essays on the Cultural Psychology of the Japanese.* Berkeley and Los Angeles: University of California Press, 1973.

Dillon, Richard. *Meriwether Lewis: A Biography.* New York: Coward-McCann, Inc., 1965.

Dinnerstein, Leonard, and Reimers, David M. *Ethnic Americans: A History of Immigration and Assimilation.* New York: Dodd, Mead & Co., 1975.

Dobbin, Muriel. "3-Year California Study Seeks Whys of Suicide," *Baltimore Sun.* 9 November 1981.

Donald, David. *Lincoln's Herndon.* New York: Alfred A. Knopf, 1948.

Douglas, Jack D. *The Social Meanings of Suicide.* Princeton: Princeton University Press, 1967.

Drieser, Theodore. *Sister Carrie.* New York: W. W. Norton, 1970.

Dublin, Louis I. *Suicide: A Sociological and Statistical Study.* New York: The Ronald Press, 1963.

———. *After Eighty Years: The Impact of Life Insurance on the Public Health.* Gainesville: University of Florida Press, 1966.

———, and Bunzel, Bessie. *To Be or Not To Be.* New York: Harrison Smith and Robert Hass, 1933.

Durkheim, Émile. *Suicide: A Study in Sociology.* Translated by John A. Spaulding and George Simpson. Glencoe, Ill.: The Free Press, 1951.

———. *The Division of Labor in Society.* Translated by George Simpson. Glencoe, Ill.: The Free Press, 1960.

Earle, Carville V. "Environment, Disease, and Mortality in Early Virginia." In *The Chesapeake in the Seventeenth Century: Essays on Anglo-American Society.* Edited by Thad W. Tate and David L. Ammerman. Chapel Hill: University of North Carolina Press, 1979, pp. 96–125.

Eissler, Kurt R. *The Psychiatrist and the Dying Patient.* New York: International Universities Press, 1955.

Ellenberger, Henri F. *The Discovery of the Unconscious: The History of Evolution of Dynamic Psychiatry.* New York: Basic Books, 1970.

Elliott, Emory. *Power and the Pulpit in Puritan New England.* Princeton: Princeton University Press, 1975.

Ellis, Richard J., and Munslow, Alun. "Narrative, Myth, and the Turner Thesis," *Journal of American Culture* 9 (Summer 1986):9–16.

Englehart, H. Tristram, Jr. "The Disease of Masturbation: Values and Concept of Disease." *Bulletin of the History of Medicine* 48 (Summer 1974):234–248.

Erikson, Erik H. *Identity: Youth and Crisis.* New York: W. W. Norton, 1968.

Falret, Jean-Pierre. *De l'Hypochondrie et du Suicide.* Paris, 1822.

Farberow, Norman L., and Shneidman, Edwin S. *Clues to Suicide.* New York: McGraw-Hill, 1957.

———, ed. *Suicide in Different Cultures.* Baltimore: University Park Press, 1975.

Faris, Robert E. L. *Chicago Sociology, 1920–1932*. Chicago: University of Chicago Press, 1979.

Fedden, Henry Romilly. *Suicide, A Social and Historical Study*. New York: Benjamin Blom, 1972.

Fehrenbacher, Don E. "In Quest of the Psychohistorical Lincoln." *Reviews in American History* 11 (March 1983):12–19.

Fernstrom, John D., and Jacoby, Jacob H. "The Interaction of Diet and Drugs in Modifying Brain Serotonin Metabolism." *General Pharmacology* 6 (1975):253–258.

————, and Wurtman, Richard J. "Brain Serotonin Content: Increase Following Ingestion of Carbohydrate Diet." *Science* 174 (December 1971):1023–1025.

————, and Wurtman, Richard J. "Control of Brain Serotonin Levels by the Diet." *Advances in Biochemical Psychopharmacology* 11 (1974):133–142.

————, and Lytle, Loy D. "Corn Malnutrition, Brain Serotonin and Behavior," *Nutrition Reviews* 34 (September 1976):257–262.

Filson, John. *The Discovery, Settlement and Present State of Kentucke*. 1784. Reprint. New York: Corinth House, 1962.

Fisher, Vardis. *Suicide or Murder? The Strange Death of Governor Meriwether Lewis*. Denver, Colo.: Alan Swallow, 1962.

Fishwick, Marshall W. "Daniel Boone and the Pattern of the Western Hero." *Filson Club Historical Quarterly* 27 (1953):119–138.

Fleming, Sandford. *Children and Puritanism: The Place of Children in the Life and Thought of New England Churches, 1620–1847*. New Haven: Yale University Press, 1933.

Fleury, Maurice de. *l'Angiosse Humaine*. Paris: Editions de France, 1924.

Flint, Timothy. *The Life and Adventures of Daniel Boone, the First Settler of Kentucky, Interspersed with Incidents in the Early Annals of the Country*. 1833; reprinted, New Haven: Yale University Press, 1967.

Fogel, Robert W., and Engerman, Stanley L. "Trends in Nutrition, Labor Welfare, and Labor Productivity." *Social Science History* 6 (Fall 1982): special issue.

Foote, Henry Wilder. *Annals of King's Chapel, from the Puritan Age of New England to the Present Day*. 2 vols. (Boston, 1882).

Forbes, Thomas Rogers. *Chronicle from Aldgate, Life and Death in Shakespeare's London*. New Haven: Yale University Press, 1971.

Forgie, George B. *Patricide in the House Divided: A Psychological Interpretation of Lincoln and His Age*. New York: W. W. Norton, 1979.

Fowler, R. C., Rich, C. L., and Young, D. "San Diego Suicide Study: II. Substance Abuse in Young Cases," *Archives of General Psychiatry* 43 (October 1986):962–965.

Friedlander, Saul. *History and Psychoanalysis: An Inquiry into the Possibilities and Limits of Psychohistory*. Translated by Susan Suleiman. New York: Holmes & Meier, 1978.

Friedman, Paul. "Suicide Among Police: A Study of 93 Suicides Among New York City Policemen, 1934–1940." In *Essays in Self-Destruction*. Edited by Edwin Shneidman. New York: Science House, 1967, pp. 414–449.

Frisch, Rose E. "Population, Food Intake, and Fertility." *Science* 199 (January 1978):22–30.

Freud, Sigmund. "Freud's Psychoanalytic Procedure." 1904. Reprint. *Standard Edition of the Complete Psychological Works of Sigmund Freud*. 23 vols. Edited and translated by James Strachey. London: The Hogarth Press, 1957, 7:249–256.

————. *Totem and Taboo: Some Points of Agreement Between the Mental Lives of Savages and Neurotics*. 1913. Reprint. New York: W. W. Norton, 1950.

————. "Mourning and Melancholia," 1917. Reprint. *Standard Edition of the Complete Psychological Works of Sigmund Freud*. 23 vols. Edited and translated by James Strachey. London: The Hogarth Press, 1957, 14:239–258.

————. *Beyond the Pleasure Principle*. 1920. Reprint. *Standard Edition of the Complete Psychological Works of Sigmund Freud*. 23 vols. Edited and translated by James Strachey. London: The Hogarth Press, 1957, 18:3–67.

————. *Civilization and Its Discontents*. 1930. Reprint. Translated and edited by James Strachey. New York: W. W. Norton & Co., 1961.

————. *New Introductory Lectures on Psychoanalysis*. 1933. Reprint. Translated and edited by James Strachey. New York: W. W. Norton & Co., 1964.

Fullinwider, S. P. "Insanity As the Loss of Self: The Moral Insanity Controversy Revisited." *Bulletin of the History of Medicine* 49 (Spring 1975):87–101.

Furman, Robert A. "Death and the Young Child: Some Preliminary Considerations." *The Psychoanalytic Study of the Child* 19 (1964):321–333.

Gans, Herbert. *The Urban Villagers*. New York: Free Press, 1962.

Gelman, David. "Teenage Suicide in the Sun Belt." *Newsweek*. 15 August 1983.

Gibbs, Jack P., and Martin, Walter T. *Status Integration and Suicide*. Eugene, Ore.: University of Oregon Books, 1964.

Giddens, Anthony. "The Suicide Problem in French Sociology." *British Journal of Sociology* 16 (March 1965):3–18.

Gilligan, Carol. *In A Different Voice: Psychological Theory and Women's Development*. Cambridge, Mass.: Harvard University Press, 1982.

Gittings, Clare. *Death, Burial, and the Individual in Early Modern England*. Dover, N.H.: Croom Helm, 1984.

Gold, Martin. "Suicide, Homicide, and the Socialization of Aggression." *American Journal of Sociology* 63 (1958):651–661.

Goleman, Daniel. "Clues to Suicide: A Brain Chemical is Implicated." *New York Times*. 8 October 1985.

Goodwin, Donald W. "Alcohol in Suicide and Homicide." *Quarterly Studies in Alcohol* 34 (1973):144–156.

Gopalan, Coluthur, and Rao, Kamala S. Jaya. "Pellagra and Amino Acid Imbalance." *Vitamins and Hormones: Advances in Research and Applications* 33 (1975):505–528.

Gordon, Linda. *Woman's Body, Woman's Right*. New York: Penguin Books, 1977.

Grabo, Norman S. *The Coincidental Art of Charles Brockden Brown*. Chapel Hill, N.C.: University of North Carolina Press, 1981.

Granberry, Mike. "San Diego Doctor Deals With Teen-Agers on Brink of Suicide." *Los Angeles Times* 23 November 1981.

Gray, John P. "Bertrand on Suicide." *American Journal of Insanity* 14 (October 1857):210.

————. "Insanity and Its Relation to Medicine." *American Journal of Insanity* 25 (October 1868):145–172.

————. "Is Insanity a Disease of the Mind or the Body?", *American Journal of Insanity* 29 (July 1872):71–91.

————. "Thoughts on the Causation of Insanity," *American Journal of Insanity* 29 (October 1872):264–283.

————. "Suicide." A Lecture Delivered at Bellevue Medical College, March 1878. *American Journal of Insanity* 35 (July 1878):37–73.

Greaves, Richard L. *Society and Religion in Elizabethan England*. Minneapolis, Minn.: University of Minnesota Press, 1981.

Greven, Philip. *The Protestant Temperament: Patterns of Child-Rearing, Religious Experience, and The Self in Early America.* New York: New American Library, 1977.

Griffen, Mary, and Felsenthal, Carol. "A Cry for Help: Teen Suicide." *Family Circle,* 8 March 1983.

Grob, Gerald N. *Mental Institutions in America, Social Policy to 1875.* New York: The Free Press, 1973.

———. *Edward Jarvis and the Medical World of Nineteenth-Century America.* Knoxville, Tenn.: The University of Tennessee Press, 1978.

———. *Mental Illness and American Society, 1875–1940.* Princeton: Princeton University Press, 1983.

———. *The Inner World of American Psychiatry, 1890–1940, Selected Correspondence.* New Brunswick, N. J.: Rutgers University Press, 1985.

———. "Rediscovering Asylums: The Unhistorical History of the Mental Hospital." In *The Therapeutic Revolution: Essays in the Social History of American Medicine.* Edited by Morris Vogel and Charles E. Rosenberg. Philadelphia: University of Pennsylvania Press, 1979, pp. 135–157.

Gutman, Herbert. "Work, Culture, and Society in Industrializing America, 1818–1919." *American Historical Review* 78 (June 1973):531–588.

H. T. "Suicide and Suicidal Insanity." *American Journal of Insanity* 12 (April 1856):351–354.

Hair, P. E. H. "A Note on the Incidence of Tudor Suicide." *Local Population Studies* 5 (1970):36–43.

Hale, Nathan G., Jr. *Freud and the Americans: The Beginnings of Psychoanalysis in the United States, 1876–1917.* New York: Oxford University Press, 1971.

———, ed. *James Jackson Putnam and Psychoanalysis: Letters Between Putnam and Sigmund Freud, Ernest Jones, William James, Sandor Ferenczi, and Morton Prince, 1877–1917.* Cambridge, Mass.: Harvard University Press, 1971..

Hales v. Petit, 1 Plowden 253, 75 Eng. Rep. 387.

Halgren, E. "The Amygdala Contribution to Emotions and Memory: Current Studies in Humans." In *The Amygdaloid Complex.* Edited by Y. Ben-Ari. Amsterdam: Elsevier/North Holland Biomedical Press, 1981, pp. 395–408.

Hall, David. D. "The Mental World of Samuel Sewall." In *Saints and Revolutionaries: Essays on Early American History.* Edited by David D. Hall, John M. Murrin, and Thad W. Tate. New York: W. W. Norton, 1984, pp. 75–95.

Hamilton, Allan McLane. *Nervous Diseases: Their Description and Treatment.* Philadelphia: Henry C. Lea, 1878.

———. *Recollections of an Alienist, Personal and Professional.* New York: George H. Doran Company, 1916.

———. "Suicide in Large Cities." *Popular Science Monthly* 8 (November 1875): 88–93.

Hammond, Lawrence. "Diary of Lawrence Hammond." *Massachusetts Historical Society Proceedings* 7 (January 1892).

Harkness, David J., and McMurtry, R. Gerald. *Lincoln's Favorite Poets.* Knoxville, Tenn.: University of Tennessee Press. 1959.

Hawthorne, Nathaniel. *The Blithedale Romance.* 1852. Reprint. New York: Dell Publishing Company, 1960.

Headley, Lee A. *Suicide in Asia and the Near East.* Berkeley and Los Angeles: University of California Press, 1983.

Hellon, Charles P. and Solomon, Mark I. "Suicide and Age in Alberta, Canada, 1951 to 1977: The Changing Profile." *Archives of General Psychiatry* 37 (May 1980): 505–513.

Hendin, Herbert. *Suicide and Scandinavia*. Garden City, New York: Doubleday & Co., 1964.

―――――. "Black Suicide." *Archives of General Psychiatry* 21 (1969):407–422.

―――――. *Black Suicide*. New York: Harper and Row, 1971.

―――――. *Suicide in America*. New York: W. W. Norton & Co., 1982.

―――――. "Suicide: A Review of New Directions in Research." *Hospital and Community Psychiatry* 37 (February 1986):148–154.

―――――. "Youth Suicide: A Psychosocial Perspective." *Suicide & Life-Threatening Behavior* 17 (Summer 1987):151–165.

Henry, Andrew F., and Short, James F. *Suicide and Homicide*. Glencoe, Ill.: The Free Press, 1954.

Herndon, William H., and Weik, Jesse W. *Abraham Lincoln: The True Story of a Great Life*. 2 vols. New York: D. Appleton & Co., 1892.

Hertz, Emanuel. *The Hidden Lincoln, From the Letters and Papers of William H. Herndon*. New York: The Viking Press, 1938.

Hinkle, Roscoe C., Jr. "Durkheim in American Sociology." In *Emile Durkheim, 1858–1917*. Edited by Kurt H. Wolf. Columbus, Ohio: Ohio State University Press, 1960, pp. 267–295.

Hoffer, Peter C., and Hull, N. E. H. *Murdering Mothers: Infanticide in England and New England, 1588–1803*. New York: New York University Press, 1981.

Holbrook, Jay Mack. *Boston Beginnings, 1630–1699*. Oxford, Mass.: Holbrook Research Institute, 1980.

Holinger, Paul C. *Violent Deaths in the United States: An Epidemiological Study of Suicide, Homicide, and Accidents*. New York: The Guilford Press, 1987.

Hollingsworth, Rogers. "Causes and Consequences of the American Medical System." *Reviews in American History* 11 (September 1983):326–332.

Hook, Sidney, ed. *Psychoanalysis, Scientific Method and Philosophy*. New York: Grove Press, 1959.

"Homicides-Suicides, &c.,—By the Insane." *American Journal of Insanity* 4 (October 1847):170–178.

Hsiao, John K.; Agren, Hans; Bartko, John J.; Rudorfer, Mathew V.; Linnoila, Markku; and Potter, William Z. "Monoamine Neurotransmitter Interactions and the Prediction of Antidepressant Response." *Archives of General Psychiatry* 44 (December 1987):1078–1083.

Hunt, E. K., M.D. "Statistics of Suicides in the United States." *American Journal of Insanity* 1 (January 1845):225–234.

Hutton, Patrick H. "The Psychohistory of Erik Erikson from the Perspective of Collective Mentalities." *The Psychohistory Review* 12 (Fall 1983):18–25.

Imhof, Arthur E. "From the Old Mortality Pattern to the New: Implications of a Radical Change from the Sixteenth to the Twentieth Century." *Bulletin of the History of Medicine* 59 (Spring 1985):1–29.

"Inquest Records and Other Material Pertaining to the Suffolk County Coroners, 1775 to 1860." Adlow Collection. Boston Public Library. Rare Books and Manuscripts Collection.

"Inquisition by Coroner's Jury." San Diego Historical Society. Library and Manuscript Collection.

Jackson, Charles O. "American Attitudes to Death." *Journal of American Studies* 11 (December 1977):297–312.

Jackson, Donald, ed. *Letters of the Lewis and Clark Expedition, with Related Documents, 1783–1854*, 2d ed. rev. 2 vols. Urbana, Ill.: University of Illinois Press, 1978.

Jackson, Stanley W. *Melancholia and Depression: From Hippocratic Times to Modern Times*. New Haven: Yale University Press, 1986.

Jackson, Stanley W. "Melancholia and Mechanical Explanation in Eighteenth-Century Medicine." *Journal of the History of Medicine and Allied Sciences* 38 (July 1983):298–319.

Jacoby, Russell. *Social Amnesia: A Critique of Conformist Psychology from Adler to Laing*. Boston: The Beacon Press, 1974.

Jarvis, Edward, M.D. "On the Supposed Increase of Insanity." *American Journal of Insanity* 8 (April 1852):333–364.

Jefferson, Thomas. The Papers of Thomas Jefferson. Manuscript Division, Library of Congress, Washington, D.C.

————. *The Papers of Thomas Jefferson*. 18 vols. Edited by Julian P. Boyd. Princeton: Princeton University Press, 1950–1971.

Jimenez, Mary Ann. "Madness in Early American History," *Journal of Social History* 19 (Summer 1986):24–44.

————. *Changing Faces of Madness: Early American Attitudes and Treatment of the Insane*. Hanover, New Hampshire: Brandeis University Press, 1987.

Johnson, Kathryn K. "Durkheim Revisited: 'Why Do Women Kill Themselves?'" *Suicide and Life-Threatening Behavior* 9 (Fall 1979):145–153.

Jones, Jim. "Extemporaneous Speech, May 31, 1977." Reprinted and edited by Richard H. Seiden. *Suicide and Life-Threatening Behavior* 9 (Summer 1979):117–119.

Jones, Kathleen. "Homicide in Nineteenth-Century America: San Diego, A Case Study, 1870–1900." Paper presented to the Pacific Coast Branch Meeting of The American Historical Association, San Francisco, August 1982.

Jordon, Philip D. "The Death of Nancy Hanks Lincoln." *Indiana Magazine of History* 40 (June 1944):103–110.

Jurnovoy, Joyce. "Shaken by Teen Suicides, School District Seeks a Cure for 'the Hidden Epidemic.'" *Los Angeles Times*. 27 May 1982.

Kenny, Courtney Stanhope. *Kenny's Outlines of Criminal Law*. 19th ed. Edited by J. W. Cecil Turner. Cambridge: Cambridge University Press, 1966.

Kessner, Thomas. *The Golden Door: Italian and Jewish Immigrant Mobility in New York City, 1880–1915*. New York: Oxford University Press, 1977.

Kilduff, Marshall, and Javers, Ron. *Suicide Cult: The Inside Story of the People's Temple Sect and the Massacre in Guyana*. New York, Bantam Books, 1978.

King, Lester F. *The Medical World of the Eighteenth Century*. Chicago: University of Chicago Press, 1958.

Kirschman, John D. *Nutrition Almanac*. rev. ed. New York: McGraw Hill, 1979.

Klein, Nathan S. "Pharmacotherapy of the Depressed Suicidal Patient." In *Suicidal Behaviors: Diagnosis and Management*. Edited by H. L. P. Resnik. Boston: Little, Brown, 1968, pp. 313–327.

Knighton, William. "Suicidal Mania." *Littel's Living Age* 148 (February 1881):376–381.

Konig, David Thomas. *Law and Society in Puritan Massachusetts, Essex County, 1629–1692*. Chapel Hill: University of North Carolina Press, 1979.

Koslow, Stephen H.; Maas, James W.; Bowden, Charles L.; Davis, John M.; Hanin, Israel; and Javaid, Javaid. "CSF and Urinary Biogenic Amines and Metabolites in Depression and Mania." *Archives of General Psychiatry* 40 (September 1983): 999–1010.

Kraepelin, Emil. *Lectures on Clinical Psychiatry*, 1904. Reprint. Revised and edited by Thomas Johnstone. New York: Hafner Publishing Company, 1968.

Kramer, Morton; Pollack, Earl S.; Redick, Richard; and Locke, Ben Z. *Mental Disorders/Suicide*. Cambridge, Mass.: Harvard University Press, 1972.

Krause, Charles A. *Guyana Massacre: The Eyewitness Account*. New York: Berkley Books, 1978.

Kraut, Alan M. *The Huddled Masses: The Immigrant in American Society, 1880–1921*. Arlington Heights, Ill.: Harlan Davidson, 1982.

Kupperman, Karen Ordahl, "Apathy and Death in Early Jamestown." *Journal of American History* 66 (June 1979):24–40.

Kushner, Howard I. "Pathology and Adjustment in Psychohistory: A Critique of the Erikson Model." *Psychocultural Review*. 1 (Fall 1977):493–506.

_____. "The Suicide of Meriwether Lewis: A Psychoanalytic Inquiry." *William and Mary Quarterly*, 3d ser. 38 (July 1981):464–481.

_____. "Immigrant Suicide in the United States: Toward A Psycho-Social History." *Journal of Social History* 18 (Fall 1984):3–24.

_____. "Women and Suicide in Historical Perspective." *Signs: Journal of Women in Culture and Society* 10 (Spring 1985):537–552.

_____. "Biochemistry, Suicide, and History: Possibilities and Problems." *Journal of Interdisciplinary History* 16 (Summer 1985):69–85.

_____. "American Psychiatry and the Cause of Suicide, 1844–1917." *Bulletin of the History of Medicine* 60 (Spring 1986):36–57.

LaCapra, Dominick. *Emile Durkheim: Sociologist and Philosopher*. Ithaca: Cornell University Press, 1972.

Lane, Mark. *The Strongest Poison*. New York: Hawthorn Books, 1980.

Lane, Roger. *Violent Death in the City: Suicide, Accident, and Murder in Nineteenth Century Philadelphia*. Cambridge, Mass.: Harvard University Press, 1979.

Laslett, Peter. "The Age of Menarche in Europe Since the Eighteenth Century." In *The Family in History: Interdisciplinary Essays*. Edited by Theodore K. Rabb and Robert I. Rotberg. New York, 1973, pp. 28–47.

_____. *The World We Have Lost, Further Explored: England Before the Industrial Age*. 3d. ed. New York: Scribner's, 1984.

Lathrop, Joseph. *Two Sermons on the Atrocity of Suicide, and the Causes Which Lead to It*. Springfield, Mass., 1805.

Lawrence, D. H. *Studies in Classic American Literature*. New York: Viking Press, 1975.

Lesy, Michael. *Wisconsin Death Trip*. New York: Pantheon, 1973.

Lifton, Robert J. *The Broken Connection: On Death and the Continuity of Life*. New York: Simon & Schuster, 1979.

Lloyd, Kenneth G.; Farley, Irene J.; Deck, John H. N.; and Hornykiewicz, Oleh. "Serotonin and 5-Hydroxyindoleacetic Acid in Discrete Areas of the Brainstem of Suicide Victims and Control Patients." *Advances in Biochemical Psychopharmacology* 11 (1974):387–397.

Loewenberg, Peter. "The Psychohistorical Origin of the Nazi Youth Cohort." *American Historical Review* 76 (December 1971):1457–1502.

_____. "Psychohistorical Perspectives on Modern German History." *Journal of Modern History* 47 (June 1975):229–279.

_____. "Psychohistory." In *The Past Before Us*. Edited by Michael Kammen. Ithaca: Cornell University Press, 1980, pp. 408–432.

London, Jack. *Martin Eden*. New York: Holt, Rinehart, & Winston, 1967.

Luker, Kristen. *Abortion and the Politics of Motherhood*. Berkeley and Los Angeles: University of California Press, 1984.

Lynch, Gary, and Baudry, Michael. "The Biochemistry of Memory: A New and Specific Hypothesis." *Science* 234 (June 1984):1057–1063.

MacDonald, Michael. "The Inner Side of Wisdom: Suicide in Early Modern England." *Psychological Medicine* 7 (1977):565–582.

_____. *Mystical Bedlam, Madness, Anxiety, and Healing in Seventeenth-Century England.* New York: Cambridge University Press, 1981.

_____. "The Secularization of Suicide in England, 1660–1800." *Past & Present* 111 (May 1986):50–100.

MacMahon, Brian; Johnson, Samuel; and Pugh, Thomas F. "Relations of Suicide Rates to Social Conditions." *Public Health Reports* 78 (April 1963):285–293.

MacPhail, Elizabeth C. *The Story of New San Diego and its Founder, Alonzo E. Horton.* San Diego Historical Society: San Diego, 1979.

Mahler, Margaret S. "Symbiosis and Individuation: The Psychological Birth of the Human Infant." *Psychoanalytic Study of the Child* 29 (1974):89–106.

Mann, J. John. et al. "Increased Serotonin^2 and β–Andrenergic Receptor Binding in the Frontal Cortices of Suicide Victims." *Archives of General Psychiatry* 43 (October 1986):954–959.

Maris, Ronald W. *Social Forces in Urban Suicide.* Homewood, Ill.: The Dorsey Press, 1969.

_____. *Pathways to Suicide: A Survey of Self-Destructive Behaviors.* Baltimore: Johns Hopkins University Press, 1981.

_____. *Biology of Suicide.* (Special issue of *Suicide and Life-Threatening Behavior*) New York: The Guilford Press, 1986.

Markowitsch, Hans J. "Thalmic Mediodorsal Nuclease and Memory: A Critical Evaluation of Studies in Animals and Man." *Neuroscience and Biobehavioral Reviews* 6 (1982):351–380.

Marks, Alan, and Abernathy, Thomas. "Toward A Sociocultural Perspective on Means of Self-Destruction." *Suicide and Life-Threatening Behavior* 4 (Spring 1974): 3–17.

Markson, David S. "The Punishment of Suicide—A Need for a Change." *Villanova Law Review* 14 (Spring 1969):463–483.

Marshall, Thomas Maitland, ed. *The Life and Papers of Frederick Bates.* 2 vols. St. Louis, Mo.: Missouri Historical Society, 1926.

Masaryk, Thomas G. *Suicide and the Meaning of Civilization.* 1881. Reprint. Translated by William B. Weist and Robert G. Batson. Chicago: University of Chicago Press, 1970.

Masur, Louis P. "The Revision of the Criminal Law in Post-Revolutionary America." Paper presented at the Conference on Law in America, 1607–1861, New York Historical Society, 17 and 18 May 1985.

Mather, Cotton. *Memorable Provinces Relating to Witchcrafts and Possessions.* Boston, 1689. Reprinted 1697.

_____. "Propositions Concerning Self-Killing." In *Thirty Important Cases, Resolved with Evidence of Scripture and Reason.* Boston, 1699.

_____. *Diary of Cotton Mather.* 2 vols. Edited by Worthington Chauncey Ford. Boston: 1911. Reprinted New York: Frederick Unger, 1957.

_____. *The Cause and Cure of a Wounded Spirit.* 1692. Reprinted in *Evans Early American Imprints, 1639–1800.* Edited by S. A. Green. Worcester, Mass., 1963. 3d Supp. List: 58–59.

_____. *A Family Well-Ordered or an Essay to Render Parents and Children Happy in One Another.* 1699. Reprinted in *Cotton Mather, A Bibliography.* 3 vols. Edited by

Thomas J. Holmes, Newton, Mass.: Crofton Publishing Co., 1974, 1:378–401.

Mather, Increase. *The Wicked Man's Portion, Or a Sermon.* Boston, 1675.

———. *A Call to the Tempted. A Sermon on the Horrid Crime of Self-Murder.* 1682. Reprinted in *Evans Early American Imprints, 1639–1800.* edited by S. A. Green. Worcester, Mass., 1963.

Mathews, Jay. "Darker Side of Sunny California, A High Suicide Rate Under Study." *The Washington Post,* 26 December 1981.

Mathews, Tom, et al. "The Cult of Death." *Newsweek,* 4 December 1978.

May v. Pennell, 101 Me 516 [1906].

McDonald, Marjorie. "A Study of the Reactions of Nursery School Children to the Death of a Child's Mother." *The Psychoanalytic Study of the Child* 19 (1964):358–364.

McGovern, Constance M. *Masters of Madness: Social Origins of the American Psychiatric Profession.* Hanover, N.H.: University Press of New England, 1985.

McIntosh, John L., and Santos, John F. "Changing Patterns in Methods of Suicide by Race and Sex." *Suicide and Life-Threatening Behavior* 12 (Winter 1982):221–233.

McKeown, Thomas. "Food, Infection, and Population." *Journal of Interdisciplinary History* 14 (Autumn 1983):227–247.

McKinney, William M.; Garland, David S.; and Greene, H. Noyes, eds. *The American and English Annotated Cases.* Northport, New York: Edward Thompson Co., 1908.

McLaughlin, Virginia Yans. "Patterns of Work and Family Organization: Buffalo's Italians." *Journal of Interdisciplinary History* 2 (Autumn 1971):299–314.

Mead, Francis H. "The Suicide Rate in San Diego." *American Medical Association Journal* 61 (November 1913):1999–2000.

Mellen, Paul F. "Coroner's Inquests in Colonial Massachusetts." *Journal of the History of Medicine and Allied Sciences* 40 (October 1985):462–472.

Menkin, Jane; Trussell, James; and Watkins, Susan Cotts. "The Nutrition Fertility Link: An Evaluation of Evidence." *Journal of Interdisciplinary History* 11 (Winter 1981):425–441.

Menninger, Karl. "Psychoanalytic Aspects of Suicide." *International Journal of Psycho-Analysis* 14 (July 1933):376–390.

———. "A Psychoanalytic Study of the Significance of Self-Mutilations." *Psychoanalytic Quarterly* 4 (July 1935):408–466.

———. "Purposeful Accidents as an Expression of Self-Destructive Tendencies." *International Journal of Psycho-Analysis* 17 (January 1936):6–16.

———. *Man Against Himself.* New York: Harcourt, Brace, & World, 1938.

———. *A Psychiatrist's World: The Selected Papers of Karl Menninger, M.D.* Edited by Bernard D. Hall. New York: The Viking Press, 1959.

Meyer, Adolf. "A Review of Recent Problems in Psychiatry." In *Nervous and Mental Disorders.* 4th ed. Edited by A. Church and F. Peterson, Philadelphia: Saunders, 1904, pp. 650–688.

Meyer, William R. *The Making of Great Westerns.* New Rochelle, N.Y.: Arlington House, 1979.

Meyers, Mary Ann. "Death in Swedenborgian and Mormon Eschatology." *Dialogue* 14 (1981):58–64.

Miller, Rev. Samuel. *The Guilt, Folly, and Sources of Suicide: Two Discourses.* New York, 1805.

"Millerism." *American Journal of Insanity* 1 (January 1845):249–253.

Mills, Jeanne. *Six Years With God: Life Inside Jim Jones's People's Temple.* New York: A&W Publishers, 1979.

Mishkin, Mortimer, and Appenzeller, Tim. "The Anatomy of Memory." *Scientific American* 256 (June 1987):80–89.

Mitchell, Juliet. *The Woman's Estate.* New York: Pantheon Books, 1971.

Mitchell, S. Wier. "Address Before the Fiftieth Anniversary Meeting of the American Medico-Psychological Association, Held in Philadelphia, May 16, 1894." *Journal of Nervous and Mental Diseases* 21 (July 1894):413–437.

Mitscherlich, Alexander. *Society Without the Father: A Contribution to Social Psychology.* Translated by Eric Mosbacher. New York: Schocken Books, 1970.

Monk, Mary. "Epidemiology." In *A Handbook for the Study of Suicide.* Edited by Seymour Perl. New York: Oxford University Press, 1975, pp. 185–211.

Morgan, Edmund S. "The Labor Problem at Jamestown, 1607–18." *American Historical Review* 76 (June 1971):595–611.

———. *American Slavery, American Freedom: The Ordeal of Colonial Virginia.* New York: W. W. Norton, 1975.

Morrison, Gilbert C., and Collier, Jenny G. "Family Treatment Approaches of Suicidal Children and Adolescents." *Journal of the American Academy of Child Psychiatry* 8 (1969):143–152.

Muhl, Anita M. "America's Greatest Suicide Problem: A Study of Over 500 Cases in San Diego." *Psychoanalytic Review* 14 (1927):317–325.

Munden, Kenneth J. "A Contribution to the Psychological Understanding of the Origin of the Cowboy and His Myth." *American Imago* 15 (Summer 1958):103–148.

Murphy, Elaine; Lindesay, James; and Grundy, Emily. "60 Years of Suicide in England and Wales: A Cohort Study." *Archives of General Psychiatry* 43 (October 1986):969–976.

Murphy, Dennis L.; Campbell, Iain C.; and Costa, Jonathan L. "The Brain Serotonergic System in Affective Disorders." *Progress in Neuro-Psychopharmacology* 2 (1978):1–31.

Murphy, Terence R. "'Woful Childe of Parents Rage': Suicide of Children and Adolescents in Early Modern England, 1507–1710." *The Sixteenth Century Journal* 17 (Fall 1986):259–270.

Murrin, John M. "The Legal Transformation: The Bench and Bar of Eighteenth-Century Massachusetts." In *Colonial America: Essays in Politics and Social Development.* Edited by Stanley N. Katz & John M. Murrin. New York: Alfred A. Knopf, 1983, pp. 540–572.

National Center for Health Statistics. "Advance Report of Final Mortality Statistics, 1984." *Monthly Vital Statistics Report* 35, 26 September 1986.

Nelson, Franklyn L.; Farberow, Norman L.; and MacKinnon, Douglas R. "The Certification of Suicide in Eleven Western States: An Inquiry into the Validity of Reported Suicide Rates." *Suicide and Life Threatening Behavior* 8 (Summer 1978): 75–88.

Neuman, Robert P. "Masturbation, Madness, and the Modern Concepts of Childhood and Adolescence." *Journal of Social History* 8 (Spring 1975):1–27.

The New England Courant. No. 132. 3 February to 13 February 1724.

Noble, David. "The Paradox of Progressive Thought." *American Quarterly* 5 (Fall 1953):201–212.

———. *The Progressive Mind, 1890–1917.* Chicago: Rand McNally, 1970.

Noble, John. "A Glance at Suicide in the Colony and Province of Massachusetts." *Massachusetts Historical Society, Proceedings* 2d ser. 16 (December 1902):521–532.

Nordhoff, C. "A Matter of Life and Death." *Harper's New Monthly Magazine* 18 (March 1859):516–520.

Nugent, John Peer. *White Night.* New York: Rawson, Wade, 1979.

Oates, Stephen B. *With Malice Toward None: The Life of Abraham Lincoln.* New York: Harper & Row, 1977.

Oddy, D. J. "Working Class Diets in Late Nineteenth Century Britain." *Economic History Review* 23 (1970):314–323.

"On Monomania Induced Through Imitation," *American Journal of Insanity* I (October 1844):116–121.

Ordroneaux, John, M.D. "On Suicide: A Lecture Delivered Before the Students of Columbia College." *American Journal of Insanity* 20 (April 1864):369–401.

Oreland, Lars. et al. "Platelet MAO Activity and Monoamine Metabolites in Cerebrospinal Fluid in Depressed and Suicidal Patients and in Healthy Controls." *Psychiatry Research* 4 (1981):21–29.

Paerregaard, Grethe. "Suicide in Denmark: A Statistical Review for the Past 150 Years." *Suicide and Life-Threatening Behavior* 10 (Fall 1980):150–157.

Palgi, Phyllis, and Abramovitch, Henry. "Death: A Cross-Cultural Perspective." *Annual Review of Anthropology* 13 (1984):385–417.

Palmer, Douglas D. "Youth Suicide Rises Fivefold." *Deseret News.* 3 April 1982.

Palmer, William, ed. *Calendar of State Papers and Other Manuscripts Preserved in the State Capital at Richmond.* Richmond, Virginia, 1883.

Parachini, Allan. "An Alarming Picture of Youthful Suicides." *Los Angeles Times.* 19 August 1984.

————. "'84 Youth Suicides a Blip in 7-Year Drop, Report Says." *Los Angeles Times.* 19 November 1986.

Peele, Stanton. "Reductionism in the Psychology of the Eighties: Can Biochemistry Eliminate Addiction, Mental Illness, and Pain?" *American Psychologist* 36 (August 1981):807–818.

Perlin, Seymour, ed. *A Handbook for the Study of Suicide.* New York: Oxford University Press, 1975.

Petchesky, Rosalind Pollack. *Abortion and Women's Choice: The State, Sexuality, and Reproductive Freedom.* New York: Longman, 1984.

Pettit, Norman. *The Heart Prepared: Grace and Conversion in Puritan Spiritual Life.* New Haven, Conn.: Yale University Press, 1966.

Phelps, Dawson A. "The Tragic Death of Meriwether Lewis." *William and Mary Quarterly* 3d ser. 13 (1956):305–318.

Phillips, David, P. "The Influence of Suggestion on Suicide: Substance and Theoretical Implications of the Werther Effect." *American Sociological Review* 34 (June 1974):340–354.

————, and Carstensen, Lundie L. "Clustering of Teenage Suicides After Television News Stories About Suicide." *New England Journal of Medicine* 315 (September 1986):685–689.

Phillips, Samuel. *The Sin of Suicide Contrary to Nature.* Boston: Kneeland & Adams, 1767.

Pierce, Albert. "The Economic Cycle and the Social Suicide Rate." *American Sociological Review* 74 (June 1967):457–462.

Pilgrim, Charles W., M.D. "Insanity and Suicide." *American Journal of Insanity* 63 (January 1907):349–360.

Pollock, George H. "Childhood Parent and Sibling Loss in Adult Patients: A Comparative Study." *Archives of General Psychiatry* 7 (1962):295–305.

_____. "Manifestations of Abnormal Mourning: Homicide and Suicide Following the Death of Another." *Annual of Psychoanalysis* 4 (1976):225–249.

_____. "On Childhood Sibling Loss and Adult Functioning." *Annual of Psychoanalysis* 6 (1978).

Pope, Whitney. *Durkheim's Suicide: A Classic Analyzed.* Chicago: University of Chicago Press, 1976.

Popper, Karl R. *Conjectures and Refutations: The Growth of Scientific Knowledge.* New York: Basic Books, 1962.

Porter, Theodore M. *The Rise of Statistical Thinking, 1820–1900.* Princeton: Princeton University Press, 1986.

Potter, William Z.; Scheinin, Mika; Golden, Robert N.; Rudorfer, Mathew V.; Cowdry, Rey W.; Calil, Helena M.; Ross, Richard J.; and Linnoila, Markku. "Selective Antidepressants and Cerebrospinal Fluid: Lack of Specificity on Norepinephrine and Serotonin Metabolites." *Archives of General Psychiatry* 42 (December 1985): 1171–1177.

Powers, Edwin. *Crime and Punishment in Early Massachusetts, 1620–1692.* Boston: Beacon Press, 1966.

Purvis, Thomas L. "The Making of A Myth: Abraham Lincoln's Family Background in the Perspective of Jacksonian Politics." *Journal of the Illinois State Historical Society* 75 (Summer 1982):149–162.

Radzinowicz, Leon. *A History of English Criminal Law and its Administration from 1750.* 4 vols. London: Stevens & Sons, 1948.

Rank, Otto. *Myth of the Birth of the Hero: A Psychological Interpretation of Mythology.* 1914. Reprint. New York: Alfred A. Knopf, 1964.

Raush, Jeffrey L. "The Neuropsychopharmacology of Serotonin Function in Psychiatric Illness." in *Psychobiological Foundations of Clinical Psychiatry.* Edited by Lewis Judd and Philip Groves. New York: Basic Books, 1986, pp. 189–205.

Ray, Issac. *A Treatise on The Medical Jurisprudence of Insanity.* 3d ed. Boston, 1853.

_____. *A Treatise on The Medical Jurisprudence of Insanity.* 5th ed. Boston, 1871. Reprint. New York: Arno Press, 1976.

Ray, Nancy. "Reasons for High Suicide Rate Questioned." *Los Angeles Times,* 14 October 1981.

Reiterman, Tim. *Raven: The Untold Story of the Rev. Jim Jones and His People.* New York: E. P. Dutton, 1982.

Reeves, Robert N. "Suicide and the Environment." *Popular Science Monthly* 51 (June 1897):186–191.

Reiser, Morton F. *Mind, Brain, Body: Toward A Convergence of Psychoanalysis and Neurobiology.* New York: Basic Books, 1984.

"Reports of the City Inspectors of New York, 1805–1843." *American Journal of Insanity* 1 (January 1845):232–234.

Restak, Richard. *The Brain.* New York: Bantam Books, 1984.

Reston, James, Jr. *Our Father Who Art in Hell.* New York: New York Times Books, 1981.

Rhodes, Albert. "Suicide." *The Galaxy* 21 (February 1876):188–199.

Rich, Charles L. "Electroconvulsive Therapy." In *Psychobiological Foundations of Clinical Psychiatry.* Edited by Lewis L. Judd and Philip M. Groves. New York: Basic Books, 1986, pp. 335–344.

Rich, Charles L; Young, Deborah; and Fowler, Richard C. "San Diego Suicide Study." *Archives of General Psychiatry* 43 (June 1986):577–582.

Rippere, Vicky. "Diet and Mental Illness." In *Diet-Related Diseases: The Modern*

Epidemic. Edited by Stephen Seely, David L. J. Freed, Gerald A. Silverstone, and Vicky Rippere. London: Croom Helm, 1985, pp. 241–244.

Roazen, Paul. *Freud and His Followers*. New York: Alfred A. Knopf, 1974.

Robertson, James Oliver. *American Myth, American Reality*. New York: Hill and Wang, 1980.

Roe, Daphne A. *A Plague of Corn: The Social History of Pellagra*. Ithaca: Cornell University Press, 1973.

Rogin, Michael Paul. *Fathers and Children: Andrew Jackson and the Subjugation of the American Indian*. New York: Alfred A. Knopf, 1975.

Rolle, Andrew. *The Italian Americans: Troubled Roots*. New York: The Free Press, 1980.

Rose, Steve. *Jesus and Jim Jones*. New York: The Pilgrim Press, 1979.

Rosen, George. "History." In *A Handbook for the Study of Suicide*. Edited by Seymour Perlin. New York: Oxford University Press, 1975, pp. 3–29.

Rosenberg, Charles E. "The Cause of Cholera: Aspects of Etiological Thought in 19th-Century America." *Bulletin of the History of Medicine* 34 (July/August 1960): 331–354.

———. *The Trial of the Assassin Guiteau: Psychiatry and Law in the Gilded Age*. Chicago: University of Chicago Press, 1968.

———. "Sexuality, Class and Role in 19th-Century America." *American Quarterly* 25 (May 1973):131–154.

———. "The Therapeutic Revolution: Medicine, Meaning, and Social Change in Nineteenth-Century America." In *The Therapeutic Revolution: Essays in the Social History of Medicine*. Edited by Morris J. Vogel and Charles E. Rosenberg, Philadelphia: University of Pennsylvania Press, 1979, pp. 3–25.

Rosenfield, Israel. "The New Brain." *The New York Review*. 14 March 1985.

———. *The Invention of Memory: A New View of the Brain*. Basic Books: New York, 1988.

Ross, Dorothy. "Woodrow Wilson and the Case for Psychohistory." *Journal of American History* 69 (December 1982):659–668.

Rost, Hans. "Suicide in Cities." *American Journal of Sociology* 10 (January 1905): 562.

Rotberg, Robert I., ed. "Hunger and History: The Impact of Changing Food Production and Comsumption Patterns on Society." *The Journal of Interdisciplinary History* 14 (Autumn 1983), special issue.

Rothman, David J. *The Discovery of the Asylum, Social Order and Disorder in the New Republic*. Boston: Little, Brown, 1971.

———. *Conscience and Convenience: The Asylum and its Alternatives in Progressive America*. Boston: Little, Brown, & Co., 1980.

Roy, Alec, and Linnoila, Marrku. "Alcoholism and Suicide." In *Biology of Suicide*. Edited by Ronald Maris. New York: The Guilford Press, 1986, pp. 162–191.

Rush, Benjamin. *Medical Inquiries and Observations Upon the Diseases of the Mind*. Philadelphia: Kimber & Richardson, 1812.

———. *Letters of Benjamin Rush*. 2 vols. Reprint. Edited by L. H. Butterfield. Princeton: Princeton University Press, 1951.

Russell, Noadiah. "Diary of Noadiah Russell." *The New England Historical and Geneological Register* 7 (January 1853):53–59.

Sainsbury, Peter. *Suicide in London, An Ecological Study*. London: Chapman & Hall, 1955.

———, and Barraclough, Brian. "Differences Between Suicide Rates." *Nature* 220 (December 1968):1252.

San Diego County Coroner's Office, San Diego, California. Coroner's Reports, 1850–1983.

San Diego Historical Society. Library and Manuscript Collection. "Inquisition by Coroner's Juries, 1853–1905."

San Diego Union. "Self-Murder." 9 November 1893.

———. "Youthful Suicides on the Rise; Experts Point to Reasons." 12 December 1981.

Sandstead, Harold H. "Clinical Manifestations of Certain Vitamin Deficiencies." In *Modern Nutrition in Health and Disease: Dietotherapy.* Edited by Robert S. Goodhart and Maurice E. Shils. Philadelphia: Lea & Febiger, 1973, pp. 593–603.

Sarter, Martin, and Markowitsch, Hans J. "The Amygdala's Role in Human Mnemonic Processing." *Cortex* 21 (1985):7–24.

Savage, William W., Jr. *The Cowboy Hero: His Image in American History and Culture.* Norman, Okla.: University of Oklahoma Press, 1979.

Schaeffer, Jack. *The Short Novels of Jack Schaeffer.* Introduction by Dorothy M. Johnson. Boston: Houghton Mifflin, 1976.

Schein, Harry. "The Olympian Cowboy." *American Scholar* 24 (Summer 1955): 309–320.

Schmid, Calvin F. "Suicide in Minneapolis." *American Journal of Sociology* 39 (July 1933):30–48.

"Scientists Ponder Diet's Behavioral Effects." *Journal of the American Medical Association* (December 1985):3407–3408.

Scott, Arthur P. *Criminal Law in Colonial Virginia.* Chicago: University of Chicago Press, 1930.

Scull, Andrew. "The Discovery of the Asylum Revisited: Lunacy Reform in the New Republic." In *Madhouses, Mad-Doctors, and Madmen: The Social History of Psychiatry in the Victorian Era.* Edited by Andrew Scull. Philadelphia: University of Pennsylvania Press, 1981, pp. 144–165.

———. "Moral Treatment Reconsidered: Some Sociological Comments on An Episode in the History of British Psychiatry," in *Madhouses, Mad-Doctors, and Madmen: The Social Hsitory of Psychiatry in the Victorian Era.* Edited by Andrew Scull. Philadelphia: University of Pennsylvania Press, 1981. pp. 105–118.

Sena, John F. "Melancholic Madness and the Puritans," *Harvard Theological Review* 66 (July 1963):293–309.

Sewall, Samuel. "Sewall Papers." *Massachusetts Historical Society, Collections.* 5th ser. Boston, 1878–1882, vols. 5, 7.

———. *The Diary Of Samuel Sewall, 1674–1729.* 2 vols. Edited by M. Halsey Thomas. New York: Farrar, Straus, & Co., 1973.

Shayless, John B., and Shortridge, Roy M. "Biased Underenumeration in Census Manuscripts: Methodological Implications." *Journal of Urban History* 1 (1975):409–439.

Shneidman, Edwin, ed. *Essays in Self-Destruction.* New York: Science House, Inc., 1967.

Shneidman, Edwin S., and Farberow, Norman L. "Statistical Comparisons Between Attempted and Committed Suicides." In *The Cry for Help.* Edited by Norman L. Farberow and Edwin S. Shneidman, New York: McGraw-Hill, 1961, pp. 19–47.

Edward Shorter. "L'âge des premières règles en France, 1750–1950." *Annales* 36 (Mai-Juin 1981):495–511.

Sicherman Barbara. "The Paradox of Prudence: Mental Health in the Gilded Age." *Journal of American History* 62 (March 1976):890–912.

———. "The Uses of Diagnosis: Doctors, Patients, and Neurasthenia." In

Sickness and Health in America: Readings in the History of Medicine and Public Health.
Edited by Judith Walzer Levitt and Ronald Numbers. Madison: The University of
Wisconsin Press, 1978, pp. 25–38.

————. *The Quest For Mental Health in America, 1880–1917.* New York: Arno
Press, 1980.

Sidransky, Herschel. "Tryptophan: Unique Action by an Essential Amino Acid."
In *Nutritional Pathology: Pathochemistry of Dietary Imbalances.* Edited by H. Sidransky.
New York: Marcel Dekker, 1985, pp. 1–62.

Simon, Julian. "The Effect of Income on the Suicide Rate." *American Journal of
Sociology* 74 (November 1968):302–303.

Simon, Paul. *Lincoln's Preparation for Greatness: The Illinois Legislative Years.* Norman, Okla.: University of Oklahoma Press, 1965.

Silverman, Kenneth. *The Life and Times of Cotton Mather.* New York: Harper &
Row, 1984.

Slotkin, Richard. *Regeneration Through Violence, The Mythology of the American Frontier, 1600–1860.* Middletown, Conn.: Wesleyan University Press, 1973.

————. *The Fatal Environment: The Myth of the Frontier in the Age of Industrialism,
1800–1890.* New York: Atheneum, 1985.

Smith, Henry Nash. *Virgin Land, The American West as Symbol and Myth.* Cambridge, Mass.: Harvard University Press, 1950.

Smith-Rosenberg, Carroll. "Beauty, the Beast, and the Militant Woman: A Case
Study in Sex Roles and Social Stress in Jacksonian America." *American Quarterly* 23
(October 1971):562–584.

————, and Rosenberg, Charles E. "The Female Animal: Medical and Biological Views of Woman and Her Role in Nineteenth-Century America." *Journal of
American History* 60 (September 1973):332–356.

Snyder, Solomon H. "Biology." In *A Handbook for the Study of Suicide.* Edited by
Seymour Perlin. New York: Oxford University Press, 1975), pp. 113–129.

————. "Brain Peptides as Neurotransmitters." *Science* 209 (August 1980):
976–983.

"A Southern Physician." "Suicide." *The American Whig Review* 6 (August 1847):
137–145.

Spangler, George M. "Suicide and Social Criticism: Durkheim, Dreiser, Wharton,
and London." *American Quarterly* 31 (Fall 1979):496–516.

Spink, Wesley W. *The Nature of Brucellosis.* Minneapolis, Minn.: University of Minnesota Press, 1956.

Sprott, S. E. *The English Debate on Suicide: from Donne to Hume.* La Salle, Illinois:
Open Court, 1961.

Squire, Larry R. "Mechanisms of Memory." *Science* 232 (June 1986):1612–1619.

Squire, Susan. "Shock Therapy's Return to Respectability." *The New York Times
Magazine.* 22 November 1987.

Stack, Steven. "Youth Suicide Rates." *Newslink of the American Association of Suicidology* 12 (December 1986):6.

Stanley, Michael; Stanley, Barbara; Träskman-Benz, Lil; Mann, John J.; and
Meyendorff, Elaine. "Neurochemical Findings in Suicide Completers and Suicide
Attempters." In *Biology of Suicide.* Edited by Ronald Maris. New York: The Guilford
Press, 1986, pp. 204–218.

Stannard, David E. *The Puritan Way of Death: A Study in Religion, Culture, and Social
Change.* New York: Oxford University Press, 1977.

————. *Shrinking History: On Freud and the Failure of Psychohistory.* New York:
Oxford University Press, 1980.

Starr, Paul. *The Social Transformation of American Medicine*. New York: Basic Books, 1983.

"Statistics of the Suicides." *American Journal of Insanity* 3 (April 1847):349–352.

"Statistics of Suicides," *American Journal of Insanity* 4 (January 1848):247–253.

"Statistics of Suicides," *American Journal of Insanity* 5 (April 1849):303–310.

Steele, Richard, et al., "Life in Jonestown." *Newsweek*, 4 December 1978.

Strozier, Charles B. *Lincoln's Quest for Union, Public and Private Meanings*. New York: Basic Books, 1982.

Styles, G. "Suicide and Its Increase." *American Journal of Insanity* 57 (July 1900): 100.

"Suffolk County Bills, 1770–1822." Adlow Collection. Boston Public Library, Rare Books and Manuscripts Collection.

Suffolk County Court. "Records of the Suffolk County Court, 1671–1680." *Publications of the Colonial Society of Massachusetts* 29. Boston, Colonial Society of Massachusetts, 1933.

"A Suicide." [August 25, 1661], *William and Mary Quarterly* 1st ser. 15 (January 1907):181.

"Suicide in Bavaria." *American Journal of Insanity* 16 (October 1863):246–247.

"Suicides in New York City in 1860." *New York Times*, 17 January 1861.

Sym, John. *Lifes Preservatives Against Self-Killing. or, an Useful Treatise Concerning Life and Self-Murder*. London, 1637.

Tanner, James M. *A History of the Study of Human Growth*. Cambridge, England: Cambridge University Press, 1981.

Taylor, Maurice, and Wicks, Jerry. "The Choice of Weapons, A Study of Suicide by Sex, Race, and Religion." *Suicide and Life-Threatening Behavior* 10 (Fall 1980): 142–149.

Taylor, Steve. *Durkheim and the Study of Suicide*. New York: St. Martins Press, 1982.

Theilman, Samuel B. "Madness and Medicine: Trends in American Medical Therapeutics for Insanity." *Bulletin of the History of Medicine* 61 (Spring 1987):25–46.

Thimm, B. M. *Brucellosis: Distribution in Man, Domestic and Wild Animals*. New York: Springer-Verlag, 1982.

Thomas, Benjamin P. *Abraham Lincoln, A Biography*. New York: Alfred A. Knopf, 1952.

———. *Lincoln's New Salem*. Chicago: Americana House, 1961.

Thompson, Richard F. "The Neurobiology of Learning and Memory." *Science* 233 (August 1986):941–947.

Thorpe, Francis Newton, ed. *The Federal and State Constitutions, Colonial Charters, and Other Organic Laws of the States, Territories, and Colonies Now or Heretofore Forming the United States of America*. 7 vols. (Washington, D.C.: GPO, 1909).

Thwaites, Reuben G., ed. *Original Journals of the Lewis and Clark Expedition, 1804–1806*. 8 vols. New York: Dodd, Mead and Co., 1904–1905.

Timnick, Lois. "Researchers Think Suicide Factor Test May Save Lives." *Los Angeles Times*. 11 July 1981.

Tocqueville, Alexis de. *Democracy in America*. 2 vols. Edited by Phillips Bradley. New York: Alfred A. Knopf, 1966.

Träskman, Lil; Åsberg, Marie; Bertilsson, Leif; and Sjöstrand, Lars. "Monoamine Metabolites in CSF and Suicidal Behavior." *Archives of General Psychiatry* 38 (June 1981):631–636.

Turner, Frederick Jackson. "The Significance of the Frontier in American History." *Annual Report of the American Historical Association for the Year 1893*. Chicago, 1893.

―――. *The Frontier in American History*. New York: Holt, Rinehard, & Winston, 1963.

U.S. Census Office, 7th Census, 1850. *Mortality Statistics of the Seventh Census of the United States, 1850*. Edited by D. B. DeBow, superintendent of the United States Census. Washington, D.C.: A. O. P. Nicholson, Printer, 1855.

―――. 8th Census, 1860. *Statistics of the United States, (Including Mortality, Property, etc.)* Washington, D.C.: Government Printing Office, 1866.

―――. 9th Census, 1870. *Census Reports*. 3 vols. Washington, D.C.: Government Printing Office, 1872.

―――. *Mortality of the United States*. Washington, D.C.: Government Printing Office, 1870.

―――. 10th Census of the United States, 1880. *Census Reports*. 22 vols. "Mortality and Vital Statistics." vols. 11–12. Washington, D.C.: Government Printing Office, 1883–1888.

―――. 11th Census of the United States, 1890. *Census Reports*. 25 vols. "Vital and Social Statistics." 23: pt. 4 Washington, D.C.: Government Printing Office, 1892–1897.

―――. *Abstract of the Eleventh Census: 1890*. 2d ed. Washington, D.C.: Government Printing Office, 1896.

―――. 12th Census of the United States, 1900. *Census Reports . . . Twelfth Census of the United States Taken in the Year 1900*. 10 vols. "Vital Statistics." vols 3–4 Washington, D.C.: Government Printing Office, 1901–1902.

U.S. National Center for Health Statistics. *Monthly Vital Statistics Report*. Washington: D.C.: Government Printing Office, 1952 to Present. Monthly.

Valenstein, Elliot S. *Great and Desperate Cures: The Rise and Decline of Psychosurgery and Other Radical Treatments for Mental Illness*. New York: Basic Books, 1986.

Van Praag, Herman. "A Critical Investigation of MAO Inhibition as a Therapeutic Principle in the Treatment of Depressions." Ph.D. diss. University of Utrecht, 1962.

―――. "Evidence of Serotonin-Deficient Depression." *Neuropsychobiology* 3 (1977):56–63.

―――. "Significance of Biochemical Parameters in the Diagnosis, Treatment, and Prevention of Depressive Disorders." *Biological Psychiatry* 12 (1977):101–131.

―――. "Central Monoamines and the Pathogenesis of Depression." *Handbook of Biological Psychiatry*. Part 4: *Brain Mechanisms and Abnormal Behavior—Chemistry*. Edited by Herman van Praag et al. New York: Marcel Dekker, 1981, pp. 159–205.

Vinovskis, Maris A. "Angels' Heads and Weeping Willows: Death in Early America." *Proceedings of the American Antiquarian Society* 86, pt. 2 (1977):273–302.

Wägner, Anna; Åberg-Wistedt, Anna; Åsberg, Marie; Bertilsson, Leif; Mårtensson, Björn; and Montero, Dolores. "Effects of Antidepressant Treatments on Platelet Tritiated Imipramine Binding in Major Depressive Disorder." *Archives of General Psychiatry* 44 (October 1987):870–880.

Walker, Nigel. *Crime and Insanity in England, Volume One: the Historical Perspective*. Edinburgh: Edinburgh University Press, 1968.

Warren, Louis A. *Lincoln's Youth, Indiana Years, Seven to Twenty-one, 1816–1830*. Indianapolis: Indiana Historical Society, 1959.

Watkins, Susan Cotts, and van de Walle, Etienne. "Nutrition, Motality, and Population Size: Malthus' Court of Last Resort." *Journal of Interdisciplinary History* 14 (Autumn 1983):210–224.

Weightman, Judith Mary. *Making Sense of the Jonestown Suicides: A Sociological History of the People's Temple*. New York: Edwin Mellon Press, 1983.

Welter, Barbara. "The Cult of True Womanhood: 1820–1860." *American Quarterly* 18 (Summer 1966):151–174.

Wendling, Aubrey. "Suicide in the San Francisco Bay Region, 1938–1942 and 1948–1952." Ph.D. dissertation. University of Washington, Seattle, 1954.

Wenk, Gary; Hughey, Donna; Boundy, Virginia; Kim, Anna; Walker, Lary; and Olton, David. "Neurotransmitters and Memory: Role of Cholinergic, Serotonergic, amd Noradrenergic Systems." *Behavioral Neuroscience* 101, 3 (1987):325–332.

Wharton, Edith. *The House of Mirth*. New York: Charles Scribner's Sons, 1905.

Wherry, J. W., M.D. "Melancholia, The Psychical Expression of Organic Fear." *American Journal of Insanity* 62 (January 1906):369–406.

Whitmore, William H., ed. *The Colonial Laws of Massachusetts* 1660. Reprint. Boston, 1889.

Whitney, Henry C. *Life on the Circuit with Lincoln*. Introduction and notes by Paul M. Angle. Caldwell, Idaho: The Caxton Printers, Ltd., 1940.

Willard, Samuel. *Covenant-Keeping the Way to Blessedness*. Boston, 1682.

———. "A Brief Account of a Strange and Unusual Providence of God Befallen to Elizabeth Knapp of Groton." In *Remarkable Providences, 1600–1760*. Edited by John Demos. 1672. Reprint. New York: George Braziller, 1972, pp. 358–371.

Williams, Solomon. "The Frailty and Misery of Man's Life." (Boston: Draper, 1740).

Williams, Tom A. "The Prevention of Suicide." *American Journal of Insanity* 71 (January 1915):559–571.

Wingate, Edmund. *Justice Revived, Being the Whole Office of a Countrey Justice of the Peace*. London, 1661.

Winnicott, David W. *The Maturational Processes and the Facilitating Environment: Studies in the Theory of Emotional Development*. New York: International Universities Press, 1965.

Winson, Jonathan. *Brain & Psyche: The Biology of the Unconscious*. Garden City, New York: Anchor Press, 1985.

Winthrop, John. *Winthrop's Journal, "History of New England," 1630–1648*. 2 vols. Edited by James Kendall Hosmer. New York: Charles Scribner's Sons, 1908.

———. *Winthrop Papers*. 4 vols. Boston: Massachusetts Historical Society, 1944.

Wister, Owen. *The Virginian*. New York: MacMillan, 1904.

Wolfenstein, Martha. "Effects on Adults of Object Loss in the First Five Years." *Journal of the American Psychoanalytic Association* 24 (1976):659–668.

———. "How is Mourning Possible?" *The Psychoanalytic Study of the Child* 21 (1966):93–112.

Wooley, D. W., and Shaw, E. "A Biochemical and Pharmacological Suggestion about Certain Mental Disorders." *Proceedings of the National Academy of Sciences, USA* 40 (1954):228–231.

World Health Organization. *World Health Statistics, Annual, 1980: Vital Statistics and Causes of Death*. Geneva: United Nations, 1980.

Wright, Donald. "Criminal Aspects of Suicide in the United States." *North Carolina Central Law Review* 7 (Fall 1975):156–163,

Wurtman, Richard J., and Growdon, John H. "Dietary Enhancement of CNS Neurotransmitters." *Hospital Practice* 13 (March 1978):71–77.

Zee, Hugo J. "The Guyana Incident: Some Psychoanalytic Considerations." *Bulletin of the Menninger Clinic* 44 (July 1980):345–363.

Ziff, Lazar. "A Reading of *Wieland.*" *Proceedings of the Modern Language Association* 77 (1962):51–57.

Zilboorg, Gregory. "Differential Diagnostic Types of Suicide." *Archives of Neurology and Psychiatry* 35 (1936):270–291.

———. "Suicide Among Civilized and Primitive Races." *American Journal of Psychiatry* 92 (May 1936):1347–1369.

———. "Considerations on Suicide, With Particular Reference to that of the Young." *Journal of Orthopsychiatry* 17 (1937):15–31.

INDEX

abandonment, 77, 125–127, 192; Meriwether Lewis and, 128. *See also* desertion; object loss
Abernathy, Thomas, 106, 108
accident, determination of, in suicides, 32, 33, 104
accidental suicide, 107n
Achille-Delmas, François, 61
Adams, John, 28
adolescents, suicide among, 117, 208n39. *See also* teenage suicide; youth suicide
Adventures of Col. Daniel Boon (Filson), 186
Advice to Sinners Under Conviction, &c. with some Scruples of the Tempted Resolved, 27
affective disorders, 39n, 55, 56; serotonin and, 83. *See also* depression; melancholia
afterlife, 139, 141, 164
age, 149; memory development and, 7–8; suicide and, 71
aggressive behavior, 68
"Alarming Increase of Suicides," 156
Albert Einstein College of Medicine, 86
alcoholism, 66, 71, 86–87, 99, 148; in adolescents, 117; Meriwether Lewis and, 129–131; suicide and, 223n75, 231n42. *See also* drink and drunkenness
alienation, social, 119
alienists, 37–39, 41–42, 45, 51, 57, 59
altruistic suicide, 2, 143

ambition, Abraham Lincoln and, 141–143
ambivalence, 78, 125–126
American Association of Suicidology, 70, 117
American dream, 60–61
American frontier. *See* frontier, myth of
American Indians, 24; wars with, 182
American Journal of Insanity, 35–37, 41–43, 45–47, 50, 52, 106, 151, 157, 214n33, 214n35
American Journal of Sociology, 65
American Medico-Psychological Association, 52, 55, 56, 159n
American Neurological Association, 52
American Psychiatric Association, 37, 52
American Psychoanalytic Association, 75
American Public Health Association, 101
American Revolution, 30–31, 131
American Whig Review, The, 45
amino acids, 171–173
amygdala, 169, 170, 175, 176
Anderson, Olive, 65n, 99n, 235n9
Andreasen, Nancy C., 173–174
anger, 4, 77, 120; Jim Jones and, 196; Meriwether Lewis and, 122; Abraham Lincoln and, 132, 139–140, 144
Anglican Church, 16
Angoisse Humaine, L' (de Fleury), 61